# Pursuing Intersectio
# Dominant Imaginaries

*Pursuing Intersectionality, Unsettling Dominant Imaginaries* offers a sustained, interdisciplinary exploration of intersectional ideas, histories, and practices that no other text offers. Deftly synthesizing much of the existing literatures on intersectionality, one of the most significant theoretical and political precepts of our time, *Pursuing Intersectionality* invites us to confront a disconcerting problem: though intersectionality is widely known, acclaimed, and applied, it is often construed in ways that depoliticize, undercut, or even violate its most basic premises. Cogently demonstrating how intersectionality has been repeatedly resisted, misunderstood, and misapplied, *Pursuing Intersectionality* shows the degree to which the concept can be undermined by supporters and critics alike. A clarion call to more meaningfully engage intersectionality's radical ideas, histories, and justice orientations, *Pursuing Intersectionality* answers the basic questions surrounding intersectionality, attends to its historical roots in Black feminist theory and politics, and offers insights and strategies from across the disciplines for bracketing dominant logics and for orienting toward intersectional dispositions and practices.

**Vivian M. May** is Associate Professor and Chair of Women's and Gender studies at Syracuse University. She is author of *Anna Julia Cooper, Visionary Black Feminist* (Routledge, 2007), and of numerous articles and chapters focused on Black feminist intellectual history, feminist theory and literature, and theorizing Women's Studies methods and practices. Recently, May was elected President of the National Women's Studies Association for a two-year term (2015 & 2016).

## Titles of Related Interest

*Feminist Theory Reader: Local and Global Perspectives*
Carole McCann and Seung-kyung Kim

*Gender Circuits: Bodies and Identities in a Technological Age, Second Edition*
Eve Shapiro

*Reproduction and Society: Interdisciplinary Readings*
Edited by Carole Joffe and Jennifer Reich

*Routledge International Handbook of Race, Class, and Gender*
Edited by Shirley A. Jackson

*Transforming Scholarship: Why Women's and Gender Studies Students are Changing Themselves and the World, Second Edition*
Michele Tracy Berger and Cheryl Radeloff

*Women Science, and Technology: A Reader in Feminist Science Studies, Third Edition*
Edited by Mary Wyer, Mary Barbercheck, Donna Cookmeyer, Hatice Ozturk, and Marta Wayne

# Pursuing Intersectionality, Unsettling Dominant Imaginaries

Vivian M. May

NEW YORK AND LONDON

First published 2015
by Routledge
711 Third Avenue, New York, NY 10017

and by Routledge
2 Park Square, Milton Park, Abingdon, Oxon, OX14 4RN

*Routledge is an imprint of the Taylor & Francis Group, an informa business*



*Library of Congress Cataloging-in-Publication Data*

May, Vivian M.
Pursuing intersectionality, unsettling dominant imaginaries / Vivian M. May.
pages cm — (Contemporary sociological perspectives)
Includes bibliographical references and index.
1. Feminist theory. 2. Discrimination. 3. Social justice. 4. Equality. I. Title.
HQ1190.M3835 2015
305.4201—dc23
2014030155

ISBN: 978-0-415-80839-2 (hbk)
ISBN: 978-0-415-80840-8 (pbk)
ISBN: 978-0-203-14199-1 (ebk)

Typeset in Caslon, Copperplate, and Trade Gothic
by Apex CoVantage, LLC

# Contents

# PREFACE

I came to this project through two related paths: via the women's and gender studies classroom and exploring how best to invite students to shift toward and practice "matrix" or intersectional analytics, expectations, and imaginations, and via many years of research on Anna Julia Cooper, a nineteenth-century Black feminist intellectual, educator, and activist. In exploring Cooper's life and work, and noting how frequently her perceptive ideas have been misunderstood, I began to consider how intersectionality, a concept Cooper anticipated in many ways, is often similarly misconstrued.

In other words, not only does intersectionality have a longer history than usually is recognized: systematic resistance to intersectional premises and outlooks has been equally long-standing. Intersectionality seems, for many, hard to grasp or hold on to—the force of conventional ways of thinking (via categorical, either/or logics, for instance) keeps it just out of reach. What critical race and feminist philosophers have come to call "epistemologies of ignorance" thus play a significant role in curbing its social, philosophical, and political impact.

Thinking through how intersectionality has repeatedly been "checked" has, in turn, impacted how I approach teaching intersectional texts and politics—a question that many colleagues, in various disciplines and interdisciplines, also wrestle with. Intersectionality is meant to be applied to real-world problems, to unsettle oppressive logics, to plumb gaps or silences for suppressed meanings and implications, and to rethink how we approach liberation politics. This requires examining intersectionality not merely as a content area, fixed idea, or historical moment, but as a sustained and ongoing practice, a way of perceiving and engaging the world that runs against the grain of established (and oppressive) imaginaries. For example, an intersectional orientation is particularly useful for pinpointing hidden forms of collusion between resistance and dominance, or for showing the relational nature of privilege and oppression. It entails problem solving, recognizing how prevailing worldviews may not be as comprehensive or accurate as they may first appear, and keeping a razor-sharp focus on eradicating inequity via coalitional and collective means.

Because "matrix" logics can seem illogical in a "single-axis" world, or can readily slip away (even when one's intent is to engage intersectionality), I invite students at all levels to read (and to enter the historical contexts and follow the nuanced meanings of) primary intersectionality texts from across Black and women of color feminist intellectual/political history (texts often *cited* in contemporary intersectionality literatures though not necessarily engaged with care). As students, researchers, or activists, we must not only learn to employ an intersectional lens in our own applied, creative, and analytic work but also notice, in the work of others, when intersectional aims or goals seem to slip away or fall short. Across the book, then, several examples of this problem of "slippage," or of intersectionality's disappearance in well-intentioned contexts, derive, in part, from an array of rich (and sometimes thorny) classroom discussions and research questions.

Throughout this project, I emphasize the degree to which intersectionality's roots in women of color politics and ideas, and its historical moorings in Black feminist theorizing and politics in particular, *matter*—materially, philosophically, and politically. From these particular contexts, lived conditions, and sociopolitical horizons, intersectionality offers a deep critique of a range of established ideas, normative political strategies, and ingrained habits of mind that have long impeded both feminist and anti-racist thought and politics. However, too often, intersectionality critiques (e.g., charges of essentialism, of repetition without innovation, or of 'parsimony'—meaning ever-smaller, fragmented constituencies) attribute its ostensible shortcomings to its moorings in Black and women of color feminist theorizing and political action. Subtle and overt forms of delegitimizing intersectionality (or, alternatively, legitimizing it by making it more 'universal' via deracialization and depoliticization, such that its deep focus on critical race theorizing and on inclusive social justice are ignored) are commonplace and need to be addressed.

A persistent inability to take up intersectionality's alternative logics and expectations, even by those who advocate intersectional views and aim to apply them meaningfully, suggests the need to examine both *how* and *why* intersectional, multidimensional ideas are regularly (and readily) set aside. By synthesizing diverse intersectionality literatures, across time and discipline, I illustrate a troubling paradox: in order to follow many of the arguments or practices offered in intersectionality's name, one must drop its most central premises and dismiss its radical history and transformative vision. Furthermore, reductive ideas about Black womanhood, cursory readings of Black women's ideas (as descriptively rich but theoretically dilute, for instance), and reductionist notions of intersectionality often go hand in hand: interpretive distortions are often read onto the concept, but also ascribed (via an ever-tightening circular logic) to intersectionality itself as an internal flaw.

We must question why intersectionality is misconstrued as endorsing essentialist identity models or political approaches, caricatured as a narrow lens focused "only" on Black women and solely on "oppression" (the two are often homogenized and conflated), or used by practitioners in ways that uphold single-axis thinking, rather than align with its matrix orientation (wherein lived identities are treated as interlaced and systems of oppression as enmeshed and mutually reinforcing: one form of identity or inequality is not seen as separable or superordinate). From an intersectional orientation, no one factor is necessarily given explanatory or political priority: multiple factors are treated as enmeshed. Yet many intersectionality critiques and applications alike reinforce anti-intersectional assumptions (e.g., by upholding a hierarchy of oppressions model, or by bolstering rather than contesting transparent privilege).

This book thus takes up a range of troubling interpretive politics, methodological norms, and philosophical distortions facing intersectional work and ideas. Though intersectionality infuses much of contemporary feminist studies, several of the power moves and structural dynamics it has long critiqued continue on, suggesting it has not been adequately engaged with even as it has been widely cited or celebrated. Uses of intersectionality in feminist research, theory, or policy, for instance, are frequently superficial: it is often employed merely as a demographic factor, descriptive device, or "diversity" tool. Claiming intersectionality as a key feminist lens, without meaningfully engaging its analytical and political implications, is problematic.

Thus while intersectionality is regularly referenced and taught, and several of its key ideas are viewed as axiomatic in feminist studies, critical race studies, and in many other fields of inquiry (e.g., that there are multiple and enmeshed forms of both identity and oppression that need to be addressed simultaneously), basic intersectional insights are also regularly distorted or flattened. For instance, intersectional approaches clearly demand recognition of how multidimensionality and heterogeneity (of bodies, lives, ideas, experiences, harms, and possibilities) are rendered inadmissible, unimaginable, or invisible by single-axis categories (and gender-first or race-first politics): so, why do gender-first logics or gender-primary political expectations prevail in much feminist theorizing and practice?

Intersectionality is both recognized far and wide and commonly construed in ways that deny its nuances, violate its central premises, ignore its historical literatures, or dismiss its antisubordination politics. Perhaps even more unnerving is how frequently it is undermined in contexts where one might least expect it: in much contemporary feminist and anti-racist work, for example, an intersectional lens is often deployed in ways that buttress settler–colonial mindsets and histories. These more subtle forms of derailment need far more consideration: we must ask what it means, philosophically and politically, if intersectionality is undone in the ways it is applied or interpreted, especially when such distortions are enacted by those who aim to realize its promise and potential. Furthermore, while intersectionality does not come with any political guarantees, it does place interpretive and political demands on us: I therefore illustrate and delineate several strategies for bracketing dominant logics and taking up intersectional approaches more adequately.

Intersectionality is a form of resistant knowledge developed to unsettle conventional mindsets, challenge oppressive power, think through the full architecture of structural inequalities and asymmetrical life opportunities, and seek a more just world. It has been forged in the context of struggles for social justice as a means to challenge dominance, foster critical imaginaries, and craft collective models for change. In the end, my goal is to underscore the degree to which intersectionality's historical and intellectual origins, diverse philosophical premises, and range of political nuances need to be attended to more rigorously and with far more care. This book is offered as an invitation both to actively orient toward an intersectional political/intellectual disposition and to depart from a host of (interrelated) oppressive logics that uphold inequality and rationalize violation and harm.

# Acknowledgments

At various stages of this project's development, I received insightful and thoughtful feedback from several anonymous reviewers: my sincere thanks for your collegiality and careful readings. My editors at Routledge, Samantha Barbaro and Steve Rutter, have been generous and shared many astute suggestions: thank you for your conviction in the value and timeliness of this book. Thanks also go to Margaret Moore, editorial assistant at Routledge, who has been helpful behind the scenes with countless details, and to Mhairi Bennett and Renata Corbani in production. For her invaluable encouragement and acute insights over the past twenty-five years, I thank Beverly Guy-Sheftall, Anna Julia Cooper Professor of women's studies and founding director of the Women's Research and Resource Center at Spelman College.

I deeply value the aid and support of many colleagues at Syracuse University. Given the burgeoning global literatures on intersectionality, I am indebted to the tireless staff at Syracuse University's Bird Library—behind the scenes, many books have been delivered, articles located, and various electronic resource/database problems solved: without your collective help, this book would not have been possible. The Dean's office in the College of Arts and Sciences provided some financial assistance for permissions: thank you. My department chair, Gwendolyn Pough, offered both intellectual and structural support at crucial times, for which I remain grateful. Many colleagues in the women's and gender studies department and across campus provided scholarly and political community, which I appreciate greatly. Last, but never least, my students have consistently engaged with intersectional writings, politics, and imaginings in meaningful ways and have asked hard questions that needed answering, which I hope this book has begun to do: thank you for your enthusiasm and excitement.

The loving support of friends and family always helps to mitigate the solitary nature of research and writing. Allison Kimmich, Executive Director of the National Women's Studies Association, and Elizabeth West, Professor of English at Georgia State University, thank you for your friendships since graduate school and for many a long-distance chat on the phone. To my loving parents and sister, thank you for your steadfast affection and encouragement. And to my wonderful partner, Beth, thank you for all that you do, each and every day: the ordinary things in life are the most important—it has been many a walk or a swim (or skiing or snowshoe adventure), no matter the weather, and many a laugh at the end of a long day, that have made this sustained work possible.

# INTRODUCTION

## *The Case for Intersectionality and the Question of Intersectionality Backlash*

This book starts from the premise that intersectionality is important for what it has already made possible and for what it can still help to achieve: it offers a compelling vision of a more just world and should not be considered an intellectual or political relic, to be put on the shelf. Without question, intersectionality has set in motion considerable innovations in critical theory, research, policy formation, and activist practice: it has substantially shifted how we conceptualize individual and group identities, craft and sustain political alliances, and examine and transform systems of inequality. In short, it remains germane for analyzing and contesting systemic inequality and for reimagining how we think about agency, resistance, and subjectivity.

While intersectionality has been widely influential, its approach to subjectivity, knowledge, power, and social systems has also encountered quite a degree of resistance and continues to do so. This is not necessarily surprising, in that counterhegemonic ideas and political orientations generally face opposition since they challenge the status quo. Intersectionality, for instance, contests several taken-for-granted ideas about personhood, power, and social change: in particular, its multidimensional "matrix" orientation is often at odds with "single-axis" sociopolitical realities, knowledge norms, and justice frameworks.

However, it is the relatively subtle and indirect ways of resisting or undermining intersectionality that have called my attention, rather than overt forms of opposition. Via a variety of mechanisms, intersectionality is often undermined or even violated by its supporters and practitioners. In other words, it is regularly dismissed, contained, or undone in contexts where one might least anticipate it. These less obvious forms of epistemic pushback need far more consideration: they have significant philosophical and political implications and present a considerable obstacle to realizing intersectionality's wider potential.

For instance, feminist scholars who espouse a deep commitment to thinking more complexly about gender, and about feminist and anti-racist politics, often critique or apply intersectionality in ways that reinforce the kinds of single-axis, gender-first thinking (and thus erasures and hierarchies) that intersectionality opposes. Likewise, practitioners clearly committed to intersectionality in principle frequently engage it via methods that fundamentally undermine some of its core precepts and principles, whether by depoliticizing the concept or by narrowing its scope (seeing it as an equity instrument for "race" or "ethnicity" but not for "gender," for instance). In many respects, intersectionality is regularly treated in ways that suggest it is not really understood, though in fields like women's and gender studies, for example, it seems to be assumed that everyone already "knows" what it is and is about.

A review of a range of intersectionality literatures, debates, and applications readily substantiates that these occurrences (i.e., distorting or falling away from intersectionality) are not uncommon: in fact, they are ubiquitous. Since intersectionality has its roots in radical resistance politics, particularly in Black feminist, critical race, and women of color theorizing and praxis, these origins and histories are relevant, rather than immaterial, to how intersectionality, as a disposition, has been (mis)read, resisted, and (mis)used, whether overtly or inadvertently. In other words, the degree of sustained resistance faced by intersectional ideas should not be seen as inconsequential or incidental but as connected to its origins in collective social movements to contest hegemonic logics and systems of dominance.

If we remain dedicated to intersectionality, not just as an abstract idea (or as a theoretical/intellectual tradition simply ripe for the 'taking' or for instrumentalizing), but as a set of active and ongoing intellectual and political commitments that are fundamentally oriented toward antisubordination and social transformation, then we must think more about what these puzzling dynamics (i.e., patterns of marginalizing, undermining, or even negating intersectionality, as a critical/political orientation, even by its supporters) signify and identify strategies for addressing them. I therefore trace sites of intersectionality's undoing across various contexts, examine their meanings and implications, and think through what those of us committed to realizing intersectional forms of justice and social change might do, collectively, to shift the terms of its interpretation and use. However, before introducing the book's larger scope in more detail, a brief overview of intersectionality is in order, for those newer to the concept.

## What Is Intersectionality?[1] What Can It Help Us "Do"?[2]

Intersectionality is an analytical and political orientation that brings together a number of insights and practices developed largely in the context of Black feminist and women of color theoretical and political traditions. First, it approaches lived identities as interlaced and systems of oppression as enmeshed and mutually reinforcing: one aspect of identity and/or form of inequality is not treated as separable or as superordinate. This "matrix" worldview contests "single-axis" forms of thinking about subjectivity and power (Crenshaw 1989) and rejects hierarchies of identity or oppression (Combahee 1983; Lorde 1984; B. Smith 1983). An intersectional justice orientation is thus wide in scope and inclusive: it repudiates additive notions of identity, assimilationist models of civil rights, and one-dimensional views of power.

Focusing on the interplay of identities and the push–pull of multiple forms of power, intersectionality highlights the workings of racist sexism: for instance, its matrix model changes the terms of what "counts" as a gender, race, sexuality, disability, nation, and/or class issue or framework. Intersectionality also approaches lived identities, and systemic patterns of asymmetrical life opportunities and harms, from their interstices, from the nodal points where they hinge or touch. As Alison Bailey explains, "Race and gender should be conceptualized not as 'race + gender,' instead they should be thought of in terms of 'gendered racism' or how 'gender is racialized.' It makes sense [from an intersectional approach] to talk about capitalist patriarchies rather than capitalism and patriarchy" (Bailey 2009, 17). This nodal approach, in turn, leads to an understanding that what is needed, to effect change, is a politics of coalition: to contest shared logics across systems of domination, solidarities need to be forged via mutual commitments, not via principles of homogeneity or sameness.

Thus an intersectional orientation (to assessing social reality, questioning established mindsets, examining the impact of past practices on the present day, and imagining and fighting for a transformed future) is intrinsically multidimensional. However, intersectionality was not devised simply to achieve rich description and contextualization. Developed in the context of struggles for social justice, intersectionality offers a means to question and to challenge dominant logics, to further antisubordination efforts, and to forge collective models for social transformation that do not replicate or reinforce the inequalities, erasures, and distortions animated and buttressed by either/or logics, or what Audre Lorde characterizes as "divide and conquer" thinking (Lorde 1984, 112).

Rather than a fixed method with set boundaries, hard-and-fast tenets, or predetermined subjects and schematics, intersectionality can be best understood as an interpretive orientation that leaves these factors as open questions to be taken up, to help expose how subjection and dominance operate, sometimes subtly. Oppressive practices can be hidden in plain view or subtly embedded in liberatory frameworks or political strategies: central to intersectional analyses and applications, then, is pursuing its invitation to think beyond (or against the grain of) familiar boundaries or categories, to perceive sites of omission, and to consider their meanings and implications.

In examining power's multiple domains, and drawing on a "both/and" worldview, intersectionality contests conventional ways of thinking about domination, subordination, and resistance: it approaches privilege and oppression as concurrent and relational and attends to within-group differences and inequities, not just between-group power asymmetries.[3] This matric, relational model underscores how we can participate in forms of dominance, harm, and subordination even as we also fight hegemonic relations and pursue justice. Consequently, intersectional approaches to social transformation aim to account for multiple forms of power and inequality simultaneously, instead of in single-issue or sequential ways.

Karen Soldatic and Lucy Fiske, for example, highlight how race and disability must be understood as intersecting factors in their analysis of detention and incarceration rates in Australia. Studying race and disability from an either/or model impedes an understanding of these compounding relationships and patterns. Additionally, protesting incarceration via single-axis frames can leave wider carceral logics in place: their underlying, interconnected rationales slip from view. Such models of protest may also normalize (or justify) incarceration as a practice of subjection or serve to mitigate harm for one group while increasing harm for (or ignoring carceral effects upon) other populations, especially those in the "gaps" or interstices between the usual categories of analysis (Soldatic and Fiske 2009; see also Ben-Moshe 2013).

By focusing on how patterns and logics interact, and how systems of oppression interrelate, intersectionality highlights various ways in which, unwittingly, we can be engaged in upholding the very forms of coercion or domination we seek to dismantle. It is thus indispensable for identifying paradoxical outcomes (as meaningful and not just as anomalous or accidental) and for revealing unexpected or hidden points of contact between the liberatory and the coercive. Via its matrix orientation, and attention to relational power and privilege, simultaneity, and underlying shared logics, intersectionality needs to be understood to have explanatory power, analytical capacity, and a normative political component, one focused on eradicating inequality and exploitation.

Finally, intersectional concepts of liberation approach the world's possibilities pragmatically, in the here and now, and idealistically, with an eye toward more utopian goals of eradicating inequity, exploitation, and supremacy, both at the micropolitical level of everyday life and at the macropolitical level of social structures, material practices, and cultural norms. Its radical roots offer a transformative vision, one that calls for dismantling systemic oppression (in its myriad forms and guises) so that, to echo Audre Lorde (1984), we can all flourish equally.

In a world rife with persistent forms (and new iterations) of exploitation, inequality, and violence, intersectionality remains indispensable, politically and philosophically. An interrogative, antisubordination impetus informs its approach to tracing shared logics across seemingly disparate domains and contexts. By illuminating how structural, philosophical, and material factors interact, it offers a vital means of contesting domination. In particular, intersectionality provides tools for questioning default explanations about status quo reality and for probing the everyday logics that sustain and rationalize inequality; it is equally useful for identifying gaps between stated goals and actual practices, including unexpected sites of collusion between dominance and resistance.

### What Is Intersectionality Backlash?

While some attention has begun to be paid to the interpretive dynamics that shape intersectionality's reception and circulation, and to the politics of its use,[4] more focus on these issues is needed because, when looked at comprehensively (across the bounds of discipline, time period, and nation), what emerges is a portrait of a deep-seated (though not necessarily conscious) resistance to intersectional ideas and politics. To better illustrate how widespread the problem of distorting and/or slipping away from intersectionality is, I analyze examples from across diverse intersectionality literatures[5] and historicize its development (and ongoing resistance to its vision) over time. Beyond simply demonstrating the ubiquity of this dynamic, I contend we must consider subtle and overt forms of intersectionality "backlash" to be both philosophically meaningful and politically significant.

As a critical orientation, intersectionality is forward-looking and historically focused. It asks that we imagine future possibilities and reconsider omissions, past and present, from a "matrix" mindset: it also helps to expose historical silences and to understand oppression and privilege as lived experiences and processes situated in and shaped by material, political, and social conditions. For instance, in nineteenth- and twentieth-century contexts, to challenge the limits of one-dimensional political and philosophical frames, Black feminist scholars and activists used intersectional lenses[6] to render visible assumptions of whiteness embedded in ideas about womanhood and feminism and to lay bare the androcentrism at work in ideas about race and civil rights. They developed models of power, personhood, and justice that traverse categorical logics and account for complexity: at the same time, they contested either/or approaches that misconstrue subjectivity, occlude interlocking power dynamics, and distort how domination and subordination (or privilege and oppression) operate. Today, intersectionality continues to be used to contest exclusionary, one-dimensional models of personhood, groups, rights, and power.

Unfortunately, binary logics and hierarchical practices endure, despite their clear role in maintaining inequity and rationalizing harm. The ongoing impact and power of single-axis mindsets also shapes how intersectional ideas are regularly contained and resisted, in ways subtle and overt. In other words, though it is widely cited and extensively applied, and as such would not seem in need of much further explanation or justification, the fact is that many uses and common understandings of intersectionality regularly: circumscribe its analytical and political vision, turn away from its radical roots, or flatten its capacity in other ways. Even in contexts where the stated goals are to meaningfully take up the concept, the ways in which it is engaged often contravene core intersectional premises, philosophically and politically.

Any approach that contests prevailing mindsets and seeks to lay the ground for social transformation does (naturally) face outright opposition. But what I have found more compelling (and in some ways more troubling) are what might be characterized as indirect, inadvertent, or unintentional forms of resisting, even refusing intersectionality: it is often disciplined or dropped in the very ways it is taken up. For instance, it frequently is discussed or applied without much apparent grounding in its present literatures or longer histories: in fact, scholarly norms of reading and studying a tradition with care and rigor do not always seem to apply when it comes to referencing, debating, or operationalizing intersectionality (Bilge 2014; Bowleg 2014). In many ways, this mirrors a heedlessness that has faced Black feminist intellectual and political traditions at large and evokes the kinds of dismissal and disregard faced by Black women knowers over time.

As Cho, Crenshaw, and McCall (2013) observe, much of "what circulates as critical debate about what intersectionality is or does reflects a lack of engagement with both originating and contemporary literatures on intersectionality" (788). It is not uncommon to find it treated as a gesture or catchphrase, for example, used in a token manner to account for a nebulous, depoliticized, and hollow notion of "difference." In both intersectionality debates and applications, an odd disconnect emerges, one that is remarkably consistent whether the approach is critical or favorable: it is often acknowledged but then simultaneously put aside. If not dropped entirely, intersectionality may be absorbed into conventional practices—it is frequently misrecognized, or even violated, in the terms and conditions of its uptake.

In other words, intersectionality seems to face a remarkable degree of epistemic intolerance, though much of its undermining takes place via indirect rather than outright forms of dismissal. Rather than approach intersectionality *intersectionally*, scholars frequently rely on non-intersectional (or even anti-intersectional) methods and thereby evacuate intersectionality of its history, meanings, and promise. Its analytics frequently are divvied up, for example, as if its call to attend to the interfaces of context, structure, identity, power, and privilege, on multiple scales, was *optional* rather than intrinsic. Critics and practitioners alike also often ignore an intersectionality fundamental: the need to analyze, as meaningful factors (and not just as descriptive elements), the *interconnections* (of different aspects of identity, various forms of domination [and also liberation], and micropolitical and macropolitical scales). Instead, intersectionality is read as a rationale for atomization and hierarchy. Some thus argue that intersectionality should attend primarily to structure rather than identity (placing these in opposition and as separable) or that class should be viewed as prior to other factors since it is most crucial (because ostensibly more structural, material, or universally experienced), thereby positing one form of identity and structure of oppression not only as separate from others but also as primary.

The very terms of reading, discussing, and applying intersectionality can therefore distort, whether by breaching fundamental precepts, artificially dividing up its multifaceted analytics, taking up the concept ahistorically (and with little accountability to its origins), or even by using intersectional insights that have radical aims and origins, but in ways that reinforce or merely "manage" status quo inequality. Insidiously, to follow the logics of many of these arguments or practices, offered in intersectionality's name, one must actually relinquish many of its most basic ideas and commitments and dismiss its radical history and transformative vision.

In the tradition of intersectional thought and practice, I take up such contradictions as politically and epistemically significant and as instructive about the workings of power. This lack of meaningful engagement cannot simply be due to the fact that intersectionality is "complex" or in need of a more precise or rigorous definition. In other words, though this book includes in-depth discussions of intersectionality's meanings, the troubling interpretive patterns that have materialized across sites of its application are not simply "definitional" in nature. While the various examples of resistance discussed may be subtle, indirect, or unintended, they should be understood, nevertheless, to constitute forms of epistemological "backlash" with real political and material outcomes.

Philosophical intransigence and long-standing structural inequalities seem to join forces to prevent intersectionality from being fully realized (meaning our collective quests for inclusive justice models and for eradicating inequality on intersectional terms also are stymied). Such distortions delimit the full potential of intersectionality as a politic, an analytic, and a justice orientation. More attention must be paid to the means by which it is constantly sidestepped, why this might be so, and what this might indicate—not only for intersectionality scholars and practitioners but also for understanding the politics of knowledge more widely and for developing and enacting nuanced interpretive methods and strategies for social change.

### History Lessons

Intersectionality is interdisciplinary in orientation and draws on multiple sites of knowing, from the micropolitical scale of lived experience and personal reflection to the macropolitical scale of structural, political, philosophical, and representational inequities (such an impetus is clear, for instance, in Kimberlé Crenshaw's body of work: it is equally evident in nineteenth-century iterations of intersectional thought). This multiscale interdisciplinary legacy is an important part of intersectionality's usefulness for identifying gaps in conventional logics, pinpointing distortions, and introducing alternatives by thinking across ways of knowing: therefore, whenever possible, and to align analytic form with intersectional content, I follow this impulse.

Throughout this volume, I explore a series of interrelated issues. Since some confusion seems to persist with regard to its meanings and implications, I first aim to answer a basic question: what are central intersectionality ideas and orientations? Given my wider interests in tracing Black feminist intellectual histories, and in examining the politics of the reception and use of Black feminist ideas, in answering this question, I not only reference some earlier iterations of the concept but also ask why curtailed or cursory genealogies of intersectional thought seem so readily accepted. As I have argued, the

> notion that intersectionality is a recent development in feminist thought relies upon a truncated theoretical genealogy. While the late 20th century certainly marks the emergence in the critical lexicon of the term "intersectionality" by [Kimberlé] Crenshaw, and while the 1970s and 1980s were shaped by wide-ranging discussions of the interplay among systems of race, gender, class, and sexuality, it is inaccurate to suggest that the last forty years constitute the only historical moment in which the examination of *intersections* among systems, identities, and politics has been pivotal in the history of feminist thought in general and within black feminist thought in particular. (May 2012a, 18)

In other words, intersectionality's full complexity cannot be adequately understood if one attends only to its most recent examples, or even to its late twentieth-century formations: as an orientation, it has a history and thus, to echo Toni Morrison's discussion of African American literary history, it, too, has pivotal "structures," "moorings," and "anchors" (Morrison, in McKay and Morrison 1994, 151) that need to be more adequately recognized and drawn on.

However, more than simply render visible intersectionality's longevity, a historicized approach illuminates patterns of ongoing resistance (meaning, here, prolonged efforts to transform structural inequality as well as tenacious resistance to those struggles and repeated dismissal of contestatory ideas like intersectionality). A historicized approach helps demonstrate that intersectionality is longer-lived than many acknowledge and that it has also been long misunderstood or resisted. Just as the concept is not 'new,' its undertheorization and distortion are not, either. By undertheorization, I do not mean intersectionality is theoretically weak, focused on a naïve and essentialist identity framework, or too metaphorical or ambiguous to be viable (these assertions are out there, and shall be taken up, but this is not my meaning here).

When one accounts for historical Black feminist writings that introduce matrix thinking, and examines their reception, what becomes clear is that, whether presently or historically, intersectional ideas have repeatedly been misconstrued or treated reductively. Efforts to conceptualize personhood and agency in ways that acknowledge the multifaceted nature of subjectivity as well as the complexity of multiple social structures have not always been received well or even understood: intersectional ideas have been accompanied all along by overt and indirect forms of political and philosophical resistance. This dynamic may well help explain why key intersectionality concepts (e.g., matrix of oppressions, intertwined identities/positionalities, or coalition politics) have had to be reiterated for well over a century: furthermore, it has been largely Black and women of color feminists who have taken up this rearticulation and who have insisted on the meaningfulness and relevance of these ideas.

Since simplistic understandings of intersectionality are not inevitable, even if they may be commonplace, it is necessary to ask what a repeated inability to take up intersectional ideas might signify. This ongoing misconstrual and interpretive distortion deserve exploration, particularly as intersectionality is currently being mobilized in a variety of ways, some of which could well be considered anti-intersectional. Intersectionality runs against the grain of dominant logics, challenges accepted political models, and contests conventional ideas about subjectivity and agency: however, it is also subjected to the very hegemonic practices and divisive logics it contests. Furthermore, much of this absorption, assimilation, or flattening is taking place within discourses, research models, and policy contexts characterized as feminist. It is essential to explore more fully how intersectionality has been interpreted, translated, and/or applied and to examine what notion(s) of justice, subjectivity, and knowledge have been animated in its name. (On the flip side, it is equally imperative to ask what gets discarded or relinquished if we set aside intersectionality or treat it as something to supplant or move "beyond.")

### Schematics: A Synopsis of the Book's Structure

Since any in-depth review of the considerable literatures (in theoretical, methodological, activist, and policy work) readily shows that many intersectionality "basics" frequently are ignored, if not violated, I begin (in Chapter 1) by delineating and contextualizing its central premises and orientations. I proceed from the perspective that, while intersectionality is not "one" homogenous concept with set practices or fixed assumptions, it does have a historical trajectory that needs to be accounted for meaningfully and a set of commitments that, likewise, need to be engaged substantively (not nominally or via empty gestures).

I suggest intersectionality has several key qualities that must be kept in mind, together: it is an *orientation for engagement or praxis*; it *entails matrix thinking* (in terms of identities, knowledges, inequalities, and forms of power); it is relevant to and *"about" all of us*; and *it is not neutral.* Instead, it is concerned with eradicating injustice and skeptical of claims that we have fully disaffiliated from pathologizing mindsets or wholly broken from past discriminatory practices that have served to rationalize and buttress systemic harm and inequality. I then map out four additional intersectionality "facets" to flesh out its implications. I explain how intersectionality is an *epistemological project* that contests dominant mindsets; an *ontological approach* that accounts for complex subjectivity and offers different notions of agency; a *radical political orientation* grounded in solidarity, rather than sameness, as an organizing principle; and a *resistant imaginary* useful for intervening in conventional historical memory and prevailing social imaginaries. A multilevel, antisubordination impetus is at the heart of all of these characteristics.

Though I offer a sustained analysis of its meanings, I also contend, whether in the context of forming equity policies, crafting feminist theories and methods, or engaging in forms of social action, that discussions about intersectionality must shift beyond a definitional impetus. Undue focus on the definitional can draw attention away from wider political dynamics, ongoing issues of cognitive authority and power, and persistent patterns of co-optation and distortion: furthermore, it can imply that all "problems" or "issues" with intersectionality are internal to itself, replicating a victim-blaming, pathologizing logic.

Since intersectionality is an analytic meant to be applied with an eye toward justice, we must examine how it has been interpreted and instrumentalized, understand how it has (or has not) been realized as a practice, and identify what obstacles it faces. In Chapter 2, I begin to flesh out the surprisingly intractable nature of the "either/or" philosophical norms and "single-axis" political practices intersectionality has long contested: myriad forms of binary thinking (mindsets that rationalize inequality and uphold hierarchy) remain entrenched. At the same time, I offer some concrete examples of the ways in which intersectionality can be misrecognized or distorted to begin to show how frequently it is avoided, even when seemingly engaged with, extensively invoked, but then absorbed and made deferential to normativity.

How can this be so? How can a concept that is widely taught, frequently cited, and even referenced by some supranational governing bodies on one hand be so regularly misunderstood or misrepresented on the other? Unpacking this dynamic helps to illuminate how established frameworks and dominant imaginaries continue to impede intersectionality's reception and application. Because interpretive discourses are sites where material and epistemic power play out, the terms of how intersectionality is taken up (i.e., how it is read, written about, circulated, and applied) matter. In the context of women's and gender studies, for instance, interpretive politics play a part in establishing (or reinforcing) feminist theoretical norms and in delineating the bounds of political relevance and analytical significance (Tomlinson 2013b).

Consequently, in Chapter 3, I trace patterns of intersectionality's interpretation and examine feminist critiques of the concept as one central site of its disciplining and even dismissal. Oddly, critics often use nonintersectional lenses, or even anti-intersectional logics, to assess its alternative vision: via an either/or interpretive approach, intersectional both/and analyses are rendered illogical or dispensable, for example. Likewise, by using norms and measures that begin from an additive notion of identity or inequality, critics frequently obliterate its matrix thinking and cross-cutting vision of change. To illustrate, I examine several common critical motifs: *intersectionality is just "Black feminism" recycled; intersectionality's approach to identity is unsophisticated; intersectionality is disadvantaged by its focus on disadvantage*; and *intersectionality is destructive to feminism ("Sapphire" rises, beware!)*.

I then analyze some proposed solutions or "cures" for what "ails" intersectionality and discuss how many suggested improvements violate, rather than engage, its premises and politics. For instance, some seem (indirectly) to advocate deracializing or "whitening" intersectionality to make it more universal or usable,[7] while others support a return to single-axis logics and politics as the way forward (especially common are class-first or gender-first solutions). Throughout, I discuss how the stories we tell about intersectionality "matter" (Hemmings 2011): how it is portrayed or rendered, the citational practices used, the affects drawn upon, the analytic frames applied, and the "plots" it is made to fit are all important considerations.

In Chapter 4, I turn to intersectionality's operationalization (as method, theory, and policy) to illustrate how well-intentioned applications can be equally problematic. In addition to offering an overview of how intersectionality is being applied across a range of contexts, I examine whether applications *claiming* intersectionality are adequately intersectional. This "mapping" of applications is crucial because most discussions do not take up intersectional activism, policy formation, research methods, and theorizing together: furthermore, many discussions are bound by disciplinary (and national) borders that can obscure wider patterns and shared logics. I thus examine several sites of intersectionality's current application (in the twenty-first-century university, in research methodologies, and in state-level and supranational equity policies) to highlight various kinds of "slippages."

What becomes clear is that, even as practitioners may aim to use intersectionality meaningfully, how it is practiced or instituted frequently departs from or even undermines intersectional aims. For instance, researchers may set out to do an intersectional study, but will not use intersectionality as an analytic lens to shape questions, design research models, or interpret data: it will, instead, be used only as a demographic or descriptive device (see Choo and Ferree 2010; Harnois 2013; Shields 2008). In this way, its explanatory, political, and analytical capacities are abandoned: intersectionality is transmogrified into a descriptor of "difference," with no apparent utility for unpacking normative logics or challenging the workings of power and privilege therein. In fact, the sheer number of "slippages" away from intersectionality is fairly astounding, whether in critical or applied contexts.

Furthermore, the distortions and departures to be found in numerous intersectionality applications are, in many ways, not all that different from the forms of flattening found in many intersectionality critiques. In both contexts, it can be rendered amenable to prevailing analytical/political norms. For example, practitioners and critics alike may approach intersectionality as a form of binary thinking (not as a deep critique of this logic's harmful outcomes); disarticulate its interconnected precepts; interpret it via frameworks that buttress, rather than contest, normative/deviant binaries; or engage intersectionality in ways that rank identities and place forms of oppression in a hierarchy.

In short, normative frames and expectations are often imposed onto intersectionality: rather than continue to slip away from intersectionality, we must find ways to more adequately *depart from dominant logics* and approach, interpret, and utilize it more *intersectionally* and in line with its multifaceted justice orientation. In the end, this book aims to do more than pinpoint different means by which, paradoxically, as we engage with intersectionality, we may continue to uphold the very mindsets it contests and seeks to change. Once such practices and habits of mind become more discernible, we must also ask what to do about it. How can we intervene in this containment, distortion, and slippage? What are some strategies for taking it up more adequately?

In Chapter 5, I discuss the problem of the sheer force of dominant logics, and the correlative question of how to counter them, as they play a considerable role in making intersectionality perpetually "unheard," even as it is widely referenced and reiterated. Since many of the practices and norms intersectionality has long contested continue to hold sway, I take inspiration from feminist and anti-racist philosophers interested in issues of testimonial injustice, unequal rhetorical space, and epistemologies of ignorance[8] and suggest the need for a twofold practice: that of actively *bracketing* dominant logics while also being vigorously *biased toward* intersectionality's alternative worldviews. Drawing on a range of methodological and philosophical discussions, I begin to outline what practicing "bias" and "bracketing," with regard to intersectionality, might entail.

Given that intersectionality places interpretive and political demands on us, I conclude with some strategies for orienting toward intersectionality, once the first and pivotal step of bracketing/bias is under way. Rather than employ intersectionality in ways that assimilate it to conventional logics and dominant norms, we must identify how to better align intersectional aims, form, and content. This is not to suggest that our practices must be flawless; rather, it is a call to continually think about what it means to imagine and to practice an intersectional philosophy and politic by actively turning away from hegemonic expectations.

Norm emulation, assimilation to the status quo, and reinforcement of oppressive logics and processes are *not* intersectional dispositions or goals. To go about "doing" intersectionality more adequately, in ways that are more commensurate with its principles, aims, and histories, we must not make it deferential to dominant (and anti-intersectional) ways of thinking.

## Notes

1. Chapter 1 provides a more comprehensive overview of the concept's key ideas, the importance of its historical origins, and its wider political relevance and philosophical scope.
2. Recently, quite a bit of focus has been placed on intersectionality definitions (as if to pin down its complex parameters once and for all, rather than appreciate the value of unruly concepts or narrative logics as philosophically and politically meaningful, as Barbara Christian (1990) might have suggested). However, less attention has been

paid to illuminating what it can *do*, as Crenshaw (2011c) recently argued (see also Cho, Crenshaw, and McCall 2013).

3. See Brah and Phoenix (2004), Collins (1990, 1998), Mingus and Talley (2013), Parent, DeBlaere, and Moradi (2013), and Zinn and Dill (1996).
4. See, for example, Bilge (2013), Carastathis (2013b), Carbado (2013), Cho (2013), Crenshaw (2011c), and Tomlinson (2013a, 2013b).
5. I occasionally engage in close readings of particular uses of intersectionality or of common interpretations of intersectionality. The intent is not to single out an author, debate, or context of application but to: help illustrate patterns and dynamics across contexts that may not usually be examined together (due to disciplinary bounds, for instance); facilitate thinking about using intersectionality as a lens for pinpointing collusion between hegemony and resistance; and underscore the need to use intersectionality to analyze and assess the concept's own use and interpretation (i.e., to think about how to interpret and apply intersectionality *intersectionally*).
6. As many scholars have documented, intersectional ideas can be found in Black feminist intellectual/political history, well back into the early nineteenth century. For instance, see Carby (1987), Crenshaw (1989), Giddings (1984), Gines (2011, 2014), Guy-Sheftall (1995), May (2007, 2012a), Moody-Turner (2013), and Waters (2007).
7. This dynamic has also recently discussed by Bilge (2013), Carbado (2013), Crenshaw (2011c), and Tomlinson (2013a).
8. For example, Babbitt (2001, 2005), Campbell (1999), Code (1995, 2011), Fricker (2007), Lugones (1987, 1994), Mills (1997), Narayan (1997), Ortega (2006), Pohlhaus (2012), Schutte (2000), and Wylie (2011).

# 1
# What Is Intersectionality?
## *Matrix Thinking in a Single-Axis World*

On the cusp of discussing intersectionality definitions, I hesitate. Since intersectionality is a complex concept with growing impact across disciplines, policy formulations, and sites of political struggle, much time has been spent defining the concept or delineating typologies (e.g., McCall 2005). Yet while definitional work might clarify, it can also distort by disarticulating key intersectionality ideas that fundamentally link. Definitions can flatten in other ways as well. For instance, mapping out intersectionality via linear time can treat its political/intellectual origins, in Black and women of color feminisms, as (implicitly or explicitly) passé or naïve. Even if cited, earlier intersectionality texts may not be given nuanced readings but treated casually or deemed theoretically underwhelming.[1] This dynamic can also be relatively subtle: today, for instance, the secondary intersectionality literatures often are more widely referenced and taught than are many foundational writings and practices.

Time spent defining or classifying intersectionality can also draw critical energies away from asking key questions, such as: Are the examples at hand adequately "intersectional" in nature? Are intersectionality's groundings and histories, crafted within Black feminist, critical race, and women of color politics/theorizing, attended to meaningfully (and not just nominally)? Does the form align, in terms of philosophy and practice, with intersectionality's key insights and inclusive social justice objectives? Does the analytical approach or classification system artificially compartmentalize intersectionality's interrelated premises?

Laying out intersectionality definitions clearly has potential pitfalls, so why embark on this chapter? Though widely recognized, intersectionality also is regularly used or talked about in ways that flatten its complexity, ignore its historical literatures, or depoliticize its approach. Many applications let intersectionality drop or systematize it in ways that may render it more usable as an instrument, but in so doing also obviate key premises. This suggests intersectionality might *not* in fact be so fully or easily understood. Intersectionality invites us to bracket hegemonic mindsets and resist the lure(s) of oppressive power so as to achieve a more just world: are any of us so fully "liberated" from conventional ways of thinking and being that we need not engage in any further thought about intersectional meanings, practices, and histories? Instead of presuming everyone knows what intersectionality is, (re)turning to its central ideas and orientations is an apt place to begin.

## Intersectionality as a Form of Social Action

My approach to intersectionality is oriented toward what it *does* or *can do*, not simply toward its definitional status as a noun. This is in keeping with Kimberlé Crenshaw's emphasis that intersectionality is *heuristic* in nature: it is akin to a "prism" to be used to "amplify" and highlight specific problems, particularly by drawing attention to dynamics that are "constitutive" but generally overlooked or silenced (Crenshaw 2011c, 229–232). She explains her sensibility thusly: "My own take on how to know intersectionality has been to do intersectionality" (222; see also Guidroz and Berger 2009). A heuristic orientation accentuates its problem-solving capacity, one that is contextual, concerned with eradicating inequity, oriented toward unrecognized knowers and overlooked forms of meaning, attentive to experience as a fund of knowledge, and interrogative (focused on asking questions, incrementally and continuously).

Approaching intersectionality in this way also taps into its longer history. For instance, in the late nineteenth century, Black feminist educator and intellectual Anna Julia Cooper insisted that our work must never just be about "ratiocination," or knowledge merely for knowledge's sake: thought and action must be linked to do away with inequality (Cooper 1988, 285–303). During this same era, Ida B. Wells engaged in intersectional journalism and political activism to challenge lynching. Highlighting how hetero-patriarchy and white supremacy functioned together, to rationalize lynching as a tool of nationalist terror and containment during the Progressive era, Wells used a matrix lens to debunk the nation's claims to democracy (and to lay bare practices of injustice founded in racist gender nationalism, i.e., in the name of "protecting" white womanhood).[2]

Thinking about intersectionality as a heuristic orientation or disposition also echoes Barbara Christian's (1990) assertion that Black feminist theorizing, as a larger set of practices, should be conceived of as akin to an active verb, thereby allowing for flexible, nonessentialist understandings both of Black women and of Black feminisms (whereas an object/noun approach suggests stasis as well as commodity status). Many Black feminists have a deep suspicion of objects' supposed neutrality, since enslaved Black women, for instance, were categorized by the state as nonpersons/as property: the legal designation of raced and gendered property created, in turn, white masculinity as an invisible but nevertheless powerful form of accrued rights and privileges, or property, to be protected by the law (see Harris 1993).

Rather than emulate or animate the subject/object divide used historically to rank persons, Patricia J. Williams (1991) and Barbara Christian (1990) instead emphasize the value of nonlinear and narrative ways of knowing that are difficult to "control" and require interpretive engagement, such as riddles, hieroglyphs, and parables. Black feminist theorizing, they argue, rejects treating knowledge (particularly knowledge forged in and by marginalized communities) as a commodity to be extracted and traded. Approaching theorizing as active, and as engaged in by (variously) situated (and subjugated) knowers, is also a long-standing impetus in Latina and Indigenous feminisms:[3] intersectionality connects to (but does not stand in for the whole of) these traditions.

To contest false binaries, reveal links among systems of oppression, and forge political coalitions, intersectionality attends to patterns that cut across scales, focuses on unstated assumptions, and explores the meanings of gaps and absences. By accounting for multiple registers of existence, entangled forms of domination, and the simultaneity of identities, it is "applicable to both the structural level of analysis, and individual-level phenomena, via its domains of power thesis, which recognizes the various terrains on which politics plays out—structural and interpersonal" (Hancock 2007b, 74; see also Collins 1998). This focus on power's different formations across scales is not simply diagnostic or descriptive: it is oriented toward dismantling oppressive practices and forging a more just world for us all.

In other words, intersectionality is political, philosophical, and pedagogical in nature: it invites us to think from "both/and" spaces and to seek justice in crosscutting ways by identifying and addressing the (often hidden) workings of privilege and oppression. Weaving the structural and the personal, the particular and the universal, intersectional approaches offer a means to think against the grain and bridge false divides. In turn, this leads to asking new questions about power, inequality, and marginalization: intersectionality can be used to disrupt conventional philosophical frames, dislodge the usual explanations, and question default analytic categories. Intersectionality's interrogatory, antisubordination impetus is crucial and stems from its origins as a form of resistant knowing, one interested in seeking liberation on new terms and in eradicating epistemological, material, and structural inequality.

### Intersectionality Is about Matrix Thinking

Intersectionality highlights how lived identities, structural systems, sites of marginalization, forms of power, and modes of resistance "intersect" in dynamic, shifting ways. As Audre Lorde explains, "there is no such thing as a single-issue struggle because we do not lead single-issue lives" (Lorde 1984, 183). Likewise, Pauli Murray aptly notes that "the lesson of history [is] that all human rights are indivisible and that the failure to adhere to this principle jeopardizes the rights of all" (Murray 1995, 197). Over a century prior, in 1866, Frances Ellen Watkins Harper offered a similar vision at the inaugural meeting of the American Equal Rights Association: "The white women all go for sex," she remarked, "letting race occupy a minor position." Instead, we must remember (and act upon the fact that) "we are all bound up together in one great bundle of humanity" (Harper, in Foster 1990, 217–219).

This matrix philosophy has several important implications. First, it dispenses with "add and stir" political strategies, analytical premises, or research methodologies: assimilative strategies are problematic because they simply tinker within status quo frameworks (Mingus and Talley 2013), reinforce the "notion of the dominant group as standard," presume underlying sameness, and ignore "norm-constructing operations of power" (Choo and Ferree 2010, 137). Intersectionality also is not a cumulative or arithmetical identity formula (race + gender + class + sexuality + disability + citizenship status, and so on, as if these were sequential, separate factors).[4] Instead, it focuses on simultaneity, attends to within-group differences, and rejects "single-axis" categories that falsely universalize the experiences or needs of a select few as representative of all group members.

Thinking in terms of enmeshed multiplicities (of identity and power), or what Deborah K. King described as "multiple jeopardy," challenges the premise that "each discrimination has a single, direct and independent effect on status, wherein the relative contribution of each is readily apparent." It also rejects "non-productive assertions that one factor can and should supplant the other" (King 1988, 47). As Nira Yuval-Davis explains, "social divisions [are] constituted by each other in concrete ways, enmeshed in each other, although they . . . are also irreducible to each other" (Yuval-Davis, in Guidroz and Berger 2009, 65). In research, a "matrix" approach considers how inequalities intermingle and "span and transform structures and activities at all levels and in all institutional contexts": this, in turn, "makes it harder to imagine any social process as a singular 'main effect' for anyone" (Choo and Ferree 2010, 135). In philosophical terms, matrix logics attend to "thick" members of a group and reject "split-separation" mindsets, instead using "curdled" logics to conceive of, and achieve, liberation on multiple fronts (Lugones 1994). Intersectionality thus aims to account for relationships, collusions, and disjunctures among forms and sites of power.

Linking the structural and experiential, and the material and discursive, it does not approach different identities or systems of power as "non-interactive" or independent (Harnois 2005, 810): instead, intersectionality examines how power and privilege operate on several levels at once (experiential, epistemological, political, and structural) and across (and within) categories of experience and personhood (including race, gender, sexuality, disability, social class, and citizenship). In turn, this requires exploring how we occupy social positions and engage in knowledge practices that, because entwined and interactive, can be understood as sites where both marginalization and privilege play out simultaneously. However, which structures and institutional formations need to be analyzed, which categories are relevant, and how or whether they translate across cultural and historical contexts are not predetermined but are open-ended questions.

### Intersectionality's Matrix Thinking Is "about" All of Us

Though its focus on the (hidden but considerable) "wages" of privilege is often overlooked,[5] intersectionality scholars and activists repeatedly have shown that privilege and oppression are experienced and structured simultaneously: this means that addressing underprivilege requires identifying and dismantling overprivilege, within and between groups. Overprivilege and underprivilege are relational and are reinforced by social practices, philosophical norms, and structural inequalities. Intersectionality thus invites a complex view of power as multipronged and shifting, operating across different sites and scales simultaneously.

A matrix philosophy also requires studying "unmarked" or transparent categories, where power and privilege constellate on their own terms and in relation to "marked" ones.[6] This is why Crenshaw emphasizes that no one exists outside of matrices/relations of power, and everyone is socially located in multiple, overlapping ways. In concert with Collins (2008), who underscores that intersectionality is not a fixed analytic, Crenshaw explains that the "implications of this matrix—when certain features are activated and relevant and when they are not—are contextual," meaning they are not fixed, foreordained, or tied to any one particular group (Crenshaw 2011c, 230).

Uma Narayan, for instance, views intersectionality as pertinent to transnational feminist politics because it offers strategies for thinking "within and across communities" to address the needs of a "range of differently situated women" (Narayan 1997, 153). Narayan does not claim intersectionality, as it moves across worlds, does so without any "baggage" or that it is inherently liberatory due to its radical origins. However, by approaching it as a cross-border, cross-categorical mindset, she creates space for asking why this potential relevance is so often curtailed by binary logics that erroneously pit the transnational against the intersectional and that suppress intersectionality's both/and, same/different philosophical–political impetus.

In other words, despite its call to attend to privilege *and* disenfranchisement simultaneously, and notwithstanding its rejection of essentialist group or individual identities, intersectionality frequently is portrayed as narrowly conceived. For instance, it has been seen as focusing only on "oppression" or understood as relevant only to the particular forms of oppression faced by Black women (as if these could be predetermined and as if Black women were an undifferentiated group).[7] Thus, while McCall rightly underscores how analyzing simultaneous privilege and oppression is fundamental to intersectionality, she risks glossing its historical attention to heterogeneity within and between groups when asserting, "in its emphasis on black women's experiences of subjectivity and oppression, intersectional theory has obscured the question whether all identities are intersectional" (McCall 2005, 1774).

There is no reason that an emphasis on Black women's subjectivity should be seen to curtail intersectionality's relevance or applicability when it comes to insights about simultaneous privilege and oppression, multiplicity, and complex subjectivity, for instance. So, why is a focus on Black women as illustrative of wider dynamics often read as a fairly significant limitation of intersectionality's foundational writings, or interpreted as an assertion that Black womanhood is the only (or essential, or "paradigmatic")[8] intersectional identity (or, further, that no other identities are intersectional)? The implication is that attending to Black womanhood entails some inherent narrowness: it is as if only some parts of intersectionality's insights about simultaneous privilege and oppression and about the limits and distortions of "single-axis" logics are perceived or taken up.

For instance, many who find Crenshaw's notion of intersectionality overly "narrow," overlook how, in "Demarginalizing," she argues in part that white women, or Black men, are *as unrepresentative* of the larger groups "Women" or "Blacks" as are Black Women (or, conversely, Black women are *equally representative*). Everyone has intersecting identities and all of us live within interlocking structures of raced and gendered social stratification. Everyone "has" race and gender, though only Black women are perceived by the courts as embodying "both." White women's gender comes to the fore while their race falls from view as transparent, making them seem, from single-axis thinking, ideal representatives or case examples of sexism: their intersectionality is denied, though, as Crenshaw (1989) underscores, it is fully operative.[9]

The courts seem to recognize, implicitly, that identities intersect, but only for litigants who make claims about more than one nontransparent identity (e.g., in the cases Crenshaw discusses, for Black women) and only in a limited sense—"their" intersectionality (in this instance, Black womanhood) is seen as detrimental or confusing to the law because neither "their" race nor gender can be disarticulated (though, according to the court's logics, apparently others' can be when one factor matches the unstated, privileged transparency norm [whiteness for white women; masculinity for Black men]). However, the courts do not take up questions of *injustice, oppression*, or *redress* intersectionally: factors that would allow for analyzing and addressing asymmetrical, structured patterns of harm (and privilege) are treated as epistemologically irrelevant, even harmful, within single-axis frameworks.

The courts thus reinforce transparent race and gender privilege, willfully ignoring the unstated intersectionality of litigants characterized as representative of just one identity and, correlatively, normative benchmarks for understanding harm and discrimination, singularly conceived (e.g., sexism *or* racism) (Crenshaw 1989; see also Carbado 2013). Here, then, a thorny question arises in terms of intersectionality's wider reception and interpretation. As with the courts' reinforcement of transparency norms, reliance on privilege to address inequality, and rejection of intersectional analyses of systemic harm, is it the case that intersectionality's readership has engaged in a parallel, willfully narrow reading of its logics, its same/different thesis, its testimony regarding simultaneous privilege and oppression, and its wider applicability?

Again, intersectionality scholars repeatedly have shown that intersectionality is "for" and "about" everyone and that "Black womanhood" is neither singular nor monolithic, though age-old stereotypes and racist–sexist ideologies have portrayed it to be, whether in notions of "monstrous," long-breasted Black females in the sixteenth, seventeenth, and eighteenth centuries (Morgan 2004) or in more contemporary controlling images of Sapphire and Mammy.[10] Intersectionality, however, rejects these ideological legacies, de-homogenizes Black womanhood, insists on the need to attend to within-group differences, and uses "both/and" thinking to underscore how Black women's experiences are not delimited in their relevance only to Black women, via some kind of "special case" closed logic.

In fact, this both/and approach has a long and significant history in Black feminist thought. For instance, Kristin Waters identifies the development of "matrix" thinking in the work of many nineteenth-century Black feminists, from Maria Stewart early in the century to Cooper later on: both women "succeed in 'fracturing' the conceptions of race and gender while at the same time employing them, obliquely addressing concerns about essentializing that were not even to be officially raised until a century later" (Waters 2007, 382). Likewise, Hazel Carby contends Cooper and her peers "exposed the historical and ideological framework within which white women defended their own class and racial interests" (Carby 1987, 102–103, 105). She demonstrates how "the texts of black women from ex-slave Harriet Jacobs to educator Anna Julia Cooper are testaments to the racist practices of the suffrage and temperance movements and indictments of the ways in which white women allied themselves . . . with a racist patriarchal order" (6). This longer intellectual/political genealogy should not be ignored, as Crenshaw and others have argued.[11]

To return to the example of "Demarginalizing," Crenshaw references legal cases, historical examples, and personal experiences that, when considered together, do not suggest homogenous social class experiences among Black women. She neither presents a uniform portrait of Black womanhood, nor suggests Black women are to be understood as intersectionality archetypes. However, she does insist Black women's (collective yet divergent) experiences, lives, and insights should be seen as *instructive* with regard to wider patterns in the law (and in the historical archive)—that is, they have universal implications. At the same time, the particularities that emerge across Black women's lives must not be erased, collapsed, or abandoned (Crenshaw 1989).

Unfortunately, reductive readings of Black womanhood and of intersectionality texts and practices frequently go hand in hand. In discussing intersectionality and transnational stratification, for example, Nira Yuval-Davis has questioned simplistic readings of "black womanhood" that often accompany simplistic interpretations of intersectionality. She maintains that "social stratification . . . relates to the differential hierarchical locations of individual and groupings of people on society's grids of power. I find it problematic . . . that the construction of 'black woman' is automatically assumed, unless otherwise specified, to be that of a minority black woman living in white Western societies. The majority of black women in today's world are black women in black societies. This has major implications for a global intersectional stratification analysis" (Yuval-Davis 2011a, 162).

In fact, when one takes an historical view that accounts for intersectionality's precursors, the sheer tenacity of reductive ideas about Black womanhood, the persistent dismissals of Black women's ideas and analyses, and the tenacious single-axis logics that helps sustain them become far more obvious.[12] In other words, despite the longevity of intersectional premises and orientations, intersectionality's same/different premise or both/and approach (i.e., that Black women's lives and knowledges are particular and universal, highly divergent and characterized by within-group differences) cannot seem to be fully taken up.

Furthermore, an historical focus upon Black women (given intersectionality's origins, to a great extent, in Black feminist theorizing and political organizing) is often intimated (if not directly charged) with being "too particular"—and conflated with being only about oppression, if not super-exploitation. Devon Carbado persuasively argues, however, that conceiving of intersectionality simply as a "race to the bottom" (Carbado 2001) is unfounded since it aims to map out and address the full architecture of inequality, from the top to the base (and even to the substructure) of social hierarchies, as well as across them. Nevertheless, many interpretations of intersectionality ignore its call to attend to structural power and privilege and overlook its same/different thesis. Evidently, to a world used to operating on either/or logics, intersectional matrix views continue to seem illogical (Crenshaw 1989; Spade 2013).

**Intersectionality Is Not "Neutral"**

Intersectionality is not (and does not aim to be) neutral. In fact, it invites us to focus on unsettling conventional categories, analytic concepts, and political imaginaries because it is politically and socially interested: intersectionality stems from histories of political struggle and is oriented toward pursuing multifaceted forms of justice. Emphasizing context and the relevance of lived experience, it helps to expose erasures in ways of knowing and to identify forms of resistance, whether individual or collective. Being accountable to this political vision of contesting and addressing multiple forms of inequality means acknowledging simultaneous privilege and oppression within our different communities and changing the terms of how we conceptualize, and struggle for, justice and change.

Furthermore, intersectionality exposes how norms and practices declared to be impartial are often applied and enforced in (biased) ways that perpetuate systemic inequality. Part of its "bias" toward justice, then, means rejecting limited definitions of what counts as oppressive, questioning everyday assumptions that rationalize domination, and directing our attention to overlooked patterns of structural inequality. More than simply describe multiplicity, intersectional work takes a stand against inequality and harm and overtly aims for social transformation and meaningful change.

In other words, intersectionality's heuristic qualities combine with its political interests to direct attention to gaps in dominant logics or in conventional understandings of how oppression and privilege operate. This is why it is useful on many levels: intersectionality "identifies the hegemonic (ideas, cultures, and ideologies), structural (social institutions), disciplinary (bureaucratic hierarchies and administrative practices), and interpersonal (routinized interactions among individuals) playing fields upon which race, gender, class, and other categories or traditions of difference interact to produce society" (Hancock 2007b, 74) and to uphold asymmetrical life opportunities (Spade 2013).

Intersectionality also invites us to pry open and contest these asymmetries, enter the "cracks" (Springer 1999), pursue the meanings of ellipses or anomalies (May 2009), and remember that the spaces between or alongside systems of power can also be sites of knowledge and resistance.[13] This requires approaching marginalization as an ongoing, non-totalizing *process* (that is both structural and experiential), rather than a fixed state of being: marginality is also considered a "potential source of strength," not just "tragedy" (Collins 1998, 12; see also hooks 1990).

Unfortunately, this twofold engagement (with intersectionality's matrix mandate and its antisubordination legacy) is not always retained. For instance, consider Keisha Lindsay's recent work showing how intersectionality has an openness or "indeterminacy" with regard to its categories and emphases, even as certain groups have historically been its focus (Lindsay 2013, 450). Lindsay aims, in part, to add nuance to intersectionality's analytics and to show how it can be co-opted, but in building her argument about the need to attend to coercive power, she ends up offering a fairly depoliticized portrait of intersectionality.[14] She contends intersectionality's "un-specificity" means it should be understood to be a "normatively malleable heuristic" that can be used for hegemonic aims: social conservatives, in dominant and in marginalized communities alike, she argues, "are increasingly appropriating intersectionality for anti-feminist, racist, or heterosexist ends" (447).

To illustrate, Lindsay explores how conservative Black Christians in her study shore up heteronormative privilege to address raced inequalities and marginalization (Lindsay 2013, 451): several participants, invested in respectability politics, recognize that "how blacks are racially subordinated is a function of their status as heterosexuals," that is, historically characterized as pathologically or excessively heterosexual (452). The point that intersectionality is malleable and may be used oppressively is well taken: Lindsay offers a useful reminder that radical origins cannot ensure corresponding outcomes. Moreover, she rightly treats intersectionality as open to critique, not as beyond reproach or outside the contexts of oppressive power it seeks to address.

So, what is the objection? As a politic and heuristic, intersectionality is about more than describing or capturing "how identities, social categories, or processes of identification and categorization gain meaning from each other" (Lindsay 2013, 447). This characterization is too apolitical and detaches intersectionality from its antisubordination moorings (which include contesting both homophobia and heteronormative respectability politics). For instance, Lindsay maintains that "while black Christian critics of gay marriage do not explicitly acknowledge or deploy intersectionality," how they conceptualize their disadvantage is clearly premised on a "nonadditive way of understanding social inequality" that "strikingly mirrors the logic of intersectionality" (451). "Nonadditivity" is indeed pivotal to intersectional work, but so is attending to systemic power asymmetries and to simultaneous privilege and oppression (within and between groups). More than a "nonadditive way of understanding social inequality," intersectionality emphasizes how hierarchies of social and human value are indefensible, as is shoring up privilege or seeking access to oppressive power.

Intersectionality arose out of specific historical contexts and conditions: its Black feminist origins and politics are not optional even as they are not determinist or beyond interrogation. Because intersectionality has a normative interest in eradicating interlocking forms of inequality, an intersectional reading of relational power and privilege requires more than documenting interaction. In other words, Lindsay's astute insights about how the politics of respectability and homophobia intertwine to enforce exclusionary norms of blackness and narrow measures of what counts as racial subordination would not be presented as *outside* intersectional analysis and politics if her working definition of intersectionality approached it as an analytic device fundamentally committed to broad-based justice.

I would argue that intersectionality's matrix, relational approach (to power and to identity) reveals how heteronormativity is part of what reinforces racism (both share ascriptions of sexual deviance—racism relies on an ascribed primitivist hyper-heterosexuality and homophobia relies on notions of non(re)productive hyper-homosexuality [Collins 2004]): shared logics of deviance rationalize and foster interlocking forms of inequality. However, Lindsay characterizes such abuses of power and patterns of privilege and oppression as *beyond intersectionality's scope*: intersectionality seems to have no role for analyzing or contesting power. In other words, she could more overtly take up as part of intersectional analysis misuses of power in the name of securing rights.

While the church has been an important site for political resistance in Black civil rights struggles, it has also been a place where hetero-patriarchal forms of power have reigned in pernicious ways, as Mark Anthony Neal (2005) provocatively argues.[15] Again, Lindsay *does* critique this legacy, and deservedly so, but *not* under the rubric of "intersectional" analysis. Instead, she advocates a "critical theory of power," one that is focused on "domination within social groups as self-defeating and unjust and is attentive to these groups' capacity to be simultaneously advantaged and disadvantaged" (Lindsay 2013, 448): a critical approach to relative privilege and oppression is thus located as *outside of* or *beyond* intersectionality.

What problems intersectionality can help expose, what its objects of analysis are, who its subjects are, and which dynamics are operating at any given time in a formative way are not set in stone. Intersectionality is not predetermined in focus or only relevant to one group: it is open-ended and particular and requires attending to simultaneous privilege and oppression *and* working within and across differences for change. However, it does not mean co-opting its language and insights to shore up bits of privilege and power while seeking redress and rights on other fronts, thereby retaining the exclusionary logics, unequal life opportunities, and partitioned social ontologies that are part of the problem in the first place.

My larger objection, then, is to how intersectionality's political genealogy and justice orientation are often put aside, whether in the contexts of critique or application: it is not used analytically to identify or address misuses of power. Furthermore, I think it is important to ask, *should* engagements with intersectionality that employ its matrix logics to characterize complex social dynamics, or describe interacting identity formations, yet leave out (or even actively undermine) its antisubordination legacy and liberation politics, be characterized as "intersectional" (particularly when the intent is starkly discriminatory or makes intersectionality deferential to normative/deviant, worthy/unworthy human hierarchies)? I think not. Using intersectionality entails, ideally, some expectation of accountability to its roots in, and ongoing connections to, Black feminist liberation politics that have "no use" for hierarchies of oppression, grabbing at privilege, or reinforcing hegemonic power when convenient, even within systemically disenfranchised communities (Combahee 1983; Reagon 1983; Smith 1983).

Intersectionality's interest in dismantling oppressive structures on multiple fronts, and its related vision of a more just world, are not optional. It places a range of epistemological and political demands on us, one of which is to actively depart from the comforts of conferred dominance and unpack the "blank spots" (Anzaldúa 1990a, xxi) of privilege, not just in "dominant" locations but also "marginal" ones. Intersectionality has a distinct history forged by critical thinking at the intersections of struggles for race and gender justice. More than a complexity tool, it has been developed to help identify harms and injustices, locate and explain their sources and logics, and propose directions for change.

Again, in response to common questions—"What structures or analytics does intersectionality disrupt, for whom is it relevant, and who are its 'subjects'?"—there are not fixed answers. Intersectionality's possibilities vary *and* its origins are shaped by Black feminist and women of color theorizing and politics: this historical trajectory should not be treated nominally. To conceive of intersectionality as unchanging, homogenous, or beyond critique is problematic: I do not suggest otherwise. Intersectionality has resonances, dissonances, and differing iterations (though there has been a heavier emphasis on naming flaws and less emphasis on noting distorting uses and interpretations). However, approaching it as so malleable and unspecific as to be usable for overtly discriminatory or harmful ends *and still be characterized as "intersectionality"* would mean the contexts of its use and history of its emergence are immaterial (when they are pertinent) and that manipulations of coercive power and furthering oppression in its name are fitting (when they are objectionable).

### Intersectionality Is Multifaceted

So far, I have approached intersectionality as a form of action that starts from a "matrix" philosophy informed by its historical legacy in Black feminisms, that is widely applicable, and that is "biased" toward eradicating multiple forms of inequality. In the next sections, I discuss four additional qualities or "facets," though these are not wholly different impetuses or types of intersectionality. I use the "facets" metaphor because intersectionality is often characterized as "multifaceted" and because facets are different aspects of one thing. Every facet on a prism or gem, for instance, interacts with light variously, making a stone appear different from each angle, even as each facet, or angle of light, cannot be disarticulated: the facets work together as part of the whole. However, this metaphor is not perfect by any stretch (it suggests an object, when I want to emphasize intersectionality as an active orientation, for one, and it also references gemstones, most of which have been mined historically and presently in conditions of exploited labor, material expropriation, and environmental degradation).

The point is that these qualities are correlated, interconnected, and concurrent. The boundaries between them are not absolute: they interact in important ways and need to be animated simultaneously in intersectional work. With such caveats in mind, these characteristics can be useful to think about as parts of a composite whole (especially as it is intersectionality's multifaceted quality that often seems to fall from view):

1. Intersectionality is an *epistemological practice* that contests dominant imaginaries: drawing on different foundational premises, it is useful for interrogating conventional knowledge practices and for unpacking gaps and silences therein.
2. Intersectionality is an *ontological project* that accounts for multiplicity and complex subjectivity, reconceptualizes agency, and attends to simultaneous privilege and oppression.
3. Intersectionality invites us to take up a radical *coalitional political orientation* grounded in solidarity, rather than sameness, as a basis for working collectively to eradicate inequalities.
4. Finally, intersectionality functions as a kind of *resistant imaginary*—a way of intervening in historical memory or interrupting the dominant social imagination by thinking 'otherwise.' Certainly, a contestatory quality runs through intersectionality as a whole, but examining this aspect of intersectional practice on its own terms is important.

Again, each facet fundamentally interlinks. Emerging from a legacy of political struggle, a resistant imagination and interrogatory impulse undergird an intersectional orientation toward knowing as a socially located, political practice. This, in turn, connects to and informs our understanding of complex subjectivity, wherein a capacity to resist exists alongside or within contexts of dominance—this both/and vision then shapes intersectional coalitional political philosophies and practices. Together, these factors acknowledge multiplicity and interaction, account for power's various formations, *and* seek to address inequality on multiple levels.

### Intersectionality as an Epistemological Orientation

Intersectionality can be understood as epistemological in several ways. First, it attends to knowers' social location on an intimate or personal level and within wider, macropolitical frames. It also approaches lived experience as philosophically relevant: as such, it is an important critical resource for approaching the familiar in new ways (Dill and Zambrana 2009, xi). As Collins explains, intersectionality "jettisons the implicit assumption of a normative center" (Collins 1998, 152) and invokes lived experience to do so (48). Simultaneously, it presses us to account for wider contexts of knowledge production and reception and to question received logics or methods by drawing on "both/and" thinking to examine underlying assumptions. As both Anzaldúa (1990b) and Narayan (1997) underscore, if hegemonic frames and categories remain naturalized and unquestioned, changing the content therein can only achieve so much: tinkering within the logics of domination is not really the goal. No matter the philosophical practice or methodological norm in question, the objective, from an intersectional perspective, is to identify, unpack, and contest the (various and varied) workings of dominance.

Operating from the notion that all knowers are situated in systems of power, intersectionality also highlights the inherently political nature of knowledge production and reception. Since many ways of knowing, particularly those generated by marginalized groups, have been overlooked or denigrated as inferior,[16] intersectional work entails accounting for unequal cognitive authority, epistemic inequality, and distortion within and between groups. By unmasking knowledge claims purported to be neutral and universal, it raises questions about who has been perceived to be an authoritative knower, whose claims have been heard, which forms of knowledge have received recognition (and been recorded, archived, and passed down), and who has had access to the means of knowledge production and training (including access to education, the academy, and publishing).

In other words, intersectionality shifts the terms of what it means to know and to be considered knowledgeable, which means it also changes what counts as evidence, fact, or knowledge: importantly, this introduces questions of provenance into the heart of the philosophical (e.g., where do various social norms, methodological rules, or philosophical expectations come from, by whom are they authorized, and who do they best serve?). It also rejects mind vs. body, reason vs. emotion binarics which undergird positivist legacies in the sciences and social sciences and that have been used to devalue and disauthorize ways of knowing from disenfranchised groups.[17] Many factors intersectionality finds philosophically *relevant*, even central, then, often are considered *liabilities*, including: lived experience, social location, embodiment, and contexts of power or inequality.

Intersectionality thus helps to expose how conventional antidiscrimination doctrine, though seemingly neutral, relies on bias and privilege to operate (see, e.g., Carbado 2013; Crenshaw 1989; Spade 2013). It is equally useful for showing how ostensibly objective methods of observation, information gathering, and dissemination are often inadequate for addressing socially sanctioned bias or for unpacking oppressive habits of mind (Fusco 1995; Narayan 1997; Spelman 1988). For instance, as Spelman explains, while observations about 'women' and our commonalities or differences may *seem* to be "matters of simple observation" that draw on "unproblematic" categories and descriptors, these very categories, and their logics, are often part of the problem at hand. The descriptors distort via "pop-bead" or single-axis notions of the categories' ostensibly neat separability and supposed internal homogeneity (Spelman 1988, 15, 136).

Moreover, those who historically have had access to (more) power tend to be granted greater rhetorical or cognitive authority and are thus better able to assert "their" prerogative to tell the larger story (i.e., to be the narrator of "women's experiences" at large), thereby preserving the right to be the observer (not the observed). Intersectionality interrupts these narrative norms and disrupts easy male/female binaries about "men telling women's stories," for instance, to expose how structural power asymmetries also play out *among* "women" (and among "men")—some of whom have historically had more symbolic power as knowers (Spelman 1988, 152; see also Babbitt 2005).

Furthermore, an intersectional approach exposes how impartiality can be more partial than it seems, often requiring erasures to function, though we are taught to ignore these absences or to see them as natural, not as forms of enforced bias. To clarify, it is not that intersectionality abandons the pursuit of empiricism or objectivity, since part of its aim is to make normative claims about injustice. However, it uses different measures of philosophical adequacy and offers alternative notions of the empirical. Its attention to multiplicity is particularly significant in this regard: multiplicity, from an intersectional approach, is seen to have its own coherence, logic, and validity. Multiplicity is not viewed as inherently contradictory or as lacking coherence and thus in need of parsing via either/or schematics.

This impetus toward the multiple *as logical*, which has been described as a "multiplex" epistemological quality (Phoenix and Pattynama 2006, 187), stems in great part from intersectional "both/and" analytics forged in women of color and Black feminist contexts. Rather than emphasize convergence or unification of differences as necessary grounds for political or philosophical coherence, "divergent thinking, characterized by movement away from set patterns and goals" (Anzaldúa 1999, 101), is not just considered *possible* from within intersectional frameworks but *valuable* for its insights and potential, particularly as a countermeasure to the distortions resulting from either/or binary logics that emphasize sameness, are attached to the logics of oneness (Alarcón 1990; Lugones 1994) and therefore are "deadly" (Maracle 1994). Intersectionality asks that we note how sameness, as a concept, has a history, one forged at the nexus of coloniality, patriarchy, capitalism, and Western modernity: monological norms are fundamental to crafting (and staying within the bounds of) Western reason.[18]

The monological, for instance, informs "single-axis" logics of antidiscrimination doctrine and conventional models of liberation politics. With an emphasis on the universal and the generalizable as ideals (and the particular and different often characterized as corrupting 'true' knowledge), 'mono'-logics have both philosophical legacies (e.g., othering, dehumanization) and structural ones (e.g., systemic, enforced subordination). In other words, the "idea of encountering and dealing with the 'other' presupposes 'a same' who enjoys epistemic and discursive privileges. . . .—that is, the invention of the other was and is always an imperial construct of the same" (Tlostanova and Mignolo 2009, 15). It is this legacy of enforced sameness that Crenshaw (1989) contests in arguing that Black women's claims should be acknowledged both as *the same as and as different* from other groups' claims.

This same/different logic, that contests the singular, has been derived in great part from (consciously engaging with and inhabiting) multiplicity, a complex positionality. Lugones describes how "the oppressed create a clear sense of standing in a dual reality, one in which we use double perception and double praxis. One eye sees the oppressed reality, the other sees the resistant one" (Lugones 2006, 78). Intersectionality thus invites us to approach knowledge and knowers as located within multiple interpretive locations or horizons. To clarify, this is not a romanticized view of multiplicity, since the different angles of vision one takes up, and the many "worlds" one occupies, can be in tension or even opposition since they operate from different cognitive norms, have divergent analytic expectation and goals, or draw on worldviews that cannot be merged (Lugones 1987). As Norma Alarcón explains, if one's personhood is displaced or denied in myriad discourses and across several contexts, then one can end up "speaking from a position in conflict" because there is a "struggle of multiple antagonisms" (Alarcón 1990, 356, 366). Consequently, thinking about form, and stretching the parameters of genre and voice one examines (and approaches as meaningful and relevant), is important.

By widening the scope of what 'counts' as knowledge, and who 'counts' as a knower, and in pushing for strategies that can accommodate what Gloria Anzaldúa (1999, 77) has characterized as speaking in a "forked tongue," intersectionality also entails (and requires) cognitive flexibility and skill, as Sandoval's (2000) metaphor of a car's clutch implies. Holding contradictions in tension, exposing unstated assumptions, and attending to sites of collusion that, on the surface seem unrelated, entails a type of "hybrid knowledge" (Barvosa 2008, 55), a form of "conjoint attention" (Narayan 1997, 153), "multiple consciousness" (King 1988; Matsuda 1989), or what was described in the early 1900s as double or split consciousness (see Adell 1994).

In addition, intersectionality has long had an interdisciplinary orientation in large part because critical interdisciplinarity not only requires crossing knowledge divides and navigating disciplinary boundaries, but also broadening spheres of accountability—it expands the communities and groups to whom we hold our work accountable (Harnois 2013, 140). Furthermore, thinking beyond disciplinary borders is essential if one is interested in political/philosophical dissent. As Nelson Maldonado-Torres writes, "heresy needs to take an interdisciplinary and comparative approach" to draw connections across a range of identities, "knowledges, histories, and struggles" usually treated as unrelated (Maldonado-Torres 2012, 204). In this way, intersectionality can be understood as a cross-categorical counterlogic grounded in multiplicity.

Finally, because it is practice-oriented and has a social justice mission, intersectionality approaches analysis and advocacy (or theory and practice) as necessarily linked, even though philosophical work and political action are often conceived of as ideally separate (to blend them, conventionally, is thought to undermine, or impede, knowledge-making at its "best"). To draw on a metaphor from Anzaldúa (1999, 102), intersectionality might well be understood as a way of "straddling" the intellectual and the political: one can imagine physically stretching across domains to bring them together. She also characterizes bridging work in more integrative ways, where different "ingredients" combine and interact to form something new, thanks to the labor of "kneading" (103). In using verbs like "to straddle" and "to knead," Anzaldúa emphasizes the skill and effort involved: this is an achieved philosophical and political consciousness that has been forged, developed, and passed down over time.

## Ontological Multiplicity, "Survival-Rich Ambiguity," and Agency

Just as intersectionality is useful for approaching knowledge as contextual and multiple, for showing how the social world can be distorted via single-axis logics, and for shifting the terms of what counts as knowledge and who counts as a knower, it also entails a fundamental reconceptualization of the citizen–subject. As Chela Sandoval explains, though often interpreted reductively as advocating an essentialist identity politics, the wider philosophical–political tradition crafted by women of color within which intersectionality lies should be understood as a form of "critical theory for political action that allows for no single conceptualization of our position" as subjects (Sandoval 1990, 66). Intersectionality understands people as ontologically plural, not only in terms of multiple identities, but also in terms of locational and relational power. We are situated in, constrained by, and able to resist within, myriad forms of power: at the same time, we are capable of complicity with dominance on various fronts.

This attention to multiplicity at the level of the subject is important. For instance, intersectionality rejects "pop-bead metaphysics," or the notion that each identity is sequential, homogeneous, and separable, like pull-apart beads on plastic toy necklaces (Spelman 1988, 15, 136). This also has implications for politics (as I shall discuss more fully in the next section), as demonstrated by Linda LaRue's denunciation, in 1970, of "common oppression" frames that impose an either/or ontology. Refuting that Black liberation, on androcentric terms, must come "first," she underscores how such logics suggest "black women will be able to separate their femaleness from their blackness, and thus they will be able to be free as blacks, if not free as women; or, that male freedom ought to come first; or, finally, that the freedom of black women and men and the freedom of black people as a whole are not one and the same" (LaRue 1995, 169).

This insistence on recognizing ontological plurality in ways that do not slip into primary and secondary identities, or primary and secondary forms of subordination (see Cohen 1997, 1999), is long-standing. Consider Cooper's nineteenth-century anecdote about entering a train station in the Jim Crow South. To illustrate the limits of binary categories (also known as the "ampersand" problem in feminist thought; see Spelman 1988), Cooper describes a waiting room with "two dingy little rooms with [a sign] 'FOR LADIES' swinging over one and 'FOR COLORED PEOPLE' over the other." She then finds herself "wondering under which head I come?" Cooper sees herself as belonging to both, yet recognizes that these categories are falsely presented as separate then violently enforced as distinct so as to uphold white supremacy via the specter of white femininity, the "LADIES" (Cooper 1988, 96, capitals original).

Furthermore, intersectional approaches treat subjectivity as "mediated," not as given or static. Embodiment, lived experience, social location, and historical context are all relevant factors: intersectionality "foreground[s] the social dynamics and relations that constitute subjects, displacing the emphasis on the subjects (and categories) themselves as the starting point of inquiry" (Cho, Crenshaw, and McCall 2013, 796). Conceiving of identities as "schemes" and not as fixed essences allows us to approach them as salient frames "in and through which the subject thinks, feels, judges, and acts in the world" (Barvosa 2008, 62). As "interpretive horizons" (see Alcoff 2006b), identities are understood to interact with and to be shaped by macropolitical ideologies and social structures.

This is why Irene Gedalof underscores how, from an intersectional model, identity categories are not conceived as "straightforward descriptions of pre-existing realities but are discursive constructs that continually produce the realities they claim to describe; . . . they operate at both structural and subjective levels; and . . . must be understood as intersecting and mutually constitutive" (Gedalof 2012, 3). Moreover, Gedalof's discussion points to an often-overlooked aspect of intersectionality: its vision of subjectivity is not just multiple, but coalitional.[19] As Anna Carastathis explains, intersectionality highlights how identities are inseparably intermeshed, and "internally heterogeneous, complex unities constituted by their internal differences and dissonances and by internal as well as external relations of power" (Carastathis 2013a, 942). A coalitional model entails a both/and philosophy of the self as "at once diverse and self-contradictory in its identities, and yet also a cohesive whole capable of shifting its social identifications from context to context" (Barvosa 2008, 11).

Groups, and not just individuals, are also understood as internally heterogeneous from an intersectional model. Using both/and, same/different thinking, groups can be characterized by their potential to organize around "heterogeneous commonality" rather than homogeneity (Collins 2003, 221). Lugones thus advocates taking up "curdled" logics that allow for the multiplicity of the subject as nonfragmentable and that conceive of coalescing, politically, not as homogeneity (since homogenization requires the breaking down of molecules to create oneness), but as more akin to an "emulsion," wherein the suspended molecules are understood as both separate and linked, one and many simultaneously (Lugones 1994).

Yet this coalitional approach to subjectivity (whether individual or collective) runs against the grain of conventional ideas about identity (and political organizing), which tend toward singular, "common-denominator" logics (Alarcón 1990). Intersectionality contests ideals of the allegedly universal subject of human rights doctrine, policy, and advocacy and exposes the limitations, and exclusions, of the universal by focusing on the hierarchical nature of single-axis models of personhood and rights infused throughout the law and political organizing (Crenshaw 1989). As Spade explains, "the purportedly universal subject of rights is actually a specific and narrow category of persons. The ability to avail oneself of supposedly universal rights in fact often requires whiteness, wealth, citizenship, the status of being a settler rather than Indigenous, and/or conformity to body, health, gender, sexuality, and family norms" (Spade 2013, 1039).

Certainly, liberal notions of sameness (we are all the "same" underneath due to our common humanity) are persuasive, and not just because they are ubiquitous: such ideas can appeal because they seem to offer a path to equality that many yearn to see realized and struggle for (suggesting if we can identify our underlying sameness, our differences will be resolved). In discussing contemporary equity policies in the United Kingdom, Gedalof (2012) argues:

> The liberal notion of equality that underpins contemporary policy is premised on valuing sameness over difference. It does this in its taking of the autonomous, undifferentiated and universal individual as the basic unit of analysis, stripping away particularistic ties of kinship, sub-national community or "culture," personal belief and tradition to reveal an essential sameness that we can all share as moral, economic or political actors. . . . When applied to the question of how best to manage the social diversity that nevertheless persists, this liberal perspective assumes that recognizing and respecting difference needs to start by identifying some underlying shared perspectives or commonality. (4)

Though they may pull at the heartstrings, such frames undermine intersectional premises and stymie a multifaceted approach to social change. Insisting, instead, we are the *same and different*, simultaneously, intersectional models do not discard differences for some underlying essence, or focus solely on our similarities, in terms of oppression, yet overlook complicity in forms of dominance.

In many instances, however, "common-denominator" logics prevail (Alarcón 1990, 358), suggesting we are the "same underneath." For instance, treating gender as foundational to the feminist subject can imply that, beyond our differences, we all "have gender," unmitigated and separable from other factors. This ignores that "nobody experiences themselves as solely gendered. Instead, gender is configured through cross-cutting forms of difference that carry deep social and economic consequences" (Zinn, Hondagneu-Sotelo, and Messner 2007, 153).[20] It also erases power asymmetries among women, which poet Pat Parker (1999, 76) emphasized in 1978, stating: "SISTER! . . . your foot's smaller,/but it's still on my neck." In refusing the idea that gender (or any other identity) is primary, intersectionality emphasizes a "relational position to a multiplicity of others, not just white men" and, at the same time, acknowledges "multiple registers of existence" (Alarcón 1990, 359, 365).

By conceiving of multiplicity as nonfragmentable (Lugones 1994), an intersectional view of subjectivity roundly critiques ideas about feminist subjectivity wherein gender is treated as the "foundational moment" of differentiation. In contrast, a hierarchy of identity model erases complex subjectivity and undermines social change by artificially dividing up interrelated factors (Combahee 1983; Smith 1983), a violent process Anzaldúa describes as akin to being chopped into "little fragments" and "split" by labels (Anzaldúa 1983, 205). Lorde similarly objects to "constantly being encouraged to pluck out some aspect of [herself] and present this as the meaningful whole, eclipsing and denying the other parts of the self" (Lorde 1984, 120). Just as Nellie McKay discusses the pain of being asked to "take sides against the self" (McKay 1992, 277) among friends or in one's communities of belonging, Evelyn Alsultany explains that to be recognized, even by others who are also marginalized, she must often fragment herself, hide "los intersticios" (the interstices), and contain her "moving" selves (Alsultany 2002, 107–108). Ontological complexity, then, can also be (painfully) denied within one's "home" spaces (Lugones 1994; Martin and Mohanty 1986; Reagon 1983).

As discussed earlier, intersectionality's matrix philosophy means one may perceive the world in ways that are *more* than simply plural: they may be in conflict. There may be no "resolving" the differences, as doing so could require erasing differences or denying important disconnects. Such disjunctures matter and hold meaning, so one retains the tension, using "both/and" logics to keep open the "fissures" between perceptions. Likewise, intersectionality does not approach ontological complexity merely as plurality: here, too, one can "be" in opposition, be "selves" that cannot mesh without distortion, harm, or erasure. This has implications for how we conceive of subjectivity (as complex and in tension) but also for how we identify forms of feminist agency and resistance, as Conny Roggeband's discussion of the "victim–agent dilemma" illustrates, for instance (Roggeband 2010).

Analyzing strategies used by "migrant women's organizations" in the Netherlands,[21] Roggeband explores how migrant women navigate state assumptions and norms. To be recognized as agentic by the Dutch state, they are asked to self-present as victims of patriarchal cultures (from elsewhere) willing to become modern subjects (women) in accord with a white European sense of gendered agency (as mothers and educators, primarily) and of state belonging (even as many do not agree with the state's given terms of agency, gender, and culture). Given these parameters, several organizations refuse state funding altogether, but others seek to reframe and "contest negative policy and public discourses about their religion and culture" (Roggeband 2010, 946). To disrupt the state's dualist frame and its pathologizing gaze at "other" cultures (and to shift the gaze back upon structural inequalities in Dutch society), retaining a sense of *multiplicity* as meaningful (and as possibly agentic, not inherently tragic) is pivotal. Holding on to their various "selves" is politically and personally strategic and affords room, in the interstices, to "criticize the government for setting migrant women apart as a problem category, and . . . [to] oppose the culturalization of their problems" (Roggeband 2010, 962).

To further understand how intersectional approaches to knowledge and subjectivity intertwine, consider Lugones' discussion of "worlds" and "selves." The cognitive shift toward multiplicity permits one to perceive and keep hold of divergent premises: it also reveals gaps in conventional logics, allowing one to understand dominant worldviews as non-totalizing, even as incorrect. This, in turn, Lugones explains, creates space to inhabit more than one "world" and to "be" more than one self, at once—a self who exceeds what those with conferred dominance may perceive or imagine (Lugones 1987, 2010). Depending on structural factors and contexts as a Latina lesbian decolonial feminist philosopher, Lugones, for instance, is *and* is not "playful"—she is and is not at "ease" in the world: she exceeds the binary and is both, sometimes simultaneously, though this claim can seem implausible according to notions of a singular, coherent self in a singular (or monological) world (Lugones 1987).

The way out of this conundrum should not be seen to lie with Lugones individually: she is not the source of damage or locus of the needed structural/systemic repairs (though she does not deny internalized oppression or the lived wounds of injustice). Her ability to "be" more than one self, to retain contradictions, is an achievement, a form of "survival-rich" ambiguity, not brokenness (Lugones 1987). Nevertheless, her plurality and ambiguity are likely to be (mis)perceived as evidence of ontological fragmentation that needs mending, as deficits that need addressing, even though to approach multiplicity as "fragmentable" is to *not* understand it intersectionally. In other words, to do so is an error of the imagination that lets go of the logic of the multiple and returns to the harmful logics of atomization and false homogenization (Lugones 1987).

So, the intersectional solution, as Lugones delineates it, is not to work, individually, on "her" being or discomfort: this would require that *she* become more psychologically "at ease" with oppression by adhering (or conforming) to oneness, making herself amenable to dominant logics. To become (or be) at ease, she would have to let go of ontological multiplicity and survival-rich ambiguity: to become "one," she would need to self-violate and conform her "selves" to the logics that deny, distort, or cannot perceive her multiplicity in the first place. The intersectional subject is constantly invited to break apart, to become "fragmented," to be recognized or to receive redress in terms that align with and support a single-axis world. Instead, the world(s) in which she is not "at ease" would have to change (Lugones 1987).

Lugones' discussion helps illuminate (and contest) a common misconception of intersectionality's emphasis on lived multiplicity—that it is a naïve theory of identity with inadequate attention to sociopolitical and epistemological structures.[22] More than a rich account of multiple-category demographics (Bowleg 2008; Shields 2008), an intersectional approach to subjectivity focuses on how subjects are *systemically* constrained (or advantaged) and fragmented (or, in terms of systemically conferred privilege, made to seem whole, seamless, and agentic). In this vein, intersectionality calls for structural transformation, but again, this fundamental aspect of its approach is often overlooked. Epistemological and ontological binds are not just individual problems with individual solutions but are structural—though they are also personal (which is why lived experience is philosophically and politically salient to intersectional analysis). Intersectionality's focus on ontological complexity highlights how many of the problems faced by subjects who speak and think from a "matrix" place, and insist on justice on these terms, require collective organizing and macrolevel transformations.

Furthermore, the "survival-rich ambiguity" Lugones points to, in delineating experiences of multiplicity, helps explain why intersectional models reconceptualize subjectivity away from the unified liberal subject and common-denominator frames but also reframe agency away from the default framework of a liberal, autonomous self (Alarcón 1990). As Sirma Bilge demonstrates, "agency is a deeply liberal concept in its philosophical sense, closely linked to the transcendental humanist subject, a rational, free-willed, choosing agent": it is no accident, moreover, that "women, non-whites, minors and the insane were historically excluded from this liberal account of agentic subjects" (Bilge 2010, 11). A liberal model of agency (both classically liberal and neoliberal) also "orders responsibility toward ready-made choices," toward choosing among options that, even if numerous, all tend to be relatively "congruent with domination." As Lugones explains, many of these "choices" take for granted "ready-made hierarchical worlds of sense in which individuals form intentions, make choices, carry out actions in the terms of that world/s" (Lugones 2005, 86).

In contrast, intersectionality highlights how one can be a resistant subject yet unable to "act" or resist in a conventional sense, since all readily available means of action or agency entail forms of self-annihilation, on some level—a signature aspect of systemic oppression.[23] Intersectionality thus involves rethinking either/or notions of freedom versus coercion and a "breaking with the attachment to agency as autonomy . . . as a self-evident ground of feminist solidarity" (Hutchings 2013, 26). To clarify, the goal here is not merely to *stretch* the parameters of modernist subjectivity to "include" ontological complexity but to alter the possibilities for selfhood and action by transforming the contexts and structures in which we live. Intersectionality can thus be used to question the usual frames of resistance and subjectivity and even for "shattering" established notions of agency (see Bassel 2012).[24]

This is not to say an intersectional approach downplays how people negotiate and play an "active role . . . in asserting their identities" (Warner and Shields 2012, 208; see also Choo and Ferree, 2010). Intersectional identity research, for instance, highlights how subjects navigate, and deploy, multiple overlapping identities as a way to negotiate with multiple forms of power and inequality (to varying degrees of success and often at great cost) (e.g., Bowleg 2013). Linking the ontological and epistemological, Sandoval, for instance, describes a matric "topography of consciousness," one comprising points around which individuals constitute themselves as oppositional subjects. Rather than fixed positions, these are *orientations* (toward the world and the self) developed to seek "subjective forms of resistance other than those determined by the social order itself" (Sandoval 2000, 54).

Illustrating the "survival-rich ambiguity" Lugones discusses, and the consciousness articulated by Sandoval, Anneliese Singh describes how transgender youth of color strategically modify and adjust their gender-racial-ethnic self-definitions as one way to cope with and manage racist transprejudice. She highlights different forms of resiliency but does not suggest a resilient sense of self is inherent or guaranteed—it is both a developed skill and a stance that can be a struggle to maintain (particularly in the face of what can seem to be insuperable structural and social obstacles to becoming one's complex, full self) (Singh 2013). Via its "both/and" approach to subjectivity, an intersectional orientation accounts for our ability to act within oppression yet also emphasizes how we can be impeded by systemic structures of possibility and constraint.

Intersectionality seeks to shift the terms of agency and personhood by transforming social reality. Its larger point is to insist that the world change, that our basic assumptions about knowledge and the self transform by departing from the singular to the plural. Intersectional approaches to identity as not just multiple but also coalitional (Cole 2008; Greenwood 2008) thus help illuminate possibilities for forging coalitional justice agendas. Intersectionality, then, is inherently a political orientation grounded in solidarity and collective contestation, as much as it is an epistemological practice and ontological framework.

### Intersectional Politics: "You Do Not Have to Be Me . . . for Us to Fight Alongside Each Other"[25]

Intersectionality's political genealogy connects to larger struggles to eradicate inequality and emphasizes the degree to which meaningful contestation requires *collective* action (Collins 2000; Combahee 1983; Reagon 1983). Intersectionality entails more than integrationist "demands for inclusion within the logics of sameness and difference": it accounts for "ideological structures" that shape everyday practices and assumptions (Cho, Crenshaw, and McCall 2013, 791) and offers a lens for analyzing and *contesting* the workings of power across multiple domains (Collins 1990, 1998; Spade 2013; Yuval-Davis 2011b).[26] By attending to lived experience, and to how identities are shaped by social structures, an intersectional approach examines how politics play out on both structural and personal levels (Hancock 2007a, 2007b; Yuval-Davis 2011b). Intersectionality also defines the political, and political action, inclusively: intervening in dominant logics is understood as politically necessary, as is departing from narrow notions of personhood and agency—in other words, what "counts" as political action or coalitional work is broadly conceived.[27] In this way, its philosophical, ontological, and political qualities intertwine: intersectionality's multipronged models of subjectivity, knowledge, and justice require political practices constellated around solidarity, not sameness or single identities.

For example, in the early 1970s, the Combahee Collective[28] insisted on "the development of an integrated analysis and practice based upon the fact that the major systems of oppression are interlocking" since "the synthesis of these oppressions creates the condition of our lives"

(Combahee 1983, 261; see also Reagon 1983; Smith 1983). A similar outlook lay beneath Lorde's pointed question, "Can any one of us here still afford to believe that the pursuit of liberation can be the sole and particular province of any one particular race, or sex, or age, or religion, or sexuality, or class?" (Lorde 1984, 140). Likewise, a century prior, in her 1893 speech at the Columbian Exposition in Chicago before an audience of white women, Cooper insisted that *all* women "take our stand on the solidarity of humanity, the oneness of life, and the unnaturalness and injustice of all special favoritisms, whether of sex, race, country, or condition" (Cooper 1998a, 204).[29]

Yet coalitional visions can be controversial and made to seem the cause of schisms. Ironically, though single-axis thinking enforces splitting and divisiveness (of the subject and of political aims), intersectional logics and hybrid strategies are often perceived as unwieldy and unrealistic, or worse, as ruinous or traitorous. For instance, forty years prior to Cooper's 1893 Columbian Exposition speech, the American and Foreign Anti-Slavery Society (AFASS)[30] was founded by a group of men who protested the inclusive vision of the AASS (American Anti-Slavery Society). As "A Colored Man" explained in his 1841 letter to the editor of *The Liberator*,[31] the AASS seemed too radical because "too leveling in principles: it places us all on a common platform, without regard to age, sex, color, or condition" (cited in Jones 2007, 53). A coalitional, "leveling," multipronged philosophy is presented as divisive, whereas a hierarchical, single-axis one is seen as unifying (though, of course, it is only cohesive for some members of the group, the "thick" members [Lugones 1994]—those with access to normative power and privilege "but for" one quality [Crenshaw 1989]).

Such rifts are not unique to anti-slavery movements: several examples can be found in the history of U.S. feminist organizing also. At the 1925 meeting of the International Council of Women (ICW) in Washington, D.C., "because Afro-Americans would be in attendance, the Daughters of the American Revolution refused to allow the ICW to use the auditorium of Memorial Continental Hall. When it was agreed among the whites that Afro-Americans would not have open seating but would be required to sit in a segregated gallery, the members of the NACW [National Association of Colored Women] walked out" (Neverdon-Morton 1989, 201). Such actions by white feminists constitute a pattern that early Black feminists had previously critiqued. Nevertheless, in 1903, the National American Women Suffrage Association (NAWSA) board "endorsed the organization's state's rights position, which was tantamount to an endorsement of white supremacy in most states." Moreover, "Despite endorsement of black suffrage, Anna Howard Shaw [president of NAWSA from 1901 to 1915] had been accused of refusing to allow a black female delegate at the Louisville suffrage convention in 1911 to make an antidiscrimination resolution" (Terborg-Penn 1997, 24).

An unconscious "common platform" approach to social justice would also turn out to be an internal obstacle to political organizing for the Combahee River Collective in the 1970s. Despite a deep commitment to eradicating multiple oppressions, and despite the group's matrix-oriented aims and radical philosophies, questions of sexuality and global capitalism served at times to fracture or impede coalitional ideals. Learning from their own internal contestations, they would come to more overtly identify both capitalist exploitation as well as homophobia (and the conferred privileges of heteronormativity), for instance, as core issues to be addressed among and between Black women (see Combahee 1983), as would others.[32]

Coalitional models of social change, grounded in an intersectional vision of personhood and justice, have historically faced resistance, internally and externally, in part because they attend to privilege and oppression as relational and simultaneous. This both/and coalitional logic seems, at times, too great to take up or retain. Even as single-axis politics have repeatedly proved ruinous to social change organizing and activism (Spade 2013), and although such divisive hierarchical principles uphold hegemonic inequality, notions of *intersectional approaches as fractious* (because they break up false universals and reject single-axis political and philosophical norms) continue today, in various iterations.[33]

Those interested in intersectional approaches to rethinking political organizing and group membership must, therefore, often rearticulate why a coalitional mindset focused on solidarity, not sameness, is essential. In this vein, Alison Kafer examines three sites of coalition (trans/

disability bathroom politics, environmental justice, and reproductive justice) which entail contestations and contradictions "that are not easily resolvable." She contends it is essential to remember that coalition politics do not mean the mere bringing together of discrete groups and issues ("women as a discrete group working with disabled people as a discrete group," for instance): instead, intersectional politics entail "a process in which the interests and identities themselves are always open" and understood as in relation and potential contestation (Kafer 2013, 150). As Chandra Talpade Mohanty explains, solidarity requires thinking in terms of mutuality and accountability as the political basis for relationships. Rather than assume a commonality of oppression or of identity, defined singularly within the logics of sameness, "the practice of solidarity foregrounds communities of people who have chosen to work and fight together. . . . [It] is always an achievement, the result of active struggle" (Mohanty 2003, 78).

By grounding its philosophy of liberation in multiplicity, intersectionality aims to unpack mindsets that not only conceal injustice but inhibit political organizing (Doetsch-Kidder 2012; Mingus and Talley 2013; Spade 2013). Intersectionality's "polyvocal" (Harris 1999, 16) social-justice orientation focuses on how issues that *seem* singular actually cut across multiple contexts. Defining "commonality in terms of shared interests rather than shared identity" (Cole 2008, 447) also means that some *loss* (of systemically conferred unearned privilege, for instance) may be required, as James Baldwin eloquently put it in 1954: "Any real change implies the breakup of the world as one has always known it, the loss of all that gave one an identity, the end of safety" (Baldwin 1993, 117). Anna Julia Cooper's sarcastic analysis, in 1892, of the conferred advantages of whiteness that many women's rights advocates at the time counted on (and sought to protect), also points to this thorny issue (Cooper 1988, 80–81).

Whether in nineteenth, twentieth, or twenty-first-century contexts, intersectional analyses have exposed how redress strategies intended to facilitate alliances and foster change can be so singular in focus that they reinforce social hierarchies or maintain structural inequalities. For instance, feminist reproductive rights models have historically been formed around a gender-first, common-denominator logic as the basis for advocacy, drawing on narrow ideas of womanhood and reproductive politics. However, an intersectional reproductive justice agenda shifts what "counts" as reproductive politics. It also directs attention to systemic patterns and practices the state has long been involved in, such as population control, usually presented as salvific (e.g., proposals to sterilize women who receive public assistance [see Roberts 1997], or involuntary sterilization of Native women, incarcerated women, and women with disabilities[34]). Intersectional "reproductive justice for women of color [thus] requires interventions into criminalization, child welfare, environmental regulation, immigration, and other arenas of administrative violence" (Spade 2013, 1032).

In other words, intersectional models account for multiple and interacting sites of power and also the role the state plays in maintaining inequality, even as it tends to self-present as neutral, protective, or redemptive in its future intent, present practices, and historical origins. The Women of Color Resource Center's approach to organizing (in the San Francisco Bay area) has amply illustrated this justice model, for instance (see Brown and Sánchez, 1994), as does the work of *Somos Hermanas/We Are Sisters* as part of the AAWO/alliance against women's oppression, also in the Bay area.[35] Once the state is thus understood, via intersectional analytics, as fully capable of harm and violation (even as one also fights for state recognition of one's personhood and rights on new terms, not just on terms that tinker with the state's hierarchical "but-for" norms of settler-class citizenship), addressing the state's practices of "administrative violence" (including incarceration and criminalization, immigration and citizenship, and child and family welfare) is understood as *integral to* reproductive justice agendas.

Spade spells out how this crosscutting political vision requires practicing "articulation" as a means of pivoting away from the atomized logics of liberal individualism:

> The articulation of reproductive justice as concerned with population control turns away from the individual-rights narrative that centers the question of whether the government is affirmatively and explicitly blocking a given woman from accessing abortion or contraception. Instead, it argues that all of the conditions that determine reproductive

> possibilities—subjection to criminalization, displacement, immigration enforcement, and environmental destruction; the unequal distribution of wealth and access to health care; and more—are the terrain of contestation about the politics of reproduction. This shift toward conceptualizing harm at the population level generates an analysis of the relationship between multiple vectors of harm and of how systems of meaning and control like sexism, racism, and ableism might interact in particular ways to affect the various populations managed through their articulation. (Spade 2013, 1036–1037)

Pivotal to intersectionality's justice orientation and political capacity, then, is its adeptness at pinpointing and unpacking overlooked forms of partnership between the radical and the coercive, and the resistant and the dominant, whether those alliances occur within and between grassroots communities or within state and social service structures that appear (and may even intend to be) beneficial yet can also be sites of perpetuating harm.

## Intersectionality as a Resistant Imaginary and Historical Intervention

Intersectionality's attention to multiplicity is key to its invitation to intervene in historical memory and to *un*learn prevailing social imaginaries: it directs our attention to alternative worldviews and focuses attention on "disremembered subjects" (Foreman 2013, 316). These landscapes of memory, and the "disremembered" who inhabit and inherit them, are often erased in conventional frames or are missing from the usual historical timelines. However, because intersectionality is interested in identifying omissions and approaching them as meaningful, gaps or interstices must be engaged politically and philosophically rather than viewed as incidental (Jordan-Zachery 2007; Springer 2005). Attending to multiple historical realities and to internal heterogeneities is also significant because doing so can render visible diverse forms of resistance (and not just readily recognizable forms of resisting), allowing for their particulars to be examined across time, place, and circumstance (Schueller 2005, 53).

To clarify, intersectional memory work is not "nostalgic" (hooks 1990, 147; see also Mann 2011) but a form of countermemory that reads existing archives and historical narratives against the grain—unpacking assumptions, noting gaps, and questioning official versions of events. As Maldonado-Torres explains, in discussing Anzaldúa's body of work, she does more than model a "critical" form of memory: he finds, for example, that "in *Borderlands/La frontera*, history is part of a decolonial form of traveling through time"[36] (Maldonado-Torres 2012, 197)—a form of thinking/moving/being that, in a different context, Black lesbian poet Cheryl Clarke (2008) has named a legacy of "itinerancy" in Black feminist histories. In this vein, Maylie Blackwell discusses the importance of "retrofitted memory." She writes, "Retrofitted memory is a practice whereby social actors read the interstices, gaps, and silences of existing historical narratives in order to retrofit, rework, and refashion older narratives to create new historical openings, political possibilities, and genealogies of resistance" (Blackwell 2011, 102).

History, on intersectional terms, entails journeying to other possibilities, unearthing past potential as a means of crafting a different path ahead. In Cooper's nineteenth-century version of this notion, intersectional thought, such as her own, is at once "retrospective," "introspective," and "prospective" (Cooper 1988, 26–27; see also May 2009). The Combahee River Collective, for instance, clearly tapped into collective historical struggles via their choice of name (Combahee 1983; Harris 1999). Barbara Smith describes how they chose it not only to recall past group actions but also to engage others in learning about this forgotten past. She explains, "People looked at their conditions and they fought back, they took great risks to change their situation; and for us to call ourselves the Combahee River Collective, that was an educational [tool] both for ourselves and for anybody who asked, 'So what does that mean. I never heard of that?' It was a way of talking about ourselves being on a continuum of . . . Black women's struggle" (Smith, in Harris 1999, 10).

In examining intersectional interventions in historical memory, what becomes clear is that history cannot be told in the singular voice or via the lone, iconic figure (see May 2014b). This is why, for instance,

Bonnie Thornton Dill and Ruth Zambrana (2009, 3) lay "claim to a U.S. scholarly tradition that began in the nineteenth century with women like Maria Stewart and men like W.E.B. DuBois." Similarly, in discussing why race–gender must always be understood as interlinked, Valerie Smith references a range of nineteenth-century U.S. Black women, including Sojourner Truth, Harriet Jacobs, and Anna Julia Cooper, who all approached race and gender as co-constituted categories of experience and analysis (Smith 1998, xii–4). She likewise points to Ida B. Wells, who debunked the myth of the Black rapist and documented how gender relations were used to propel and facilitate racial oppression (see Giddings 2009).

This retrospective technique, as a means to locate one's ideas (and self) in legacies of struggle, is not a new rhetorical or political phenomenon. In 1892, to highlight how women's contributions had been left out of history, to question what these absences signified, and to place her Black female self squarely inside the category "woman," rather than at its periphery (or outside its bounds), Cooper queried, "who shall recount the name and fame of the women?" and referenced women often forgotten or dismissed across history, from Ruth to the Amazons, Sappho to Madame de Staël (Cooper 1988, 129, 48–49). She also invoked a range of Black women artists and activists who were her contemporaries, but who remained overlooked "sisters in the service" despite their substantial work for social change, among them Frances Watkins Harper, Sojourner Truth, Charlotte Grimke, and Hallie Quinn Brown (140–142).

Citational practices in intersectional work are thus especially important: they offer a way to mark collectivity, delineate historical precedence, and claim legacies of struggle. For instance, in 1951, Claudia Jones referenced Harriet Tubman to chart a longer history of insurgent Black women intervening in capitalism's exploits: via an intersectional race-gender-class analytic, Jones rejects a class-primary Marxist approach and androcentric notions of Blackness and Black liberation (Davies 2008, 152; see also Weigand 2001, 186). The Combahee Collective also remind us that their non-hierarchical model of race-gender-sexuality-class politics has a history: they mention a host of nineteenth-century Black women, including Sojourner Truth,

Harriet Tubman, Frances Harper, Ida B. Wells-Barnett, and Mary Church Terrell—who, despite their marked differences, nevertheless had a "shared awareness of how their sexual identity combined with their racial identity" (Combahee 1983, 211).

Similarly, in 1972, Angela Davis demonstrated why a gender-differentiated analysis of slavery is requisite: de-homogenizing Blackness and the lived geographies of enslavement means that notions of resistance need to account for domestic spaces as political sites and render visible enslaved women who led "household[s] of resistance" (Davis 1972, 90). Likewise, analyses of (and political organizing around) rape must account for its racially differentiated politics. Davis reminds us that Ida B. Wells and Frederick Douglass cogently illustrated this in the nineteenth century: their insights offer antecedents to her own critique of how systemic violence (e.g., slavery and rape) and liberation politics were being narrowly conceptualized in the late twentieth century (Davis 1983). In challenging the limits of contemporary and historical rape discourses and modes of activism, when arguing for the need to turn away from single-axis logics, Crenshaw (1989) also underscores this longer genealogy.

Intersectional historical contestation, as a means of refusing to forget alternative landscapes and geographies of memory, is both individual and collective. Intersectional reinterpretations (or interruptions) of history have what Lugones would characterize as a "sociality"—they are a means of situating oneself, or one's group, within histories of resistance. Acknowledging this wider trajectory effects an important "rupture" in collective and individual consciousness: it opens up possibilities, past and present, by denaturalizing oppression and presenting it as an ongoing process, not an accomplished (and implicitly unchangeable) fact (Lugones 2005, 93–96). Consequently, in asking whose voices have been heard, documented, or recognized, intersectionality not only raises questions about who "counts" as a knower, but also what counts as evidence of resistance or insurgency: in so doing, it entails a redefinition of the past, a rethinking of the archive.

As an interpretive tool, intersectionality offers a "lens through which to lay bare issues of power and inequality and to question conventional historical terms, timelines, and values. . . . [It] is invaluable for plumbing history's silences; for understanding oppression as having a history and as existing within a set of cultural, political, and social conditions; and for unearthing a vision of historical agency for those whose personhood and agency have been denied" (May 2012a, 19). Furthermore, I suggest Anna Julia Cooper did just this, in her 1925 Sorbonne dissertation, where she opens her history of the Age of Revolution by pivoting time frames to discuss, first, the emergence of chattel slavery: she also inserts resistant Black subjectivity (that is not merely mimetic) into the archive. Examining race, class, and capital as intertwined, Cooper illustrates that the periphery (Haiti) was central to and shaped politics in the metropole (France) and shows how supremacist mindsets permeated the political imaginary, both in France and in St. Domingue (see Cooper 2006 [trans. Keller]; May 2007).

Certainly, then, intersectionality refuses an inclination toward erasure or forgetting that progress narratives tend to encourage: it disrupts (and distrusts) celebratory "narratives that declare that the US legal system has broken from the founding violences of slavery, genocide, and heteropatriarchy" (Spade 2013, 1033). Intersectional approaches help to rupture stories of the nation's evolution and to unsettle its settler logics in great part because their both/and approach is amenable to "apposition," a flexible and destabilizing interpretive method capable of reading time periods and multiple identities concurrently, in syntactical relation (Smith 1994, 671–672). As a critical heuristic, intersectionality could thus also be useful for tracing systematic patterns of "precarity," a "politically induced condition in which certain populations suffer from failing social and economic networks of support and become differentially exposed to injury, violence, and death" (Butler 2009, 25).

Thus because an intersectional approach helps to trace how "state-making, racializing, and gendering functions of founding violences like enslavement and settler colonialism continue in new forms" (Spade 2013, 1033), it invites us to understand that many "declared breaks [from the past] are fictions," as prison abolitionists have persuasively argued. For instance, intersectional juxtaposition reveals how the contemporary "criminal punishment system" in the United States can be viewed as "an extension of the racial control of slavery" (Spade 2013, 1043; see also Davis 2003). Its cross-cutting analytics expose how the nation's carceral logics extend to: using biomedical rationales for institutionalizing people with disabilities (Ben-Moshe 2013), criminalizing immigration, engaging in violent deportation practices, and using Islamophobic justifications for secret "detainments" and trials in the name of protecting the state (Razack 2008).

In a similar vein, both Joy James (1996, 2002) and Andrea Smith (2004, 2012) (differently) contend that gender violence and racial genocide, historically interlinked phenomena, were not aberrations in the genesis of the U.S. state but foundational. Likewise, in thinking through instances of contemporary racism across the European Union, which "entangle" with gender, class, empire, and sexuality, Gail Lewis finds they "derive their power and pertinence from the historical sediments of colonial modernity that was so central to the formation of Europe as an idea and a collective identity" in the first place, though official EU narratives pronounce a definitive departure from this past (Lewis 2013, 878).

In short, intersectionality is useful for tracing continuities, for showing how old logics take new forms. It offers tools for developing "counterhistories" and "counternarratives" (Dill and Zambrana 2009, 6) in great part because drawing on multiple categories of analysis at once is fundamental to reimagining the past and "re-writing" history (Anzaldúa 1990a, xxv). This interpretive (re)orientation rejects singular views (of history, time, place, and subjectivity): furthermore, the methods required to animate lost memories, or to excavate history's missing subjects, are often not conventional. Thus while some intersectional historical techniques may be fairly traditional, as in seeking to unearth and reference forgotten facts/actions (such as the Combahee Collective's referencing the Combahee River uprising, or Cooper's analysis of the Haitian and French revolutions), others may not adhere to the "facts" because these often are so partial, or biased, as to be unusable. The documented or archived facts must sometimes be doubted, or set aside, to pursue history adequately and intersectionally.

Consequently, the creative has often been an important way to analyze (or even create) the missing archive, to reimagine the past, to reconsider what counts as adequate evidence or knowledge, and who counts as a knower or an historical agent. As writer Alice Walker (1983) and filmmaker Cheryl Dunye (1996) both suggest, when it comes to Black women's history, whether in terms of folklore traditions (Walker) or queer subjectivity (Dunye), when confronted with a patently racist, sexist, and homophobic intellectual, narrative, and visual archive, sometimes one has to *craft* the stories and histories one should have been able to access, and study, but could not. Similarly, in examining novels by Toni Morrison, Sherley Anne Williams, and J. California Cooper, Elizabeth Ann Beaulieu argues that a contemporary genre such as the neo-slave narrative "opens up a new way of reading and re-reading America's slave past": the enslaved mothers' perspectives interject a raced-gendered understanding of slavery as lived experience into the larger social imaginary. Moreover, these novelists invoke women of resistance in their works (though the forms of resistance do not necessarily align with conventional ideas about what opposition or struggle might entail) (Beaulieu 1999, 21).

Intersectionality insists that submerged histories, disregarded forms of knowing, and long-forgotten or misinterpreted examples of agency and resiliency be acknowledged: memory is politicized (or, rather, its inherently political nature is tapped into). This helps draw our attention to examples of the "resistant oppressed" (Lugones 2006, 78) but also to sites of contact between the dominant and the resistant, the coercive and the insurgent, and the past and present. This plumbing of history, which unearths legacies of violence as ongoing and rejects "postracial" or "postfeminist" progress narratives, is not cynical. Rather, intersectionality is both critical and hopeful: it taps into our collective yearnings for the possibility that such "breaks" from systemic oppression, coercive exploitation, and endemic violence are *possible,* even if not (yet) fully achieved or guaranteed.

Unearthing evidence of past resistance, and tapping into the collective, to history's sociality and multiplicity, suggests that some of us, in some ways, some of the time, *have* "broken" from dominance—have viewed other possibilities, caught glimpses of other worlds, selves, and mindsets, and have willfully pursued them, contrary to conventional wisdom or against the grain of dominant logics. Intersectionality is fundamentally committed to the potential that change is possible, meaning that it is conceivable and feasible, though not guaranteed.

## Notes

1. See Bilge (2013), Crenshaw (2011c), Gines (2011), Lewis (2013), May (2014a).
2. See Giddings (2008), Gines (2011, 2014), Wells-Barnett (2014), Wells-Barnett and DeCosta-Willis (1995).
3. See, for example, Allen (1986), Alarcón (1990), Anzaldúa (1990a, 1990b, 1999), García (1989, 1997), Hurtado (1997), Maracle (1994), Mignolo (2012), Moraga (1983), Moraga and Anzaldúa (1983), Pérez (1999), Saavedra and Nymark (2008), Saldivar-Hull (2000), Sandoval (2000), Smith (2005a, 2005b), L. Smith (2012), Soto (2010), Torres (2003), Trujillo (1998).
4. See Bowleg (2008), Cole (2009), Collins (1990), Crenshaw (1989), Guidroz and Berger (2009), Hancock (2007a, 2007b), Harnois (2013), King (1988), Martinez (1993), Phoenix and Pattynama (2006), Spelman (1988), Squires (2008).
5. I contend intersectionality aims to widen the concept of the "wages of whiteness," as articulated by Harris (1993), Roediger (1999), and earlier, in 1935, by W.E.B. Du Bois (see Du Bois 2013), to account for multiple "wages" granted for various forms of conferred privilege.
6. See Choo and Ferree (2010), Crenshaw (1989), Jordan-Zachery (2007), Saldanha (2010), Staunaes (2003).
7. See Carbado (2001, 2013) for a critique of this "race to the bottom" notion of intersectionality.
8. Jennifer Nash contends, for instance, "black women have become quintessential intersectional subjects (or quintessential intersectional metaphors). Intersectionality's preoccupation with black women has produced a body of scholarship that often posits black women as the paradigmatic marginalized subject, neglecting the host of ways that black women's experiences are often marked by the complex simultaneity of privilege and oppression" (Nash 2009, 590).
9. See also Devon Carbado's (2013) discussion of the constitutive nature of whiteness at work in questions of raced-classed heteronormative gender expectations, and employment discrimination in *Jesperson v. Harrah's* (2006) litigation, discussed here in more detail in Chapter 3.
10. See Beauboeuf-Lafontant (2009), Collins (1990), Guy-Sheftall (2002), Harris (1982), Hobson (2013), O'Grady (1992), Pough (2012), Wallace-Sanders (2008).
11. See Carby (1987), Collins (1990), Crenshaw (1989), Foster (1993), Giddings (1984), Gines (2011, 2014), Guy-Sheftall (1995), May (2007, 2012a ), Waters (2007).
12. I discuss this more fully in Chapter 2.
13. See Anzaldúa (1990a), Hoagland (2001), hooks (1990), Lugones (2005, 2007, 2010).
14. My goal is not to single out Lindsay's approach, but to take it up as but one concrete example of a common way of reading and applying intersectionality as primarily an identity descriptor or complexity tool.
15. Neal parallels the socially praised preacher and socially maligned pimp to expose (heteronormative, masculinist, and exploitative) continuities between ostensibly opposite forms of Black masculinity and moral character (Neal 2005). See also Collins' (2004) analysis of the connected logics of the prison and the closet and James Baldwin's classic 1952 coming of age novel, *Go Tell It on the Mountain*. Neal and Collins (and implicitly, I would argue, Baldwin; see May 1996) contend that, until race liberation politics

take up a Black feminist, anti-homophobic politic, the logics of deviance that uphold myriad systems of domination shall remain intact.

16. See Alcoff and Kittay (2007), Anzaldúa (1999), Christian (1990), Code (1995), Collins (1990), Dill and Zambrana (2009), Williams (1991).
17. See Code (1995), Collins (1990), Hawkesworth (1989), Jaggar (1989), Lindsay (2013), Shields (2008).
18. See Alarcón (1990), Anzaldúa (1990b), Christian (1990), Lugones (1994, 2010), Maracle (1994).
19. See Carastathis (2013a), Cole (2008), Crenshaw (1991), Greenwood (2008).
20. Gender-primary logics continue (in advocacy, research, and curriculum) and still undergird ideas about who, or what, is "feminist." Gender-universal thinking also shapes intersectionality critiques and is a site of "slippage" for applications, as I shall discuss.
21. Meaning "organizations set up by women of Turkish and Moroccan descent . . . [that] are sometimes ethnically more diverse and may reach out to other ethnic minority women as well" (Roggeband 2010, 945).
22. E.g., Carastathis (2008), Conaghan (2009), Cooper (2009), Kwan (1997, 1999), McGinley and Cooper (2013), Puar (2007).
23. See Bartky (1990), Frye (1983), Lugones (1994, 2005), Young (1990).
24. Though she does not overtly use intersectionality, Sumi Madhok's insights about sociality, contextualization, and shifting the terms of what counts as 'action' are useful: "a conceptual shift in our thinking of agency would pay attention to the sociality of persons and to the particularities of social and historical circumstances in which persons fulfill their moral obligations and pursue life plans and choices . . . [and] it would be predicated upon a non-insistence on maximal or free action" (Madhok 2013, 106–107).
25. See Lorde (1984, 142).
26. For example, Pratt-Clarke (2010) discusses Transdisciplinary Applied Social Justice (TASJ) frames.
27. Researchers thus advocate using methods and models that *overtly* aim to tap into an intersectional social justice orientation. For instance, Greenwood (2008) explores how feminists can work collectively when race relations structure activist groups. She argues solidarity in a racially heterogeneous group is possible via forging an intersectional political consciousness, one attendant not only to the *fact* of multiple intersecting identities, but to the implications and consequences of this multiplicity (e.g., simultaneous privilege and oppression).
28. A radical Black feminist organization founded in the United States in 1974. To signal their commitment to coalition politics and radical social change, the Collective named themselves not after a particular individual or historical figure, but after the guerrilla military operation, during the Civil War, at the Combahee River in South Carolina in 1863, led by Harriet Tubman, which freed around 750 enslaved persons. For more on the Collective and its history, see Harris (1999), Roth (2004), and Springer (2005).
29. The other Black women who spoke were Hallie Quinn Brown, Frances Ellen Watkins Harper, Fannie Barrier Williams, Fanny Jackson Coppin, and Sarah J. Early (for all six speeches, see Sewall 1894). Notably, Ida B. Wells did not speak: she protested by handing out a booklet, *The Reason Why the Colored American Is Not in the World's Columbian Exposition*. It contains five essays, including one by Frederick Douglass (see Wells 1893).
30. On the AFASS, the AASS, and their ideological differences, see Jones (2007, 44–57).
31. An abolitionist newspaper founded in 1831 by William Lloyd Garrison and Isaac Knapp.

32. See Clarke (1983a, 1983b), Harris (1999), Lorde (1984), Roth (2004), Smith (1983), Springer (2005).
33. Chapter 3 takes up critiques charging intersectionality with ruining cohesive feminist politics (or subjects, or logics). Drawing inspiration from Gwendolyn Pough's work in progress (see Pough 2012) on new iterations of Sapphire, I explore how tales of intersectionality's destructive force reinforce the Sapphire stereotype and animate a kind of reverse-racism logic, placing causative blame on the "both/and" thinkers who have dared to point out that the cohesion feminist theory and/or politics has claimed (or mourned) was always exclusionary and thus only possible in the first place via fragmentation (which favored rather than contested privilege).
34. See Asch and Fine (1988), Kluchin (2009), Largent (2008), and Saxton (2013).
35. See Carastathis (2013a) for an in-depth analysis spanning six years of this group's multiracial, transnational work.
36. Here Maldonado-Torres builds on Lugones' conception of a "pilgrimage" as a particular type of decolonial journey that Anzaldúa pursues and performs (Maldonado-Torres 2012, 196–197). I would argue that other contestatory journeys, as in Harriet Tubman's, for example, could be thought of in this way as well—as crossing borders, as requiring a changed consciousness, and as reliant on collective knowledge and coalitions to be enacted (see May 2014b).

# 2

# Intersectionality's Call to Break from Single-Axis Thinking

## *Still Unheard, Still Unanswered?*

Given intersectionality's widespread use in academic, policy, and activist contexts, my suggestion, in this chapter's title, that its call to take up matric logics and forms of justice has not (yet) been adequately answered may seem counterintuitive. Certainly, intersectional approaches have had a marked influence on feminist and anti-racist practices, in a range of institutional contexts (from the classroom to the courtroom, from research to policy) and beyond formal institutional contexts (even anti-institutional ones, as in prison abolition activism [Spade 2013]). Intersectionality studies is also emerging as a field in its own right, one that encompasses "three loosely defined sets of engagements: the first consisting of applications of an intersectional framework or investigations of intersectional dynamics, the second consisting of discursive debates about the scope and content of intersectionality as a theoretical and methodological paradigm, and the third consisting of political interventions employing an intersectional lens" (Cho, Crenshaw, and McCall 2013, 785).

At the same time, however, its philosophical and political nuances are not always sufficiently understood: in turn, intersectional ideas and practices are often inadequately taken up. While many champion intersectionality's ongoing possibilities, others suggest it has "peaked" or is "outmoded"—its potential exhausted (e.g., Conaghan 2009; Kwan 1997; Taylor, Hines, and Casey 2011). Intersectionality could thus be described as existing in a somewhat contested state: unpacking this contradiction offers important insights into how hegemonic mindsets (in this case, the subtle workings of single-axis logics) exert power, often in unexpected ways.

The chapters that follow highlight specific patterns of intersectionality's interpretive distortion and examine instances of its nominal use across different contexts. Here, I introduce more generally how ubiquitous reference to, or widespread application of, intersectionality does not necessarily translate into contextualized understandings of the concept. Even when we are committed to eradicating injustice, invested in social change, and seek to transform our practices, we can also pick up and wield "the master's tools" (Lorde 1984) often unwittingly. An intersectional orientation thus emphasizes the need to pinpoint and contest the unconscious workings of oppressive power, even within resistance projects and liberation struggles.

Yet, when it comes to interpreting and applying intersectionality, acknowledging the capacity to distort, even in "loving" contexts (Ortega 2006), often seems forgotten. As feminist scholars, educators, researchers, policymakers, and activists, we must think about how to more adequately take up intersectional ideas and justice orientations. Understanding some of the nuances of intersectional orientations, histories, and commitments is only a first step: if the terms of applying or interpreting intersectionality fundamentally undermine its central premises, we must think through this paradox. This chapter begins this project.

### Intersectionality Is Employed Widely *and* Frequently Misunderstood?

Imagine being asked to answer a survey question about intersectionality's current status: *Which statement is correct?* "*Intersectionality has 'arrived:' it is firmly established, widely recognized, and broadly utilized,*" or "*Intersectionality remains misunderstood and its time is still yet to come: despite its longevity and impact, it is often treated carelessly.*" Should one follow the line of reasoning, answer the question as posed, and select the most accurate statement via an either/or evaluation? Or should one respond by setting aside the question's binary lens and draw on intersectional both/and thinking to answer?

Certainly, the first way of responding is more (conventionally) "logical": it aligns with the question's given structure and produces less ambiguous outcomes. The forced-choice tactic seems to offer precision and clarity (though it does so in part by hiding complications from view). Conversely, the second approach leads to a messier place: it departs from the question's either/or sensibilities and affords the seemingly contradictory conclusion that *both* assessments are accurate. "Both/and" conclusions are not easily understood without contextual analysis: they require more explanatory work. However, by opening up space for thinking beyond the question's parameters, the second approach also allows for paradoxes to be considered potentially meaningful.

In a nutshell, the either/or approach, while straightforward, can suppress contradictions and alternative possibilities: by adhering to a dichotomous view, it may also create conflict or enforce divisions where there may, in fact, be none. The both/and lens, though a less tidy, more difficult place to begin (and end), offers ways to evaluate a situation from multiple standpoints, creates room to identify shared logics while accounting for differences, and can be used to approach tensions or contradictions as having logics and implications of their own, rather than treating them primarily as problems to smooth over.

In my view, an intersectional, layered approach to interrogating and unsettling dominant ways of thinking remains generative: its "time" has not passed us by, but has been deferred or delimited in various ways. It thus seems unlikely that intersectionality could be outdated if it has not yet been fully understood. To qualify as passé, it would need to have been engaged with more adequately in the first place. In other words, I find both conclusions to be accurate: intersectionality has arrived, but not yet come. On one hand, it is referenced and used widely (suggesting it is readily understood). On the other hand, if one looks beyond the mere fact of its frequent citation or widespread use and examines *how* it is interpreted and applied, it becomes clear that intersectionality is also commonly misconstrued and used in ways that depart from and even abrogate its key premises. How can this be so?

To start, bell hooks' insights about the politics of language and interpretation are useful. hooks reminds us that being widely talked about does not necessarily signal transformed social, philosophical, or institutional relations: she remarks, "Often this speech about the 'Other' is also a mask, an oppressive talk hiding gaps, absences, that space where our words would be if we were speaking" (hooks 1990, 151). For marginalized groups, interpretation can involve simultaneous recognition and violation: dominant ways of reading or understanding can perpetuate co-optation, avoidance, and even suppression of Black women's work and words. Drawing on hooks' observations, it just must *mean* something that intersectionality is so widely cited yet so unevenly applied. In fact, some of the ways in which it has been interpreted and implemented are surprisingly reductive: beyond being unsophisticated, they depart from (and even undermine) its premises and goals.

This current (and historical) contradiction needs more attention: the sheer array of slippages away from intersectional logics, as if basic intersectionality premises remain intangible, and the frequent trivialization or disappearing of key intersectionality concepts, ideas, and arguments, should not be brushed aside.[1] What does it mean if intersectionality is often erased in the very ways it is recognized—that it disappears or becomes flattened (and often unrecognizable, even nonintersectional) in how it is used or interpreted? Why are central intersectional premises and insights (e.g., simultaneous privilege and oppression, complex subjectivity, multilevel and contextual analysis, contestation of categorical logics) so often approached as optional or discardable, such that "intersectionality" becomes reconfigured as a mere demographic device in research modeling[2] or a simplistic diversity management tool (see Ahmed 2012; Mohanty 2013)? We must be more curious about these peculiar dynamics and explore why intersectional worldviews seem, for many, difficult to grasp or hold on to, easy to ignore or discount, or, perhaps, viewed as ripe for extraction or expropriation.

These interpretive patterns suggest a kind of incapacity (and/or willful refusal) to fully engage intersectional logics: it is as if its multifaceted view of subjectivity, power, knowledge, and social change cannot (or will not) be retained. How does intersectionality slip away, even as it is reached for? How do its alternative orientations get so quickly distorted? Normative ideas (including either/or thinking, gender-first models of feminism, and hierarchies of oppression) seem to have a kind of magnetic force that keeps intersectionality just out of reach, even as intersectionality seeks to render visible the deep violations built into these very same mindsets and invites us to pull away from them, even to divest from them. As Barbara Tomlinson has discussed, "societal and disciplinary power relations give utterances that are friendly to prevailing power relations an overdetermined reasonableness while rendering most oppositional arguments automatically suspect" (Tomlinson 2013b, 994).

Asymmetrical cognitive authority is thus another impediment: not all knowers are granted the same degree or kind of political, philosophical, or experiential authority. Subjugated knowers are often denied equal (or any) cognitive authority, in part because "marked" embodiments are seen as a "drag" on rationality (though 'unmarked' or transparent bodies do not undergo this same epistemic indictment—in fact, 'transparent' bodies are accorded invisible epistemic privilege).[3] As María Lugones argues, "legitimacy, authority, voice, sense, and visibility are denied to resistant subjectivity": this means that resistant speech or actions often take unconventional forms (Lugones 2010, 746). However, too often, critics and practitioners alike use modes of interpretation or application that cannot "meet" intersectionality's alternative visions, unconventional approaches, and different forms of knowing: instead, as I shall illustrate, many of the methods used can suppress or even violate intersectionality.

In sum, dominant logics tend not only to "make sense" without much cognitive effort, but we, too, are more likely to be perceived as making sense when keeping to the usual rules of analysis or argument. Ironically, this is a fundamental intersectionality insight: power operates to continually deny complexity and delay social transformation, both at individual and structural levels. However, whether in debates about intersectionality, or in applications of it, what we may not have accounted for adequately is how we are regularly invited to adhere to and think within the confines of existing and established frameworks.

"Single-axis" mindsets continue to hold sway: they consistently seem more logical or plausible and those who use them, or adhere to their norms, are more likely to be perceived as rational or as making reasoned claims. This is what intersectionality, in great part, has to teach us: and this is also, in great part, how it gets dropped or distorted.

### Echoes across a Century: The Problem of Speaking "Into the Void"[4] Is Not New

I came to this project in large part through my body of work on Anna Julia Cooper, an early Black feminist intellectual, educator, and activist.[5] In exploring Cooper's life and work, and in examining how her prescient ideas have been undertheorized and distorted, in her own time and thereafter, I began to think more fully about how intersectionality, a concept she anticipated to a great degree, likewise seems regularly misunderstood, read simplistically, and even carelessly dismissed. Whether in Cooper's more widely known 1892 volume, *A Voice from the South by a Black Woman of the South* (the first book-length articulation of U.S. Black feminist thought; see Cooper 1988), or in her nearly forgotten 1925 Sorbonne dissertation on the Haitian and French revolutions (see Cooper 2006), her writings (and speeches) offer some of the clearest examples of intersectional scholarship from the period.[6] Her analytical and political vision lies at the foundation of contemporary intersectional work.[7] Though nearly a century spans the period between Cooper's *A Voice* and intersectionality's emergence in the lexicon (by Crenshaw [1989] in "Demarginalizing"), the remarkably similar ways in which their analyses and political visions have (and have not) been taken up stood out and called for more attention.

Of course, Crenshaw herself draws on this longer history of Black feminist theorizing to support her line of reasoning: she also crafts alternative genealogies to interrupt conventional historical memory. For example, when delineating intersectionality's utility for unpacking exclusions embedded in the law's binary logics and models of redress and rights, Crenshaw (1989) underscores that her analysis builds on ideas from nineteenth-century Black feminists, including Anna Julia Cooper and Sojourner Truth. She populates her arguments with previous voices: more than documenting a collective intellectual and political impetus, Crenshaw shows precedence for her claims (in the tradition of legal argument, but rather than reference case law alone, she cites alternative intellectual histories and archives, including the archive of personal experience).

Indeed, Cooper employed similar tactics in her own writings: referencing numerous other Black women thinkers and activists to paint a more collective view, she refused individualist norms of authority and refuted potential charges that her ideas were merely her own opinion or singular standpoint (Cooper 1988, 140–142). She also combined established forms of theological, philosophical, literary, and sociopolitical analysis with more personal forms of reflection to illustrate key problems. For instance, when naming the issue of internalized oppression, Cooper recalled how she had accommodated herself to living in constraint and fear, like a beaten dog (88–89). Delineating the related issue of internalized dominance, she reprimanded Black men for sexist practices and adhering to patriarchy (32, 78), protested white feminists' following the logics of white supremacy and xenophobia (117–126), and censured white men for their ignorance, egotism, and unbridled violence, condemning white mob rule (Cooper 1998a, 210) and the problem of "Angry Saxons" (Cooper 1998b, 259).

Also notable is the fact that the silencing and elision Crenshaw critiques in contemporary feminist theory and in civil rights doctrine's either/or analytics, which foster testimonial inequality and impede meaningful social change (Crenshaw 1989), are not that different in kind from the biases and obstacles preventing an "equal hearing at the bar of the nation" that Cooper anticipated as a writer, educator, and activist a century prior (Cooper 1998a, 202). Cooper was unsure as to whether her "voice" would be heard or taken up as legitimate, due to outright epistemic and material inequalities she faced as a Black woman knower. However, she forged ahead and underscored that the "colored woman of to-day occupies . . . a unique position in this country. . . . She is confronted by both a woman question and a race problem, and is as yet an unknown or an unacknowledged factor in both" (Cooper 1988, 134). Sojourner Truth's memorable 1851 question, "Aren't I a woman?" (Truth 1995), likewise pinpoints, and rejects, such erasures and elisions. Using the rhetorical form of a question, Truth invites her audience to take up her point of view, at the nexus of race-gender-class, not only shifting the terms of feminism's dominant logic, but also alluding to new (intersectional) terms of accountability for its exclusions.

More than simply point out how Black women's ideas and voices have been ignored, Cooper added that much of what Black women had to say was *unspeakable* in conventional terms—as when she eloquently references (but does not elaborate on) the "Black Woman's . . . unnamable burden inside" (Cooper 1988, 90, ellipses in original). This insight is echoed in Crenshaw's referencing the "untellable" nature of Black women's experience and knowledge, due in part to the court's refusal of both/and race-gender logics (Crenshaw 1991). Cooper, Truth, and Crenshaw, in different contexts and eras, and from different lived experiences as Black women, assert their right to speak and be heard as Black feminist knowers. Simultaneously, they underscore how Black women (collectively) have had to confront indifference, ignorance, and silence, due to their social locations: a nexus of compounding structures of privilege and oppression have resulted in patently asymmetrical (between-group and within-group) patterns of opportunity, material disparity, and epistemological inequality.

In retrospect, much of what has not been adequately understood about Cooper's and Truth's intellectual and political contributions can be tied to an inability or even an active refusal to take up their fundamentally different logics and expectations—ideas that, to a large degree, would now be characterized as "intersectional" in nature. Whether the context was religion, education, economics, literature, or history, Cooper refused to homogenize race or gender, or to treat any one factor as singular or primary. Instead, she insisted on recasting the contours of analysis and of liberation politics to account for race and gender together.[8] At the same time, she knew that using these different ways of thinking could readily lead to charges of illogic.

Crenshaw discusses this dynamic as well. In "Demarginalizing," she demonstrates how the U.S. courts cannot engage with both/and logics when it comes to civil rights claims. The notion that Black women are *both* "unique" *and* "central," that is, the same as *and* different from

White women and/or Black men when it comes to group claims, rights, and redress, seems to lie outside the realm of the possible in the law's conventional imagination (Crenshaw 1989, 150). Black womanhood, as a lived and structural conjunction (and not as a mathematical addition of separate factors, race + gender), has no place, other than to be subsumed under race *or* gender.

Reflecting on these constraints, Crenshaw writes, "Perhaps it appears to some that I have offered inconsistent criticisms of how Black women are treated in antidiscrimination law. . . . It seems that I have to say that Black women are the same [as White women or Black men] and harmed by being treated differently or that they are different and harmed by being treated the same. But I cannot say both" (148–149). She can and does say both—and asserts the rationality of her analysis, but the question she raises is: can her both/and statements, as with those of countless Black women in the justice system, be heard? Refusing the charge that her analysis lacks reason and merit, Crenshaw identifies the court's either/or "single-axis" logic as sorely lacking, not her own. She concludes, "This apparent contradiction is but another manifestation of the conceptual limitations of the single-axis analysis that intersectionality challenges" (149).

Cooper and Truth knew they might not be heard: likewise, Crenshaw anticipated she would likely be perceived as engaging in unsound arguments, due to her insistence on using a both/and approach to critique the law's either/or governing imaginary. Being compelled to arrive at such conclusions—that one may not be heard (or, if heard, likely in a way that distorts, so that even the 'hearing' one garners can be a form of misrecognition)—has been an ongoing consideration for, and context of, Black feminist intersectional work. Truth's, Cooper's, and Crenshaw's multidimensional analyses and premises have, indeed, been both recognized and misrecognized, often in the same instance.

In other words, epistemic differences, when combined with asymmetrical power relations, can lead to interpretive violence. As Ofelia Schutte explains, "To the culturally dominant speaker, the subaltern speaker's discourse may appear to be a string of fragmented observations rather than a unified whole. The actual problem may not be incoherence but the lack of cultural translatability of the signifiers for coherence from one set of cultural presuppositions to the other" (Schutte 2000, 56; see also Narayan 1997). Thus merely offering more "information" about intersectional Black feminist analyses, or more detailed definitions, cannot, alone, ameliorate the situation: fine-tuning intersectionality definition(s) does not adequately address these larger interpretive politics and dynamics. This is why Uma Narayan argues that "historically constituted discursive inequalities . . . need to be dealt with and cannot be wished away" (Narayan 1997, 135).

The abyss into which intersectionality scholars (particularly women of color scholars/activists engaging in intersectional work) continue to find their words descending (or disappearing) is politically and philosophically significant. Even as intersectionality highlights the problem of testimonial inequality in terms of exclusions in the courts' logics, gaps in the historical archive, or narrow (but ostensibly universal) notions of the citizen-subject embedded in rights discourses, as a body of work, intersectionality likewise (and paradoxically) faces substantial, and sustained, testimonial injustice (see Fricker 2007).[9] This rhetorical/political chasm has sometimes led to the reiteration of basic intersectional ideas: in turn, such rearticulation often leads to charges that intersectionality is stagnant or merely repetitive. Unfortunately, it rarely sparks exploration of how epistemological resistance or backlash may continually leave intersectionality "unheard" even as it is repeated (May 2014a).[10]

How and why has it come to pass that those who employ intersectional analytics often confront being dismissed or perceived as insufficiently coherent, particularly, I would argue, Black feminist thinkers and activists? For example, is it simply coincidental that many earlier intersectionality texts, the majority of which were crafted by Black women and women of color, are frequently read reductively? More than simply document that superficial notions of intersectionality are common, it is important to ask why intersectionality frequently is interpreted as if it were monolithic or merely descriptive—and not understood as a dynamic form of inquiry with normative commitments, internal tensions and differences, and analytical and political capacities. I would suggest that this asymmetrical treatment, in terms of interpretive and discursive politics, can be explained in part by intersectionality's fundamentally different worldview, one that challenges dominant mindsets by drawing on alternative logics. It can also likely be traced to its genealogy within radical women of color theorizing.

### Race versus Gender Binaries and the Enduring Power of Single-Axis Mindsets

In addition to helping to trace how intersectional ideas have been read reductively across time, and to consider what this signifies, an historicized approach also reveals that many of the narrow-minded yet widely condoned ways of thinking contested by Black feminists in the nineteenth century continue to this day, sometimes practically unmodified in terms of their underlying premises (meaning, the contexts have changed, but the underlying logics have a certain constancy). I do not mean that there have been no substantial material, structural, legal, and philosophical changes that have occurred thanks to collective struggles over the past century. However, the *tenacity* of mindsets that Anna Julia Cooper and others in her time identified as patently violent and distorting is striking and worth thinking about, since intersectionality has long sought to intervene in and eliminate many of these ways of thinking.

For example, the 2008 and the 2012 presidential elections in the United States were saturated with simplistic (and distorting) "race versus gender" logics, ones largely indistinguishable, in terms of underlying premises, from those Cooper decried over a century prior. Patricia J. Williams, for example, noted countless "media depictions of white women as sole inheritors of the feminist movement and black men as the sole beneficiaries of the civil rights movement"; she also asked, poignantly, "What happened . . . to the last four decades [or, I might add, the last century's worth] of discussion about tokenism and multiple identities and the complex intersections of race, gender, sexuality, ethnicity, and class?" (Williams 2010, 29).

As Tracy A. Thomas persuasively argues, the 2008 campaign "continue[d] the false dichotomy between race and sex" in ways that virtually mirror arguments and rhetorics proffered in acrimonious nineteenth-century deliberations over suffrage, abolition, and civil rights. Many such debates pitted 'women's suffrage' against civil rights (e.g., the Fourteenth and Fifteenth amendments to the U.S. constitution) (Thomas 2010, 33–35), dropping from view (and also from coordinated/coalitional political struggle) the rights of "women" who were Black and "Blacks" who were women. Crenshaw also pinpointed "troubling polemics that bore discomforting connections to the arguments of suffrage-feminists such as [Susan B.] Anthony and [Elizabeth Cady] Stanton" (Crenshaw 2011a, 228). Numerous "Hillary versus Barack" controversies showed the degree to which ideas about group coherence, based on (falsely universalized) singular identities (e.g., gender-primary frameworks or common-denominator racial logics), are still presumed necessary for effective advocacy and viable politics, even as women of color feminists have contested these divisive political strategies for at least two hundred years.

It is not as if these tired "race versus gender" mindsets went unchallenged, as Williams' (2010) and Thomas' (2010) discussions illustrate, for instance. Yet, even in many critical assessments of the elections, aimed at unpacking the ongoing legacies of racism and sexism, one can find substantial reliance on binary analytics (or slippages away from intersectional ones). Consider as illustrative Jane Caputi's provocative reading of political cartoons, rhetorics, and media images from the 2008 election. Caputi documents prejudice and hatred expressed in election paraphernalia and public rhetoric. She creates a valuable archive of such ephemera and identifies and contests an array of "smear techniques" (including othering, demonization, threats to the nation, "pornification," gay-baiting, and dehumanization) that connect to more overt lies, threats, and stereotypes also in circulation at the time. However, though she explicitly aims to take up the "intersecting meanings of race, sex, age, class, gender, religion, and sexuality" (Caputi 2010, 122), she falls away from these intersectional goals in a variety of (subtle) ways.

Sometimes this departure occurs via mismatches between analytical intent, interpretive methodology, and organizational structure. In examples that could be drawn on to illustrate how multiple vectors of power are deeply imbricated, for instance, Caputi tends to highlight only particular aspects (in part because she divides the essay into thematic sections). Referencing a bumper sticker invoking O. J. Simpson ("Obama loves America like O. J. loved Nicole" [cited in Caputi 2010, 126]), she discusses how "Alien/Nation" works to position Obama as an outsider, a stranger, but also a sham and perhaps an otherworldly or monstrous (inhuman) figure.

Yet, Caputi does not take up many of the simultaneous race–gender notions at work here, though they function to increase the affect of impending national threat (to render it more palpably menacing): the phrase analogizes the nation to a White female body (Nicole) who, in the event of Obama's election, might risk harm, and perhaps death (he may *seem* heroic, but could be capable of violent harm). Another lost opportunity is tracing these rhetorics and stereotypes back to nineteenth-century justifications of white mob rule with impunity. The bumper-sticker analogy trades in similar "logics" of patriarchal, white supremacist fear-mongering that Ida B. Wells took on in the 1890s, for instance, to contest racist–sexist rationales for lynching as a means to "protect" the national body politic. Wells carefully documented how lynching was an explicit tool of social control used in a widespread effort to eradicate civil rights and dismantle reconstruction (e.g., Wells-Barnett 2014; see also Carbado 1999a; Giddings 2008).

At other times, Caputi uses an implicitly gender-first (and patriarchy as primary) mode of analysis to explain the workings of systemic prejudice. Discussing "Mind-Body Splitting," she asserts, "patriarchal culture conceptually severs the mind from the body and elevates the mind over the body, associating the male with the mind and culture, and the female, as well as exploited and marginalized groups, with the body and with what we come to think of as an external 'Nature,' consisting of wilderness, animals, and the elements" (Caputi 2010, 133). Here, her syntax lumps together all "women" and divides them from other "exploited and marginalized groups." Patriarchy is identified as the root source of this mind/body splitting—that is, it does impact other groups, but patriarchy is the origin and cause of this objectification that justifies domination. Multiple other historical factors, including racism, coloniality, and what Lugones describes as the "heterosexualism" of the "colonial/modern race/gender system" (Lugones

2007, 2010), are invisible as causal and thus implicitly secondary or ancillary.

This invites a hierarchy of oppressions model of thinking, though Caputi aims to take up intersectional analysis. In this same section, she homogenizes gender in other ways, reinforcing a gender-primary lens. For example, she remarks, "Women, paradigmatically, are reduced by sexists to their specifically female body parts and powers. Hillary was not only repeatedly labeled a *cunt*, but also, more euphemistically, 'the vajority choice'" (Caputi 2010, 133, italics in original). However, as critical analysis of the life of Sarah Baartman amply illustrates (including the politics of her capture as a Khoikhoi in what is now the Eastern Cape of South Africa, her forced display as a curiosity in England and France, and, later, the dissection of and display of Baartman's genitalia and brain by French naturalist and anatomist George Cuvier), which "parts" of a woman's body are her "female body parts" (to be objectified and maligned) are not the same for all "women": furthermore, the medicalization, cataloguing, and objectification of "female" parts is heavily racialized.[11]

A third means by which Caputi departs from intersectional analysis occurs when she artificially divides up "racist" and "sexist" stereotypes. Notions of Michelle Obama as "Obama's Baby Mama" (cited in Caputi 2010, 138) are characterized as *racist*, though this phrase is also deeply gendered, classed, and heteronormative. (Furthermore, intersectionality demands that we not rely on "respectability" tactics for rebutting such notions: simply arguing the "Baby Mama" charge is inaccurate because the Obamas are married, respectable, and family-oriented, for example, would not disrupt the underlying hierarchy of worthy/unworthy persons at work here.)

Conversely, denunciations of Michelle Obama's alleged rage (e.g., as an "angry black Harridan" [cited in Caputi 2010, 140]) are categorized as *sexist*, despite a long history of the trope of angry Black womanhood used to disparage Black women and to reinforce ideals of white, middle-class norms of gender and family formation. Notions of uncontrollable, irrational (and even emasculating) anger are not solely (or primarily) misogynist:[12] here, race interweaves with gender to characterize a particular vision of a wrathful hag (or uncontrollable worn-out horse,[13] or irate, sexually loose woman, all etymological possibilities for a "Harridan"). Inadvertently, Caputi reinforces an atomized logic of race and gender as separate factors, even as her aim is to raise awareness about the poisonous intersections of these enduring mindsets. Minimally, these examples are both racist and sexist and draw on notions of a monstrous, oversexed, and (in)human (primitivist, even bestial) nature to create lines of distinction between the normative and the perverse.

Simplistic (and distorting) race versus gender binaries emerged in other contexts as well during these U.S. presidential election cycles. For instance, much of what was (or was not) considered to be a "women's" issue, or considered illustrative of endemic sexism, was still based, to a large degree, on the apparent representativeness of white, middle-class, heterosexual women for all women (Russo and Spatz 2010; Simmons 2010). In 2012, proposals by some states (e.g., Virginia) for vaginal probes (via handheld wands for transvaginal ultrasound imaging) to be compulsory for women seeking an abortion were fairly readily understood by much of the wider public and by national feminist organizations to be a "women's issue."

Yet matters tied to *intersectional* reproductive justice agendas were generally overlooked or, if acknowledged, treated as distinct from "women's" issues or feminist political agendas. These issues include widespread poverty and an ever-increasing wage gap; environmental hazards and pollution in poor rural and urban areas; increased disparities in access to health care and in life span and rates of illness; immigration and citizenship policies which unduly impact women; ongoing anti-natalist policies and practices with regard to disability, race, poverty, and citizenship; endemic and escalating forms of violence against women, much of which remains underreported and unaddressed; and intensified rates and forms of incarceration and their gendered politics and implications.

While misogyny certainly underlay efforts to formally require an invasive and medically unnecessary vaginal probe to access and undergo a legal medical procedure, hyperfocus on this proposal, almost in isolation from violent factors *presently* in practice that already disproportionately and negatively impact many women's lives, can serve to replicate old exclusions in reproductive politics, particularly an over-emphasis on issues of choice and pro-natalism, with underattention to anti-natalism in its various guises and histories. What is recognizable as "sexist" still tends to be limited to issues that fit neatly or obviously within gender-primary, common-denominator logics—the imaginary for what is "feminist" or who "women" are, and the affective sites of coalesced energy and protest, remain relatively single axis, in other words, and not intersectional.

"Race versus gender" binaries were omnipresent in other public debates and popular discourses during the 2012 election cycle as well. Consider an editorial cartoon (by Mike Lester) that portrays President Obama as a pimp (shown wearing a flashy fur coat and oversized accessories) and that suggests Sandra Fluke[14] is (akin to) a prostitute.[15] Part of how this image functions, and indeed underlying the entire incident, is deep misogyny and racism. Fluke faced excruciating criticism and had to deflect what could be described as a misogynist frenzy in the halls of Congress and in print, social, and televisual media. But part of the *outrage* against how Fluke was publicly maligned ties into the "wages" of class and race privilege and the politics of respectability. The "offense" of the comments was seen as greater or more contemptible in part because Fluke is a "nice," white, middle-class, educated, eloquent woman—not only a top student at Georgetown Law (at the time) but also a minister's daughter.

More than "racist" logics are also in play in the depiction of President Obama: stereotypes of hyper-heterosexual (and criminal) Black masculinity have long saturated the American social imaginary. Portraying the president as a crass, buffoonish pimp is objectionable, but not just in terms of "race." Race is imbricated by gender, class, and sexuality simultaneously, by norms of national belonging, and by unspoken but powerful codes of worthy versus contemptuous personhood. No one factor alone offers an adequate lens for unpacking the highly racialized, hyper-heterosexual, yet clownish (and thus implicitly impotent) "thug" masculinity portrayed. The image paints President Obama as a felonious fool (a representation/stereotype that fits squarely in the minstrelsy tradition [see Riggs 1983]), and an intersectional approach would highlight how these racist ideologies and visual rhetorics rely on heterosexist, middle-class, and white gender norms of nationhood and citizenship simultaneously.

The stereotype of deviance or pathology attributed to Black masculinity at large, and, in this case to the president in particular, is a form of racism that requires sexist, heterocentric, and middle-class norms (and hierarchies of human worth and value) to play out—they cannot be disarticulated and monocausal analyses are not up to the task of evaluating and addressing these notions (Carbado 1999a, 1999b; Collins 2004; McWhorter 2009). Attending to simultaneous privilege and oppression, across sites of power and within-group, illuminates far more about the image, the debates it references, and the stereotypes and assumptions they trade in, than thinking about sexism or racism in isolation. Multiple power vectors and various sites of representation, discourse, and institutionalized oppression are *already present and in play*.

To clarify, there is no predetermined list of factors to be addressed by intersectionality: rather, the aim is to identify the many forms of power at work, to show how they constellate, interrelate, and intermingle, and to then address how these intersections maintain subordination and inequality (and also uphold power and privilege). From a single-axis perspective, what is explicitly at work, or even intended, can appear to be one factor alone, or at least one as primary (with other factors posited as secondary, or following from the most causal factor). However, since intersectionality attends to and interrogates normativity, the invisible effects and workings of privilege, and transparent sites of power and subjectivity, it also highlights logics that are implicit, unstated, and unsaid—yet still operative and formative.

This detour into recent U.S. presidential elections[16] illustrates how either/or race versus gender logics prevail and continue to operate in detrimental ways. While intersectionality starts from the premise that our various identities and the many structures of power we live within and navigate should be understood as interconnected and enmeshed, conventional ways of conceptualizing identity or examining inequality tend to rely on either/or thinking and be "single-axis"—meaning that we are asked to examine (and address) race *or* class separately, or perhaps think about disability *and* sexuality, but insist that one factor be "primary" (they are still conceived of as separate, since one must be first or more significant). Unfortunately, despite the fact that single-axis thinking distorts and dehumanizes, it still saturates the collective social imaginary. Certainly, part of its perversion lies in the stereotypes and biases it trades in: it is just as pernicious in how it invites us to engage in simplistic strategies for redress and rights and to overlook how inequalities and privileges can be about race, gender, class, disability, citizenship status, and sexuality simultaneously.

That such mentalities persist is not necessarily surprising, since contemporary identity (and group) categories and logics were forged within historical contexts of domination and violation, from chattel slavery to settler colonialism, systems which relied on stark binaries and comparative differentiation between groups.[17] Since these logics connect to long-standing structural forces and institutional practices, that they endure is not unexpected, and that we fall prey to their normative force is not either. As Crenshaw explains,

> Owing to the unique history of the mutual construction of racism and patriarchy in the American state, the intertwining of both has been a profoundly salient feature of American life. Yet despite these structural features, the dynamic interface between these systems was rarely politicized or contested either within anti-discrimination law or within the political formations organized to contest patriarchy and racism. Black feminist theory and advocacy sought from its earliest iterations to draw attention to this interface, not simply as a demand for self-recognition, but as a critique of the limitations of feminism and anti-racism and as a demand for accountability. (Crenshaw 2011c, 227)

As Crenshaw suggests, there is ample evidence of repeated and ongoing insistence, particularly (but not exclusively) from Black feminists, for the need to attend to the "interfaces" of multiple sites of power and, likewise, to develop terms of accountability and politics for social change from this viewpoint. Beverly Guy-Sheftall's (1995) volume *Words of Fire* documents, for instance, nearly two hundred years of Black feminist analysis starting at and asserting the need to examine the nexus of race–gender–class as a way to develop more adequate models of personhood, politics, and liberation. Yet, at the same time, there is equally abundant evidence of a repeated inability to hear, recognize, or answer this demand, which is why Crenshaw recently wondered if Black feminists shall continue to speak "into the void" (Crenshaw 2011c, 228). Single-axis thinking perpetuates systemic privilege, obscures the interplay of systems of inequality, and masks within-group differences via homogenization: it rationalizes inequality and fractures or impedes cross-categorical coalitions for social change. For these reasons and more, we must take up more adequately intersectionality's call to divest of these logics.

### Why Turning Away from Single-Axis Logics Is Imperative

As I have suggested, single-axis imaginaries continue to permeate political organizing, policy formation, research modeling, and philosophical and theoretical work: they also emerge in new forms all the time. Rejecting either/or mindsets (philosophically, politically, and ethically) is thus an ongoing (and not a one-off) project, as new iterations of either/or politics emerge, even under the guise of progress and positive social change. For example, intersectionality scholars and practitioners must be wary of, and voice our criticism of, moments when one set of rights is (implicitly or explicitly) pitted against another, as in 2013, when the U.S. Supreme Court effectively eviscerated the Voting Rights Act and, simultaneously, struck down the Defense of Marriage Act (DOMA) and California's Proposition 8 (that state's ban on same-sex marriage).

Moreover, an ongoing inclination toward the singular and the tenacity of binary thinking constitute more than theoretical curiosities or abstract academic problems: these logics have real, detrimental consequences when it comes to our collective yearnings and efforts to abolish unjust practices and systemic inequality. As intersectional thinkers and activists have long underscored, conceptualizing group identity or the workings of oppression via "common denominator" (Alarcón 1990) or "but-for" (Crenshaw 1989) frameworks leads to inadequate and distorted understandings of discrimination and often leaves the operative logics (and existing systems of privilege and inequality) in place.

When single-axis models are relied on, the experiences and knowledge of some are often (falsely) universalized as if they could adequately represent the experiences, needs, and claims of all group members: this obscures within-group differences, the relationality of power, and interactions among and permeability between categories. Likewise, single-axis forms of redress adhere to, rather than challenge, the conceptual "building blocks" of domination—they leave the foundations of inequality intact and also reinforce them. Intersectionality is thus especially useful for unpacking how it is that many equality strategies paradoxically legitimize and even expand the forms of violence or harm they seek to dismantle, in large part because they do not depart from the binary logics and hierarchical processes that undergird inequality.

Crenshaw illustrates, for example, how conventional antidiscrimination frameworks require conferred advantage to function. Those with access to the most privilege within oppressed group(s) are most likely to benefit from the court's single-axis approach to inequality and more likely to have their claims recognized and seen as "representative" (Crenshaw 1989, 151). She highlights the court's historic inability and outright "refusal to acknowledge compound discrimination" (149) and exposes how other forms of antidiscrimination practice, including civil rights and feminist organizing, likewise rely on and reinforce systemic privilege. Single-axis models of redress may seem clearer, more logical, and more workable than intersectional ones: however, they are highly distorting and unable to adequately account for or address the interacting nature of systems of oppression.

Intersectionality thus helps unpack how advocacy tactics and redress models can be misleading in their promise of equality, since they may reinforce structural inequality. Dean Spade shows, for instance, how intersectionality is useful for thinking through the implications of law-enforcement models of antiviolence advocacy. Though a common (and widely accepted) strategy, a law-enforcement approach can serve to increase (and rationalize) criminalization, reinforce a culture of violence at large, and buttress the state's paternalistic power, even if it offers a degree of justice or protection for some (Spade 2013, 1037; see also Williams 2009). This contemporary discussion echoes, and builds on, long-standing insights from Black feminist thought and politics that have used a "both/and" analytic, at the intersection of race, gender, and class, to show how a law-enforcement response to the crime of rape was an inadequate tactic, particularly when pursued via a gender-first lens that erased the (gendered) politics of class and race (and the raced and classed politics of gender).

For instance, Ida B. Wells,[18] in the late nineteenth century, and Angela Davis (1983), in the late twentieth century, both questioned single-axis approaches to rights and redress. They also asked us to be wary of seeking (and furthering) paternalistic state protection. Such strategies can perpetuate harm by: justifying an increased (and unwarranted) criminalization of Black men, rationalizing white men's violence against Black women as reasonable and not as criminal, ignoring how Black women suffer from sexual violence as a form of racial terror, and reanimating the carceral logics of enslavement and of the prison via the specter of the Black rapist. The problems resulting from leaving a single-axis approach unquestioned and from adhering to the state's operative logics (which are just two key intersectionality insights, not its sum total) can be both tangible and significant.

Intersectionality's critical utility for identifying gaps and erasures in conventional social justice models, theoretical frames, and political practices, continues to hold much promise. For instance, Menah Pratt-Clarke uses an intersectional approach to document how health disparities, asymmetrical life expectancies, economic inequities, and differing rates of incarceration intertwine: a multisystem analysis of economics, politics, health, educational access, and prisons, combined with a multiple/interacting identity model, is fundamental to understanding these dynamics. The usual frames used to define and understand inequality, assess health, measure economic disparity, or think about incarceration must shift, for without attending to multiple processes and forms of inequality (via intersectionality), significant interactions, like those delineated by Pratt-Clarke, fall from view and our capacity to identify and intervene in structural disenfranchisement likewise slips away (Pratt-Clarke 2013, 105).

Many also draw on intersectionality's same/different thesis and both/and logics to combat within-group disparities, such as differential patterns of economic inequality *among* women, while simultaneously challenging *collective* patterns, such as women's and girls' increasing rates (and lengths) of incarceration. Naming and addressing a group pattern (e.g., women's and girls' incarceration rates) requires attention to in-group differences among women, but also within other categories that are already "within" gender, in particular race, disability, class, and sexuality. In this vein, Monique Morris uses intersectionality to question the adequacy of a framework used to expose and dispute the endemic incarceration of youth of color: the "school to prison pipeline" metaphor (Morris 2012). Certainly, this metaphor highlights the enmeshment of two public institutions with ostensibly different aims and roles: the school and the prison. It also emphasizes the correlation between "the securitization and privatization of public schools and local prison systems" (Isoke 2013, 3). So, how is the "pipeline" metaphor a single-axis concept? It obscures girls' educational conduits to prison.

Morris suggests the metaphor, in its conception and in terms of how it has been used to protest carceral logics, has been fundamentally androcentric and overly homogenous in terms of underlying assumptions about race, education, and prison. Much research on the "pipeline" dynamic fails to encapsulate "the education-system pathways to incarceration for Black girls" because, to a great degree, "the behaviors for which Black females routinely experience disciplinary response are related to their nonconformity with notions of white, middle class femininity, for example, by their dress, their profanity, or by having tantrums in the classroom" (Morris 2012, 6). Likewise, Priscilla Ocen contends that conventional analyses of incarceration capture neither the prison's massive social impact nor the interconnected raced and gendered logics buttressing its power. Much scholarship thereby masks the significance of Black women's gender by focusing primarily on Black men. Instead, "Mass incarceration and imprisonment . . . should be better understood as mechanisms of racial control that trade on gendered logics" and that function "through the policing of racialized gender norms" (Ocen 2013, 479–480).

An intersectional focus on within-group differences is also valuable for identifying intensifying economic disparities among women.

Without it, Julianne Malveaux suggests it would be far more difficult to name and to protest the fact that, according to a 2010 study by the Insight Center for Community Economic Development, in the United States, "the average net worth of single middle aged (36 to 49) Black women (including those who head households and have children) is just $5, compared to $42,600 for single white women of the same age" (Malveaux 2013, 16).[19] In examining the last twenty years of Critical Race Theory, Crenshaw also documents persistent, if not worsening, raced asymmetries that are clearly structural. She references a continuing wealth gap, an increasing health gap (e.g., asymmetrical access to health care, life expectancy, rates of illness and treatment), intensified incarceration, and underscores the disproportionate impact of the recent mortgage and foreclosure crisis on people of color. Attending to within-group racial differences, Crenshaw notes that the wealth gap is particularly prominent for women of color (Crenshaw 2011b, 1337–1340, n255–258).[20]

As these few examples illustrate, intersectional, multilevel analytics, which attend to several systems and structures of power at once, remain invaluable for identifying overlooked or undertheorized sites of injustice and harm and for developing cross-categorical ways of thinking about redress and social change. Intersectionality's time is not "over." The fact that its promise may not (yet) have been entirely realized, or that it has sometimes been co-opted or distorted, should not serve as a rationale for letting go of its vision: intersectionality remains a fruitful means of identifying hidden workings of power, unpacking structures of oppression, and calling for social transformation to address endemic inequities.

### Intersectionality Does Not Come with a Political or Liberatory Guarantee

Unquestionably, intersectionality taps into our collective desires for a changed, more just world. It has been developed as a tool of protest, to communicate outrage against the fact that many of the means and mechanisms for recognition of one's personhood and claiming of one's rights often rely upon exclusionary logics and hierarchical norms of justice that maintain, rather than dismantle, privilege and inequality. Since it is meant to be applied, and not just theorized about as a hypothetical, many have sought to instrumentalize it—to turn it into a readily usable method, policy model, equity norm, or rights framework.

However, in thinking about how to apply intersectionality, reflexivity about the terms of its uptake is necessary. For instance, while many groups interested in social transformation seek recognition (by the state, for instance) as one means to enact change, acquiring legibility in this way can have its perils (Ferguson 2012; Spade 2013): it can require self-violation and abandoning a comprehensive justice orientation to gain any traction within given systemic constraints (Crenshaw 1989). Intersectionality's status has also risen to such a degree that some characterize it as an obligatory, if not hegemonic, tool of feminist "Occidentalism": as Julia Roth discusses, for example, it can seem requisite as a referent or framework if one hopes, from the Global South, to be acknowledged as having anything of import to say by feminists (and publishers, organizations, and funders) in the Global North (Roth 2013).

Likewise, Jasbir Puar has pushed for recognition that liberatory ideas or frameworks for social change cannot be presumed to be incontrovertibly progressive (due to their origins in struggles for civil rights and social change): furthermore, the contexts and modalities of their use matter. As Puar argues, both queer liberation and intersectionality, as concepts and political impetuses, can be wielded as emblems of Western reason or used as weapons of religious "modernity," which is why she finds troubling forms of intersectionality or of queer politics that do not account for Islamophobia within structures of inequality and the workings of the nation, for instance (Puar 2005, 2007).

Thus, more attention must be paid to how intersectionality *can* be used coercively, as in contexts of nationality and settler-colonial nation building. At the same time, we should not (re)enact a false binary between women of color feminisms, as if these were "domestic" or bound by nation, and transnational feminist practices (Lewis 2013; Patil 2013): doing so erases the substantial history of Black women's (radical) transnational activism (Coogan-Gehr 2011; Tomlinson 2013b). Furthermore, intersectionality can be used to contest powerful state rationales and ideologies because, as Spade argues, it highlights how "legal reforms can expand violent systems by mobilizing the rhetoric of saving women combined with frameworks of deservingness that reify racist, ableist, antipoor, and colonial relations" (Spade 2013, 1032).

Just as the need for intersectional analyses continues, concomitantly, so does the need for thoughtful attention to *how* it is used, in what contexts, by whom, and to what ends. Rather than drop intersectionality because some have engaged it in ways that buttress oppressive practices and logics, I would argue intersectionality (used reflexively, not as a lens with a liberatory guarantee) has continued political relevancy and efficacy, whether one seeks to intervene in state-level debates over multiple inequalities or to question sexualized and gendered rationales for engaging in war.[21] An intersectional analysis can help unpack how Islamophobia has been utilized to justify state violence and war transnationally (Razack 2008; Riley 2013) or to govern religious dress codes and police women's bodies within national boundaries, as Sirma Bilge discusses regarding France's debates over the meaning of headscarves, which rely on unstated norms of secularism, feminism, and democracy (Bilge 2010; see also Rottman and Ferree 2008).

Intersectionality *can*, in other words, be used as a tool of resistance and change. Van der Hoogte and Kingma (2004) find much promise in intersectionality for critical NGO and development contexts since it is context-specific and can be useful for dismantling coloniality and paternalism. In the context of CEECs (Central and Eastern European Countries), Koldinská raises the question of coercive or forced sterilizations of Roma women as an instance of discrimination that can better be understood and addressed via intersectionality (Koldinská 2009, 556–560).[22] In fact, intersectionality has been employed across various scales, at local levels (e.g., to change domestic violence response policies [Crenshaw 1991; Sokoloff 2008; Sokoloff and Dupont 2005]) and supranational ones as well. At the 2001 United Nations Conference on Racism, the NGO forum declaration invoked intersectionality as a fundamental (see Van der Hoogte and Kingma 2004; see also Zambrana and Dill 2009, 12). In Canada, intersectionality is being used to address structural health disparities and inequalities (see Hankivsky

2011). And, in Europe, the "GENDERRACE" project addresses the lack of research about intersectionality and multiple discrimination in EU juridical contexts (Burri and Schiek 2009, 5, 22).

Intersectionality has been equally generative when it comes to grassroots politics. Mia Mingus, for example, articulates how a radical intersectional disability justice orientation both helps to account for relational differences within the category/politic of disability and to forge complex affinities with queer, anti-racist, and feminist struggles (Mingus and Talley 2013). Anna Carastathis (2013a) also offers a snapshot of intersectionality's promise to engage in political action and community organizing in ways that are "bottom-up." Likewise, Jennifer Jihye Chun, George Lipsitz, and Young Shin examine the history of AIWA (Asian Immigrant Women Activists, in the San Francisco Bay area) to highlight "social movement intersectionality" as a key tool of political organizing, a central means of exposing multiple sites of oppression, and as an essential way "for immigrant women workers to become active and visible leaders in movements for social and economic justice" (Chun, Lipsitz, and Shin 2013, 917).

At the same time, intersectionality applications can fall short, or, worse, buttress state violence in the name of protection (whether these uses should be characterized as, in fact, "intersectional" is another key question). For instance, Emily Grabham worries the state's approach to (or appropriation of) intersectionality shall result in an increase of the state's "scopic" power while appearing to be an inclusive or emancipatory effort (Grabham 2009). Similarly, Toni Williams documents how formally instituting intersectionality can exacerbate the state's oppression of Indigenous communities (Williams 2009).[23] Since intersectionality may be employed in liberatory and coercive ways (even both simultaneously), the circumstances and modes of its use matter and are relevant. Attending to contexts and outcomes can help gauge whether applications *claiming* intersectionality as their paradigm are, in fact, adequately or equally intersectional, and whether there are slippages at work, or forms of co-optation involved.

In this vein, Marta Cruells and Gerard Coll-Planas show how intersectionality has been distorted in some EU equity initiatives, used as a "strategy for assigning less funding to equality policies" rather than transforming notions of equity and changing the processes for achieving it (Cruells and Coll-Planas 2013, 135). The logics here nearly mirror some forms of repackaging intersectionality in the contemporary (and increasingly corporatized) academy as a tool for maximized efficiency (not as a critical heuristic), such that in the name (though not the spirit) of intersectionality, it can be invoked as a rationale to downsize or eradicate ethnic studies, women's and gender studies, Black studies, and so on (Dill and Zambrana 2009, xiii).

For instance, in the United Kingdom and in Ireland, the government has closed some women's studies units, citing both the success and the failure of feminism as the rationale (Hemmings 2011, 10). Clare Hemmings' (2011) provocative analysis of the state's rhetorical maneuverings with regard to women's studies suggests intersectionality, too, could be narrowly interpreted as an efficiency technique, and lauded as such (its multiplicity a value-added factor for cash-strapped governments or institutions), but, then, eliminated, either for "failing" to be as efficient as it was supposed to be or for "succeeding" and thus claimed to be no longer needed after "consolidation" has been achieved.

Moreover, "efficiency" models for restructuring knowledge practices in the academy are often accompanied by the restructuring of economic and material realities in the wider society, frequently by co-opting the language and rhetorics of feminism while further policing and constraining women's lives. Toni Williams thus sounds a warning regarding intersectionality's increased popularity in academic and policy sectors, paralleling it to feminist theory's prior successes. She writes, "As feminist theory consolidated its place in universities and as references to women's equality started to appear in policy discourses and decision-making fora of national and international institutions, changes associated with neo-liberal economic restructuring began to make the conditions of life for most women harder and less secure" (Williams 2009, 79).

## The Need to Interpret Intersectionality *Intersectionally*

Clearly, intersectionality is at an interesting historical juncture. Its recognition and use have increased exponentially, in the academy and beyond: however, as it "travels,"[24] it is engaged with unevenly or in ways that blunt its multifaceted vision of justice. Rather than dismiss these issues as an unfortunate, inevitable "cost" of popularity, or as trifling examples of sloppy or inconsistent scholarship, we must take intersectionality's being regularly misrecognized *as meaningful*, as having something to teach us. In so doing, we can better identify some of the interpretive barriers or constraints that make such slippages and disciplinings possible and plausible. Since social justice origins cannot guarantee intersectionality will be used for radical, resistant, or liberatory ends, questions of its uncritical adoption or assimilation in academic or policy contexts, as a methodological lens, or as a political organizing tool, need careful consideration.

It is time to further explore the different ways in which intersectionality is being normed, depoliticized, regulated, or assimilated to the needs of the state or of supranational governance, for instance. Intersectionality may be corporatized, used rhetorically to invoke "good feeling" or manage institutional or national image, but not to address inequality (Ahmed 2007, 2008). In the academy and beyond, is it being invoked as a means to allow "business as usual" to go forward—ignoring its social justice origins and imperatives (Zambrana and Dill 2009, 275)? Both Sara Ahmed (2012) and Chandra Talpade Mohanty (2013) note intersectionality applications that "manage" diversity or assimilate difference to sameness, in ways antithetical to its impulses.

This, then, leads to another pivotal question: are all intersectionality applications equally (or at all) *intersectional*? Without becoming determinist, and without policing intersectionality, so to speak, it is still possible to consider whether there are some basic qualities or requisite factors for something to "count" as an adequate use of intersectionality. Though it can be tempting simply to celebrate intersectionality's wide deployment, more questions must be raised about how it is being used. In so doing, we must also remember that intersectionality *does* have a history, one that it is oriented toward eradicating inequality: it thus seeks to make normative claims. Merely descriptive, demographic, rhetorical, or otherwise nominal uses of intersectionality are not, in my book, adequately intersectional.

Since intersectionality has been developed as a means to intervene in and to resist oppressive mindsets, structures, and processes, it does more than draw on different logics, ones that are "matric" in nature: it is expressly interested in eradicating inequality. It has long had a "liberation framework" as part of its driving force (Jordan-Zachery 2007, 256), one that seeks to identify and eradicate inequalities, be they rhetorical, epistemological, ontological, and/or structural. Unfortunately, many descriptions or applications of intersectionality set aside this legacy. As if intersectional political aims and orientations were happenstance, it is often treated as a depoliticized "complexity" descriptor without much history and without normative commitments to eradicating injustice or exposing the workings of privilege.

Indeed, there has been quite a bit of debate about the cause of intersectionality's uneven application and about the root of such confusion about its meanings and aims. Unfortunately, many such discussions do not draw on intersectional analytics or insights to think through these questions and dynamics. Instead, its apparent shortcomings are sometimes intimated to be traceable to its origins in Black feminist theorizing (itself also homogenized, approached as static and unchanging, and suggested to be insufficiently generalizable for feminist praxis writ large [see Lewis 2009, 2013]). Bilge also discusses examples of "genealogical recalibration" (e.g., Lykke 2010) that add in a host of white feminist thinkers to the intersectionality canon, oddly displacing Black feminist work in intersectionality's name (Bilge 2013, 417). Whether via a critical "diagnosis" of intersectionality's limits or via more seemingly positive discussions about developing a "wider" and more inclusive scope or future (despite a 'narrower' past), such discursive moves can invite readers to take up a kind of raced paranoia (or eugenic diagnostics) and to disregard several key intersectionality premises at once.

First, the idea that intersectionality is constrained, or too narrow, due to its moorings in Black feminist theorizing, seems both to support and deploy the either/or logics of sameness versus difference that intersectionality challenges. In addition, rather than a principle with a fixed set of subjects or applications, intersectionality is flexible in its applicability *and* tied to its history in Black feminist theorizing.

Moreover, Black women are not intersectionality's only, or essentialist subjects (despite Nash's [2008a] critique). Rather, as Crenshaw, for instance, argues, Black women's (varied) experiences of refusal in the courts and erasure in social justice movements are illustrative of wider patterns: these particulars help pinpoint insidious structural dynamics and underlying logics that must be addressed (Crenshaw 1989). In addition to implying that intersectionality is held back (or overdetermined) by its origins in Black feminist theorizing, this line of critique implies that *other* forms or genealogies of feminist theorizing and research are not dragged down by any such 'particularity' or determinist, overbearing quality: it indirectly reinforces the "but-for" ways of thinking intersectionality seeks to dismantle.

Others suggest intersectionality's uneven applications and interpretations are due primarily to flaws in intersectionality theorizing itself, particularly the intersection metaphor, where cars meet or crash (referenced by Crenshaw 1989). Intersectionality has thus been critiqued as too rigid in its geospatial imaginings, as instituting notions of fixity on a grid (in terms of space/place), and as implicitly requiring separability both of vectors of power and of categories of identity (in terms of separate roads and cars).[25] Oddly, Crenshaw's other metaphors introduced across her writings are rarely discussed. For instance, even in "Demarginalizing," where the "intersection" metaphor appears, Crenshaw also uses the metaphor of a basement with a small (single-axis) trap-door opening.

It is rather surprising how rarely the trap-door/basement metaphor is discussed (given critics' seeming preoccupation with Crenshaw's metaphors), as it helps to emphasize the law's hand in maintaining structural stratification and to show how the logics of sameness play out, in that those who "but for" one aspect of their identity tend to represent (or be seen as representative of) a marginalized group, since they most closely approximate the "transparent" universal citizen-subject, a constraint that erases within-group differences, denies compound subjectivity, and renders impossible intersectional justice claims (Crenshaw 1989). Yet, this metaphor is generally ignored (for an unusual, extended discussion, see Carastathis 2013b).

Furthermore, few if any critics have noted that Crenshaw's spatial imaginary of the trapdoor can be read as alluding to a host of other spaces of containment—and resistance—in the African American intellectual tradition, such as Ralph Ellison's basement apartment in his 1952 novel, *Invisible Man* (Ellison 1995), which functions as an architectural manifestation both of existential invisibility and social containment. There is also Harriet Jacobs' attic, described in her 1861 *Incidents in the Life of a Slave Girl* (Jacobs 1987), wherein concealment takes on a resistant (and collective) form—it is a space of withdrawal from exploitation and physical coercion: it is also an open secret which the enslaved community keeps, helping Jacobs survive for years before she can escape. Crenshaw's basement and Jacobs' attic also call to mind Katherine McKittrick's discussion of "garrets": spaces for political organizing and resistance that are crafted, and hiding, within unreceptive institutions (McKittrick 2006; see also Isoke 2013).

In the case of the metaphor debates, beyond overattention to the intersection metaphor, as if it were intended or offered literally (e.g., scrutinizing its static geospatial imaginary without discussing the condoned asymmetrical violence implied by crashing vehicles and drivers who leave the scene, unharmed and unaccountable), and underattention to the metaphor of the basement trapdoor, Crenshaw's scholarship frequently is treated as if it were static and as if she had only ever written one or two essays twenty-five years ago. How many bother to read (and not just hastily reference) her larger and rather extensive body of work, attend to how she has shifted (and used various) metaphors over time, or consider how she has further explicated what it means to think of intersectionality as a heuristic, for example?

Certainly, devising adequate metaphors has importance, since they help convey a concept's meaning. My point is not to resolve these metaphor debates, per se: rather, this factor alone (adequate vs. inadequate metaphor) cannot sufficiently explain why many applications or interpretations of intersectionality fall short. While metaphors offer powerful snapshots of sociopolitical imaginaries and worlds, and thus must be thought through in terms of their possible sites of distortion or mismatch in terms of philosophical and political aims, they are not so powerful as to wholly cause a concept's cavalier use, co-optation, or distortion across disciplines, contexts, and scales. The metaphor of the intersection, for instance, cannot be both the origin of intersectionality's apparent shortcomings and the cause of its interpretive distortion.

Given my interest in discursive politics, I neither suggest metaphors are immaterial or unimportant nor dismiss out of hand dialogue about the implications of intersectionality's origins in Black feminisms and women of color theorizing more widely and what this might mean as intersectionality continues forward as a form of inquiry and "travels" across geopolitical and disciplinary boundaries. However, I concur with Carastathis, who argues that "detaching the concept of intersectionality from its context in the existential conditions of Black women and the theoretical concerns of Black feminist thought, and harnessing it to diametrically opposed representational purposes. . . . [is] ethically and intellectually indefensible" (Carastathis 2013b, 14; see also Bilge 2013).

Furthermore, attributing widespread interpretive distortion of intersectionality's key insights solely to its own shortcomings in isolation is too akin to a pathologizing diagnostic approach. Such models narrow the analytic scope to such a degree that wider contexts and practices fall from view and whereby a determinist (and internalist) explanation for any failings seems reasonable. Pathologizing diagnostics have also long been used in service to domination. Instead of relying primarily on a deficit model of analysis both to assess and interpret intersectionality, it is vital to widen the analytic gaze.

Intensive focus on the definitional has also served as a distraction from these broader patterns and dynamics that must be noted, and addressed, if we are committed to realizing intersectionality's vision and promise. To clarify, thinking through what constitutes an intersectional approach is useful (and not necessarily an easy or straightforward endeavor). However, in so doing, we should not overlook interpretive models that fragment or distort intersectionality to animate an argument or operationalize it as a practice. "Disciplinings" of intersectionality that assimilate it to hegemonic norms and let go of its alternative logics, or applications (in theoretical, policy, research, and political contexts) that aim to take up intersectionality, but are lacking in some significant ways, cannot just be brushed aside.

Intersectionality seems to risk misrecognition on nearly every front, whether co-opted by the state, corporatized in the neoliberal academy, or regulated by feminists committed to intersectionality but who inadvertently norm it to disciplinary logics, methodological conventions, or gender-primary theoretical premises. Intersectionality can be used in interrogative, creative, and visionary ways, not just as a descriptive or demographic factor, as is too often the case. Yet, too many portrayals of intersectionality in the wider literature are frankly facile: near caricatures of its central insights and careless readings of its founding literatures (if they are read or referenced at all) seem regularly to pass muster. It is time to examine how intersectionality's alternative logics and multifaceted vision of justice and personhood go unheard, are undertheorized, or are set aside.

In other words, these constitute *more than misreadings*: they violate basic intersectional insights and normative commitments. The epistemic violence involved (or animated) in intersectionality's deployment and/or interpretation cannot solely be attributed to intersectionality itself, in a kind of acontextual vacuum in which it is both the origin and cause of its own misapplication or distortion. Those of us who utilize and interpret intersectionality also have (and have had) an impact on its meanings, implications, and discursive and political life: we have both responsibility and power as communities of knowers.

Beyond identifying troubling patterns, then, it is equally imperative to think about what to do about them. As practitioners committed to social change and transformation, we must consider how intersectionality places *interpretive and political demands* on us: not just a mere commodity or tool, it is, in other words, an achieved imaginary (hooks 1990; Sandoval 2000), one that may need to be struggled for, worked through, and, also, continually reexamined. In short, there is a need to draw more fully on intersectional analytics and insights to better understand, interpret, and apply intersectionality. Rather than simply *integrate* intersectionality into "business as usual," whether in policy, research, theoretical, or political contexts, conventional logics and practices need to be actively set aside. Simultaneously, engaging in a kind of focused orientation toward intersectionality is also needed. Otherwise, we risk norming intersectionality to hegemonic practices, making it deferential to dominance.

## Notes

1. These dynamics are taken up in Chapters 3 and 4.
2. See Bowleg (2008), Choo and Ferree (2010), Hancock (2007a, 2007b), Harnois (2013), Shields (2008).
3. See Alcoff (2012), Dotson (2011a, 2011b), Fricker (2007), Ortega (2006), Wylie (2011). The politics of cognitive authority are discussed in more detail in Chapter 5.
4. See Crenshaw (2011c, 228).
5. See May (2004, 2007, 2008a, 2008b, 2009, 2012a, 2012b).
6. See Gines (2011, 2014), Guy-Sheftall (1995, 2009), May (2008a, 2012a), Moody-Turner (2013).
7. I do not suggest Cooper emerged from nowhere, *in vacuo*: many of her nineteenth-century peers advocated more complex ways of thinking about personhood, rights, and justice (including Maria Stewart, Hallie Quinn Brown, Sarah Parker Remond, Harriet Jacobs, Frederick Douglass, Sara Early, Sojourner Truth, Ida B. Wells, W.E.B. DuBois, Victoria Earle Matthews, and many others). See Carby (1985, 1987), Foster (1993), Giddings (1984, 2008), Gines (2011, 2014), Guy-Sheftall (1990, 1995), Jones (2007), Logan (1999), May (2007, 2012a), Peterson (1995), Waters (2014), Waters and Conway (2007).
8. In her 1925 Sorbonne dissertation, Cooper continued to focus on simultaneous privilege and oppression. Therein, she pinpoints how internalized dominance and a colonized consciousness on the part of *gens de couleur* (people of color) in St. Domingue at first undermined what would become a fruitful coalition between the slaves and the gens de couleur to overthrow the French state in the Haitian revolution. To fight alongside the enslaved, rather than align with white colonists and property owners, gens de couleur had to let go of their property, including slaves, but also their attachments to a hierarchy of personhood (see Cooper [trans. Keller] 2006; see also May 2007, 2008b).
9. I discuss the contours and implications of this rhetorical inequality more fully in Chapter 5.
10. Critiques of intersectionality as "mere repetition" are more thoroughly addressed in Chapter 3.
11. See Gordon-Chipembere (2011), Guy-Sheftall (2002), Hobson (2013), Nash (2008b).
12. There are echoes of the Moynihan Report's pathologizing "matriarchy thesis" (see Crenshaw 1989) here and in the "Baby Mama" stereotype.
13. It should be noted that species-ism, a form of "'dehumanization' [that] depends on a prior oppression of nonhuman animals" (Taylor 2012, 214), is also implicitly at work here, as part of the hierarchical logics that pivot on the distinction between humans and animals. As Chloë Taylor explains, species-ism "entails and depends on the view that humans are more developed than nonhuman animals, just as some humans are more developed than others. If you can show a human being to be closer than average on this developmental scale to nonhuman animals, then it becomes more permissible to mutilate, kill, involuntarily sterilize, incarcerate, or enslave that person, just as we do to animals of other species all the time" (Taylor 2012, 215).

14. Fluke was asked to testify before Congress in favor of federal funding for birth control and for women's right to engage in sexual activity outside the parameters of reproduction, marriage, and state moralizing or monitoring (she was denied the right to testify by House Republicans but did speak to House Democrats).
15. The idea of Fluke as akin to a prostitute is presented in the image by President Obama who explains, in a dialogue bubble, that she wanted to get "paid for having sex": this obscures the actual source of this defamation (right-wing radio personality Rush Limbaugh).
16. What also tends to get lost in examining race and gender politics in recent U.S. elections is the fact that, in 2008, two women of color ran for president and vice president on the Green Party platform: Cynthia McKinney and Rosa Clemente. Though their running is historic, and though their partnership bridged traditional (McKinney) and alternative (Clemente) sites of the political (electoral politics and hip-hop protest), they remain invisible in most discussions. As Zenzele Isoke argues with regard to the 2008 election, "When black women were mentioned, the debate settled on whether 'race' would trump 'gender' in their vote choice. The impoverished quality of these debates rested upon ignoring or, rather, *denying* the existence of two extraordinary political women who have consistently spoke out against the combined effects of race, gender, class, and national oppression in US politics" (Isoke 2013, 146).
17. See Lugones (2007, 2010), McClintock (1995), Morgan (2004), Murphy and Spear (2011), Smith (2010).
18. See Wells-Barnett (2014) for "Southern Horrors" (1892), "A Red Record" (1895), and "Mob Rule in New Orleans" (1900).
19. Malveaux draws on a 2010 study by the Insight Center for Community Economic Development, www.insightcced.org/uploads/CRWG/LiftingAsWeClimb-WomenWealth-Report-InsightCenter-Spring2010.pdf.
20. See also United for a Fair Economy (www.faireconomy.org/) for more data on wealth and income disparities and how they have been deeply racialized, historically and presently.
21. See Hunt and Rygiel (2008), Puar (2007), Puar and Rai (2002), Riley, Mohanty, and Pratt (2008).
22. See also Kóczé (2009), who advocates a grassroots intersectional activist orientation with regard to Romani women's rights.
23. Williams' analysis of how state uses of intersectionality can serve as a new mechanism to enforce long-standing settler-colonial logics and inequities is taken up more fully in Chapter 4.
24. For more discussion of the notion (and implications) of intersectionality as a "traveling" concept, see Lutz, Hererra Vivar, and Supik (2011). For a critique of how intersectionality is (and is not) discussed in many of the writings included in Lutz et al., see Bilge (2013), Crenshaw (2011c), and Lewis (2009, 2013).
25. See Chang and Culp (2002), Carastathis (2008), Conaghan (2009), Cooper (2009), Garry (2011), Grabham (2009), Grabham et al. (2009), Grosz (2010), Yuval-Davis (2006).

# 3
# Why Are Intersectionality Critiques All the Rage?

Intersectionality critiques have become something of their own genre—a form so flourishing, at times it seems critique has become a primary means of taking up the concept and its literatures. Certainly, in the academy, as in political and public spheres, engaging an idea via debate and argumentation is not unusual.[1] In fact, one way a theoretical or political framework evolves is to have its premises questioned and puzzled over:[2] critiques *can* signal heightened regard for a concept and be a key means by which an idea endures. At face value, then, the mushrooming intersectionality critique industry may be nothing to worry about.

Yet, there is something about the sheer number of critiques as well as their nature that deserves consideration: *how* intersectionality is read and portrayed (and not) can be troubling, particularly when basic intersectional premises (about 'both/and' thinking, relational power and privilege, ontological multiplicity, and intermeshed oppressions, for instance) are violated by a critic's operative assumptions and interpretive methods. What might this mean—that a critic's approach, or terms of assessment, may animate the very logics (and approaches to self, reason, and inequality) intersectionality contests?

I am not alone in my concerns. Devon Carbado has mapped out several common intersectionality critiques that circumscribe its longer history, inclusive scope, and wider possibilities.[3] In reviewing the turn from intersectionality to multidimensionality theory, in critical race legal scholarship, Sumi Cho questions reductive portraits of intersectionality's "categorical hegemony" with regard to race and sex as a means to critique its limits and to present multidimensionality theory as avoiding intersectionality's ostensible errors (e.g., upholding single-axis logics of identity or the dominance of race [meaning Blackness] and sex [meaning women] as analytic/identity frames, to the exclusion of others, such as sexuality) (Cho 2013).[4] Gail Lewis (2013), Sirma Bilge (2013), and Barbara Tomlinson (2013a, 2013b) question another form of presenting intersectionality reductively: the "whitening" of intersectionality, particularly (though not exclusively) in European debates. The patterns they identify echo the philosophical border-patrol tactics Cynthia Saavedra and Ellen Nymark also critique, in discussing the epistemological policing of feminist theory's parameters more widely, wherein "hegemonic feminist scholars act like the *migra* of feminist praxis, building *parades* to keep the *ilegales* and illegitimate out" (Saavedra and Nymark 2008, 261).

In short, interpretive frames exert a normative force, epistemologically and politically. In examining U.K. equality policies, Irene Gedalof demonstrates that "how an issue is framed, how social life and subjects are figured in such documents, establishes limits on what counts as meaningful" (Gedalof 2012, 2). Likewise, I contend that how intersectionality is critiqued, and how its ideas about power, subjectivity, knowledge, and oppression are interpretively represented, also "establishes limits on what counts as meaningful." Furthermore, since feminist and anti-racist scholars have long challenged research norms (and philosophical ideals) wherein the contexts of discovery are considered analytically irrelevant or even sites of bias (also known as the "fact/value" distinction),[5] the contexts in which we do our work should be considered germane for crafting feminist analysis and for assessing feminist interpretation itself. In other words, intersectionality researchers have repeatedly asserted that context is relevant to knowing (including contexts of structural inequality, affective economies, ideological forces, history, social location, material structures, philosophical norms, and more): these same contexts are, in turn, relevant to assessing how intersectionality is (and is not) being read or debated.

Karla Holloway has persuasively shown that "inquiry is not empty of social histories" and institutionalized knowledge practices have "regulatory heft" (Holloway 2011, xv). Since (feminist) critical knowledge practices are not immune from functioning as forms of "socializing pedagogies" (Wiegman 2010, 83), and because interpretation is a crucial epistemic (and political) practice, we must consider whether (and how) intersectionality critiques may invite us to take up assumptions or reinforce premises that are profoundly anti-intersectional. Though intersectionality, as a theoretical and political concept, has been crafted, in part, to render visible and address systemic epistemic distortion and social injustice, it also faces ongoing forms of epistemic misrecognition.

To clarify, I am not suggesting intersectionality is beyond debate. Rather, the terms of critique, the forms of rhetorical containment used, the politics of plausibility in play, and the wider implications of discursive practices all "matter"[6] (i.e., they are both philosophically significant and have material consequences). As Gail Lewis persuasively argues, *how* intersectionality circulates as a concept and a practice holds weight: since "inequalities of opportunity and recognition tied to structures of race, class, and gender remain, questions of provenance also remain central to the politics of knowledge production" (Lewis 2013, 872).

In light of the politics of intersectionality's circulation and interpretation, we need to ask more questions, including: What are the diagnostic strategies commonly used, and the kinds of conclusions reached about intersectionality, that then pass as consensus beliefs or are cited as accurate assessments? What solutions are offered to improve (or go beyond) intersectionality? When examining rhetorical tactics, affective states, and analytical politics, it is also important to ask why certain critiques seem more readily plausible, persuasive, and ideologically intelligible: is it because they rely on (or return to) logics that are familiar, even if these same logics are, from an intersectional viewpoint, part of the problem at hand?

## Remedial Approaches to Reading Intersectionality

Pinpointing flaws in an idea's conceptualization then offering alternatives is common academic practice and not unique to intersectionality debates. Nonetheless, a critical race-disability studies lens would contest the ready acceptance of interpretive norms that pivot on wider cultural "fantasies" of measurement and assessment (Samuels 2014) and that aim, analytically, to identify deficits or pathologies so as to "cure" them.[7] Furthermore, many intersectionality critiques also rely upon, and invite readers to take up, forms of white solipsism (Rich 1979) to understand and to apply intersectionality in more "comprehensive" ways.[8] Many critiques can thus feel remedial in nature, even quasi-Eugenic (particularly when the means offered to improve intersectionality deracialize its history and constrain its political reach to render it more robust and universally applicable).

In this vein, Tomlinson examines European critiques of intersectionality (in particular, portrayals of its U.S. women of color origins and writings) and highlights several analytic strategies that mirror the logics and rhetorics of colonial racism in the name of furthering and strengthening intersectionality, which is seen to lack rigor. She notes how critics "deploy rhetorics of racial hierarchy that depict a gulf between what they present as their own perspicacious thinking and the collectivized and caricatured thinking that they attribute to intersectionality's originating black feminist scholars in the U.S." Moreover, she contends, "these rhetorics map closely to structures of thinking described by Albert Memmi in his analysis of colonial racism" (Tomlinson 2013a, 255).

The repositioning of intersectionality as a problem to surmount can be quite subtle. Stephanie Shields discusses, for instance, how disciplinary norms can quietly aid in this reframing: in social science research, "intersectionality frequently becomes redefined as a methodological challenge. . . . Psychological scientists have typically responded to the question of intersectionality in one of three ways: excluding the question; deferring the question; limiting the question" (Shields 2008, 304). These insights about how researchers evade intersectionality by treating it as a problem parallel Audre Lorde's incisive observations about how differences generally are approached. Lorde explains, "We have *all* been programmed to respond to the human differences between us with fear and loathing and to handle that difference in one of three ways: ignore it, and if that is not possible, copy it if we think it is dominant, or destroy it if we think it is subordinate" (Lorde 1984, 115). Likewise, Alarcón discusses how "difference" is dealt with, at the level of the feminist subject: it tends to be appropriated, negated, or subsumed via a common-denominator logic (Alarcón 1990, 358).

Whether implicit or overt, many such containment practices (philosophical and physical) stem from a longer history of minoritized groups being characterized as problems, often via an individualizing gaze that turns attention away from systems of oppression and the institutionalized social structures and cognitive norms that rationalize and maintain them. Early in the twentieth century, both W.E.B. Du Bois (2007, 7–32) and Anna Julia Cooper (1988, 299–300; 1998a) discussed the implications of being perceived as an ontological and political problem: they delineated how the "Negro Problem," for instance, was an ideological distortion invented to distract from the maintenance of brute supremacy and demonstrable, systematic white privilege. Furthermore, argued Cooper, the real problems at hand (including white arrogance, mob terror, and supremacist mindsets) are rendered invisible by a pathologizing gaze: remedial diagnostics and (white) racial panics distract from and obscure the actual distortions and violations at work (Cooper 1998a). More recently, Eli Clare has described how "dominant paradigms of disability—the medical, charity, supercrip, and moral models—all turn disability into problems faced by individual people, locate those problems in our bodies, and define those bodies as wrong" (Clare 2001, 359–360). Via individualizing logics, the problem of the "problem body" can seem to be solved not by political and structural transformation, but by means of individual cure/intervention or by (medicalized) eradication strategies like eugenics targeted at specific "problem" bodies or groups.

Turning a critical lens back onto the anxieties and underlying assumptions that surface in many intersectionality critiques, and pointing to a range of control mechanisms frequently used to curb intersectionality's reach and potential, Crenshaw notes that "intersectionality has engendered some of the same disciplining moves *among* feminists that have also been deployed *against* feminism" (Crenshaw 2011c, 223, italics added). In fact, many of the discursive tactics questioned by Bilge (2013), Carbado (2013), Cho (2013), Crenshaw (2011c), May (2014a), and Tomlinson (2013a, 2013b) evoke the hyper-surveillance and micro-aggressions faced by women of color in the culture at large but also in the academy.

Heidi Mirza describes how women of color regularly find they are viewed "suspiciously" for being in the academy, with any "mistakes made along the way" (even minor ones) zeroed in on and paraded about as evidence of one's "misplaced authority" or inauthenticity as a knower (Mirza 2006, 106). Certainly, Mirza is discussing how Black women in the academy are read, observed, and discounted—but it can be instructive to trace parallels between how particular bodies (here, Black women) are engaged with and how bodies of thought associated with those bodies (i.e., intersectionality) are treated. For example, intersectionality texts, particularly writings/practices developed in the context of Black feminist politics and theorizing, are often read hastily if not inaccurately (e.g., merely as a demographic diversity mandate or a naïve identity model), then critiqued for conceptual provinciality or political narrowness, as if in a "straw (wo)man" argument. This, too, could be considered a form of discursive surveillance or scrutiny: the ongoing misrecognition of intersectionality as an idea is not unlike the institutionalized micro-aggressions and systematic dismissals faced by women of color in the academy and in society at large.

In addition, it cannot be considered irrelevant when critics fall back on norms of theoretical, political, or methodological adequacy that have been identified by intersectionality scholars as flawed but also as profoundly tied to dominance and traceable to violent ways of thinking about, and treating, disenfranchised populations and groups. For example, as I shall discuss more fully, many worry intersectionality undermines feminism's philosophical and political coherence by splintering gender. To resolve this alleged fragmentation (or proliferation of genders), some call for a renaissance of gender-first or gender-universal approaches (e.g., Gunnarsson 2011), while others see social class as primary (Conaghan 2009; Giminez 2001; Valentine 2007) and push for a (return to a) materialist, class-first political and analytical model. Both lines of critique (and types of remedies) seem to downplay, if not ignore, that intersectionality scholars have repeatedly shown the deep violence of (false) coherence[9] and downplay how single-axis approaches, in fact, require fragmentation to function.

That intersectionality is debated, or its premises, aims, and implications contested, is not the issue: it is the means and mechanisms of scrutiny, the terms of reading and characterizing intersectionality, that need to be examined more fully. What does it mean, for instance, when critics render intersectionality as the fixed ground against which more viable ideas or practices are mobilized—a figure/ground rhetorical move that is often also accompanied by relatively superficial portraits of intersectionality (or of particular essays or well-known theorists), rather than close readings? As I shall discuss, co-opting intersectional ideas, then (re)introducing them as new and improved concepts, is another common analytical maneuver: critics frequently draw on views crafted largely in the contexts of intersectionality but without attribution. The allegedly missing insights are often ones elucidated time and again by intersectionality scholars: however, their voices, contributions, and texts are rendered invisible.

This leads to some rather odd assertions. Apparently, for example, intersectionality could be improved upon, or advanced, by taking into consideration its very own insights (e.g., a "both/and" approach to understanding and addressing oppression that is both structural and individual, macropolitical and micropolitical, in scope).[10] Since the "new" insights often are not connected to intersectionality's history or meaningfully tied to its literatures, the circular reasoning, and the extraction and violation of the (past and ongoing) intellectual labors of women of color, tend to be occluded. The improved concepts are thus often presented in contrast to (or as the answers to fixing) an unsophisticated version of intersectionality. Gloria Anzaldúa has suggested that such interpretive practices signal a "collector's mentality" (Anzaldúa 1990a, xxi) of expropriation, a mindset attached to (and framed by) legacies of settler colonial rule.

Mobilizing affect, even indirectly or subtly, is another common means of rhetorical persuasion, and intersectionality critiques are no exception. As Clare Hemmings underscores, affect tends to be drawn on in ways that invite readers to go along with an interpretive account. Rhetorical glosses, as a "textual mechanism" (Hemmings 2011, 17), have affective effects that help to generate agreement between the author and reader of an argument. Hemmings explains, "glosses appeal to the common sense of their reader without detailed discussion. . . . through the mobilization of affect" (20). These affective strategies tend to position the knower(s) wielding them (and the readers invited to follow the critique) as rational and knowledgeable. Furthermore, I would argue, emotions and ideas that feel "common sense" often align with hegemonic norms and assumptions.

As shall become clear in discussions of different intersectionality critiques throughout this chapter, at least three forms of affect are commonly invoked. One is pity or condescension (as in, *Isn't it a shame intersectionality is so naïve and narrow when it could have paid attention to structural inequality and more 'universal' groups/issues?*).[11] Another is fear or horror (as in, *Beware! Intersectionality causes social/political/ philosophical ruination via fragmentation*).[12] Finally, there is the affect of mature reason and responsibility, in contrast to intersectionality's rendering of the social world, which is seen as underdeveloped, hazy, or too romantic (as in, *Intersectionality needs to mature and become more rigorous and systematized*).[13] These affective states, in turn, align with roles ubiquitously ascribed to intersectionality—roles that are quite telling in terms of expectations and underlying assumptions.

For example, intersectionality is sometimes painted as a villainous destroyer of a once-coherent (and ostensibly more viable) feminist project (e.g., Gunnarsson 2011; Zack 2005). However, if intersectionality, as a praxis rooted in large part in Black feminist intellectual genealogies, political histories, and justice orientations, is portrayed (even implicitly) as akin to an angry, disruptive "Sapphire" figure, ruining feminist philosophical and policy worlds, this characterization cannot be meaningless. Intersectionality is also often suggested to be unimaginative, short on epistemic competence, and theoretically unsophisticated (even if its experiential value or descriptive capacity may be acknowledged as important) (see Bilge 2013). For instance, Gines (2011) critiques Gunnarsson (2011) for characterizing (women of color) intersectionality theory as "rhetorical," as opposed to more nuanced feminist analyses described by Gunnarsson as "theoretical."

Underlying assumptions that intersectionality is simplistic also emerge in the seemingly opposite critique: that it is harder to take up than anticipated.[14] Why is it surprising that intersectionality requires a substantial cognitive shift, some "world-travelling" (Lugones 1987), and achieved craft or skill (Sandoval 2000)? Does such incredulity suggest intersectional analytics are presumed unsophisticated from the start? As Crenshaw recently argued, "That it is easier to call for intersectional analysis rather than to perform it is not a failing of the concept but a recognition that performing intersectional analysis is neither a simplistic symbolic signifier nor is it a paint-by-numbers analytic enterprise" (Crenshaw 2011c, 231).

In sum, schematically, intersectionality turns up regularly in the critical literatures as akin to: a destructive, unruly Sapphire figure (who needs to be tamed/taken down); a theoretically unsophisticated concept (while, at the same time, often lauded as experience's poster child); a dated idea in need of a makeover; or a deficient body of thought in need of a remedial/eugenic cure. These clichés have long distorted the bodies, and bodies of thought, of women of color: they are neither random nor innocuous. Such roles and interpretive frames impact the discursive field, shape interpretive possibilities, and have bearing on cognitive authority (Narayan 1997). Moreover, these narrative arcs, while tired, should not necessarily surprise, if one recalls that ignorance about, and dismissal of, Black women's ideas and creativity is deeply connected to being viewed and characterized as "a discredited people" (Christian 1990, 338).

Again, I do not object to differing philosophies of identity, varying analyses of oppression, or conflicting ideas about how best to go about transforming inequitable social practices and structures: in fact, in line with Anna Julia Cooper's early philosophy of the generative nature of differences (Cooper 1988, 285–303), debate and divergence are important and potentially fruitful. However, forms of epistemic violation or backlash at work in intersectionality debates should be noted and challenged: how feminist critics deploy "technologies of power" in discursive contexts matters (Tomlinson 2013b, 994). Given the widespread nature of intersectionality's discursive containment, it also seems a bit overstated to characterize it as enjoying "*theoretical monarchy*" (Nash 2011, 448, italics added), suggesting dominion and ascendancy. Its cavalier treatment in the critical literatures suggests, instead, that its power and authority are fairly "checked."

In far too many readings, intersectional ideas (e.g., about the problems inherent in hierarchy of oppressions thinking) cannot really be taken up because hierarchical approaches to identity and structural oppression prevail as interpretive norms and political measures. Rather than engage intersectional thinking and its counterlogics, critics often impose dominant logics onto the concept, such as gender-primary lenses, "pop-bead metaphysics," or either/or thinking. What does it mean if intersectionality is rendered *illegible* by a critic's reliance on (and readers' implicit recruitment into) "interpretive templates" (Crenshaw 2011c, 228) that contravene its basic premises? What does it mean if, by the terms of critique offered, we are invited to take up affective states and follow storylines or plots that essentially rely on racist–sexist stereotypes?

## Intersectionality Is Just Black Feminism "Recycled"

This line of critique has a tendency to characterize intersectionality as a tired if not static body of thought that offers nothing "new." Some critics affirm intersectionality, at one time, offered innovation, but find it now mostly rehashes "old" Black feminist ideas and has run its course (Conaghan 2009). Nash, for instance, claims: "intersectionality recycles black feminism without demonstrating what new tools it brings to black feminism to help it fashion a more complex theory of identity" (Nash 2008a, 9). Some suggest intersectionality lacked innovation from the start. Early intersectionality theorists (usually meaning from the late 1980s/early 1990s—the decades of work prior to this era are rarely discussed) are cast as simply having reiterated or mimicked existing concepts already developed by women of color feminists in the 1970s, such as Frances Beale's "double jeopardy" (Beale 1970) or

*Triple Jeopardy* (the name of the Third World Women's Alliance newsletter addressing sexism, imperialism, and racism simultaneously),[15] but without advancing these ideas further, politically or intellectually (e.g., Aguilar 2012). Essentially, intersectionality is presented as derivative and as gutted of (or as never really having had) radical political potential.

Others acknowledge intersectionality's contributions as having been important, in their (bygone) era, but suggest the time has come for a new term to more adequately capture what intersectionality may have aimed to encompass, but failed, ultimately, to accomplish (either due to *internal flaws* [e.g., its ostensible fixation on separate strands of identity, inattention to structure, or failure to attend adequately to flows or interwovenness] and/or *external constraints* [e.g., it has been distorted/misused to such a degree the term has become meaningless and needs replacing]). One can find a long list of suggested alternatives, including: *configurations* (Bhavnani and Bywater 2009),[16] *assemblages* (Puar 2007),[17] *cosynthesis* (Kwan 1997),[18] *symbiosis* (Ehrenreich 2002),[19] *interdependency* (to emphasize interrelatedness rather than separability) (Walgenbach 2007), *social dynamics* (Cooper 2004, 2009),[20] *interactions* (Dhamoon 2011),[21] *multidimensionality* (Hutchinson 2000; Mutua 2006, 2013), or *interconnectivity* (to account for "situational commonalities") (Valdes 1995), to name a few.[22]

However, like Carbado (2013), Cho (2013), and Yuval-Davis (2012), I remain in favor of retaining the term "intersectionality," not for sentimental purposes or adulatory motivations, but for political, historical, and epistemological reasons. First, too often, in narrating feminist histories and in thinking about feminist futures, linear notions of time and progress are relied on, such that "black and lesbian feminist engagements become firmly identified with the past, become anachronistic, as do their presumed subjects" (Hemmings 2011, 6). Second, "thresholds of disappearance" can operate as a silencing tactic, even in practices intended to be inclusive. As Coogan-Gehr explains, "A threshold of disappearance is not the same as disappearance *tout court*. In the case of a threshold of disappearance, one conceptual framework is subsumed under another emerging conceptual framework, which provides new explanatory concepts, ideas, and theories to account for related phenomena. Complex relationships among concepts, ideas, and theories central to the disappearing framework come to be understood in the language of the new framework" (Coogan-Gehr 2011, 90).

Offering new or substitute metaphors can be taken to signal that intersectionality is tragically out of date or politically defunct, even as countless other approaches or concepts would not be (and have not been) cast aside in this same way. One insinuation, then, is that intersectionality itself (and the legacy/history it names and derives from) is *disposable*. Dropping the term 'intersectionality' can thus play into a wider politics of dismissal and reinforce forms of presentism or futurism that (mis)treat earlier scholars of intersectionality (predominantly women of color) as just old hat or unsophisticated. Even when scholars are (rightly) frustrated with constant misreadings and misuses of intersectionality (e.g., Puar et al 2008), I would argue that abandoning the term can, in effect, leave such distortions alone and even allow them to flourish.

Moreover, too many critics dispense with intersectionality by employing a figure/ground strategy,[23] meaning an "over-and-against stand" (Cho 2013, 395), a "rhetoric of rejection and replacement" (Tomlinson 2013b, 1001) that tends to portray intersectionality as stagnant or stuck (in the past or in clunky frameworks) as a means to introduce and animate an alternative metaphor or lens.[24] As Carbado notes, "wittingly or not, proponents of the [new] frameworks artificially circumscribe the theoretical reach of intersectionality as a predicate to staging their own intervention" (Carbado 2013, 816). Many critics inadequately address the broader politics of supplanting or going "beyond" the term, a move that can easily be taken up in the wider discourse as a rationale for extraction or amelioration that is deeply racialized and tied to the logics of both of development and dominion.

"Intersectionality is recycled/passé" critiques can thus be used to justify expropriating the intellectual labors of women of color, as if their ideas were "raw materials" to be further developed (or refined) and made amenable to/usable for more 'universal' purposes (and commoditized for wider markets). Tomlinson, for example, finds that

> many European social scientists and philosophers . . . appear to find valuable a 'purified' intersectionality, quarantined from its exposure to race. Establishing the Black feminist scholars who originated intersectionality as 'unworthy,' parochial, 'race-bound,' incapable of 'theorizing,' justifies extracting from them the valuable tool of intersectionality. Such justification also reinforces the self-conceptions of racial Europeanization and its construction of its own innocence with regard to its colonial histories and contemporary racisms. (Tomlinson 2013a, 266; see also Bilge 2013)

Replacing or superseding an 'outmoded' intersectionality can also inadvertently solidify notions of linear time tied to legacies of conquest (Allen 1986), enforce "chrono-normativity" (Freeman 2010), and invoke progress narratives that deny temporal (and ontological and epistemological) co-evalness. This, in turn, occludes an enduring "coloniality of being" as well as an equally persistent resistance to coloniality (Lugones 2010). Furthermore, what many critics implicitly drop, when supplanting the term intersectionality, is an insistence that its meanings (and histories) be read more adequately, including its vision of collective justice and social change. Too frequently, this contestatory impetus is ignored in critiques of intersectionality as "passé."

However, "to re-retrieve forgotten, unarchived meanings is an act of memorial consciousness" (Gillman 2007, 107). Resignifying the meanings of existing categories, offering counterhistories and counternarratives, confronting omissions, and addressing enforced silences and gaps are all pivotal to intersectionality's interrogative impulses (Dill and Zambrana 2009; Hancock 2007b; Jordan-Zachery 2007), though this seems quickly forgotten when it comes to charging intersectionality with repetitiveness. In the face of ongoing resistance to intersectional ideas and politics, repetition of key/basic concepts might well signal the *re-retrieval* Gillman highlights.

Sometimes, it seems, we have so busied ourselves offering "cures" for what ails intersectionality, or devising new terminology so as to better interrupt hegemony's workings via linguistic perfection, that a key question remains largely unasked and unanswered: "*why this recurrence*?" Rather than use intersectionality's repetition as a rationale for its dismissal or replacement, we need to ask, "What larger dynamics are at work such that intersectional analyses bear repeating, time and again?" The answer simply cannot be that intersectionality theorists have had no innovative ideas as of late or are so devoted to unwieldy categories (e.g., monolithic Black womanhood) as to have forgotten about simultaneous privilege and oppression and within-group differences (and, thus, forsaken their own basic ideas and assertions). Exploring the question "why repetition?" requires examining wider contexts, including unyielding philosophical norms and ongoing social inequality.

Too few critics seem interested in thinking about the costs imposed, largely on women of color, to have to repeat the same analyses, time and again, though Anne DuCille already named some of the history of this labor and asserted, twenty years ago, "this is not a new dilemma" (DuCille 1994, 597). In assuming nothing analytical, innovative or resistant lies in repetition, many seem also to have forgotten Audre Lorde's keen observation about how intransigent forms of power drain our energies and distract us from moving ahead, collectively. She remarked, "We find ourselves having to repeat and relearn the same old lessons over and over." Lorde then asked, pointedly, "how many times has this all been said before?" (Lorde 1984, 117). From the angles of vision offered by DuCille and Lorde, restating intersectionality "basics" could be read to signal indignation at being continually misunderstood, not intellectual stagnation. Repetition could well indicate the degree to which the logics of "purity" (Lugones 1994), "single-axis" thinking (Crenshaw 1989), and "monolithic" reason (Christian 1990) prevail—that is, sets of assumptions and worldviews that render intersectionality unrecognizable, unhearable, and illogical.

Examining repetition *intersectionally* requires shifting critical energies toward analyzing wider material conditions and epistemic structures, asking questions (e.g., "why might something need repeating, time and again?"), and looking to larger social contexts for answers. By acknowledging the constancy of structural inequality, the "changing same" (McDowell 1987) of dominance can emerge as analytically relevant. In turn, intersectionality's repetition can be interpreted as having a different impetus and origin (i.e., other than intellectual cloddishness or political stagnation). An intersectional approach to asking, and answering, "why repetition?" requires recognizing how one state of obduracy can necessitate that another, equally persistent worldview be continually rearticulated. Repetition needs to be approached as having potential meaningfulness (i.e., being open to the possibility that these dynamics represent more than mechanical reiteration). Rather than signal intellectual/political inertia or stuck-ness, repetition could symbolize rearticulation as a form of steadfast defiance, a way to confront being persistently refused, silenced, and ignored.

As a form of interstitial thinking aimed at social critique and transformation, it seems logical for intersectionality to have been (and have to have been) re-uttered, rearticulated, and repeated. It is this history of intersectionality as a means of political intervention and interpretive resistance (and the accompanying persistence of hegemonic mindsets that repeatedly render it illegible/illogical) which the name helps keep visible, as an epistemological *and* political problem to be addressed (not dropped or put aside). I am in favor of retaining "intersectionality" as a term in part to insist that we recall, and tap into, this genealogy: furthermore, perhaps insipid, apolitical, one-dimensional, anodyne, and even coercive uses of intersectionality should be called out (or called something else).

### Intersectionality's Approach to Identity and Power Lacks Nuance

As Gail Lewis (2013) discusses, intersectionality is often imputed to be short on theoretical sophistication and political robustness due to its apparent over-attention to identity in ways that are rigid, lack depth and nuance, and are not fine-tuned (e.g., Staunaes 2003). By extension, it is also seen to engage in equally simplistic views of power and inequality (e.g., Prins 2006). Practitioners and critics of intersectionality alike often "intimate a certain parochialism in its origins that compromises its theoretical comprehensiveness" (Crenshaw 2011c, 224). As Collins (2014), Hancock (2007a, 2007b), and Jordan-Zachery (2007) argue, critics also erroneously present intersectional approaches as removed from sustained antisubordination efforts, some even going so far as to equate intersectionality with an apolitical, positivist approach. Gunnarsson, for example, asserts we must distance ourselves from intersectionality's unsophisticated ideas about identity, particularly its "empiricist fixation with physical appearances and directly accessible entities" (Gunnarsson 2011, 27). In addition to ascribing a naïve understanding of identity onto intersectionality, she suggests it unquestioningly assents to and actively relies on "technologies of surveillance" used by the state to pathologize and contain Black women's bodies (Collins 2008, 75).

Such claims abound and often persuade by glossing the intersectionality literatures. One would hardly know that intersectionality illuminates how inequalities play out "institutionally, intersubjectively, representationally as well as in the subjective constructions of identities" (Yuval-Davis 2006, 205). Likewise, such glosses tend to ignore how doing intersectional research requires asking "what role inequality plays": this question, in turn, "draws attention to the ways that multiple category memberships position individuals and groups in asymmetrical relation to one another, affecting their perceptions, experiences, and outcomes. This question helps psychologists to view constructs such as race and gender as structural categories and social processes rather than primarily as characteristics of individuals" (Cole 2009, 173). In other words, although an intersectional approach to identity can be taken up with a phenomenological and hermeneutic orientation (e.g., Alcoff 2006b), and understood as a way to think about identities as ideologically powerful, experientially salient (but not essentialist), and as fluid (Dhamoon 2011), it is more frequently read as a "static list of structural locations" (Ferree 2009, 87) that reinforces simplistic notions of atomized, additive identities and that either ignores structural/institutional power altogether or relies on an elementary understanding of power.[25]

Furthermore, to solve intersectionality's supposedly reductive either/or modeling, and imbalanced analysis, some call for intersectionality to attend *both* to contexts of lived experience *and* to structural constraints and power relations, rather than one (identity) or the other (structure) (Arya 2009; Hunter and de Simone 2009; Smooth 2013), as, it is implied, intersectionality has (foolishly) advocated (at least in its less nuanced, past iterations—i.e., when first elaborated by women of color feminists and critical race scholars). Reading these critiques, one would hardly know that the earliest intersectionality writings called for lived experience to be examined in the context of structural oppression and vice versa (as part of intersectionality's "both/and" multilevel political and analytical approach). Instead, intersectionality frequently is portrayed as accepting (and promoting) an "alleged elementary conceptualization of power that leads to a framing of problems at an individual or identity level" (Cho 2013, 393). Its same/different thesis (to bridge the particular and the universal) is also read as a call for particularism (Rahman 2009). Furthermore, Cho remarks, "What is perplexing about this . . . claim is that intersectionality was explicitly about systems and structures" (Cho 2013, 393). A more thorough reading of intersectionality literatures would reveal that a both/and approach to (multiple) identities contextualized within myriad social structures and attendant to the relational nature of power and privilege within and between groups is (and has long been) fundamental to intersectionality.

In addition to overlooking much of intersectionality's genealogy and literatures, to render a more persuasive portrait of its philosophical and political naïveté, critics often deploy either/or interpretive practices. Some critics assert that intersectionality has, in error, decoupled identity from structural power relations and has thereby promoted reductive identity formulations that need correcting. Intersectionality is also commonly presented not only as adopting identity categories (without questioning their history, ideological function, or boundaries) but also as delving into the experiential at the expense of the "bigger" picture (i.e., empirical, material, and structural issues). To its detriment, the argument goes, intersectionality has focused too much on identity and undertheorized categories, social structures, and institutions (Conaghan 2009; Yuval-Davis 2006).

For instance, Kerri Froc identifies "multidimensionality theory" as an (enhanced) outcome of intersectionality: multidimensionality is distinct from intersectionality since it focuses on contexts and systems of oppression, unlike (apparently) intersectionality (Froc 2010, 25). Trapped in retrograde notions of experience and identity, intersectionality is portrayed as unequipped to attend meaningfully to structural inequality, discursive politics, or materialist analysis. Similarly, Rosemary Hunter and Tracey de Simone, in examining how best to understand subordination, present *intersectional* and *contextual* analysis as separate choices—one focused on identity, the other on structure. Intersectionality falls short because it focuses on "identity" or "experience in categorical terms," whereas their model entails "paying attention to context, institutional dynamics and local practices" (Hunter and de Simone 2009, 177). This portrait of intersectionality erases repeated assertions by intersectionality theorists about the need to start from the very type of multivalent, multilevel analysis[26] they identify instead as their own contribution, one that adds to or improves intersectionality.

Many scholars also read intersectionality as affirming (or uncritically adopting) a sequential ontology which leads to additive models of identity and inequality (Barvosa 2008) and a simplistic identity politics (Yuval-Davis 2007) that overstates agency and undertheorizes power (Valentine 2007). That intersectionality aims to *challenge the limits* of such reductive ontological frameworks and roundly critiques a "logic of separation" (Bassel and Emejulu 2010), whether at micropolitical or macropolitical levels, disappears. Instead, intersectional approaches are portrayed as accepting categorical identity logics at face value, undertheorizing classification as a process, and offering little to no consideration of the categories' sedimentation, deployment, and wider implications.[27]

Ironically, many critics locate rigid, ahistorical, single-axis identity formulations within intersectionality so as to introduce the value of focusing on heterogeneity, complexity, and fluidity. Thus even as intersectionality rejects views of identity categories (at individual or group levels) as internally coherent, separable, and rankable, Grabham asserts, "There is a foundational assumption that the categories are distinct" (Grabham 2009, 191), and Nash finds intersectionality theory reifies categories as mutually exclusive and as internally homogenous or monolithic (Nash 2008a, 6, 8, 12). Likewise, though many intersectionality scholars have emphasized lived identities as intermeshed, inseparable, and inextricably shaped by structures of power,

Puar remarks that "an intersectional model of identity . . . presumes components—race, class, gender, sexuality, nation, age, religion—are separable analytics and can be thus disassembled, [whereas] an assemblage is more attuned to interwoven forces that merge and dissipate time, space, and body against linearity, coherence, and permanency" (Puar 2005, 127–128).

Thus although "attention to intersecting identities has the potential to create solidarity" (Roberts and Jesudason 2013, 313), intersectional approaches are often critiqued for causing rifts and ruptures. Intersectionality's atomizing effects are traced to its apparent "ontological fallacy," wherein each axis of identity or oppression is assumed a priori to "have an existence apart from the ways in which they combine" (Cooper 2004, 48). In this vein, though her recent work illuminates how intersectional identities are deeply coalitional in nature, and not fragmentable (Carastathis 2013a), in her earlier work Carastathis asserted that the "mutual exclusivity of the categories of race and gender is the condition for the possibility of their intersecting. . . . [T]he intersectional model of identity essentially inherits the ontology that its predecessors, the unitary conception of "woman" and the "additive" model of identity, were criticized for assuming" (Carastathis 2008, 28).

Yet numerous foundational intersectionality texts approach identities as multiple and *enmeshed*: furthermore, they overtly consider categorization as a complex social process tied to domains of power, a dynamic that entails both hegemonic ascription and, in turn, continual resistance. Take, for instance, Crenshaw's (1991) discussion in "Mapping the Margins." She clearly recognizes "the process of categorization is itself an exercise of power" and explains,

> First, the process of categorizing—or, in identity terms, naming—is not unilateral. Subordinated people can and do participate, sometimes even subverting the naming process in empowering ways. One need only think about the historical subversion of the category 'Black' or the current transformation of 'queer' to understand that categorization is not a one-way street. Clearly, there is unequal power, but there is nonetheless some degree of agency that people can and do exert in the politics of

> naming. And it is important to note that identity continues to be a site of resistance for members of different subordinated groups. (Crenshaw 1991, 1297)

Using a both/and approach to subjectivity, Crenshaw suggests categories can be employed in ways that disrupt their hegemonic structures and that shift their meaning toward different frames of rationality, personhood, agency, and justice.

In addition to acknowledging the doctrinal erasure or denial of marginalized claims and claimants, she also takes on testimonial injustice and ontological asymmetry in calling for the law to acknowledge its hidden subjectivities, structured absences, and historicity. As Crenshaw reiterated nearly twenty years later, critical race legal scholars did not have a romantic or naïve idea about the law: they knew it "was an indeterminate and sometimes counterproductive tool in social struggle." A both/and approach to its workings, including an intervention into the law's simplistic (and reductive) categorical logics, was requisite, and required "acknowledging that law was obviously a discourse of domination, but at the same time, it constituted an arena through which the rules of racial subordination might be engaged," contested, and transformed (Crenshaw 2011c, 227).

How is it, then, that intersectional contestations are read as indicating a naïve view of identity and as promulgating an unquestioning faith in the law's categories? For instance, Conaghan contends that because intersectionality has "its roots in law"[28] it is profoundly constrained, even determined, by law's logics, which cannot capture "complex multiplicity" and "cannot unpick or unravel the many ways in which inequality is produced and sustained" (Conaghan 2009, 22). Furthermore, she claims intersectionality thoughtlessly adheres to a "grid-like aesthetic" (22) and this "grid with perpendicular vectors whose coordinates can be neatly plotted" cannot match the realities of inequality, which are fluid and interactive (26; see also Staunaes and Sondergaard 2010).

Using a central intersectionality precept (about multiple forms of oppression operating simultaneously and in a relational dynamic), Conaghan reads an impetus toward separability and a faith in static mappings of power onto intersectionality as a crude grid (contra its claims). With regard to transsexuality, she then finds intersectionality deficient as it "directs our focus to points of intersection, to places where separate strands of inequality cross." Instead, what is requisite, "in the case of transsexuality and sexual orientation, . . . is a conception of inequality in which strands never operate separately; indeed, are always in some form, working together" (Conaghan 2009, 22). Here, she draws on a pivotal intersectionality insight—the simultaneity of identities and of systems of inequality—to pinpoint its failings.

Not only does this critical maneuver co-opt, it obscures how intersectionality pushes for reconceiving subjectivity *at the intersection*. Echoing Crenshaw's critique of antidiscrimination doctrine's inability to account for within-group differences and power dynamics, Lugones finds that, despite a deep understanding of the politics and structures of difference, Iris Marion Young's (1990) philosophy of difference, in its vision of group politics and representation, "lacks a conception of a multiple subject who is not fragmented" (Lugones 1994, 473). Likewise, I would argue that in reading the logics of fragmentation onto intersectionality, Conaghan erases its different approach to subjectivity, consciousness, and power (as multiple, relational, and shifting) and instead introduces fluidity and multiplicity as her own correctives to an intersectionality weak spot.

Yet implied in Crenshaw's (1989) assertion of "irreducibility,"[29] and overt in Lugones' (1994) notion of "curdling," is that simultaneity is about more than multiple identity strands added or woven together. Lugones explains, contrary to the either/or "logic of purity," which perceives the multiple as fragmentable, "according to the logic of curdling, the social world is complex and heterogeneous and each person is multiple, nonfragmented, embodied" (Lugones 1994, 463) with the potential to resist (133). "Curdled" logics/approaches have political and analytical utility for foregrounding, and addressing, intersected oppressions: furthermore, "unification and homogeneity . . . [are] related principles of ordering the social world" which erase multiplicity and fragment the identities (and lived realities) of women of color (Lugones 1994, 463).

## Intersectionality Is Disadvantaged by Its Focus on Disadvantage

Another common critique is that intersectionality is merely about "Black women," only focuses on (and is only about) "the oppressed," or over-attends to the "multiply oppressed" (suggesting these groupings are homogenous). Often, such critiques deploy a series of conflations—that intersectionality is 'about' Black women exclusively, that Black womanhood is monolithic, and that Black women are symbolic stand-ins for super-exploitation. Alluding to how this oversimplification of intersectionality functions in neoliberal academic and policy settings, Crenshaw underscores how, increasingly, "there is a sense that efforts to repackage intersectionality for universal consumption require a re-marginalising of black women" (Crenshaw 2011c, 224). Likewise, Bilge confronts "European disciplinary feminism" for downplaying "the importance of race in intersectional thought—for instance, by declaring race an irrelevant category for Europe" (Bilge 2013, 414).

Ignoring altogether its same/different thesis and both/and thinking, intersectionality's (ostensibly narrow) origins in Black feminism and (alleged) focus exclusively on the multiply oppressed are seen as reductive and as curbing its potential scope, usability, and relevance. Challenging the "predictable" oversimplification of power and identity that intersectionality has apparently promulgated, Baukje Prins argues that the origins for this problem stem from research that "focuses on groups who are positioned on the fringes of society, for whom mechanisms of social power have indeed become reified. But it is highly questionable to base one's general framework of identity upon such 'extreme' cases in which power works in a near totalitarian way" (Prins 2006, 282). Focusing on the margins is presented as a unidirectional endeavor that undermines intersectionality's wider applicability and relevance (apparently, knowledge crafted in and about the margins offers no insights about hegemony): furthermore, the margins, at their outermost "fringes," are presented as hopeless sites where domination succeeds fully and oppression is totalizing.

Notably, "narrowness" critiques are far from new: intersectional Black feminist analyses have long been charged with needing to become more refined, robust, and universal. In answer to such notions, Barbara Smith explained, "I have often wished I could spread the word that a movement committed to fighting sexual, racial, economic and heterosexist oppression, not to mention one which opposes imperialism, anti-Semitism, the oppressions visited upon the physically disabled, the old and the young, at the same time that it challenges militarism and imminent nuclear destruction, is the very opposite of narrow" (Smith 1983, xxxi).

Just because "much of the literature on intersectionality has been theorized from the standpoint of those who experience multiple dimensions of disadvantage" does not mean intersectionality is unable to "also inform how privileged groups are understood" and to understand how privilege operates across scales (Cole 2009, 171). Unfortunately, intersectionality's same/different thesis is often dispensed with. Furthermore, "framing intersectionality as only about women of color gives masculinity, whiteness, and maleness an intersectional pass." This, then, leaves what Carbado calls "colorblind [*sic*] intersectionality and gender-blind [*sic*] intersectionality unnamed and uninterrogated, further naturalizing white male heterosexuality as the normative baseline against which the rest of us are intersectionally differentiated" (Carbado 2013, 841).[30]

Also embedded in many of these critiques is the inference that intersectionality's focus on "the disadvantaged" is just too unhappy a place, one not invested enough in progress or moving forward: intersectionality does not perform or invoke the right affect, and specifically it fails to comply with the onus to be "happy." (I find this insinuation rather ironic, in that a deep commitment to contesting and transforming systemic inequality runs through intersectionality's history—revealing an underlying yearning and hope for a better world.) In thinking through how happiness politics inform racialized, gender-normative, imperialist governmentality, Sara Ahmed describes how "bad feelings are seen as orientated towards the past; as a kind of stubbornness that 'stops' the subject from embracing the future." Furthermore, she suggests, "it is the very assumption that good feelings are open and bad feelings are closed that allows historical forms of injustice to disappear. The demand for happiness is what makes those histories disappear by reading them as a form of melancholia (as if you are holding onto something that is already gone). These histories have not gone" (Ahmed 2008, 12).

Not only is intersectionality too particular, and perhaps too depressing, but an ostensible over-attention to marginalized groups and inattention to members of dominant groups means, apparently, that it has undertheorized power to such a degree that it *hinders* and even undermines important empirical, materialist, and justice-oriented work that is wider in scope and applicability (e.g., Valentine 2007; Staunæs and Søndergaard 2011). As Carbado has suggested, it seems "the genesis of intersectionality in Black feminist theory limits the ability of some scholars both to imagine the potential domains to which intersectionality might travel and to see the theory in places in which it is already doing work" (Carbado 2013, 815).

Using rhetorics of improvement, many advocate a "majority-inclusive principle" (Staunes 2003, 105), suggesting majority populations (and their conferred advantages and access to power) have been overlooked (Hulko 2009). Some critics call for more "complexity" and argue that both whiteness and masculinity should be accounted for more fully by intersectionality.[31] This line of critique often calls for intersectionality to address simultaneous privilege and oppression, focus on within-group differences, and unmask transparent sites of power, suggesting these ideas are *missing* in intersectionality theories/applications (even though they are central intersectional insights).

Introducing these ideas as "improvements" overlooks how intersectionality has always, of necessity, accounted for systematic, structural privilege, in part by attending to within-group differences and relational power (Alarcón 1990; Anzaldúa 1990a; Dill and Zambrana 2009; Zinn and Dill 1996). An intersectional focus on between-group *and* within-group asymmetries, and on multiple social positionings, means that simultaneous privilege and oppression—for all involved—must be considered. However, these key premises are rarely understood as having already been presented by intersectionality scholars or are posited as an unacknowledged or unresolved dilemma for intersectionality research and practice.

In raising the question of "how to conceptualize the intersections so that bringing the agency of the disadvantaged into focus does not leave the actions of the powerful out of sight," Walby, Armstrong, and Strid suggest, for example, that Crenshaw "loses sight of the actions of the powerful and the racist structures" and that, in fact, "much of the work that uses concepts of 'category' and 'strand' tends to obscure the powerful within them" (Walby, Armstrong, and Strid 2012, 228). But, if one returns to Crenshaw's earliest writings, including "Demarginalizing," it is clear that she does focus on the powerful, lays bare transparent sites of privilege, and highlights how within-group relational power is situated within, and impacted by, structures of dominance. Her writings offer clear examples of how to pierce dominant ideologies and reveal the workings of power within categorical logics and strands. Furthermore, she models how to begin to show transparency is an artifice used to maintain status quo power relations: in other words, hegemonic or "representative" identities are also intersectional, even if their intersectionality is unarticulated (and in fact, actively hidden and denied).

Certainly, Crenshaw insists that we stop using the most privileged members of any group as representative, as the measure and referent for justice, personhood, and knowledge: she illustrates, for example, that a doctrinal focus on the most privileged marginalizes those who are multiply burdened and obscures claims that cannot be understood as resulting from discrete sources of discrimination (Crenshaw 1989, 140). Crenshaw shows how the law repeatedly focuses on and serves the powerful, even when it seems not to be. Furthermore, by focusing both on masculinity and whiteness, she illustrates how the law takes privilege as a given in discrimination claims, paradoxically requiring that one already have access to power and privilege on some counts to seek redress for discrimination on others.

More recently, Carbado has analyzed racialized gender normative expectations at work in the Jesperson employment discrimination litigation (*Jesperson v. Harrahs*, 2006) to underscore how "whiteness is doing racially constitutive work in the case but is unarticulated and racially invisible as an intersectional subject position." Carbado finds Jesperson's whiteness to be a pivotal but unnamed factor in Harrah's efforts to require Jesperson, as an employee, to adhere to middle-class, heteronormative, binary gender performance standards in terms of comportment, dress, hairstyle, and makeup. Likewise, he demonstrates that whiteness is a silenced but central factor in the framework of Jesperson's sex discrimination suit since, "throughout the litigation, whiteness anchors the intelligibility of Jesperson as a woman and the intelligibility of her claim as an alleged instance of sex discrimination. Thus, gender is intersectionally but invisibly constituted as white" (Carbado 2013, 823–824). Again, an intersectional reading reveals how false universals operate to safeguard power: here, gender-universal logics function as a repository for white privilege which in turn makes Jesperson's claim of sex discrimination both legible and intelligible.

Earlier examples in the intersectionality literatures also demonstrate the merits of focusing "up" and "down" social hierarchies at once, from a matrix view. Consider Anna Julia Cooper's analysis, in 1892, of a (white) women's art and culture club. Her sharp assessment of "Wimodaughsis (. . . a woman's culture club whose name was created using the first few letters of *wi*ves, *mo*thers, *daugh*ters, and *sis*ters)" offers a criticism of white solipsism, false gender universalism, and overt adherence to status quo power relations (in terms of race and class). Sarcastically, she describes how "Pandora's box is opened in the ideal harmony of this modern Eden without an Adam when a colored lady, a teacher in one of our schools, applies for admission to its privileges and opportunities." Cooper astutely retains the phonetic sound of the club's name, but changes the spelling to "*Whimodaughsis*" to reveal and to discredit the workings of white supremacy (Cooper 1988, 80–81, italics in original).

As an aside, I find it interesting that Cooper references "Pandora's box" springing open when *Wimodaughsis/Whimodaughsis* denied a "colored lady" entrance to their club, just as the courts, a century later, would deny Black women's right to claim gender discrimination under Title VII in the 1976 decision *De Graffenreid v. General Motors* (see Crenshaw 1989). In both instances Pandora's box is opened by those in power when the pretense of inclusivity and representativeness of single-axis, gender-first logics is exposed. When 'universal' gender is revealed, by the applicant or plaintiff, to be narrow and particular,

Pandora's box is opened by the members of the Club (or the Court) to maintain status quo power relations.

Cooper also employed an intersectional lens in public debates about personhood, citizenship, civil rights, and freedoms. As her remarks before an audience of white feminists at the 1893 Chicago World's Exposition illustrate, the Black feminist worldview she drew upon was collective, grounded in a vision of solidarity, and pivoted on a same/different thesis. Cooper stated, "We take our stand on the solidarity of humanity. . . . The colored woman feels that woman's cause is. . . . not the white woman's, nor the black woman's, nor the red woman's, but the cause of every man and of every woman who has writhed silently under a mighty wrong" (Cooper 1998a, 205). Starting from the premise of the indivisibility of all aspects of the self and from the insight that systems of oppression are interlocking, Cooper advocated a matric model of rights and activism.

Additionally, when critics suggest intersectionality's sole focus has been a unidirectional (and simplistic) margin-to-center politics, with inadequate attention to the "center," what gets suppressed is how intersectional approaches focus on relational and shifting power but also *margin-to-margin* hostilities and possibilities. Again, this is evident in its long-standing call for coalition politics and equally persistent criticism of false universals and internal hierarchies within resistance movements and intellectual traditions. Assertions that intersectionality "only" focuses on "the oppressed" do more than distort intersectional histories and premises: they treat "the oppressed" and "the powerful" as neatly bifurcated (not as positionalities sometimes occupied simultaneously) and imply that "the oppressed" (or the privileged) are fully (and only) so. Not only do intersectional questions of relative power and inequality fall away, so do pivotal concerns about ongoing resistance to subordination in the face of persistent, structural inequality.

In sum, this line of critique can distort intersectionality's history and literatures in multiple ways. Intersectionality theory, from its earliest writings, has focused on debunking "transparent" power and has contested privilege, both within and between groups. It not only theorizes "up" and "down" structural, political, epistemological, and ontological hierarchies (Carbado 2013, 814), but highlights how transparent privilege insidiously functions to render dominance, and dominant subjectivities, invisible yet also normative. In refuting transparency, intersectional approaches underscore that everyone (differently) occupies intersectional locations, even as the multiplicity of the powerful is denied and rendered invisible via pretenses to unified subjectivity (Lugones 1994). To take up these assertions, then, one must ignore key intersectionality arguments about domains of power, relative privilege and oppression, both/and analyses of sameness/difference, simultaneity, and matric approaches to subjectivity.

### Intersectionality Is Destructive to Feminism ("Sapphire" Is Rising, Beware!)

Though intersectionality is multilevel, matrix-focused, and both/and oriented, it is often critiqued for having a splintering effect. As a "wedge" (Nash 2008a), it is charged with fragmenting feminism and/or gender: again, this assertion seems somewhat ironic, in that part of intersectionality's central analysis is to reveal how either/or logics and single-axis models of identity and forms of political action fragment because *they* rely on hierarchy and division. In other words, internal differences "within" gender have always been present but denied (as Cooper's exposé of "*Whimodaughsis*" suggested): certainly, intersectionality *exposes* internal wedges, but is it accurate to say it *creates* and *wields* them?

Thus while some find ambiguity might well be intersectionality's deepest value (Davis 2008), it is frequently attributed with an immense power to irreparably split apart gender and/or feminism, leaving no meaningful political ground to work from (or on) together (Gunnarsson 2011).[32] In methodological debates, for instance, it is often seen to violate the "rule of parsimony" because it proliferates categories of analysis without apparently adding any meaningful explanatory power or analytical insight to empirical research (Hancock 2007b, 66). In political contexts, intersectionality's speciation is seen to thwart collective action (Arya 2009, 334–344). In philosophical debates, the "parsimony objection" emerges in charges that intersectionality creates "too many genders" or makes gender, as a category of analysis, meaningless because too varied and unstable (suggesting this variability, instability, and multiplicity are *new* and not always already present within gender[s]) (see Bailey 2009). (I would add that trans* feminisms are also seen, differently, to violate gender parsimony, and treated as a threat for this reason: this only adds to my prior assertion [May 2014a] that gender needs to be further troubled as feminism's go-to governing imaginary.)

In other words, even as intersectionality advocates coalition, its detractors worry instead about what they see as its fragmenting capacity to create "vanishingly small constituencies" (Carasthathis 2008, 447). Many scholars have documented how intersectionality offers paths to alliance and solidarity, not separatist fragmentation,[33] but it is often misconstrued as an identity model and political approach that both creates and focuses on smaller and smaller (and relatively meaningless) groups. Intersectionality also is seen to waste energies that, it is implied, could be used for real, meaningful change. Conaghan, for instance, finds it to be "a project of limitless scope and limited promise. Not only does it preclude the deployment of equality categories in other ways, for example, to explain or elaborate structures, relations and/or processes of inequality, it ensures that the focus of intellectual, political and legal energy is directed towards the infinite elaboration of inequality subgroups, engendering a slow but steady march towards conceptual fragmentation and, ultimately, dissolution" (Conaghan 2009, 31).

Similarly, Naomi Zack suggests intersectionality "lends to a fragmentation of women that precludes common goals as well as basic empathy" (Zack 2005, 7) because it reinforces incommensurability among women by focusing on differences, not shared relations and goals (8–18). Furthermore, it promotes "the view that race, class, sexual preference, ethnicity, religion, nationality, ableness, and anything else combine in individuals or groups to result in distinct women's genders" (73). In contrast to this disquieting ontological proliferation, she advocates an "egalitarian discourse of duties and practical exchange." Zack contends, "Assistance based on duties and claims constitutes real membership in a world that is unevenly advantaged. . . . The benefactors may be able to learn from those they assist, once they are able to relate to them as equals on the ground of shared relations of being women" (9).

Once again, the (historical and ongoing) call by Black feminists to acknowledge that gender is always already differentiated, because it is fundamentally inseparable from and shaped by myriad other factors, seems inadequately engaged with. For example, consider Frances Beale's analysis from 1970 of how the powerful illusion of universal "womanhood" can be ruptured by drawing on knowledge gleaned from lived experiences of structural inequality. Beale highlights the connected workings of capitalist, race, and gender ideologies, and contends, "Though we [Black women] have been browbeaten with this white image, the reality of the degrading and dehumanizing jobs that were relegated to us quickly dissipated this mirage of 'womanhood'" (Beale 1970, 91).

Moreover, just as Alison Bailey mistrusts Zack's implicit support of *noblesse oblige* as grounds for feminism and for women's actions on behalf of other women (Bailey 2009, 30), I am skeptical of a faith in positive duty and an impetus to "help" others that pivots on self-interest as a motivator. Ahmed's discussion of the United Kingdom's "'new equality regime' premised on the redefinition of equality as a positive duty" is illuminating here. She finds, within a positive duty framework, "a set of processes that maintain what is supposedly being redressed"—a racist "inequality regime given a new form" (Ahmed 2012, 8). Zack does not offer enough detail to explain what tactics and ethics must be taken up so that positive duty does not devolve into boomerang perception (Spelman 1988) or pity (Code 1995) as the basis for privileged women "seeing" (themselves in) less privileged women's lives (see also Boler 1999; Narayan 1997).

Many intersectionality crisis narratives/critiques also seem to adhere to a (neo)liberal notion of difference and suggest an underlying sameness, of one kind or another, remains a necessary foundation for social cohesion, philosophical consistency, and political viability. Irene Gedalof sums up this philosophy thusly: "Difference can only be accommodated if, first, there is a secure and stable ground of sameness upon which our differences can be allowed to flower" (Gedalof 2012, 6). Mourning the loss of a "group unity equals group uniformity logic" (Hancock 2007b, 65), even as these forms of unity frequently require secondary marginalization to cohere (Cohen 1999), discussions of intersectionality's destructive force can indirectly reinforce the very logics of sameness it contests. As Gedalof explains, "The privileging of sameness over difference results, not in the production of universal values, but rather in the effective universalizing of the particular interests and perspectives of dominant groups. In a context of inequality, assuming a common good as the shared desired end point can end up perpetuating the existing privilege of some, as their perspective on the common good is likely to dominate" (Gedalof 2012, 4).

In various versions of this "Sapphire" threat, intersectional approaches are portrayed as both shortsighted and aggressive, characterized as harmful to feminism because they abandon (and impede the possibility for) commonality and unity among women due to an excessive focus on multiplicity and an overpropagation of "distinct and incommensurable identities" (Zack 2005, 18). However, the language of proliferation relied on in many such critiques echoes long-standing and inflammatory rhetorics of (over)breeding and excess used to vilify Black women (and to justify an array of state practices of containing and/or exploiting Black women, from slavery to anti-natalist policy and healthcare, to incarceration). These rhetorics also parallel those used to disparage faculty of color in the academy, as Sara Ahmed discusses: she writes, "If only we had the power we are imagined to possess, if only our proximity could be such a force. If only our arrival was their undoing" (Ahmed 2009, 41).

As the villainous destroyer of a once-coherent, more viable, and potentially (re)unified gender-primary feminist project, intersectionality has also been charged with being "against feminist theory" (Gunnarsson 2011, 25) or presented as in favor of race and class (but not as strongly in favor of gender) (Lykke 2006). These discussions discursively mobilize gender, race, and class in atomized ways and ignore how an intersectional ontology is complex, compound, and coalitional.[34] In other words, intersectionality is portrayed (and then critiqued for) being a form of pop-bead thinking ("for" class and race, but "against" feminist theory or gender): furthermore, single-axis logics are required to follow these arguments.

Such critiques also imply that intersectionality, as a body of thought and as a political impetus, is another kind of "killjoy" (Ahmed 2010; Rollock 2012), one that is insufficiently deferential to gender-primary feminism, and/or whiteness, or, more generally, inadequately deferential to dominance (Carbado 2013; DuCille 1994; Tomlinson 2013b). Lamentation over lost opportunities and a shattered feminism often combines with an affect of fear about the present and anxiety about the long-term implications of intersectionality's detrimental forces. Rhetorically centering attention on "gender" in ways that turn focus away from intersectional logics, questions, and assessments, an intersectional vision of a more just world transmogrifies here into an alarming threat that must be warded off or quarantined.

Notably, the role of a feminism-destroying anti-hero(ine) has, over time, also been attributed (variously) to postmodern, queer, and trans* feminisms. However, as Clare Hemmings argues, no matter what group or concept is characterized as the villain of the moment, the "heroine" of narratives about feminism (and the supposed "victim" of these harsh and unruly margins) has been fairly consistently cast: the proper subject of Western feminism remains Western, bourgeois, able-bodied, and white (Hemmings 2011, 191–193). Via reversal and transference, exclusions in gender-universal feminism are ignored and these more coherent feminisms or more usable feminist theories/methods/frames are rendered the casualty of intersectionality's ruinous splinterings (while violations engendered by gender-universal feminisms, which intersectionality contests, slip from view).

### How to "Cure" What Ails Intersectionality? Return to Single-Axis Hierarchies!

In answer to intersectionality's ostensible fragmentation, undertheorization of power, and uncritical approach to categorical thinking and identity, many critics advocate a return to single-axis, hierarchical models, usually via a collective good rationale that draws on common-denominator *gender-first* or *class-first* logics. Against the threat of (an already present, but widely denied) heterogeneity, and to repair the harmful fissures apparently caused by an intersectional focus on relational power, multiplicity, and within-group differences, one should batten down the hatches and mobilize the unitary!

In European debates, for example, one can readily find calls to depart from intersectionality's identity-based particularism and return to a materialist analysis or approach. Generally, the argument goes as follows: social class should have priority because it ties into our commonalities and because other structures of social inequality are subordinate to material and economic forces. In contrast to the vision and political roadmap offered by materialist politics, intersectionality is perceived as deeply divisive of (more authentic/viable) progressive politics ("progressive" here meaning class-based thought and action) (Valentine 2007).

Often, this critique is fairly subtle: for instance, Grabham, Herman, Cooper, and Krishnadas contend that intersectionality "should not overwhelmingly focus on subjective experiences and questions of identity but should instead account for material conditions and social practices" (Grabham et al. 2009, 6). Similarly, Conaghan argues, "Intersectionality has become too bound up with notions of identity and identity formation." She adds, "While identity analyses tend to highlight experiences of inequality and law's characterisation of and response to those experiences, class discourse tends to focus on the structured processes and relations which produce and mediate experience" (Conaghan 2009, 29–30).

However, positing the material as the way for feminism to regain an ability to meaningfully address macrolevel issues essentially "evacuate[s] Western feminist theory of its history of critical race work" (Hemmings 2011, 127). As Quijano's (2007) and Lugones' (2007, 2010) analyses of the coloniality of power demonstrate, modernity was established via a concerted project of sexual-racial exploitation and carefully crafted (and enforced) ontological hierarchies that explicitly benefited and furthered European empires. This means "any serious materialist critique . . . [should not] bypass the colonial encounter, because it is constitutive of the historical development of modern society and of capitalism" (Grech 2012, 53).

Additionally, a class-first strategy, argues Gedalof, often "defines class as something we all have, while gender, race, ethnicity and sexuality are reduced to 'the politics of identity,' a kind of special pleading."

This rhetorical and political move "undoes the possibility of any kind of intersectional understanding of these categories of difference, by de-linking the socio-economic from the gendered, sexualized and racialized ways in which socio-economic positioning is lived, and situating it solely in the undifferentiated space of 'class.' Class then becomes a way of stabilizing sameness" (and sameness is then often linked to whiteness and to masculinity) (Gedalof 2012, 13).

Furthermore, as Linda Martín Alcoff underscores, this type of solution to the "problem" of intersectionality obscures the fact that there are not really any "pure" class issues or demands anyway—only from within (or colluding with) the logics of dominance are other identities seen as particularist and divisive and other systems of oppression (racism and sexism, for instance) understood as immaterial to explaining and addressing class inequality. She explains,

> there are demands of skilled or unskilled workers, of the trades or the service professions, of migrant workers, of women workers, of immigrant workers, and so on. Sometimes these groups can make common cause, but the very project of doing so will require a clear understanding of how identities mediate class relations to produce specific workplace hierarchies and conflicts of interest. Class reductionists argue here that conflicts will dissolve if we can only wean ourselves from our identity attachments. It is in just this way that the left colludes with the right in portraying ethnic group politics today as special interest agendas with opportunistic leaders who never take into account the common good. (Alcoff 2011, 74)

Positing the material in opposition to (and as the remedy for apparent oversight within) intersectionality also obliterates intersectionality's long-term and *insistent focus upon the material and structural aspects of oppression and lived identity*. As Coogan-Gehr persuasively demonstrates, "critiques of capitalism and imperialism have been at the heart of black feminism since its beginnings, and hasty associations of black feminist scholarship with an unrefined U.S. multiculturalism mask this intricate history" (Coogan-Gehr 2011, 95).

For instance, the Combahee River Collective clearly asserts that capitalist exploitation is a fundamental factor, historically and presently, shaping Black women's lives transnationally: "We realize that the liberation of all oppressed peoples necessitates the destruction of the political-economic systems of capitalism and imperialism as well as patriarchy." Furthermore, they explain, "Although we are in essential agreement with Marx's theory as it applied to the very specific economic relationships he analyzed, we know that his analysis must be extended further in order for us to understand our specific economic situation as Black women" (Combahee 1983, 279; see also Davies 2008 on Claudia Jones, a radical Black feminist Marxist). Unfortunately, however, to highlight the radical nature of class-first approaches, many critiques offer a depoliticized portrait of intersectionality and overlook its long-standing critiques of material forces and structural power, particularly capitalist, settler colonial, and (neo)liberal forms of exploitation and extraction (Bilge 2013; Tomlinson 2013a, 2013b).

Correspondingly, the remedy frequently presented to mitigate intersectionality's splintering of gender and/or women and/or feminism is common-denominator thinking: gender is offered as a means of rescuing feminism from intersectionality's failings. For example, Zack finds intersectionality creates an infinite number of genders, each more particular than the next. She writes, "In the paradigm instance of intersectionality, a black woman is understood to be not merely a woman in the white feminist sense, who is in addition black. No, a black woman is understood to be someone with a distinct identity of gender because *race is supposed to be a principal determinant of gender*: race + class = gender!" (Zack 2005, 7, italics in original). This proliferation of genders furthers incommensurability among women because it "precludes common goals as well as basic empathy" (7): intersectionality undermines feminism's feasibility because it fractures women's commonality into infinitesimal, atomized bits.

As an alternative, she advocates a "nonsubstantive" form of gender commonality. Zack contends, "All women share the nonsubstantive, relational essence of being assigned to or identifying with the historical, socially constructed, disjunctive category of female birth designees, biological mothers, or heterosexual choices of men—category FMP" (Zack 2005, 162). By "FMP" she means women's "shared assignment to, or identification with, the historically defined category of human beings who are designated *f*emale from birth, biological *m*others, or *p*rimary sexual choices of men" (Zack 2005, 61, italics added). By using an FMP model, she argues, "specific or local women's genders can be viewed as variables that are culturally contextualized" (61).

However, this "all women share" approach has several embedded silences and Zack does not really account for how "relations of oppression . . . mark otherwise neutral physical features as determinants of sex" (Hall 2005, 113). For instance, she does not adequately address gender variance or genders that do not readily fit this umbrella vision for all "real women" (such as MTF women or FTM men). Likewise, intersex babies are regularly "designated" female or male at birth by a doctor. This "designation" can entail gender violence via surgical enforcement of dual sex embodiment (Fausto-Sterling 2000, 2012; Hall 2005; Stryker and Whittle 2006). Moreover, she does not explain whose "genders" might turn out to be understood or categorized as "*variables*" (versus whose will be seen as normative, neutral, or transparent).

As with class-primary remedies to intersectionality's ruinous (and unsophisticated) fragmentation, gender-primary correctives often reinforce common-denominator logics and hierarchies of identity and oppression. These single-axis solutions forcibly break from (and break apart) a matrix justice orientation and suppress the multiplicity of lived identities. For instance, Gunnarsson advocates for the category "women" to regain priority, as "people belonging to the group are intrinsically tied to a common position in a materially (and discursively) constituted gender structure" (Gunnarsson 2011, 34). In a rhetorical move that homogenizes and atomizes groups and disarticulates vectors of power as distinct,[35] she argues that "the structures of race, gender and class have distinct existences in so far as they exercise their causal force on our lives in ways relatively independent from each other" (Gunnarsson 2011, 32).

However, intersectionality illustrates that such causal forces interdepend and play out simultaneously as interwoven, such that what sexual harassment looks like and feels like for racially marginalized women, some of whom might also be queer, disabled, or noncitizens, is qualitatively different because such forces of power interdepend. Furthermore, as Cole succinctly argues, "treating race and gender as independent variables suggests that these social categories are primarily properties of individuals rather than reflections of macrolevel social practices linked to inequality" (Cole 2009, 178).

In approaching these causal forces as distinct and independent, Gunnarsson also asserts that gender commonality can readily be found in shared, everyday forms of gender performance and in women's collective material inequity. She writes, "The position as woman will make its occupant apt to act in ways commonly understood as feminine and experience things that males do not tend to experience. She will tend to earn less than her male colleagues, since those who decide her wages are in positions motivating them to discriminate against women, and in order to promote her short-term interests she will be motivated to dress in feminine clothes" (Gunnarsson 2011, 33). The notion that 'women' experience things that 'men' do not requires that gender be understood both as fundamentally binary and as readily separable from (rather than inextricably entangled with) other sites of identity and power.

Here, Gunnarsson's notion of intersectionality is instructive for understanding how a (dualistic) gender commonality is, in her view, a better path for feminism and for understanding how, also in her view, "gender" can readily be extricated from other factors. According to her "unusually broad sense" of the concept, intersectionality focuses on "the complexities stemming from women's different positioning in power relations *other than gender*" (Gunnarsson 2011, 25, italics added). In her view of intersectionality, gender is posited as operating independently, in embodied, ideological, material, and structural terms: this is why the "feminine" ways of acting and the forms of discrimination alluded to are not understood or presented by Gunnarsson as always already also classed, racialized, heteronormative, able-bodied and tied to citizenship norms. Her gender-atomized approach also reinforces the norm/centrality of those "men" who are at the top of the earnings ladder and in positions of leadership—erasing myriad other factors shaping and embedded within masculinity, such as citizenship status, race, sexuality, disability, and social class standing.

Furthermore, as Lugones has argued persuasively, and repeatedly, atomized identity logics and notions of universalized gender are fundamental to the colonial/modern gender system wherein the "light" side of modernity reserved (and continues to reserve) gender for itself, the human—whereas the "dark" side of modernity, and of the colonial/modern gender system, is understood to have biological (animal) "sex" characteristics, but not gender (Lugones 2007, 202–207; 2010, 743–750):[36] this is why, according to Lugones, the answer to Sojourner Truth's infamous query "Aren't I a woman?" must be understood to have been, and to remain, "no," from within the logics of coloniality (Lugones 2010, 745).

If, as Lugones carefully illustrates, the concept of gender has been "light" from its start, conceived within the structures of coloniality, the emergence of capitalism, and the expansion of empire and slavery, then to argue for a "return" to gender-as-universal, or for atomized/separable gender, is to reiterate and reinforce the excruciating logics of coloniality, race and racism in the name of a viable and workable feminism, rather than to take up the call to decolonize feminist projects and praxes. This (eugenically) improved (yet retrograde) feminism is one cured of attending to a matric liberation politics and absolved of the fundamental need to engage in sustained coalitions to eradicate multiple forms of structural inequality.

### Attending to the Politics of Legibility and Plausibility

Critique can be a vital way to engage with and further an idea, but also to disengage and flatten a concept. Critique can provide a means by which conventional worldviews and hegemonic mindsets prevail because they are more familiar (and hence transparent), understandable (and thus persuasive), and can seem, generally, more logical, particularly when critics take on a concept, like intersectionality, that contests and seeks to transform conventional logics. I have suggested that intersectional ideas are often disciplined and dismissed by the terms of interpretation at hand. Many critiques are framed within (and reinforce) narrow ways of thinking (about gender, feminism, politics, research, policy, etc.), even when these are the very same ways of thinking intersectionality has challenged. Specifically, modes of perception identified by intersectionality theorists as fundamentally violating (e.g., binary logics, falsely homogenized categories, or primary and secondary oppression frameworks) are consistently used to assess and characterize intersectionality.

Too often, critics adhere to entrenched rationalities and use, as their primary reference points or measures of political or philosophical sufficiency, the very ideas and practices intersectionality has contested and asked us to divest from. This renders intersectionality unknowable on its own terms. That intersectionality is often read carelessly or reductively, or presented as a threat in need of containment, matters. Ironically, for instance, the forms of ideological and philosophical containment that Crenshaw sought to expose in "Demarginalizing" are regularly used to suppress her own arguments, in particular, and, more generally, to render intersectional approaches illegible or illogical.

Thus while reading and interpretation are usually thought of as practices of understanding, they are also potential sites of distortion: conventional terms of analytic legibility can enforce intersectionality's illegibility. Furthermore, many critical approaches seem to focus only on intersectionality's deficiencies without accounting for how intersectional work has exposed substantial shortcomings and absences in an array of established ways of knowing: the attention to questions of lack is unidirectional. The intersectional invitation to forge reflexive, dialogic solidarities and to depart from the inaccuracies and violating consequences of single-axis mindsets is regularly set aside. This presents more than a mere philosophical conundrum: as Tomlinson has argued, many everyday but "uninterrogated scholarly and social conventions and habits of argument lead to distorted and destructive critiques of intersectionality that are damaging to feminist antisubordination scholarship and activism" (Tomlinson 2013b, 993).

Intersectionality contests the pull of prevailing mindsets, in part, by drawing from political expectations, lived experiences, analytic positions, and philosophical outlooks not crafted solely within the bounds of dominant imaginaries—often forged in resistance alongside or outside of them (Lugones 2005). However, when adhering to hegemonic epistemological assumptions in terms of the questions asked, the assessments offered, and the expectations brought to bear, critique narratives can shore up normativity, flatten such resistance, and erase intersectionality's fundamentally different approach to subjectivity, knowledge, and power.

Rather than seek interpretive perfection, my argument is that it is imperative to attend more fully to the politics of reading, interpretation, and reception. Interpretive politics are not to be underestimated, as they are connected to larger terrains of struggle over political, philosophical, and ethical worldviews and practices. This is why we must ask which critiques (and/or uses) of intersectionality seem readily accepted and why this might be so. In fact, I would argue, a wide range of issues (many of which I take up in Chapter 5) must be more fully considered, including: hermeneutic marginalization and interpretive violence; the impact of power on the politics of writing and reception; and the influence of established social imaginaries on meaning-making.[37]

However, first, in the next chapter, I show that intersectionality applications can also distort and even drop its key premises. When using or instrumentalizing the concept, researchers and policymakers often slip into hegemonic logics as well. Though intersectionality applications often entail quite a different affective dimension (e.g., a more favorable rather than critical approach), a more positive take on intersectionality offers no guarantee of methodological, interpretive, political, or philosophical adequacy. As critics and practitioners, we must more fully consider whether the analytic expectations and interpretive tools brought to interpreting and applying intersectionality are adequate to the alternative geographies of knowing and being it offers. We must aim to meet, not suppress, intersectionality's radical multiplicity, justice orientations, and epistemological demands.

## Notes

1. Kristie Dotson asks whether this mode of engagement, particularly its combative aspects, should be primary, particularly when accounting for highly gendered and racialized asymmetries of power and cognitive authority in the academy (Dotson 2011b).
2. This is why both Lugones (2005) and Alcoff (2006a) have called for more nuanced readings of figures such as Gloria Anzaldúa: they seek to intervene in empty adulation of or passing reference to Anzaldúa's ideas and innovations.

3. Carbado discusses, and succinctly responds to, six "standard criticisms of the theory: 1. Intersectionality is only or largely about Black women, or only about race and gender. 2. Intersectionality is an identitarian framework. 3. Intersectionality is a static theory that does not capture the dynamic and contingent processes of identity formation. 4. Intersectionality is overly invested in subjects. 5. Intersectionality has traveled as far as it can go, or there is nothing more the theory can teach us. 6. Intersectionality should be replaced by or at least applied in conjunction with (fill in the blank)" (Carbado 2013, 812).
4. In brief, multidimensionality theory in critical legal studies has emerged as a way to more overtly account for masculinities (e.g., McGinley and Cooper 2013; Mutua 2013) and sexualities (e.g., Hutchinson 1999, 2000, 2002)—what McGinley and Cooper characterize as a "new" way of conceptualizing identity (e.g., "cubed" rather than linear or axial, contextual, shifting, and interactive [McGinley and Cooper 2013, 327–228; see also Kwan 1997]), extending other lenses, including intersectionality, which are seen to inadequately account for these qualities or for masculinities, sexualities, and more. However, others (e.g., Carbado 1999b, 2013) have theorized masculinities and sexualities in a multidimensional, contextual way within intersectionality theory. Furthermore, Cho strongly contests the distinctiveness of multidimensionality theory or the need to "supercede" intersectionality (Cho 2013, 386). She underscores, "Recognizing that both power and identity are complex and interrelated, intersectionality [already] offers a systemic and structural analysis of both, while recognizing the variability, fluidity, and contingency of specific manifestations of subordination" (385; see also Han 2006).
5. See, e.g., Alcoff (2001), Alcoff and Kittay (2007), Babbitt (2001), Code (1995), Choo and Ferree (2010), Christian (1990), Cole (2009), Collins (1990, 1998, 2004), Frye (1983), Hancock (2007a), Harnois (2013), Hawkesworth (1989), Hoagland (2001), Jaggar (1989), Lugones (1994), Martin (1991), Narayan (1997), Pohlhaus (2012), Simien (2007), L. Smith (2012), Tuana (2006), Williams (1991).
6. Arguing "stories matter" with regard to how feminist theory is narrated and its theoretical subjects conceived, Hemmings examines stories of progress, loss, and return and delineates their temporality, affective dimensions, and imagined feminist subject(s). Loss narratives lament feminism's depoliticization, professionalization, and the fragmenting of analytic categories (Hemmings 2011, 64–76); progress narratives celebrate shedding naïve "experience" and falsely homogenized "woman" (36–37); and return narratives posit materialist analysis as the way "back" to addressing macrolevel issues (127). Furthermore, Hemmings contends, each set of stories has its distortions and exacts different costs.
7. For questioning diagnostic rhetorics, frames, and legacies from a disability studies angle, see, e.g., Baynton (2005), Davis (1995), Linton (1998), and Mitchell and Snyder (2000).
8. For discussions of intersectionality's "whitening," see: Bilge (2013), Lewis (2009, 2013), May (2014a), Tomlinson (2013a).
9. See Alarcón (1990), Combahee (1983), Crenshaw (1989), Lorde (1984), Lugones (1994).
10. E.g., see Conaghan (2009), Cooper (2009), Grabham (2009), Hunter and de Simone (2009).
11. E.g., see Grabham et al. (2009) and Kwan (1997). Lykke (2010) tends toward posing a false divide between Black feminist analysis and materialist analysis (despite the fact that both sets of traditions center on thinking through material reality as a means of transforming social structures), perhaps due to a keenness to emphasize socialist-materialist analysis.
12. E.g., as I shall discuss later in the chapter, Gunnarsson (2011) and Zack (2005) both rely on different iterations of the "parsimony objection" (see Bailey 2009; Hancock 2007b; May 2014a) to decry intersectionality's fragmentation of gender.

13. This affective implication can also emerge in critiques or discussions sympathetic to an intersectional approach (e.g., McCall 2005; Nash 2008a).
14. See Nash (2010) on the issue of the "fetishization of intersectionality's difficulty."
15. For more on the Alliance, see Anderson-Bricker (1999), Kelley (2002), Springer (2005), and Ward (2006). For photos of their newsletter *Triple Jeopardy: Racism, Imperialism, Sexism* (published between September, 1971 and August, 1975), see www.flickr.com/photos/27628370@N08/sets/72157605547626040/.
16. Bhavnani and Bywater find the verb "to configure connotes more movement and fluidity. . . . Configuration also connotes agency, offering a way of thinking about how inequalities . . . work with and against each other. . . . Intersectionality is too static, too close to losing sight of agency" (Bhavnani and Bywater 2009, 53–54).
17. Puar focuses primarily on "intersectional identity theory" (a condensation of intersectionality as a wider orientation), which she finds "foregrounds separate analytics of identity" (Puar 2007, 206) thus unable to account adequately for a range of complications, including "complicities" with dominance (24) or embodiments that do not (or cannot, or refuse to) align with categorical identity logics or notions of the individuated subject, such as the "faggot Muslim body" (96) or the "intimacy of weapon with body" that becomes body-weapon in the "suicide bomber," a "newly becoming" body formation (217) that "scrambles" the subject/object divide (193). Importantly, Puar does not oppose the concepts "assemblage" and intersectionality, or necessarily suggest that assemblage should supercede intersectionality. Rather, she discusses how "intersectional identities and assemblages must remain as interlocutors in tension" (213) and argues that an intersectional analysis (i.e., as a heuristic) is in fact a pivotal analytical tool (125).
18. In contrast to intersectionality, "cosynthesis" is presented as a "dynamic model of the conditions of categorical formations whose ultimate message is that, since the multiple categories through which we understand ourselves are implicated in complex ways with the formation of categories through which others are constituted, political emancipation and the achievement of justice are realizable only when we recognize that we all have a stake in finding ways of seizing control over the legal and cultural forces that shape all of the categories that are formed to maintain systems of oppression" (Kwan 1997, 1257).
19. Since "intersectionality" and "identity theory" lend themselves to co-optation and "divisive thinking," Ehrenreich offers the metaphor of symbiosis to address missing but key pieces of the larger "puzzle," i.e., to focus on the interrelationship among systems of subordination (viewed as mutually reinforcing), to urge coalition politics that account for a same/different analytic and vision, and to discuss simultaneous (and relational) privilege and oppression (Ehrenreich 2002, 251–252). As with many alternative lenses offered by various critics, these seem key premises *of* intersectionality, not beyond it.
20. Davina Cooper aims to focus on "dynamic processes" of power and relational inequalities in a multiscalar way rather than approach identity/power as separable or singular strands, which she asserts intersectionality analysis is prone to given its linear imaginary and spatially static or fixed focus on specific points of contact (Cooper 2004, 2009).
21. Rather than rely on the metaphor of "intersections," Dhamoon has "tended to use the language of interactions as a way to describe, explain, and critique the ways in which processes of differentiation dynamically function through one another and enable each other; they do not exist apart from one another" (Dhamoon 2011, 232). At the same time, she underscores its value for studying "how various oppressions work together to produce something unique and distinct from any one form of discrimination standing alone" (231).

22. The intent is not to collapse these notions, many of which account for intersectionality's influence in their genesis and vision (though, many authors inadequately distinguish the "new" frame from the "old," rely on static or reductive notions of intersectionality, or are so frustrated with simplistic interpretations of intersectionality that devising a more adequate term is seen as requisite). While space prohibits an in-depth discussion, there are extensive debates in the wider literature about these alternate frames or metaphors.
23. Building on Biddy Martin's (1996) questioning of how "femmes" get portrayed as duped as a means of imagining queer liberation and unfettered (and perhaps disembodied) futures, May and Ferri (2005) critique the use of this rhetorical strategy, particularly in ableist metaphors and language, in a wide range of feminist theoretical arguments: we contend that a more adequately intersectional analytic and politic would not rely on ableist imaginaries to animate its premises, or on notions that present embodiment as a "drag" on freedom to conjure a vision of liberation.
24. See, e.g., Bhavnani and Bywater (2009), Conaghan (2009), Hunter and de Simone (2009), Hutchinson (2000), Kwan (1997).
25. See Chang and Culp (2002), Carastathis (2008), Conaghan (2009), Cooper (2004, 2009), Garry (2011), Grabham (2009), Grabham et al. (2009), Grosz (1994), Yuval-Davis (2006).
26. See Choo and Ferree (2010), Hankivsky and Cormier (2011), Zambrana and Dill (2009).
27. E.g., Chang and Culp (2002), Conaghan (2007, 2009), Grabham (2009), Hornscheidt et al. (2009), Hutchinson (2000), Knapp (2011), Kwan (1997), Mehrotra (2012), Staunaes (2003).
28. While Conaghan traces the impact of law as a disciplinary practice and mindset, as a tradition and framework with discursive and political impact, this tale of intersectionality's 'roots' is only partially accurate: Crenshaw's "Demarginalizing," while taking up antidiscrimination legal doctrine, makes clear reference to Sojourner Truth and Anna Julia Cooper, neither of whom were legal scholars or practitioners (though both were subject to the law's terms of property and citizenship, as they were born enslaved). She also references nineteenth-century civil rights and feminist movements as sites of single-axis distortions and oversights: law was not the sole focus of the essay by any means.
29. See also Carastathis (2014) on the question of irreducibility.
30. I support Carbado's analysis but not his use of blindness. Though common legal terminology, it naturalizes ableism and able-bodiedness (as, in his words, a "normative baseline") to reveal other discriminatory/normative mindsets. For more on political and philosophical problems animated by ableist metaphors, see May and Ferri (2005) and Schalk (2013).
31. See Choo and Ferree (2010), Christensen and Jensen (2012), Hearn (2011), Nash (2008a), Yuval-Davis (2011a).
32. See Hemmings' (2011) discussion of return narratives and Ahmed's (2012) discussion of diversity in higher education for more analysis of rhetorics that present "difference" as grievous threat (to feminism and to the academy at large).
33. See Carastathis (2013a), Cohen (1997), Cole (2008), Mingus and Talley (2013), Spade (2013).
34. See Alarcón (1990), Carastathis (2013a), Cole (2008), Crenshaw (1989), Phoenix and Pattynama (2006), Tarver (2011), Taylor (2012)
35. Such a move serves to "attribute false uniformity" and aligns with neoliberal state ideals and norms (see Butler 1993, 116).
36. For a clear illustration of this racialized sex/gender distinction as part of the project of modernity, see Jennifer Morgan's (2004) historical/archival research.
37. See Babbitt (2001), Campbell (1999), Code (2011), Dotson (2011b), Fricker (2007), Mills (1997), Narayan (1997), Schutte (2000), Wylie (2011).

# 4
# Intersectionality—Now You See It, Now You Don't

## *Slippages in Intersectionality Applications*

The previous chapter examined how critics often dilute intersectionality via interpretive motifs that flatten its complex vision, analytic methods that draw on the very logics it identifies as fundamentally distorting, and discursive tactics that circumscribe its scope. Here, I attend to the politics of intersectionality's use and show that applications that drop intersectionality, even while employing it, are not uncommon. Practitioners can blunt its critical edge and transformative aims by moving away from a multilevel approach, delimiting it to the descriptive, or turning it into a version of pop-bead identity logics or single-axis notion of oppression. While the purpose may be to apply intersectionality meaningfully, the outcomes can be wanting.

In fact, intersectionality's analytical, epistemological, political, and normative possibilities are set aside in a variety of ways, as when researchers or policymakers render the concept deferential to hierarchy, align it with liberal individualism, or norm it to forms of reason it censures. For instance, applications may claim intersectionality but be devoid of context and structural analysis (Berger and Guidroz 2009), such that its call to address institutional biases and to work toward social transformation goes unheeded. Likewise, passing reference to intersectionality to invoke an abstract notion of "difference" performs an empty theatrics that do not lead to substantively changed outcomes (Gillman 2007; Puar, Pitcher, and Gunkel 2008; Ringrose 2007). Exhortations to "complexity" without substantive actualization in terms of methodological design, analytic approach, or political orientation do not suffice, but persist (as when intersectionality is rhetorically hailed while the work at hand continues as usual, unmodified and untransformed).[1]

Also common are analytic gestures wherein scholars engage intersectionality, but without much intellectual "vigor" or academic rigor (Bailey 2011; Bilge 2014; Bowleg 2014). Its usage also varies widely by discipline. For instance, it is "neglected" by philosophers overall and cannot be said to drive most Anglo-European philosophical inquiry, feminist or otherwise (Bailey 2010). It also can be "used in feminist educational spaces in ways that water down the approach and relativize, individualize, and liberalize issues of oppression and power" (Ringrose 2007, 265): this infuses intersectionality into the curriculum, but via principles of individualism and meritocracy (even as such notions run counter to its focus on institutionalized systems of oppression and its critique of meritocracy and individualism).

In policy contexts, intersectionality can be presented apolitically, as if to temper its critique of power relations or soften its social justice orientation. It emerges repackaged as amenable to neoliberal governance, useful for managing the status quo via an assimilationist (not transformational) impulse. Institutional and governmental actors may, in the name of intersectional reform, steer away from structural change and, instead, focus on ineffective, individual-focused 'diversity' measures as a means to rhetorically recognize, but not meaningfully address, discrimination (Squires 2008). In research, its heuristic capacity and political aims are likewise downplayed: it can seem to have no apparent analytic value or methodological role, other than a descriptive one (Hancock 2007b; Shields 2008). In particular, intersectional research studies and policy formulations continue to seek out "primary" sociopolitical relations or treat identities and forms of power as isolatable, though doing so uses single-axis logics and reinforces hierarchies of identity and oppression, ideas and values at odds with its emphasis on matrices of oppression, contextualization, relational power and privilege, and both/and thinking.

Operationalizing intersectionality can thus result in puzzling departures from its vision. It can be used without substantive focus on dismantling inequality and with little attention to simultaneity, interaction, and context. Many examples align it with established practices, while others animate it in ways that render it in service to furthering, rather than dismantling, exploitation and harm. The means of its adoption or operationalization can even attempt to commoditize and "whiten" intersectionality and to thereby render it amenable to neoliberal governance or neoliberal professionalized feminisms (Bilge 2013). Numerous intersectionality applications, in terms of processes, mechanisms, or outcomes, animate philosophies, politics, and strategies which intersectionality contests (e.g., single-axis logics, false universals, hierarchies of oppression, or difference as mere demographic descriptor [not as a site of structural power, ontological meaning, or epistemological insight]).[2]

More than merely misguided, such applications "disappear" intersectionality and render it unknowable (on intersectional terms). We must think more closely about what this "slipping" away from intersectionality might mean: how it is modeled and enacted, how it is (and is not) applied, and the terms of its validation (and invalidation) are important considerations. When used in ways that contravene its critiques of social hierarchies and ignore its challenges to divest of divisive logics, as when intersectionality is taken up as a means to *continue* patterns of silencing and delimiting Black women plaintiffs and reinforce unitary categories of identity (see Carastathis 2013b),[3] we must trace how it comes to be erroneously presented as supporting such outcomes. When applying intersectionality results, minimally, in its tokenization, or, maximally, in its antithesis, something is awry. If our collective goal is political, institutional and epistemological change, we must pinpoint how intersectionality can disappear, even when invoked as central, and think through how to change this dynamic. It is time to map out more fully how intersectionality is used in ways that, even if inadvertently, render it a helpmeet to dominance.

## Intersectionality Is Not Fail-Safe

Intent to achieve a more inclusive account of knowledge, or determination to dismantle systemic inequality across multiple fronts at once, cannot guarantee transformative outcomes. Social-justice origins and aims do not assure how, and in what contexts, intersectionality will be used. As Uma Narayan reminds us, with regard to the politics of knowledge and asymmetrical power relations, positive aims do not mean collusion with dominance is absent (Narayan 1997, 125). Crenshaw anticipates this early on, when discussing how antidiscrimination law's successes can be fleeting.[4] She describes "an ongoing ideological struggle in which the occasional winners harness the moral, coercive, and consensual power of law" and warns, "the victories it offers can be ephemeral and the risks of engagement substantial" (Crenshaw 1988, 1335). Even as intersectionality is ever more widely applied and crosses national, disciplinary, and political borders, it can also be (mis) used as a tool of epistemic hegemony.[5]

Such incongruities suggest sites of difficulty or contest: attention to lack of fit, and what it might signify, is pivotal to intersectionality's capacity to challenge the role erasure plays in perpetuating dominance. Seeking intersectional purity, or requiring a political guarantee in advance (or finding the absence of such a guarantee to signal an inherent failing), is not my point. Intersectionality is meant to be applied reflexively in an ongoing, contextual way, since power is elastic and institutions can shape-shift to incorporate, even weaken, challenges to their foundational premises. We must be able to discern among different kinds of intersectionality's "use" (and consider whether all applications are equally adequate), to identify instances of co-optation or distortion, and to recognize modes of application that reproduce harm or legitimate oppression.

For instance, Dorothy Roberts (2011) illustrates how the global pharmaceutical industry and the field of biogenetics employ language and concepts that seem intersectional, at least at the level of demographics. Yet, *how* they employ these notions matters. Quasi-intersectional ideas can be invoked to suggest meaningful methodological change, yet still reinforce acontexual and determinist arguments about health and genetic predisposition. Despite inclusive demographics, for instance, Roberts shows how research methods and medical aims may not account for systemic, cumulative effects of oppression on bodies and populations. The lived body as it is impacted by various factors (including environmental toxins, access to food and housing, impacts of stress and prejudice, and endemic violence), the politics and processes of different groups' medicalization, and norms of medical diagnosis, intervention, and cure can still be approached ahistorically. Power, as it imbricates the methods and resulting data, the medical gaze, and the body alike, can thus once again be framed as having no scientific relevance.

Looking at how intersectionality is being taken up across disciplinary, national, and intellectual terrains helps illuminate the prevalence of such "slippages" or departures. That these are frequent does not mean we should forego using intersectionality (or proclaim its impossibility, defer it to a future day, or declare it obsolete). Instead, we can identify how it comes to be rendered more "palatable" and then find ways to intervene in such distortions.

## Doing Intersectional Research, but Delimiting Intersectionality's Role

Intersectionality is increasingly claimed as central to research in the disciplines and interdisciplines, yet delimited in both scope and role.[6] Its analytical potential, coalitional justice orientation, and historical moorings are set aside in various ways. Rather than employed to guide research, shape theoretical questions, develop assertions, flesh out claims, problematize methodological norms, or interpret data, it is often used merely for descriptive aspects of a study or applied selectively in other ways, such that the research design undercuts key intersectional concepts, thwarts its analytical potential, and abandons its social justice orientation and roots. Intersectionality should be engaged at all levels of research, from initial conceptualization, through data/textual/archival collection and analysis, to drawing conclusions: however, multilevel applications remain less common.

This may be due, in part, to the fact that intersectionality is also distorted by established disciplinary norms: it can be assessed via a discipline-specific lens, then put outside the field's core practices and central parameters (leading to claims like, *That's not Psychology!* [Shields 2008], or, *That's not Philosophy!* [Bailey 2010]). Intersectionality may also be treated as a subspecialty, recognized but restricted.

Even then, it can slip away. For example, Catherine Harnois investigates "citation networks" to reveal disconnects between researchers' claims of interdisciplinarity in intersectionality research and their actual practices, which tend to be more bound by discipline than stated or intended. She contends adhering to disciplinary boundaries in "both methodological and theoretical approaches . . . limit[s] the possibility for a multiracial feminist approach" (Harnois 2013, 24–28). Intersectionality can be indirectly displaced in other ways as well, such as via "over-reliance on relatively homogenous [survey] samples" that one's disciplinary field may see as acceptable measures of social reality and as methodologically necessary for any viable (and publishable) study (38).

How intersectionality's history or origins are understood and introduced into an applied context can also be reductive, implying intersectionality has analytic promise, but only in certain eras or for certain identities, issues, or populations: moreover, its longer genealogy tends to be treated cursorily.[7] Timelines can present it simply as recent or trace its origins without meaningfully engaging Black and women of color feminisms. Chela Sandoval (2000) and Benita Roth (2004), for example, show how the "waves" motif of feminist historical periodization may present concepts such as intersectionality as "later" and primarily reactive formulations, reflecting an unstated white norm for mapping out feminism's historical trajectory and iterations. This erases intersectionality's history, obscures multiple feminisms, and reinforces common-denominator gender-first narratives of feminist thought and action (Frankenberg and Mani 1993; Ringrose 2007; Rowe 2000). Today, the window of relevance for intersectionality is sometimes even further delimited by chronologies that posit it as *both* a "late" arrival to feminist theorizing *and* as already passé (Ahmed 2012; Hemmings 2011).

"Absorption" strategies are another practice to consider: intersectionality is frequently folded into established intellectual trajectories. Mapping out multiple discourse communities is important: however, blending intersectionality into more recognized historical and intellectual genealogies, as a way to legitimize it or translate it, can perform a kind of epistemic (and political) disappearing act. For instance,

McCall describes how "writings by feminists of color . . . [are] often assimilated into and then associated with the writings of feminist poststructuralists" (McCall 2005, 1776). Specifically, its history can be traced in ways that pivot focus away from Black feminist contributions and whiten the concept (Bilge 2013; Lewis 2013; Tomlinson 2013a). Consider Conaghan's (2009) mapping of socialist feminism and intersectionality's origins, or Nina Lykke's crediting Judith Butler, in a variety of ways, for the development of intersectionality theory (Lykke 2010, 2011). Lykke (2010, 128) also names Thomas Kuhn (1962) and Paul Feyerabend (1975) as developing analytical premises (e.g., the interconnectedness of context and knower) that could as easily be traced to Anna Julia Cooper in the nineteenth century, for instance, or to Black feminist contemporaries of Kuhn and Feyerabend.[8]

Another means of restricting intersectionality's role is via consignment to pretheoretical realms (Dill and Zambrana 2009), mirroring long-standing practices of treating theorizing by women of color as experientially rich but philosophically meager (hooks 1989; Zinn et al. 1986). Conceiving of intersectionality in this way cannot capture the qualitatively different knowledge crafted at the intersections that it highlights and draws from. Here, Uma Narayan's discussion of how Western feminist theories are understood to have normative aims, whereas "third world" feminist analyses are relegated to enriching or contextualizing existing frames of reference, is useful. She writes, "The goal of a feminist politics is seldom merely to come to a refined and sensitive understanding of various points of view held by those immediately affected by an issue. In the broadest sense, feminist political projects involve commitments to normative and political inquiry, which calls for questioning, assessing, analyzing, and criticizing various points of view" (Narayan 1997, 151). Likewise, intersectionality is not always granted a full range of theoretical and political possibilities. As Crenshaw has had to reiterate, her notion of intersectionality, as first discussed in 1989, "was not simply a descriptive account of the marginalization of certain claims but a normative argument for reversing the dominant conceptions of discrimination—especially the paradigm of sameness and difference—that underwrites them" (Crenshaw 2011c, 229).

What delimitation to the descriptive looks like certainly varies by methodological and disciplinary standard. It can arise in distinctions between the experiential and analytical (e.g., by adhering to fact/value divides[9]) or in equating intersectionality with demographic diversity but not much more. Though intersectionality is widely "construed in terms of multiple group memberships," this can also curtail its analytic potential, meaning "its emergent properties and processes escape attention" (Shields 2008, 304). In both policy and research, intersectionality can also be cordoned off from "political practice and socio-economic context by translating it into a merely theoretical abstraction of slipping signifiers of identity" (Erel et al. 2011, 66). Restricting intersectionality to description or demography is a form of epistemological dismissal that must be considered more fully.[10]

Furthermore, though frequently used in research and policy focused on identity, marginalization, and social inequality, intersectionality is usually still applied primarily to those identities "marked" as different, marginalized, or subordinated. Applications tend to concentrate "on outsider or marginalized groups without analyzing the relationship to and with 'unmarked categories' (i.e., privileged or dominant groups)" and with no genealogical tracing of "the power relations that create these processes [of inequality]" (Choo and Ferree 2010, 137). This, ironically, repeats several violations intersectionality contests. The relevance of (and ability to analyze) simultaneous privilege and oppression slips away. Within-group differences are obscured. Structural privilege and transparency also go unremarked—though upholding transparency buttresses the systemic inequality under analysis. In short, status quo social relations, categories, logics, and processes are not really questioned or challenged.

It should go without saying that inclusion of multiple demographics is not synonymous with intersectionality research. Asking "additive" questions about demographic difference is also inadequate, since key "dimensions of experience," including "meaningful constructs such as stress, prejudice, [and] discrimination," are ignored (Bowleg 2008, 316): macropolitical dynamics and asymmetrical power relations are positioned as beyond the scope of research. Leaving out background contexts is another methodological and political problem, as is portraying intersectional analysis as divorced from social transformation, despite its roots in liberation politics (Jordan-Zachery 2007). Presenting intersectionality as disassociated from contesting structural injustice also obliterates its focus on how social location impacts one's experience of the social world, shapes what is known and understood about inequality, and plays a role in how one's knowledge may (or may not) be heard or understood.

Equating intersectionality with diversity or description is more than simply reductive: it can actively buttress the logics of domination. In the contexts of queer activism, for example, Kevin Duong describes how a "descriptive intersectionality" that only "conceptualizes collective identity, such as queer, as constituted [merely] on the basis of a [given] demographic characteristic ('deviant' sexual orientation)," treats the normative group, its views of other groups, and the "representational status quo uncritically." Furthermore, a descriptive approach ignores how, when "queer activists and theorists identify as such, they are also. . . . enacting a queer commons and public" (Duong 2012, 378–382). Descriptive intersectionality models omit intersectionality's contestatory logics and coalition politics, rendering them invisible and irrelevant. Furthermore, identity categories or group descriptors are not just "there": they are constructs with political, social, and experiential histories of lived impact and socio-political enforcement. They are also highly regulated and managed by the state, for example (Crenshaw 1989; Spade 2013).

In examining the vexed question of how to decolonize research methodologies, Linda Tuhiwai Smith therefore underscores that demography can replicate settler-colonial state logics and enact epistemological violence with regard to Indigenous peoples' long contestation of coloniality's "truths" and categories. Such orientations also overlook key issues, like sovereignty (L. Smith 2012, 209). Demographic categories, statistical models, and outcomes should thus be understood as rooted in processes of colonization.[11] These insights help to illuminate the importance of intersectionality's skepticism with regard to single-axis politics and universalized categories: uncritical acceptance of the state's logics, even in seemingly innocuous sites (e.g., relying on large scale data sets or common demographic categories), can reinforce coloniality.

Additionally, Liat Ben-Moshe demonstrates that entire groups can be wholly disregarded by relying on given demographic categories and default explanatory frames. In thinking about incarceration, people with disabilities, and different forms of institutionalization (many of which have not been categorized as imprisonment), she reframes what counts as incarceration and who counts as incarcerated. The containment of people with disabilities (in nursing facilities and medical institutions) is conventionally excluded from definitions of incarceration: ableist norms and ideologies are also overlooked in many analyses of carceral rationales. The resulting data distort, as do the categories of prison and prisoner. People with disabilities are obliterated as having experienced incarceration and as having resisted state-sanctioned detention and containment. Such distortions have implications for researchers and intersectional justice movements, like the prison abolition movement: if we rely on given definitions of prisons and available prison population data, inclusive carceral justice slips away (Ben-Moshe 2013, 290–293).

### Policy Applications of Intersectionality: Dismantling or Reinforcing Inequality?

Not only has intersectionality "found a place in the intellectual toolkit of scholars [and activists] around the world," it is also being "used to interrogate problems and policy issues" in regional, national, and transnational contexts (Bose 2012, 67). Yet, although it is being taken up in many policy applications, it is often applied in ways that reduce it to an anodyne notion of diversity or that downplay race and racism. For example, in her study of poverty and employment interventions used by the New Jersey Department of Labor and Workforce Development (NJDLWD) to address economic insecurity, Mary Gatta explores how "job training policy can be re-conceptualized by attending to the intersectionality of women's identities in order to provide real access to education and training to low-wage working women" (Gatta 2009, 101). Approaching intersectionality as a structural and experiential lens and as a change-oriented analytic, Gatta highlights asymmetrical life chances of living in poverty (107) and underscores that these are structural questions that require significant social change (they are not accidental issues or "personal failings") (103).

Yet in a section titled "An Important Note on Race," she reveals the "intersectional approach" taken by the NJDLWD treated "race as a given" (Gatta 2009, 116) in part because this was a "gender-based intervention." Gatta maintains "women" were not treated as a homogenous group (in that "gender, class, and marital status" were accounted for—though whether they were approached as intermeshing and relational is not clear): however, "race" seems to have been conflated with "class" as an indicator for likelihood to experience poverty, which means gendered and classed inequalities in the labor market and in educational access having to do with racism, sexuality, or citizenship status were not addressed by these policies (or by this study).

Using a diverse demographic is not, on its own merits, adequate—and intersectionality is not only about 'identity': what remains unasked (and unanswered) is, how can the goal of "real access to education and training" be attained if racism is left off the table in "intersectional" gender policy (and in research about such policy)? Furthermore, what does it mean to conflate "race" with "poverty" within the category "class"—to use "class" to make race disappear, even as gender and marital status come forward as salient structural and personal factors? While Gatta urges that future programs account for race in more meaningful ways, more needs to be said about how and why race was taken as a "given" and thus was not analyzed as meaningful or impactful, other than as an indictor for poverty—'race' here also stands in for non-whiteness, meaning whiteness' transparency was also taken for granted.

Beyond U.S. contexts, intersectionality is increasingly being used in NGO, state, and supranational contexts to address inequality via policy formation and law reform. For instance, it served as a crucial lens at the 2001 World Conference against Racism (Blackwell and Naber 2002; Falcón 2012; Yuval-Davis 2006). The South African Constitution (1996) also formally recognizes an intersectional approach to rights and redress in its equality clause.[12] Supranational organizations, including the United Nations (UN) and the European Union (EU), have begun to understand the need to account for interlocking forms of oppression. The UN thus has a "Special Rapporteur on Violence against Women," and some have used this position to apply intersectionality contextually.[13] In 2011, Rashida Manjoo issued a report on intersectional discrimination and violence emphasizing indivisibility of oppressions, within-group differences among women, and structural dynamics.[14] A decade prior, Radhika Coomaraswamy, in preparation for the World Conference against Racism, employed intersectionality to challenge the UN's tendency to compartmentalize forms of discrimination via an either/or race versus gender lens (Coomaraswamy 2001).

In the Americas, intersectionality is also being widely applied. For example, Canadian human rights law references intersectionality with the aim of recognizing interacting forms of inequality (Aylward 2010; Froc 2010); it is also being used as a policy instrument, particularly to improve national and provincial health policies.[15] In Mexico, the Zapatista movement's radical advocacy for "plural paths" illustrates how intersectionality can offer a contextually-specific social justice methodology attendant to multiplicity (Diaz, Mane, and González 2013, 98). In Uruguay, fostering intersectional community consciousness has been identified as a key strategy for change (Townsend-Bell 2011), while in Brazil, it is being applied as a regional, cross-border advocacy tactic: Afro-Brazilian activists use an intersectional approach, within the nation-state and transnationally, to address patterns of inequality in health and to fight for reproductive justice (Caldwell 2009; Franklin 2013). A report by the Central American Women's Network (CAWN) on macrolevel and microlevel forms of violence likewise stresses intersectionality's value for working across national borders (Cabrera 2010) because "multiple macro-level structures, like economic neoliberalism, politics, and patriarchy, operate at a regional and national level and are linked to the micro-level of local economic, social, sexual, or cultural forms of violence against women and women's poverty" (Bose 2012, 70).

Across the Americas, then, community organizers and grassroots activists have drawn on intersectionality in a multiscalar way in antiviolence advocacy, Indigenous sovereignty movements, transnational queer justice movements, workers' rights and immigration rights organizing, disability rights, and reproductive justice struggles.[16] However, to safeguard against intersectionality being imposed as a kind of compulsory colonialist feminist import, being accountable to the concept's social justice origins, resistant imaginary, and context-specific practical orientation, suggests Julia Roth, is pivotal. Intersectionality can continue to have radical potential by "contextualizing and decolonizing the discourse on intersectionality for researching interdependent inequalities in Latin America, rather than doing away with the concept as 'Eurocentric'" (Roth 2013, 15). Bringing decolonial and intersectional feminist frames and politics together is thus imperative (see Lugones 2010), particularly as, from Indigenous feminist perspectives, intersectionality can (and has) been used to further settler-colonialist legacies of violence (Williams 2009).

Because of the potential to use intersectionality to further coloniality, we must continually examine how it is applied, and to what ends. In the EU, for instance, there is need for a healthy skepticism about state engagements with intersectionality politics. Multipronged approaches to addressing inequality have expanded since Article 13 of the 1997 Treaty of Amsterdam, which provides grounds to address six areas of discrimination (sex/gender, race/ethnicity, religion/belief, age, disability, and sexual orientation) individually and across categories.[17] In the United Kingdom, public institutions have been charged (e.g., in the 2008 Single Equality Bill, granted Royal Assent in 2010) with devising a single equity policy that encompasses myriad forms of discrimination rather than separate policies for "separate" identities.[18] Given its utility for thinking across multiple categories, intersectionality has been lauded for its potential to reframe gender equity policies away from false universals that present gender in opposition to race or that treat gender as atomized and primary.[19] Yet many European policies continue to be nonintersectional: some employ a "'one size fits all' approach" and collapse all forms of discrimination together (Verloo 2006), while others take up, rather than contest, single-axis categorical logics.

For instance, Judith Squires (2008) and Leah Bassel and Akwugo Emejulu (2010) contend that the United Kingdom's single equality model has further reinforced atomized, individualized modes of redress rather than led to intersectional ones. In France, Bassel and Emejulu find a persistent "logic of separation," wherein issues of gender discrimination are separated from those of *intégration* in relation to minority groups. Thus "minority religious groups, and in particular Muslim women who wear the *foulard* (or headscarf), are . . . unable to make intersecting claims for social justice while participating in a republican model of citizenship that does not recognize difference" (Bassel and Emejulu 2010, 540). Invoking intersectionality to endorse assimilation is widespread, both in immigration and marriage reform. Analysis of recent LGBT gender and marriage laws in Spain shows how state-level approaches to intersectionality can "lack a multiple discrimination perspective" and lean toward assimilation, "intended to include . . . citizens previously discriminated on the basis of belonging to a sexual minority, rather than attempting to transform the social construction [and lived realities] of sexuality itself" (Platero 2008, 48). Many citizenship models and equity policies thus "reinstate sameness as a necessary ground of belonging" or even recognition (Gedalof 2012, 3). Though it critiques assimilative logics because they serve to reinforce (not contest) status quo hierarchies and exclusions, uses of intersectionality as amenable to assimilationist paradigms are common.

The affective and epistemological politics at work in state-level equity enterprises can therefore have a peculiar, even perverted quality, by rationalizing state-sanctioned racism in the name of equity, particularly in the name of gender equity (Gianettoni and Roux 2010; Siim 2013). In many EU member states, gender equity continues to be separated from (even pitted against) migrant and ethnic rights issues. Single-axis models of personhood and rights persist, whether by reinforcing competing group identities in a hierarchy via a multiple (but separate) oppressions approach, or by reverting to gender-primary models (with other factors posited as subsets of "gender"). By creating a "false dilemma" between race and gender equity (Delphy 2006), single-axis, gender-first feminisms replicate a political, ontological, and philosophical violation that intersectionality questions: that those who have the greatest resources within any particular group not only are erroneously seen to represent the group at large, but also tend to speciously claim the universal and the right to set the groups' political agenda (Crenshaw 1989).

This contravenes intersectional aims by replicating stratification processes and enforcing "secondary marginalization" (Cohen 1999), wherein the most elite members of a community articulate their legitimacy, advance their goals, and further their privileges by marginalizing and stigmatizing other community members. In particular, as Hemmings explains,

> the use of gender equality as a marker of an economic and regulatory modernity marks the subject of gender equality as Western, capitalist, and democratic and the West, capitalism, and democracy themselves as sites that create the possibility of, and reproduce, rather than hinder, gender equality. Critically, they position the objects of gender equality as non-Western or post-socialist, . . . as creating and perpetuating traditional gender inequalities not part of the modern world. A gender agenda is thus consistently harnessed to cultural or economic difference from Western subjects and sites. (Hemmings 2011, 9)

Though at face value deployed to acknowledge multiplicity and institute equity, gender-first policy models can tie into a series of anti-intersectional and colonialist distinctions among women, dividing the modern/non-modern, Western/non-Western, White/non-White. As Bilge underscores, there is a "problematic persistence of a gender-first approach to discrimination in governance feminism . . . [that] pushes [single-axis] feminist agendas within states, human rights establishments and supranational organisations" (Bilge 2010, 11).

Thus "governance feminism" (Bilge 2010), though invoking intersectional concepts and aims, can buttress systemic racism via rhetorics of "extraordinary" sexism attributed to racialized communities, who are then posited as a threat to the nation and to gender-equity (Delphy 2006). In this vein, Lavinia Gianettoni and Patricia Roux analyze contemporary debates in Switzerland to show how such attribution of (greater and intrinsic) sexism to racialized/immigrant Others[20] functions as a rationale for "protecting" the nation and, ostensibly, "gender" equality therein. Sexism already operative in the nation is obscured by means of a pathologizing lens that treats immigrants as a menace. In short, "denunciation of the sexism of the Other does not automatically reflect a feminist position": it can reinforce racist-sexist notions of deviance and "extraordinary" sexism and naturalize everyday "ordinary" sexism (Gianettoni and Roux 2010, 283).

Furthermore, as Hege Skjeiea and Trude Langvasbråten discuss with regard to Norway, while cases of multiple discrimination are beginning to be acknowledged, an intersectional model of multiplicity has not (yet) been realized. Instead, the lens being used "describes discrimination on the basis of several grounds that are/can be treated as additive" (Skjeiea and Langvasbråten 2009, 515): single-axis forms of antidiscrimination legislation and policy prevail (520). Likewise, in the United Kingdom, though "equality advocates—especially gender equality advocates—supported the creation of a single equality body, believing it to offer significant scope for institutionalizing intersectionality," Judith Squires finds "the existence of a single [equality] body does little to address cumulative and combined inequalities (while operating with separate strand anti-discrimination legislation)" (Squires 2009, 503, 498). Bassel and Emejulu concur: "institutional processes and actors characterize these multiple sources of inequality as independent and unconnected social phenomena, impeding policy that recognizes and combats the simultaneous and interacting sources of discrimination that shape the lives of minority women and men" (Bassel and Emejulu 2010, 518).

While many EU states aim to conform with Article 13 mandates, and while there is a push to infuse multiple discrimination and intersectional approaches into the EU's Gender Equity Index (GEI), for instance, many such efforts remain orientated toward pitting "diversity" strategies against gender mainstreaming (Bustelo 2009), using gender equity both as a marker of national belonging and as an us/them border-patrolling device (predicated on whiteness) (Siim 2013).[21] Policy formulations (e.g., for gender equity) that interpret intersectionality as amenable to singular (racist) logics "whiten" intersectionality (Bilge 2013), willfully ignore years of scholarship about and activism around migrant women and migrant feminisms across Europe, disregard decades of work by Black feminists (Yuval-Davis

2006), and dismiss foundational intersectionality literatures and the political struggles that shaped them.

Intersectionality *contests* antidiscrimination practices that reproduce conditions of racial domination and perpetuate nationalist structures of inequality. However, either/or race versus gender logics continue via a twin dynamic of saturation and disavowal: as Gail Lewis contends, "even while elite and popular discourses across Europe are saturated with processes of racialization, there is a disavowal of the relevance and toxicity of the social relations of race as a pan-European phenomenon, with a corresponding displacement of its relevance" (Lewis 2013, 870). In other words, "hierarchical racial orderings continue to be reproduced, even where anti-racist feminist scholarship is brought in as a tool for dealing with racial inequality" (Gillman 2007, 136). Intersectionality is thus sometimes being used to reify the logics of separation, hierarchy, and false universals it contests. State-level applications may apply intersectionality in ways that could *augment* rather than contest the state's inclination for classifying and categorizing citizens (and noncitizens), thereby facilitating population surveillance, control, and containment. In intersectionality's name, scopic regimes of state power expand via "anatomies of detail" that normalize the law's disciplinary constructions of identity and rationalize surveillance of citizens (and noncitizens) (Grabham 2009, 183).

Unease about state-level intersectionality applications can be found in the Canadian context as well. Kerri Froc finds the "failure of the Supreme Court of Canada to give more than lip service to 'context' when considering claims under s. 15 of the Canadian Charter of Rights and Freedoms arises largely from the Court's prevailing analytic framework, which resists recognizing the social relations of power inherent in complex cases of oppression" (Froc 2010, 48). Given intersectionality's call to not misconstrue discrimination by artificially parsing interlocking forms of power and inequality, many advocate that it be further institutionalized in Canadian law, not ignored (Aylward 2010): indeed, intersectionality has begun to be overtly recognized (and employed) by the courts at provincial and federal levels.[22]

Yet many Indigenous feminists are wary of state-level intersectionality endeavors (due in part to an a priori skepticism, if not rejection, of the nation state in the first place). The state often implements practices that reinforce settler-colonial logics, legitimize ongoing inequality, and naturalize mistreatment and harm (INCITE 2007). Jennifer Hamilton analyses an array of court cases, in Canada and the United States, that "rely on reductive pluralist discourses of indigineity to continue to manage and even deny the existence of a colonial past and a [neocolonial] present" (Hamilton 2009, 5). Native populations and politics are folded into the state's multicultural, assimilative logics of ethnicity, erasing Native sovereignty struggles and centuries of contesting Enlightenment notions of personhood and property (Clark 2012; Smith 2005b).

Toni Williams is thus highly skeptical of "an overly instrumental stream of policy research . . . which purports to use intersectionality strategically to change how law and social policy affect members of marginalized groups" (Williams 2009, 81). She has particular qualms about whether Canadian courts can apply intersectionality without turning it into a tool of settler nationalism, applied in the name of "protecting" Native women while strengthening carceral and colonial logics. Williams examines uses of intersectionality in federal judicial sentencing decisions with regard to Native women (since 1996 changes in sentencing law, including s.718.2 (e) of the Criminal Code). She shows how courts have: reinforced settler colonial logics, relied on pathologizing discourses about Native communities that mask ongoing forms of coloniality and inequality structures, and *increased* Native women's incarceration rates, though using intersectionality in these decisions was supposed to address, not exacerbate, these issues.[23]

Paradoxically, applying intersectionality (in interaction with legal discourses on "salience of risk to penalization") has heightened "faith in imprisonment as the appropriate response to offences committed by Aboriginal women" (Williams 2009, 80). Instrumentalizing intersectionality (in, I would argue, a *nonintersectional* manner) can reinforce oppressive stereotypes about Indigenous women, erase the ongoing impact of colonial domination, and justify their incarceration as salvific. Problematically, the court absents from sentencing decisions political and historical contexts having to do with the role the court has played (as an arm of the settler state) in perpetuating oppression of Native peoples and in buttressing white supremacy. The judiciary is encouraged to "contextualize" sentencing via a unidirectional, pathologizing gaze at Native culture: settler colonialism and its legacy in the Canadian state's assimilationism, containment, and carceral practices are positioned as beyond the scope of relevance (86–94). The courts treat as (immaterial) background "social and economic relations and the legal regimes that maintain the subordination of Aboriginal Peoples in Canada" (95).

By applying intersectionality unidirectionally, in ways that ignore coloniality and institutionalized oppression and privilege, the courts adhere to "a simple narrative that constructs Aboriginal families as incubators of risk, Aboriginal communities as containers of risk and the prison as a potential source of healing" (Williams 2009, 95). Instead, Williams advocates that intersectionality be used to advocate for prison abolition and to address settler-colonialist legacies of harm and violence (96; see also Davis 2003, 2005; Spade 2013; Smith 2005a, 2005b).

### Intersectionality's Institutionalization in Academia

Just as policy applications of intersectionality can become sites of its displacement, many scholars committed to intersectionality's antisubordination politics and practices worry about its increasing institutionalization in the academy: is it being adopted as an empty managerial rhetoric to reinforce the status quo rather than contest it? Certainly, intersectionality *can* be implemented in ways that constitute a significant departure from (if not total distortion of) its terms, intents, and goals, particularly its role in the entrepreneurial university, where efficiency and profit are at the forefront of many discussions and decisions, and where the push to instrumentalize knowledge is ever stronger. At the same time, I do not want to engage in a tale of intersectionality's inescapable devolution and dissolution, as if to suggest its growth or institutionalization in the academy inevitably signals "selling out."

Certainly, the contemporary educational climate well illustrates how insurgent practices can be co-opted into organizational servicing of the status quo (Ferguson 2012) and aligned with problematic metrics of "value" and "excellence."[24] Marketizing education (whether in K–12 schooling or in the neoliberal university) devalues students and educators as knowers, decontextualizes learning, draws attention away from exacerbated and ongoing economic inequality, and downplays the profit-making aspects embedded in most assessment and curriculum mandates. In the U.S. context, via austerity measures and alarmist tales of spiraling debt, pressure to resolve the current financial crisis has also been placed squarely on the shoulders of public schools and non-profit institutions of higher education (not the for-profit financial institutions who caused, in great part, this crisis—and who were rescued thanks to public funds, showing the degree to which the public good has been redefined as market-based).

Furthermore, if one's understanding of the academy, and its role in producing, disseminating, and archiving knowledge, already accounts for the historical workings of power (e.g., colonialism, misogyny, imperialism, patriarchy, and slavery, as these systems were crafted within and alongside capitalism), the market's relationship to knowledge, to education as a practice, and to the university as an institution is nothing "new." Certainly, this may well have become more visible to a wider audience, as the impact of various economic forces spreads to impact groups who, previously, have been relatively shielded from or had the privilege of ignoring them. Furthermore, long-standing partnerships between the university and the market are taking new forms.

However, intersectionality has never presumed knowledge practices or institutions to be neutral or set apart from structural inequality. Rather, it aims to expose how power asymmetries and structural disparity get perpetuated, even in sites where this should not, at face value, be the case (e.g., antidiscrimination doctrine's reliance on privilege and inequality). As Harnois explains, intersectionality helps expose how "'knowledge' is structured by inequalities of race, gender, and class. It is not simply that some voices are given more credibility or legitimacy than others, but that some groups have had more access to the resources (e.g., academic credentials, time, administrative support, sabbaticals, work-related benefits, and money) required to produce 'academically legitimate' knowledge" (Harnois 2013, 21). Since knowledge production, dissemination, and access to education itself have long been tied to the making and maintenance of inequality, the academy is a necessary site of intervention. Many of us located *in* universities are not fully *of* their logics. We should neither devalue struggles in the academy to enact change nor assume that transformation is "won" and done: intersectionality insists on this both/and mindset—change is possible and can quickly be undermined.

It is in this vein that we can draw on the possibilities intersectionality offers for meaningful intervention (e.g., Spade 2012) and simultaneously raise concerns about the roles it is being asked to play (e.g., Ferguson 2012; Puar 2007, 2012b). Nelson Maldonado-Torres' discussion of the structural containment of ethnic studies is illustrative of these joint considerations. Echoing facile depictions of intersectionality as a naïve identity-based impetus, which dehistoricize and flatten, he explains how ethnic studies came to be characterized, and institutionally structured, as "a matter of re-presentation within the framework of area studies, not one of decolonization or epistemic justice. The liberal university subsumed these programs into its logic, seeing them as not much more than containing measures to address social demands having to do with diversity, and then, after defining them in such limited way, faulted them for allegedly being too essentialistic" and provincial (Maldonado-Torres 2011, 4). Likewise, there is concern that intersectionality is being used simply to contend with diversity in an ornamental way, in terms of how particular fields apply the concept and in how university leadership takes up intersectionality to "manage" sociopolitical difference, rather than enact structural change.

Sara Ahmed's analysis of diversity initiatives in U.K. universities is also illuminating: she shows how documents publicly committing institutions to equality and diversity, which build on and are the result of a long history of activism and radical scholarship by people of color, function by "not bringing about the effects [of diversity and equality] they name" (Ahmed 2007, 105; see also Ferguson 2012). There is a fundamental departure from counterhegemonic practice toward shoring up (the same old forms of) privilege. Whether by owning up to "being racist," or by positing the institution as an individual subject who "suffers from prejudice but who can be treated," both the individual and the institution can be let off the hook (Ahmed 2007, 107).[25] "Admitting" to its racism, an institution can pronounce its non-racism; likewise, by individualizing the institution as the racist subject, individual persons need not account for their privileges or address their own practices.

Via rhetorics of change and accountability, or via confessions of culpability, conferred privilege can be reinforced. Theories and language from communities of struggle are thus often institutionalized in the service of whiteness (as well as masculinity, heteronormativity, ableism, and elite class interests), while the actual bodies, material conditions, political analyses, and theoretical insights of marginalized and subjugated communities are further silenced. Speech acts that appear inclusive "conceal the ongoing reality of racism" (Ahmed 2007, 110). In an "audit culture" of performance indicators used to "measure" diversity and inclusion, intersectionality can be used as a form of credentialing to bolster an institution's reputation such that managing perceptions of "good" image becomes the only tangible outcome (115). Building on Kelly Coogan-Gehr's (2011) analysis of "thresholds of disappearance" in feminist scholarship, Mohanty thus emphasizes how intersectionality can be emptied of its social transformation aims and "disconnected from its materialist moorings" to be made amenable to institutional settings, including educational ones. It can "become a commodity to be consumed; no longer seen as a product of activist scholarship or connected to emancipatory knowledge, it can circulate as a sign of prestige in an elitist, neoliberal landscape" (Mohanty 2013, 971). She is also mindful of how intersectionality's "epistemological and methodological claims" can be altered, aligned with a "privatized politics of representation, disconnected from systematic critique and materialist histories of colonialism, capitalism, and heteropatriarchy" (Mohanty 2013, 972).

As intersectionality becomes more widely adopted in academia, the risk is that its analytical and political aspects will be dropped. While some forms of leveraging intersectionality to maintain, rather than transform, social and epistemic inequalities are fairly overt, intersectional work is also stymied by a host of less explicit, but no less damaging, obstacles in the academy. Many established knowledge conventions present an impediment. Theoretical complexity and methodological multiplicity are still often treated with circumspection. Likewise, approaches overtly embracing the relevance of social location to knowledge production, both with regard to analyzing multiple systems of power and to working across disciplinary and methodological bounds, continue to confront suspicion.

It thus remains relatively difficult to get intersectional studies published and funded (McCall 2005): the size and complexity of such work can still be perceived as excessive and unmanageable, even impossible or unsound (see Shields 2008). In addition, many large-scale data sets, widely used to measure and analyze inequality (e.g., in the United States, the Schedule of Sexist Events [SSE], the Index of Race-Related Stress [IRRS], and the General Social Survey [GSS]) fundamentally adhere to single-axis and homogenizing logics, as I discuss in more detail later (see Harnois 2013). Methodological norms can also run counter to intersectional aims (e.g., emphases on demography, variance frameworks, generalizability, testing for main effects, comparative analysis, and more).[26] Most journals and funding agencies remain committed to traditional modes of (disciplinary) research, single-identity (or one factor as primary) analyses (and data), and thus to the kinds of incremental change, "special issue" tokenism, or tinkering within set patterns that do not allow for intersectionality to have meaningful impact.

However, there are "important historical reasons" why concepts like intersectionality, which "emerged from the situated, subjective experience of people who experienced multiple forms of mutually-constituting oppressions," are deeply interdisciplinary (Shotwell 2010, 119). As Sarah Hoagland underscores, "Disciplinary structures created during the four centuries of Ibero-Anglo-European colonization structure Western academic relationality and imagination today, including white and hegemonic feminism" (Hoagland 2010, 235). It is not a fluke, in other words, that when one looks at the longer genealogy of intersectional work, one can find a deep commitment not only to cross-categorical thinking in terms of identity and structures of power, but also to interdisciplinary frames and hybrid ways of knowing.

Regrettably, disciplinarity often continues to be "a hindrance to the radical border-crossing thinking intersectionality requires. Creative thinking about subjectivity and inequity in an era increasingly marked by contingent, shifting, hybrid identities necessitates scholarly exchanges across the at-times heavily policed disciplinary borders that shape the contemporary university" (Nash 2009, 593). This can leave intersectionality in an epistemological and political catch-22. Cho, Crenshaw, and McCall explain, "The institutional gravity that pulls the attention of practitioners in their respective disciplines may lead others outside the field to misrecognize or misinterpret intersectional methodologies, or to infer an absence of method altogether. At the same time, efforts to 'discipline' intersectionality within established research practice can sometimes proceed along lines that suggest that its insurgent dimensions constitute an unruliness that undermines its utility and future development" (Cho, Crenshaw, and McCall 2013, 793).

Intersectionality also can be "checked" or cordoned off in curricula—viewed as having limited relevance or framed as a narrow specialization, rather than used to problematize and transform a field's core concepts, analytics, methods, and curricular aims. Alternatively, intersectionality can be widely referenced, even celebrated, but engaged superficially. In women's studies, for example, this can allow narratives of gender oppression based on patriarchy to continue.[27] Many accepted academic practices lend themselves to using intersectionality merely as "a way to manage difference," reinforce "liberal multiculturalism," and reposition white women as the field's center (Puar 2012b, 53). In addition, while transnational feminist analytics and intersectionality are not collapsible, they can be approached, fruitfully, as "heterogeneous, irreducible, and related" (Desai, Bouchard, and Detournay 2010, 49). Unfortunately, these epistemological/political commitments are often treated as opposed or in competition, creating a false divide between the transnational and the intersectional[28] that erases longtime critiques of imperialism, capitalism, and structural underdevelopment in Black feminist and women of color theoretical and political traditions.

Intersectionality's curricular delimitation and dilution is not unique to women's studies, of course. Jennifer Puentes and Matthew

Gougherty, building on research by Myra Marx Ferree and Elaine J. Hall (1996), surveyed more recent introductory sociology textbooks and syllabi. They were interested in how Ferree and Hall had documented that "segregating gender, race, and class to different levels of analysis gives a distorted view of stratification processes and reduces gender to personality, class to structure, and race somewhere in between. Furthermore, this resulted in no attempts to discuss intersectionality" (Puentes and Gougherty 2013, 160). A decade later, Puentes and Gougherty found striking similarities in how "different dimensions of stratification" are introduced: the "continued confinement of gender to socialization, race to group relations, and class to macro-level comparisons would suggest that distributional models are still being used to explain inequality across these various dimensions." Though "discussions of intersectionality would provide evidence of a more relational understanding of race, class, and gender, where one system of privilege and oppression could not be understood without the others," intersectional approaches tend to be stymied by sociology's approaches to teaching and studying stratification (Puentes and Gougherty 2013, 160). In short, while intersectionality is widely referenced, how sociology's basic precepts are framed in these texts continues to undermine intersectionality's analytical and sociological relevance.

### Persistent "Pop-Bead" Logics: Instrumentalizing Intersectionality as a Single-Axis Strategy

Thus far, I have aimed to shed light on the highly variable, sometimes counterintuitive ways intersectionality is being taken up and the different means by which it is delimited or dropped (beyond one disciplinary location, discourse community, or geopolitical context). In rendering these patterns visible, I want to take up the question of how to take up intersectionality differently. But first, it is imperative to explore a key problem found across applications: *falling into pop-bead logics in the name of doing intersectional work.* Intersectionality is a heuristic aimed at intervening in exclusion by design (whether that design is institutional, epistemological, ontological, historical, political, etc.). However, if, as it becomes implemented, the operative logics contradict intersectionality and reinforce the enduring asymmetries it has contested, then we must question these emergent patterns. Since intersectionality is often instrumentalized as if it were a single-axis analytic (despite its deep critique of the ontological, epistemological, and political harm embedded in such thinking), the remainder of this chapter focuses on this confounding issue.

I begin by discussing intersectionality applications that do engage multiple identity factors and power formations, but in noninteractive ways that reinforce binary logics: they approach identity, power, inequality, and knowledge as atomized. This dynamic might be named "X vs. Y" models of identity and inequality (e.g., gender vs. ethnicity): they approach group categories as analogous and parallel and tend to avoid ranking oppressions or identities (though atomization is a necessary first step toward hierarchy), yet can still be competitive (either/or) in orientation. While "X vs. Y" applications artificially parse interconnected dynamics and distort, they do not necessarily reinforce notions of primary and secondary marginalization or identity. The second set of examples, however, *do* take this next step: they slip into "X-first" (e.g., gender-first or class-first) analysis, placing identities, forms of power, and modes of redress in competition, but also in a pecking order. This more deeply reinforces the false universalization, ontological erasure, and epistemological violation intersectionality has long contested.

I then conclude with a discussion of a classic essay by Marilyn Frye (1983) about oppression to illustrate how quickly an analysis can slip from intersectional aims and to show how "X vs. Y" and "X-first" patterns interrelate. Frye's essay is widely taught because she astutely describes oppression as a structural weave of systemic forces and practices, one that entails numerous no-win situations (see, e.g., Bailey 1998). Furthermore, she demonstrates why micropolitical and macropolitical analyses are requisite for understanding and dismantling oppression. However, she also departs from the complexity she aims to take up in analyzing oppression's workings. Frye is not unique in this regard (as the many examples already referenced illustrate), but looking at how she lets interactive, intersectional possibilities fall away is instructive. This essay can be taught in a way that asks students to recognize the importance of Frye's arguments about oppression's structural aspects and nuances, and, at the same time, to recognize how readily, despite intent, we can fall into both formulations of the "pop-bead" problem, atomization and hierarchy, that undermine the structural, multilevel analysis Frye advocates.

## Applying Intersectionality Means . . . Atomization?

To quickly reiterate, pop-bead mindsets reinforce either/or logics of separation and noninteraction and erroneously approach categories as internally coherent. This atomized approach to difference falsely universalizes within-group (via common-denominator thinking) and tends to focus on comparison between groups or bounded categories. Single-axis or pop-bead logics also obscure shared politics or premises, overlook simultaneous privilege and oppression, and stymie coalition politics. Furthermore, they skew our understanding of how we *all* exceed the terms of single-axis categories, both those who seem to fit them, by virtue of transparent power and privilege, and those who, by virtue of being "marked" as members of multiple disenfranchised groups, seem *not* to fit (Crenshaw 1989; Lugones 1994; Spelman 1988). While intersectionality clearly critiques pop-bead thinking, it continues to pervade intersectionality applications.

Despite a researcher's commitment to intersectionality, for instance, atomization can still be at the heart of common research practices, including "statistical models that test the separate and combined effects of two different social categories" (Cole 2008, 445), independent variable models that approach factors as noninteractive (Harnois 2005) and conceptually independent (Hancock 2007b; Jordan-Zachery 2007), practices of testing for difference (Shields 2008), reliance on additive research questions (Bowleg 2008), adding binary variables to regression models without attending to simultaneity or within-variable possibilities (Simien 2007), or using survey questions that push "individuals to attribute their mistreatment to a particular social status," thereby potentially distorting respondents' multidimensional experiences (Harnois 2013, 49; see also Bowleg 2013). Much feminist research thus continues to analyze multiple factors in simplistic, sequential ways and remains acontextual and reliant on monocausal explanations (Zambrana and Dill 2009). Springer, Hankivsky, and Bates' examination of large-scale research on gender, health and wellness bears out this observation: "most conventional gender and health research is limited to . . . looking at gender in addition to other categories . . . without fully considering and analyzing full contexts, interactional effects with other social locations and influences of power inequities" (Springer, Hankivsky, and Bates 2012, 1663).

The prevalence of pop-bead research models and outcomes, even when seeking to engage intersectionality, is partly due to an "over-reliance on relatively homogenous [survey data] samples" (Harnois 2013, 38): these data sets approach the lived experience of gender, for instance, via a distorting binary (life experienced "as men" and "as women") that presupposes binary gender, suppresses within-group differences among men and among women, and disaggregates systems of oppression. Harnois finds, for example, that the Schedule of Sexist Events (SSE) is potentially biased in that "some social-spatial contexts are over-represented and others are under-represented": furthermore, this asymmetrical representation corresponds to various "differences in social status" (54). Conclusions gleaned from the General Social Survey (GSS) can mislead equally: its questions "encourage respondents to view systems of inequality, and the discrimination that results, as distinct. . . . [and as] based on a single characteristic—gender, or race, or ethnicity, or age" (57–58). Furthermore, the Index of Race-Related Stress (IRRS), in focusing on masculinist measures and models of racial discrimination, can exacerbate "intersectional invisibility" (Purdie-Vaughns and Eibach 2008) by failing to "recognize people with multiple marginal identities (e.g., black women)" (Harnois 2013, 86–87).

In other words, many standard research practices and expectations are founded in pop-bead thinking from the start (and thus contravene intersectional both/and logics from the start as well). Researchers may claim (and desire) an intersectional research design yet employ a variance framework that implicitly treats identities as constructed, lived, and regulated independently one from the other, such that within-group differences and complex interactions between social identity and social institutions cannot be examined meaningfully. As Stephanie Shields discusses, this can lead to additive or "cumulative disadvantage models of oppression," not intersectional ones. Furthermore, "conventional quantitative research designs and statistical analyses are constructed to test for differences between groups," not to test for differences within group. She cautions, "It is neither an automatic nor easy step to go from *acknowledging* linkages among social identities to *explaining* those linkages or the processes through which intersecting identities define and shape one another" (Shields 2008, 303–304).

Such disconnects also occur in policy, where "monofocused" applications continue to hold sway (Bustelo 2009; Platero 2008). The persistence of pop-bead thinking as policy's governing imaginary is not due to lack of discussion about intersectionality's policy implications. Johanna Kantola succinctly summarizes the significance of intersectional analyses of discrimination and power, wherein "several grounds operate and interact with each other," simultaneously and inseparably. Policymakers must understand that the "relationship between the categories is an open empirical question" and that more than individual factors, biases, and intents should be accounted for. Since "Intersectionality conceptualises the categories as resulting from dynamic interaction between individual and institutional factors," multilevel policy orientations must be enacted (Kantola 2009, 26–27).[29]

Rather than use an intersectional orientation to trace how "systemic disparities align with identity-based modes of representation to channel structural vulnerabilities towards some communities and away from others" (Oliviero 2011, 2), many attempts to "operationalize intersectionality" rely on either/or thinking (a key component of pop-bead logics), leading to a series of avoidable (and artificial) methodological and policy quandaries, such as: "Should an intersectional analysis focus on the micro or the macro level? On subjectivity or objectivity? On identities or overarching societal constellations?" (Urbanek 2009, 2). However, Doris Urbanek emphasizes, "intersectional policy analysis does not need to choose between one and the other position. On the contrary, it is this dichotomous way of thinking that reduces possibilities" (2).

Other forms of applying intersectionality perpetuate notions that "different axes of inequality are similar to one another, matter to the same extent and can be treated with an anti-discrimination approach" that conceives of discrimination occurring "on the basis of several grounds operating separately" (Kantola 2009, 27). This can turn into an "oppression Olympics" frame, where inequalities are separated, conceived of as in competition, not interaction, and structured/experienced in parallel ways (Hancock 2007b; Martinez 1993). This also transpires in "double-axis" or 2 × 2 models, wherein no more than two sites of structural inequality (and privilege) can be examined or addressed, as Angéla Kóczé demonstrates with regard to policy and research on Romani women's experiences across Europe (Kóczé 2009). Via various nonintersectional mechanisms, "intersectional claims can mutate into competing claims due to 'sorting' or 'separating' influences of official state actors" (Bassel and Emmejulu 2010, 27).

Many equity policies thus still overlook how "forms of oppression shape and are shaped by one another," treating them as self-contained and distinct. As Squires asserts, "a failure to recognize this results in both simplistic analyses and ill-conceived policy interventions" (Squires 2007, 514). In discussing equity initiatives and hate crime policies in Spain, Marta Cruells and Gerard Coll-Planas argue we must distinguish between "multiple discrimination" approaches (which rely on single-axis logics) and intersectional ones focused on strategies for "taking action" in a multidimensional way, with a goal of "structural transformation." In contrast, the multiple approach proceeds from the premise that "although different forms of discrimination come under the same umbrella, each axis is dealt with in parallel, without taking into consideration how they interact. This logic generates competition between groups and runs the risk of overlooking those groups with fewer resources and less influence at an institutional level" (Cruells and Coll-Planas 2013, 134).

Similarly, Bassel and Emejulu find that France and the United Kingdom share a depoliticized, individualized policy approach, despite significant philosophical differences (the United Kingdom pursues multiculturalism, whereas France follows an integrationist republican model). In both contexts, "through a process of misrecognition, intersecting axes of disadvantage are separated and in some cases even silenced." This is not just an epistemological blunder but a political error and policy distortion: "Treating these axes as independent and unrelated categories results in the construction of institutional spaces that misrecognize inequalities and limit articulation and action to address structural discrimination." For example, the recent U.K. Single Equality Bill defines antidiscrimination doctrine narrowly, as individualized, and affords no "institutional space for understanding and practicing intersectionality more broadly as a fusion of social structures that creates specific social positions that are either privileged or devalued" (Bassel and Emejulu 2010, 519, 535–538). Pop-bead thinking reinforces acontextual, additive mindsets that artificially disaggregate identities and systems of power: intersectionality becomes impossible to conceive or practice when atomization is the operative logic.

Though some 'pop-bead' applications are fairly obvious, atomization also occurs indirectly, even when trying to make connections. Rhetorical devices like analogy, used to bridge differences, can animate a kind of misrecognition that undermines intersectionality. An emphasis on similarity can mean attention to sameness *and* difference drops out of the equation. Material differences and power asymmetries can be elided on behalf of imagined similarities.[30] Focusing on sameness, of oneself as a "co-sufferer," for instance, may obscure whatever role one plays as a perpetrator of harm (Boler 1999; Code 1995, 2001, 2011; Spelman 1998). Using analogy to identify commonality of oppressions has thus long been questioned by intersectionality scholars, as in challenges to nineteenth-century race-sex analogies equating "women's" inequality with "slavery," or suffrage with abolition (King 1988; Newman 1999). Twentieth-century parallels between women's rights and civil rights were likewise critiqued for erasing Black womanhood and collapsing material differences,[31] and Crenshaw recently noted the "curious resurrection" of suffrage/first wave feminism in twenty-first-century rhetorics (Crenshaw 2011a).

Analogies have potential to foster shared understanding but can also entail disaggregation and decontextualization. Despite its possible pitfalls, use of analogical thinking continues in many antidiscrimination applications, though not without debate. Some have challenged the ubiquitous reliance on ableism in liberatory discourses, including foundational intersectional texts that "use disability to locate objects of remediation," thereby reinforcing binaries intersectionality roundly critiques, including same/different, subject/object, and figure/ground divides (May and Ferri 2005; see also Schalk 2013). Carbado questions linking LGBT rights and civil rights in the United States, via motifs of the closet, comparisons of anti-miscegenation marriage laws and the Defense of Marriage Act, or parallels between Jim Crow military practices with Don't Ask Don't Tell military policies. Rather than render visible meaningful connections or coalitional potential, he contends such analogies lead to intersectional invisibility (Carbado 1999a, 2013). Analogy may seem like an affiliative gesture, but its impetus toward atomization, sameness as a basis of recognition, and implicit assumptions of transparency, margin to margin (see Lugones 2006), must also be recognized. Intersectionality's same/different thesis must be retained, whether in delineating differences and distinctions, or in identifying connections and tracing parallels.

### Using Intersectionality Entails . . . Establishing Hierarchies?

In exploring how intersectionality gets turned into a hierarchical formulation, it is imperative to acknowledge the degree to which pop-bead thinking creates fertile ground for an antagonistic framework: the shift from parallel, noninteractive categories to an "X-first" model takes these atomized practices a step further. Moving from the notion of competition between bounded identities or groups toward positing one identity or factor over others is basically a matter of degree, not kind. However, hierarchical ("X-first") pop-bead models *do* more deeply depart from and violate basic intersectionality insights. Certainly, both models rely on either/or thinking, ignore simultaneous privilege and oppression, erase complex subjectivity, and set aside interaction: however, an "X-first" approach also buttresses the logic of primary and secondary marginalization (not just parallel, analogous ones). Despite the harm caused by ranking identities, and the distorted worldview rendered by atomization and hierarchy, intersectionality applications that slip into ranking oppressions or identities can readily be found.

Sometimes this "X-first" dynamic is subtle, as in practices that, in intersectionality's name, treat one identity or vector of power as principal, yet still pursue intricacy. For instance, complex statistical analyses, such as multiple regressions, approach each variable as separate and as impacting a given dependent variable independently: interaction and simultaneity are not readily visible as relevant. Likewise, researchers may seek to identify a "main effect" and then incorporate other factors via comparative analysis as a means of applying intersectionality: however, atomized hierarchical results can still carry the day. Though multiplicity and complexity may be the goal, this does not mean a method, on its own, or as usually practiced, is necessarily amenable to allowing for knowledge outcomes that are intersectional in design, application, orientation, or outcome.

As Hae Yeon Choo and Myra Marx Ferree underscore, simply inserting "intersectional relations to what are typically conceptualized as persistent, untransformed 'main effects'" cannot suffice. Though this approach is "explicitly comparative and contextual . . ., by connecting particular levels of analysis or institutions with different inequalities, it [still] tends toward separating primary from secondary contradictions" (Choo and Ferree 2010, 135). To illustrate, they discuss Annette Lareau's renowned study, *Unequal Childhoods* (2003). Lareau uses class as a main variable, adding in factors of race and gender to contextualize. However, as Choo and Ferree underscore, there are "interrelated analytic problems that arise from treating gender, race, and class as separate variables and trying to find which has the 'biggest' effect. First, . . . interaction among them is not apparent as a process. . . . Second, the effects of class, race, and gender are primarily seen in the experiences of those in the subordinated or 'marked' category." In other words, this approach is, at its root, "formulated to explain only the difference of the nondominant groups from the dominant" (Choo and Ferree 2010, 140–141).

Granting class relations predominant status (implicitly or explicitly, treating other forms of inequality as subordinate to economic relations, as Giminez (2001) argues should be the case) is not that unusual in intersectionality applications, particularly those attendant to structural, material inequalities. However, using one category as primary, or even two as superordinate, can buttress existing social arrangements, reinforce sameness, and undermine intersectional politics and possibilities. As Choo and Ferree illustrate, in discussing Michèle Lamont's *The Dignity of Working Men* (2000), "nation and class are set out as the defining features of the study and their structural effects are explained first. Then all other differences are treated as extra rather than as intertwined, intersecting, and inflecting them. The dominant racial category in . . . [France and the United States] is also allowed to exercise unexamined normative authority" (Choo and Feree 2010, 143).

In "X-first" intersectionality applications, class can be deployed as a form of (unstated) assurance that white privilege will not be disrupted: it is offered as "a reunifying ground of equality," unlike the ostensible divisiveness of anti-racism, presented as something to move away from or progress beyond (Gedalof 2012, 12–13; see also Hemmings 2011). "X-first" assuagements present class as universal, suggesting other factors, like race, gender, or sexuality, are secondary or particular: not only are identities atomized, but so are the structural and material processes that enforce them (Gedalof 2012, 13). Likewise, gender-first logics can reinforce whiteness as gender's normative center.

Harnois, for instance, analyzes an array of studies using gender universalism to explore "women's relationship with feminism" across racial groups (Harnois 2005, 810) and reveals how unstated but powerful assumptions obscure how the methods and measures used, the data gathered, and the conclusions reached are all off target for Black women.[32] She shows how lack of intersectionally-conceived measures leads to distorting conclusions (e.g., that Black women are "less feminist"). "Self-identification," a common measure of feminist identity for white women, is an unreliable "indicator of how 'feminist' Black women are" (819). Moreover, reliance on "attitudinal or ideological variables to measure the salience of feminism in women's lives is also problematic," since feminism does not have one meaning or history (812).

Due to the ubiquity of hierarchical, single-axis thinking, and gender versus ethnicity binaries, questions about whose subjectivity or rights should come "first" can seem sensible. For instance, banning the wearing of headscarves is often made to appear rational and necessary via reference to gender equality "concerns"—that is, under the fear that "gender equality may lose out . . . [to] diversity," as participants in a 2007 Eurobarometer survey reported (Bagilhole 2009, 47). Such binary assessments, however, are not natural—*they are created*. The European Court of Human Rights has *constructed* an artificial and distorting rights conflict, then ruled on (and regulated) this binary: "we have—or rather—we construct—two rights in conflict, and strive to balance these, or to prioritize them" (Skjeie and Langvasbråten 2009, 524). In other words, using falsely universalized categories, disaggregated and prioritized from the beginning, leads to a host of errors, both political and epistemological.

As Bilge illustrates, in discussing debates about headscarves in France, by approaching the symbolic meaning of wearing headscarves as unitary and fixed (i.e., as menacing secularism [laïcité] and as threatening "gender" equity), the meanings of feminism, secular (liberated) gender, and national democracy also become fixed as inherently non-Muslim (and white). She explains, "What veiled women have to say about their veiling is irrelevant, and cannot change the meaning of the veil, since they are alienated and unwittingly adopt the views of their oppressors. In contrast, French feminists *qua* emancipated subjects have access to the 'real' meaning of the veil: it is both a symbol and an instrument of women's oppression by men" (Bilge 2010, 15).

Such frames reinforce colonial fantasies via gender norms, wherein gender metonymically stands in for nation. The path to modernity lies in breaking radically from (marked) culture, religion, or "tradition"—*unveiling* would then signify this rupture (Yeğenoğlu 1998, 39–67) even though the subjectivity/citizenship promised remains perpetually unavailable because it is coded (and regulated) as Western, white, modern, and because it requires an ongoing coloniality of being to operate (Hoagland 2010; Lugones 2007, 2010). The political and epistemological errors of continued reliance on, or slippage to, pop-bead, hierarchical thinking intertwine. Beyond constructing conflicting rights, relying on (and reinforcing) absolutist divides (e.g., between "free" and "subjugated" women), it contravenes intersectional thinking by hiding forms of oppression that the "free" assent to (or are asked to live with) and by masking our capacity to oppress others, to participate in (and benefit from) dominance. Stark divides also obscure how those who are subjugated resist—domination can be made to appear totalizing.

It is not a far stretch from relying on neatly bifurcated mappings of persons (free and unfree, agentic and dominated, knower and known) to participating in a series of divisions that align with social hierarchies and norms by distinguishing between "deserving" and undeserving (or less-deserving) persons, as Spade (2013) convincingly illustrates, violating intersectionality's ontological, political, and epistemological aspects all at once. Yet applications that invoke intersectionality to develop equity policy or rights advocacy can uphold this worthy/unworthy division, rather than challenge it, as in LGBTQ rights discourses that highlight the "good" queers whose life choices and political goals match middle-class, heterocentric, white values (Price 2006; Spade 2013), or immigration reform advocacy that focuses on the stories and needs of deserving "dreamers" (named after the "Dream" immigration reform act in the United States) as distinct from other immigrants (implicitly undeserving, hence criminalized) (Martínez 2012), or the stigmatization of welfare for unemployed persons, versus the acclamatory rhetorics of necessity and productivity accorded corporate welfare.

Slipping into human hierarchies, via X-first notions of identities and rights, can be found in research contexts as well. Choo and Ferree highlight, for example, how Mitchell Duneier's study, *Sidewalk* (1999), pivots on unstated "assumptions not only about the fundamental difference between the 'normal' members of 'society' and these poor black men, but of the resonance that readers will feel, seeing money-earning work as redemptive and normalizing. Duneier suggests that the sidewalk's informal economy turns a person with an unfortunate past into a 'deserving' member of society" (Choo and Ferree 2010, 138). However, relying on notions of deserving/undeserving persons reinforces a hierarchical normative/deviant dualism intersectional approaches contest: this parsing of personhood also animates a binary sameness versus difference divide intersectionality thoroughly dispenses with.

### Theorizing Oppression: Slipping from Matrix Thinking to Single-Axis Analytics

Many trained in feminist philosophy, social theory, social stratification, and women's studies, especially in the United States, have been introduced, in part, to thinking about the workings of oppression via philosopher Marilyn Frye's insightful 1983 essay "Oppression." Though Frye's stated aim is, in part, to think through systems of race, class, and gender inequality as a matrix (the term intersectionality was yet to be coined), she relies on an atomized, gender-primary lens, one obliquely reinforcing a white, heteronormative conceptualization of gender that erases within-group differences among women (and men), presently and historically.[33]

For example, Frye's analysis of patriarchy implicitly posits the divide between men and women as principal. She argues that "men" are never denigrated or oppressed "as men" and asserts, "Whatever assaults and harassments [a man] is subject to, being male is not what selects him for victimization" (Frye 1983, 16). Masculinity is presented as not impacted by disability, race, sexuality, or citizenship status in an inextricable, dynamic way (e.g., see Carbado 1999b). Gender is also presented as dual and homogenous, despite the fact that a "pursuit of a 'politics of unity' solely based on gender forecloses the 'pursuit of solidarity'" (Alarcón 1990, 364). Indirectly, Frye relies on an undifferentiated, dimorphic notion of gender in delineating a key concept, the double bind—"situations in which options are reduced to a very few and all of them expose one to penalty, censure or deprivation" (Frye 1983, 2).

In discussing the politics of anger and the smile, as illustrative of the double bind, Frye rightly contends, "it is often a requirement upon oppressed people that we smile and be cheerful. If we comply, we signify our docility and our acquiescence in our situation" (Frye 1983, 2). Yet the potential for thinking through who is asked to bear the onus to smile, for what reasons and in which contexts, falls away as Frye moves to describe the smile as instructive with regard to "women's" oppression. Via atomization, she relinquishes an opportunity to take up how systemic double binds take place within contexts of relational dominance and subordination within and across multiple vectors of power and sites of identity. To clarify, she does allude to a wider sense in which various oppressed people or groups (i.e., not just "women") are asked to take up the emotional duty to present a happy affect (often combined with gratefulness). And, though she does not specify the many possibilities, some can be readily identified.

For instance, alongside the "feminist killjoy" who is maligned because she refuses to play along with business as usual with a smile, Ahmed also reminds us of "happy queers" asked to "approximate the straight signs of civility to be accepted into civil society" (Ahmed 2010, 106) and "diversity workers" asked to perform solicitous gratitude for being "allowed" entry into institutions of higher education (Ahmed 2012). Then, there are the proverbial "happy cripples" who populate the ableist imaginary with joyful smiles and infantilized grins, accepted by virtue of being inspirational "supercrips" (Shapiro 1994), from Tiny Tim, "resolutely euphoric in his impairment, illness, and poverty" (Wasserman 2006, 215), to sentimental telethon and charity figures. Certainly, there are also the purportedly joyous Black caricatures peopling the white social imaginary, beaming and grinning thanks to the ostensible beneficence of racism, as discussed by Marlon Riggs (1983) and Kimberly Wallace-Sanders (2008), for example.

However, now consider the possibility that these various smiling people, compelled to take up their requisite happy affect as part of the binds and constraints they experience as systemically oppressed, are all "women": the meanings (and solicited or coerced performances) of happiness are not the same and cannot simply be boiled down to "gender" alone (or gender unmodified or gender as primary) to explain the oppressive and relational dynamics at work. Some women and men are expected to show docility or compliance via smiling, or other signifiers of good-humored deference, *to appease other women* (and some men to other men and/or other women as well), because race, class, disability, gender, citizenship status, and sexuality intertwine.

Later, Frye discusses the smile's counterpart: anger, usually perceived by those with more power as groundless in nature and unwarranted when expressed by those with less power: anger tends to be characterized as silly (foolish) or uncontrolled (threatening) when used by oppressed groups or persons. Furthermore, anger is an emotion unduly ascribed to oppressed groups (usually in combination with assertions of irrationality, even danger) when they do not comply with the onus to perform happy affect. To explain, Frye asserts, "it is my being a woman that reduces the power of my anger to a proof of my insanity [*sic*]" (Frye 1983, 16). What Frye does not explain or discuss is *how* she has such confidence that it is her "being a woman" alone that is causal: gender is pulled apart from race, ability, class, citizenship, and sexuality.

These factors become "transparent" sites of power and identity in such assured claims. Yet people marked as "different" by means of race, disability, and social class are also stereotyped as overly irrational and unduly "angry." Some women are also perceived as differently "angry" (or inappropriately angry) in comparison to other women (consider the stereotypes of the angry Black woman, the vengeful woman terrorist, or the predatory, man-hating lesbian). Frye's pop-bead analysis, which homogenizes gender and drops opportunities to examine how gender interacts and intertwines with multiple other sites of power and identity, cannot account for these aspects of the politics of anger as a site of oppression.

Finally, in discussing how "women's" dependency is derogated even as it is systemically reinforced (Frye 1983, 4, 7–10), Frye astutely attends to the hidden structural dimensions of oppression as well as its pervasive ideological aspects. However, she does not note that different forms of gendered dependency are differently derogated. Some are relatively idealized (e.g., women's dependence on men who are their fathers or husbands for protection and care) whereas other forms of dependency are stigmatized as dire social problems (indeed individual pathologies) in need of remediation (e.g., poor women's reliance on the state via welfare). While both types of institutionalized dependency can be understood as oppressive in structural and ideological terms, and by means of the evidence of lived experience, the fact is that public patriarchy carries social stigma and contempt,[34] whereas private patriarchy garners far more social approval and reward. This was patently clear in the 1965 Moynihan Report, for instance (Crenshaw 1989, 163–165), and in many policy efforts since that reward anti-natalism (even sterilization) and heterosexual marriage as "responsible" forms of citizenship for structurally marginalized and disenfranchised communities (Onwuachi-Willig 2005; Thomas 1998).

Questions of relational power, coercion, and constraint apply, via an intersectional approach, to "men" and to "women" (and beyond these normative genders/categories). Furthermore, gender (and patriarchy as a form of oppression) cannot be disarticulated, and then posited as primary, without distortion. Acknowledging how gender imbricates with race, sexuality, nation, and disability changes the terms markedly of what constitutes gendered behavior, expectations, representations, and politics. Valences of sameness *and* difference operate simultaneously and interactively—but to engage this requires intersectional "both/and" logics.

It is this both/and thinking that slips away in Frye's analysis, even as she invokes multiplicity and references forms of commonality across inequalities throughout. Importantly, Frye mentions (and seeks to recognize) differences among women as she unpacks the workings of oppression. Some of her most insightful claims underscore how the micropolitical and macropolitical interdepend, how oppression is structural and comprises interwoven forces, and how hegemony's restraints are evident in the most intimate details of everyday life. However, she reverts to generalizations about women and men as groups and to analyses of gender processes as homogenized and isolatable from other factors and processes: she thereby inadvertently obscures many of the workings of oppression she aims to highlight and undermines her own insights about the interacting vectors of power that must be examined macroscopically.

I do not suggest Frye is unique: in countless research applications, theoretical analyses, and policy practices, single-axis logics continue to hold sway, even when intersectional goals are stated or when key intersectional premises are employed. In intersectionality's name, one can find myriad practices that overtly buttress oppressive structures and institutions or subtly slip away from intersectional logics. Intersectionality's focus on disrupting hegemonic epistemic norms may be downplayed or let go of, its attention to historical context and contestatory memory abandoned, its clarion call for sociopolitical transformation muffled, or its attention to within-group differences and rejection of false universals discarded. Many of the intersectionality applications discussed aim for intersectional social justice and theoretical and institutional transformation, yet fall short. In relatively subtle ways, practitioners let go of the multivalent epistemology, pluralized ontology, and politics of solidarity intersectionality entails.

These "slippages" highlight a wider problem that intersectionality actually invites us to tackle—the influence of dominant logics. When we take up a contestatory imagination, begin down an interrogative path, and glimpse alternative worlds and selves, we may let go of these different possibilities, often inadvertently: Gloria Anzaldúa eloquently describes this on a personal level (Anzaldúa 2002; see also Lugones 2005), but this issue equally applies to institutional and collective contexts. Disconnects between goals and outcomes have much to teach us about the pull of dominant mindsets and hegemonic imaginaries.[35] They also help illuminate how a critical, justice-oriented, and multifaceted concept can become flattened and co-opted. By dropping an intersectional vision of justice and liberation, some applications go even further: they offer a kind of "cover" for maintaining inequality and shoring up privilege. We must think through why intersectionality seems to remain "unheard" and identify some strategies for addressing these distortions and sites of departure.

The next chapter takes up these questions. First, I discuss the normative power exerted by dominant logics and the resulting issues of testimonial inequality (Fricker 2007) and asymmetrical cognitive authority. I then identify two key epistemological strategies needed to more adequately take up intersectionality: *bracketing* dominant logics and finding ways to practice active *bias toward intersectionality*, in line with intersectionality's own bias toward marginalized lives and subjugated knowledges. In so doing, intersectionality's many facets must be kept in mind (including its praxis and justice orientation, its call for macropolitical and micropolitical or multilevel analysis, its emphasis on epistemological and ontological multiplicity, its adherence to both/and thinking, its attention to relational power and privilege, its coalitional vision, and its interrogatory and contestatory imagination). In short, it is essential to begin our work (whether political, philosophical, or institutional) from within intersectionality's logics. Then, to conclude, and given intersectionality's focus on praxis, I identify some strategies for doing intersectional work: these can be thought of as orientations to be taken up, once active bias and "bracketing" are under way. We must conjure ways to recognize, and mitigate, powerful mindsets that can impede or undermine the very changes we seek to achieve.

## Notes

1. See Choo and Ferree (2010), Cole (2008, 2009), Hancock (2007a, 2007b), Harnois (2013), Jordan-Zachery (2007), Knapp (2005), Lindsay (2013), McCall (2005), Shields (2008).
2. Debates about what constitutes an adequate form of applying intersectionality have occurred in some contexts (e.g., policy formation, state and supranational politics, and social science research methods, qualitative and quantitative) more than others. Yet, few discussions trace slippages across scales, geopolitical contexts, and disciplines. An interdisciplinary comparative snapshot of intersectionality's instrumentalization provides a more complex view of the nature of its distortion. More than just identify slippages, the goal is to intervene in these patterns.
3. Carastathis explains, "In *Harrington v. Cleburne County Board of Education* (2001), the court references 'intersectionality,' obligating the plaintiff, Mary L. Harrington, to pursue an 'intersectional' theory of discrimination to describe her claim. Harrington, an African American woman, sued the Alabama school board for violating the Equal Pay Act, Equal Protection Clause, and Title VII, claiming she was paid less than whites and males in comparable positions, was given additional work and less compensatory leave time. While hers was a claim of 'race and sex discrimination,' the court, *sua sponte* (of its own accord) gave Harrington three options. First, to limit her claim to one alleged basis of discrimination, abandoning the other. Second, she could divide her claim, alleging discrimination 'either because she is black, or because she is female.' Third, she could pursue an 'intersectional theory' of discrimination: 'that is, that the defendant treated her disparately because she belongs simultaneously to two or more protected classes' (Harrington v. Cleburne 2001). Interestingly, Harrington resisted the intersectional interpretation of her claim, unsuccessfully sought relief from the court's order, and continued to want to claim discrimination on 'distinct grounds of race and sex discrimination theory, and not on the 'intersectionality theory' that she elected under duress because of the conditions imposed on the trial of claims based on distinct discriminatory motives' (Harrington v. Cleburne 2001). Rather than remedy political invisibility, in the courtroom 'intersectionality' became a device through which the representational claims of still another Black woman plaintiff . . . were muted [sic] (Harrington v. Cleburne 2001)" (Carastathis 2013b, 707).
4. Such risks are not unique to intersectionality: Tolhurst et al. discuss, in the context of health disparities and international health policy, problematic uses of Gender Mainstreaming (GM). These include: depoliticization, rhetorical invocation with no follow-through or implementation, and state manipulations of GM to obscure gender-specific patterns of disadvantage and inequality (Tolhurst et al. 2012, 1826). GM and intersectionality are not the same: further, intersectional policy aims in part to address GM's philosophical oversights and political elisions (e.g., to question GM's gender-universalizing tendencies). However, critiques of how GM has been applied (as a depoliticized, technocratic lens) are helpful for examining intersectionality's current institutionalization.
5. See Mehrotra (2012), Patil (2013), Purkayastha (2012), Robertson and Sgoutas (2012).
6. See Bowleg (2008), Choo and Ferree (2010), Glenn (1999), Hancock (2007b), Harnois (2005), Henderson and Tickamyer (2009), Jordan-Zachery (2007), Shields (2008), Smooth (2013).
7. Some notable exceptions include Bilge (2010), Brah and Phoenix (2004), *Collins (1990)*, Guy-Sheftall (1995), Hancock (2013), Harnois (2013).

8. Including Frances Beale (1970), Toni Cade (1970), Angela Davis (1972), and Claudia Jones (see Davies 2008).
9. "Fact vs. value" binaries suggest values belong to the realm of human sentiment and emotion, seen as partial or biased states of mind, rather than neutral and impartial. These factors must therefore be abstracted out and distanced from to arrive at, and adequately observe, the "facts," which are posited as inanimate, simply out there to be discovered or observed. Social factors—such as who knowers are, and what their social locations, historical contexts, and workings assumptions are, are not seen as impacting or shaping the facts at hand. Intersectionality is one among many critical knowledge traditions that have contested this cordoning off of knowledge "proper." See Alcoff and Kittay (2007), Code (1995), Collins (1990), Hawkesworth (1989), Jaggar (1989), Lindsay (2013), and Shields (2008).
10. Intersectionality is not unique in this regard. Transnational politics and analytics are also flattened in feminist practice: "among its many meanings, the 'transnational' functions to reference migratory, mobile, and other global phenomena, hence it functions as an empirical descriptive, for example, of diasporic subjects, rather than as a mode of critique" (Desai, Bouchard, and Detournay 2010, 48).
11. For a discussion of engaging demography differently, see Axelsson and Sköld (2011).
12. Notably, Crenshaw and other feminist critical race scholars were involved in crafting it. For a comparative discussion of the South African and U.S. Constitutions, see Kende (2009). The Bill of Rights is online: www.info.gov.za/documents/constitution/1996/96cons2.htm.
13. For further discussion of the special rapporteur's role, see Ertürk and Purkayastha (2012).
14. The report is available online: http://daccess-ods.un.org/TMP/2316089.27249908.html.
15. See Hankivsky (2011), Hankivsky and Cormier (2011), Loutfy et al. (2012), Mulvihil, Mailloux, and Atkin (2001), Simpson (2009). For a discussion of jurisprudence and multiple grounds human rights claims, see the Ontario Human Rights Commission Discussion Paper (2001), prepared by the Policy and Education Branch: "An Intersectional Approach to Discrimination: Addressing Multiple Grounds in Human Rights Claims."
16. See Barker (2008), Brown and Sánchez (1994), Carastathis (2013a), Grundy and Smith (2005), Mingus and Talley (2013), Sokoloff (2008), Spade (2013).
17. See Kantola and Nousiainen (2012), Krizsan, Skjeie, and Squires (2012), Lombardo and Agustín (2012), Lombardo and Verloo (2009), Verloo (2006).
18. See Bassel and Emejulu (2010), Bagilhole (2010), Ben-Galim, Campbell, and Lewis (2007), Conaghan (2009), Gedalof (2012), Squires (2008, 2009), Strid, Armstrong, and Walby (2008), Yuval-Davis 2006, 2007).
19. See Borchorst and Teigen (2009), Bustelo (2008, 2009), Lombardo and Agustín (2012), Lombardo and del Giorgio (2013), Lombardo and Verloo (2009), Platero (2008).
20. See also Narayan's astute analysis of feminist analytics that asymmetrically attribute a "death by culture" determinist "explanation" for ostensibly greater (and inherent) murderous violence toward women in (and from) the "Third" (majority) world (Narayan 1997).
21. See: www.ecpg-barcelona.com/negotiating-equality-and-diversity-across-europe-multiculturalism-citizenship-and-transnational.
22. For example, in 1993, Supreme Court Justice Claire Hereux-Dubé noted, "Categories of discrimination may overlap, and . . . individuals may suffer historical exclusion on the basis of both race and gender, age and physical handicap, or some other combination. The situation of individuals who confront multiple grounds of disadvantage is particularly complex. Categorizing such discrimination as primarily racially oriented,

or primarily gender-oriented, misconceives the reality of discrimination as it is experienced by individuals" (qtd. in Ontario Human Rights Commission 2001, 5), www.ohrc.on.ca/en/intersectional-approach-discrimination-addressing-multiple-grounds-human-rights-claims.

23. In the 1990s, "at only three per cent of the national Canadian population, Aboriginal women accounted for one in ten federally incarcerated women, and 'nearly half' of the women admitted to provincial prisons" (Williams 2009, 84). A decade later, "the number of Aboriginal women—and men—in prisons has increased. . . . The Aboriginal female population of the federal prisons has doubled [since 1996]. . . . Aboriginal women represent close to one in three (31 per cent) federal female prisoners in 2006, up from one in five (21 per cent) in 1996" (88).
24. In K–12 education in the United States, such measures are accompanied by scripted and universalized curricula and increased bureaucratization and scrutiny, wherein schools, students, and teachers "fail" (or "succeed") in an acontextual vacuum devoid of structural analysis, then categorized as "undeserving" or "deserving" of further resources. Notably, many 'failing' schools are required to enter a commercial relationship (to purchase and follow a for-profit curriculum): capitalism enters as salvific via "common core" mandates, for example. Large conglomerates have a near monopoly on all aspects of the financial/educational relationship, selling: textbooks and accompanying scripted curricula to school districts; student assessment tests; teacher assessment tests; the college curriculum for teacher education; and selling teacher-certification tests as well. Under neoliberal norms of value and accountability, such curricula and assessments are infiltrating U.S. higher education as well.
25. This strategy in higher education, whereby the institution is made over into an individual (and antidiscrimination doctrine remains narrowly conceived in an individualist framework wherein discrimination is the act of individuals and conscious intent must be proven), could be seen as related to the push for legal recognition of corporations as individual persons.
26. See Bowleg (2008), Choo and Ferree (2010), Hancock (2007b), Harnois (2013), Shields (2008).
27. See Collins (2008), Gillman (2007), Puar (2007), Ringrose (2007).
28. See Alexander and Mohanty (1997), Cooghan-Gehr (2011), Holloway (2006), Rooks (2000).
29. Tools to apply intersectionality more adequately, in research and policy, have been devised by various organizations. The Canadian Research Institute for the Advancement of Women has a toolkit and wheel diagram about intersectionality's multilevel analytics and social change orientation (Simpson 2009). The African American Policy Forum (AAPF) offers a "primer" on intersectionality, online fora, and publications showing how intersectionality can be brought to bear to realize a more just world (http://aapf.org). Olena Hankivsky has also developed a useful "Intersectionality 101" handbook (www.sfu.ca/iirp/resources.html).
30. See Anzaldúa (1990a), Carbado (1999a), Collins (2008), Grewal and Kaplan (2003), Gillman (2007), Lugones (2006), May and Ferri (2005), Reddy (2011), Schueller (2005), Somerville (2005).
31. See hooks (1981), King (1988), LaRue (1995), Spelman (1988).
32. Zenzele Isoke underscores that conventional measures of political engagement in general are equally off target. For example, they erroneously "depict low-income black women as apolitical. . . . Political analysts interpret minimalist participation in mainstream political venues as an index of apathy based on masculinist assumptions about the nature of politics" (Isoke 2013, 1).

33. A shorter discussion of Frye's essay, and slippages from an intersectional approach, appears in May (2012b).
34. At least presently: as Hancock points out, "explanations of women's poverty have changed as the perceived race of the prototypical recipient has changed. The politics of paternalism for White Protestant widows and southern European immigrant mothers was prevalent during the nineteenth and twentieth centuries prior to the New Deal. . . . As greater numbers of women of color obtained benefits between the 1940s and the 1970s, a politics of contempt emerged" (Hancock 2004, 12).
35. See Anzaldúa (1990a), Campbell (1999), Code (2006, 2011), Hoagland (2001), Lorde (1984), Narayan (1997).

# 5

# Being "Biased" toward Intersectionality

## *A Call for Epistemic Defiance*

The previous chapters have journeyed across the terrain of intersectionality's historical and current iterations to illustrate what an intersectional disposition entails, to delineate how deeply single-axis logics distort to so as to better understand why an intersectional approach aims to pierce and dismantle their power, and to render visible patterns of intersectionality's repeated misrecognition and/or letting-go in a variety of contexts and practices. Here, I shift attention to several epistemological factors and politics that aid and abet these distortions and slippages. Furthermore, I call for practicing epistemic disobedience or defiance to more adequately take up intersectionality as a disposition.

First, I touch on recent theoretical debates about how epistemologies of ignorance function to maintain hierarchy and harm in the name of the common good or the social contract. These debates help to contextualize why an intersectional approach probes structural silences and takes up knowledges, lives, and forms of justice at the interstices. More specifically, I contend intersectionality should be understood as a heuristic useful for exposing and challenging epistemologies of ignorance. At the same time, I maintain that an ignorance effect has impeded intersectionality's uptake.

I then take up issues of credibility deficits, asymmetrical cognitive authority, and the issue of knowers' authorization (and disauthorization) to offer insight into how established single-axis logics and norms continue to exert considerable force, despite ample evidence as to the harm and violation they both animate and support. I follow this general discussion of how such logics continue to operate as an enduring social imaginary by taking up a pivotal question for feminist studies: if gender, as one example of the lasting power of monological/single-axis imaginations, can be understood to be epistemically unjust on intersectional terms, should it remain the means by which feminist projects are, still, largely signaled or authorized?

Building on decolonial and intersectional critiques of gender that show how it can violate even as it may seem a recuperable category or workable analytic tool, I then delve into questions of testimonial inequality and point to the need to reframe what "understanding" as an intellectual and political practice requires, from an intersectional orientation. Rather than presume discursive space to be equal, or presuppose understanding to entail transparency and (full) translatability, intersectionality directs our attention to the "voids" (Crenshaw 2011c) where silenced speech resides, focuses on the "residues" (Schutte 2000) that do not translate, and calls for the need to presume the meaningfulness of an alternative idea or unfamiliar worldview (Babbitt 2001), even if one cannot understand it on conventional terms.

To illustrate how its both/and logics and same/different thesis offer a means to read/interpret differently, I discuss how intersectionality is pivotal for perceiving the "resistant oppressed" (Lugones 2006), for piercing opacities, and for engaging with obscured lives and meanings, even as doing so can require a decentering of common feminist lenses and of conventional feminist subjects/protagonists. Given the considerable force continually exerted by dominant logics (which is one of intersectionality's central insights), I conclude by discussing the need to actively practice epistemic disobedience and disidentification to more adequately take up intersectionality as a radical political/philosophical disposition. Specifically, I lay out why both "[] bracketing" (Lugones 2010) and "bias" (Babbitt 2001) are called for to more fully inhabit an intersectional imagination and enact intersectional politics.

## Contesting Dominant Logics, Being Contested by Dominant Logics

Identifying and unpacking the relationship between epistemic asymmetries, cognitive distortions, and structural/material inequalities is central to intersectional scholarship and politics. Paradoxically, these same factors also often combine to impede our ability to realize intersectionality's innovative politics and possibilities. As the last chapters have illustrated, intersectionality can be sidestepped in ways that seem to pass relatively unnoticed: for instance, analyses obscuring interactions across systems of power, slippages to either/or hierarchical logics, and depoliticized notions of intersectionality are commonplace. Engaging intersectionality can transmogrify into a kind of studied indifference to its precepts, histories, and orientations in ways that reinforce, rather than upset, a politics of domination. Via a host of mechanisms, researchers and practitioners can lay the ground for intersectionality's critical lexicon, forged in political struggle, to be absorbed, co-opted, or diluted.

Aligning intersectionality with conventional frames or established methods may certainly render it more translatable or usable, but what does it mean if the modes by which it is understood and applied entail *anti*-intersectional thinking or violate its history, central premises, and commitments? As they accrue, what do such practices *do* to intersectional ideas, politics, histories, and meanings—do they make violation of intersectionality routine, or render acceptable the devaluing of its genealogy in resistance movements, particularly in Black feminisms? The quotidian nature of these dynamics underscores how established knowledge practices can interpellate us into adhering to business as usual, epistemologically and politically.

It is not ideas, in isolation, that do this work, for they connect to larger power dynamics: epistemic practices are part of the intimate fabric of everyday life and tie in to macropolitical forces and systems. Ways of knowing have both material outcomes and normative effects that authorize (and also disqualify or disauthorize) knowers: they are pivotal to maintaining status quo social relations and are, therefore, key sites of political struggle. When it comes to questions of epistemic distortion, as part and parcel of structural inequality, Lorraine Code argues that "it is not only individual acts of epistemic injustice" that must be addressed, but "the systemic, sedimented, interlocking character of sexist, racist, paternalistic, and other oppressive thought and action that makes those individual acts possible" (Code 2011, 210–211).

Intersectionality can be considered one such orientation or disposition, called for by Code, to dismantle epistemic distortions and structural power asymmetries, because it intervenes in intermeshed inequalities and traces patterns of systematic, asymmetrical harm. It contests the epistemic distortions and the material consequences that result from partitioned social ontologies (e.g., hierarchies of human value) and categorical thinking (e.g., atomization and false universals). Intersectionality has also long demonstrated the need to actively resist the violence and fragmentation sustained by single-axis logics. As Cho, Crenshaw, and McCall assert, countering structured epistemic and material injustice requires an "adoption of an intersectional way of thinking about the problem of sameness and difference and its relation to power." This, in turn, entails thinking about "categories [and, I would add, ontologies, temporalities, histories, affects, desires, embodiments, cosmologies, and epistemologies] *not as distinct but as always permeated* . . ., fluid and changing, always in the process of creating and being created by dynamics of power" (Cho, Crenshaw, and McCall 2013, 795, italics added).

Yet, interpretations and applications of intersectionality often deny this permeability, obscure power's fluid and processual nature, and drop its same/different analytics: the tools used to apply or assess intersectional ideas and aims are often the very ones it insists we must divest from to achieve a more just world. Intersectionality is thus repeatedly misrecognized in its own name—it is read or operationalized as adhering to categorical separation and as furthering atomized logics, rather than as *rupturing* these epistemes by drawing on knowledges, historical memories, and political desires derived from living/being/thinking within enmeshment *and* resistance. That single-axis mindsets cannot so easily be renounced (and that intersectionality seems regularly to slip away) can be explained, in part, by how we are continually enlisted to sustain normative frameworks and established knowledge paradigms. We are regularly pressured, via epistemological and other means, to legitimate consensus reality (Anzaldúa 1990a, xxi; Collins 1990, 2004).

### Epistemologies of Ignorance and Intersectionality

One key means by which an intersectional approach aims to trace and to rupture intermingled practices of dominance is by treating gaps in knowledge as meaningful. Absences, anomalies, and outliers are understood as potentially replete with suppressed meanings—as repositories for unheard testimony and as archives of knowledge and memory gleaned from differently oriented lives and epistemes. Such absences or silences are not approached in an intersectional reading as happenstance but as deeply structured, both philosophically (because tied to standard ways of knowing) and politically (because tied to structural inequality). Intersectionality focuses our attention on instances of "selective reality" or "blank spots," then, because such absences can provide evidence of a carefully structured "conditioned perception" that needs to be identified and challenged (Anzaldúa 1990a, xxi).

To flesh out this fundamental dimension of intersectional work, recent discussions about epistemologies of ignorance, or the "politics of unknowing" (Code 2011, 208), are invaluable. The epistemological norms an intersectional disposition invites us to unsettle and transform are as much about *not-knowing* as an institutionalized practice as about knowing. Specifically, in contesting exclusions in categorical logics, or violations in single-axis liberation strategies, intersectionality takes on willful ignorance, which is a "determined" form of "not knowing, and not wanting to know" (Tuana 2006, 10), "an agreement to know the world wrongly that is rewarded and encouraged because it serves to maintain the status quo" (May 2006, 109; see also Mills 1997; Swan 2010; Pohlhaus 2012).

Practices of refusing to know, though often imperceptible from within the (tightly regulated) bounds of conventional epistemes, play an active role in shoring up power and privilege. An inability to understand (or an ability to understand only in ways that violate or erase the differences at hand) is often not accidental but, instead, a structured skill, a trained incapacity. Not-knowing on the part of those accorded more power can signal an assiduously enforced lack, an acquired insensitivity achieved via a thorough schooling in ignorance that works both to naturalize and sustain inequality. Correlatively, marginalized groups can also take up and practice (a different form of) ignorance as a survival tactic and political technique—that is, choosing to not accept or fully attend to dominant logics and expectations—as a means of manipulating the epistemic oversights and limitations of those in power (Bailey 2007; Collins 1990; Lugones 2005).

As Code explains, unequal structural power and asymmetrical epistemic authority intertwine and serve to "inoculate" (privileged) knowers from perceiving the narrowness of their views (Code 2011, 213): they gain an "immunity" to stories and evidence not corresponding to established ideas (Code 2006, 110). Code's inoculation metaphor suggests a set of procedures instituted to protect (normative) citizen-subjects, and their privileges, from contest and harm. Furthermore, the benefits of epistemic inoculation (i.e., who in the body politic receives antigenic care and is protected by it) are differentially distributed: this is just one among an array of means of reinforcing discursive, structural, and material power asymmetries. In addition, the inoculation effect, or ignorance effect, is not merely individual, but naturalized by, and within, wider structures and practices.

Charles W. Mills (1997) describes how such agreements to engage in ignorance operate as part of the social contract that is in fact a "racial contract."[1] While I find his conception of the racial contract insufficiently intersectional, as his operative notion of Blackness is fairly homogenous and atomized (Black women as a population and as a group of knowers are nearly invisible in his formulation and citational practices, for instance), his keen observations offer important insight as to why taking up intersectionality requires questioning and intervening in socially sanctioned forms of cognitive opaqueness or not-knowing.[2]

Mills demonstrates that we are all (differently) invited to operate within the confines of "an invented delusional world, a racial fantasyland" characterized by myriad forms of cognitive "opacity" necessary to maintain and unify a "white polity" (Mills 1997, 18–19). At the same time, norms of transparency are instituted and enforced, as Crenshaw (1989) argues in "Demarginalizing." Likewise, as Sara Ahmed explains, "it has become commonplace for whiteness to be represented as invisible, as the unseen or the unmarked, as a noncolour, the absent presence or hidden referent, against which all other colours are measured as forms of deviance. . . . But of course whiteness is only invisible for those who inhabit it. For those who don't, it is hard not to see whiteness; it even seems everywhere" (Ahmed 2004, 1).

An epistemology of ignorance is thus core to regulating a (widely sanctioned but just as widely denied) human hierarchy, a "partitioned social ontology" of persons and subpersons accorded disproportionate privileges and patently unequal life chances. To rationalize these inequities, those categorized as "subpersons" (in Mills, those marked as raced, though an intersectional approach would focus on overlapping, intermingled, and relational ontological hierarchies) are characterized as, and considered to be, inherently inferior in terms of moral, political, and cognitive status and authority. This stratification of human value and capacity becomes institutionalized (in legal, political, religious, educational, cultural, and familial institutions), as does an asymmetrical distribution of privilege and power, and harm and suffering (Mills 1997, 11–16, 59–60).

Importantly, once this distinction and hierarchy have been established, instilled, and naturalized, claims about universal personhood and rights within the social polity are widely understood as relevant only to those considered full persons. Simultaneously, however, this narrowness is vigorously denied. Furthermore, the exclusions and erasures embedded in the universal are obscured by an array of knowledge conventions, state practices, and political norms that mask or render illegible these bald-faced contradictions (hence intersectionality's sustained attention to opacities as meaningful structured absences, as I shall discuss shortly). Cultural and political ideals of "universal" equality, sameness, and fairness prevail even as it is evident that these (false) universals were never designed to be all-inclusive and are demonstrably and consistently applied (because conceived) in systemically unequal ways (Mills 1997, 12, 53–60).

Though Crenshaw's contributions generally have been underappreciated in the philosophical literatures on ignorance, it is these patterns of patently false universality, of an overt (but disavowed) exclusion by design, and of a narrow sense of representative personhood that she pinpoints and critiques across her body of work. Early on, in "Demarginalizing," for instance, Crenshaw (1989) shows how antidiscrimination doctrine, feminist praxis, and anti-racist action, when conceived in an atomized way, cannot lead to meaningful forms of justice, as single-axis logics rely on, condone, and require systemic privilege, ontological partitions (personhood/subpersonhood), *and* systematized obliviousness. She also illustrates how such epistemic practices uphold entrenched patterns of differentially distributed harm and violation.

In other words, that *unknowing* or willful ignorance emerges as fundamental to Enlightenment knowledge ideals, and to the various systems (e.g., the law) that stem from this legacy, is no accident. The social contract is declared to be universal and inclusive, but it is instituted (and conceived from the start) in circumscribed, biased, and violent ways. For example, social contract theory, a central component of a "colonizer imagination," endeavored to render Indigenous populations across the globe as *background* figures (as not-persons) in "the fiction of the state of nature," thereby laying the epistemic ground for conquest, slavery, and empire (Hoagland 2010, 229).

Thus, the social contract presents, facially, as neutral and equitable but is conceived, instituted, and practiced in biased and asymmetrical ways. Furthermore, a wide range of normative conventions have been set in place to reinforce this effect, to make it appear as if the social contract is, axiomatically, not just an inclusive ideal, but one that is enacted objectively and in the best interests of (all) the people. By approaching ignorance politics from an intersectional and decolonial orientation, however, we can begin to see more fully how the epistemological force and violation of modernity and capitalism intimately intertwine, historically and presently, with forms of conquest, containment, exploitation, and genocide that are deeply marked by (and, in turn, fundamentally shape) race, gender, sexuality, and disability: moreover, these violations are embedded in the terms and norms of the social contract itself.[3]

What ignorance politics also pinpoint is how, when those with material and political power are invested in maintaining dominion, they can, without penalty (and, frankly, often with significant reward), use their epistemic privilege of not-knowing to refuse to acknowledge and to actively undermine "any newly generated epistemic resource that attends to those parts of the world that they are vested in ignoring" (Pohlhaus 2012, 728). As Gaile Pohlhaus, Jr. illustrates, this dismissal usually occurs by refusing to engage "resources that would call their attention to those aspects of the world to which they do not attend." Furthermore, the epistemic resources that would aid in shifting mindsets usually are "the very ones under contestation"—that is, the ones refused/not-seen/not-known are often the exact concepts and skills being introduced from the epistemic margins (728).

This dynamic—of reinforcing and reasserting the very ways of knowing being contested while ignoring, circumventing, or actively disparaging alternative epistemic tools or orientations—is clear in how single-axis norms are employed in intersectionality critiques and applications alike. By recognizing how knowledge practices are social and political, but also tied to material factors and historical forces, it becomes easier to understand how and why hegemonic ideas cannot simply be dismissed as false or proven wrong solely by rendering the perfect counterargument or providing the right data or information. Dominant views come to have a kind of protective coating or armor which provides them with a form of unassailability: in addition, asymmetrical power relations, past and present, shape what facts are available, what counts as factual, or even what premises are understandable (Narayan 1997).

From an epistemologies of ignorance approach, then, it is not necessarily surprising that the very knowledge norms and systemic exclusions that intersectionality contests also turn out to be the means and mechanisms of its undoing. Single-axis logics are at the heart of many of the structural, material, and philosophical inequities intersectionality objects to and aims to transform: at the same time, they help to render intersectional ideas illogical or illegible. Epistemologies of ignorance are thus instructive for illuminating how it comes to be that knowers committed to transforming and decolonizing knowledge practices and politics often unconsciously participate in forms of epistemic recalcitrance, even opposition or backlash.

Since intersectionality's focus, in great part, is on contesting (more than just identifying) unexpected sites of complicity with domination (whether in terms of political organizing or epistemological habits and practices), it is essential to take up the question of how to turn from such unwitting collusion and means of not-knowing when interpreting and applying intersectionality itself. A key step in this direction requires taking more seriously how knowledge practices enact power and have normative effects.

### Intelligibility Gaps[4] and the Normative Power of Single-Axis Logics

To begin to illustrate the degree to which established frameworks or ideas can uphold unequal social relations, significantly impede cognition, and undermine knowledge, discussions of ignorance politics at work in scientific knowledge communities can be useful. For instance, Barbara Whitten analyzes how physicist Michael Faraday's discovery of "lines of force" (magnetic fields) and electromagnetic induction was both discounted and dismissed in his day (though later it would be understood that he had anticipated key elements of Einstein's theory of relativity) (Whitten 2001). The Faraday example shows how thinking against the grain, and drawing on knowledge honed in the margins, is more than merely difficult: it is a "project" or achieved mindset, not just a natural outcome of one's social location or identity (Whitten 2001, 368; see also Alcoff 2012; Sandoval 2000).

The prevailing logics and epistemic norms of one's time (in Faraday's case, both Newton's hypothesis of gravitational force at a distance and the penchant for mathematical explanations and language as ostensibly superior means of proof, both of which ruled the day) can be so instilled, and we can be so inculcated into them, so as to render new ideas implausible. This ignorance effect is even more powerful as a normative force when new ideas or analyses are generated and introduced by those with less material, epistemic, and political power and when arrived at (and presented or proven) via practices and genres that do not have the same kind of cultural capital or epistemic weight. Whitten clarifies that Faraday's "'humble origins' [did] not guarantee a working-class standpoint" (Whitten 2001, 367), though they certainly impacted his point of entry into science and shaped his approach as an experimentalist.

In retrospect, we can see how three interlocking factors made his ideas seem implausible, even ridiculous, at the time: biases against ways and means of knowing more likely to be practiced by a working-class man like Faraday, trained via apprenticeship (e.g., hands-on experimentation), combined with the academy's inclination to find mathematical theorems (presented by scientists considered to be epistemic *and* social class peers, not underlings or assistants) more plausible, in conjunction with the epistemological influence exerted by the reigning theory of the time (Newton's theory of action at a distance) (Whitten 2001, 371–375).[5]

Though interested in and professionally committed to pursuing the unknown and the not-yet-understood, much of the scientific community nevertheless adhered to more familiar frameworks and to ways of knowing that held more cultural capital (and thus greater validity) for those inside the relatively elite community of scientific knowers. The upper-class underpinnings of scientific training, knowledge exchange, and practice meant that elite knowers and their explanations were more likely to be engaged with (even if, in the end, they were off course): scientific knowledge conventions rendered some new knowledge or discoveries, like Faraday's, less plausible and also, if indirectly, functioned as a means to maintain class privilege and power.

Whitten offers a tangible instance of how interpretation is a key means by which social hierarchies are maintained (and, therefore, also potentially interrupted or unsettled): philosophical standards and expectations have discursive effects that must be taken seriously because they set the parameters of "legitimation" by which knowers are both authorized and disauthorized (Alcoff 2011; Alcoff and Kittay 2007). Everyday beliefs and established norms can significantly impede an idea's uptake: in addition, problems of epistemic intransigence are only amplified by power disparities (i.e., when the new concepts at hand are ones that have been generated by marginalized knowers and that substantially contest prevailing worldviews and established ways of knowing). In other words, in a "socially stratified society, some persons are situated in positions that allow their experiences to count more in the development and circulation of epistemic resources" (Pohlhaus 2012, 718).

A similar lesson has been articulated by Collins, in delineating the contours of Black feminist theorizing more broadly: "An oppressed group's experiences may put its members in a position to see things differently, but their lack of control over the ideological apparatuses of society makes expressing a self-defined standpoint more difficult" (Collins 1990, 26). Barbara Christian named this circumstance as one of belonging to a "folk who speak in muted tongues" (Christian 1990, 13). A century prior, Anna Julia Cooper described herself as one among many "hitherto voiceless" Black women who had been forced to be "one mute and voiceless note": collectively, they comprise an "uncomprehended cadenza," a "muffled strain" struggling to be heard (Cooper 1988, i–ii). This same problem is also, in part, what Crenshaw would allude to when asserting that Black women occupy "a location that resists telling" (Crenshaw 1991, 1242).

Drawing on this long-standing Black feminist intellectual and political legacy, intersectionality challenges a host of everyday logics that uphold inequality and reinforce silences, some of which are tied to institutionalized patterns of unequal cognitive authority and systematic ignorance. At the same time, the politics of reception constitute a significant impediment to engaging intersectional ideas once they have been articulated. In other words, in addition to dominant views having a kind of protective shield, insurgent ideas and politics confront a credibility deficit (Wylie 2011) that facilitates their dismissal or distortion.

Consider some of artist Renée Cox's photographic self-portraits in which she claims her aesthetic and political authority both to contest racist-sexist visual ideologies and to represent and embody the sacred (e.g., in "Yo Mama's Pietà" as the Virgin Mary holding Jesus [who, likewise, is Black], or in "Yo Mama's Last Supper" as a nude, Black female Jesus figure at the last supper [where the only white male is Judas]).[6] Cox's visual affirmation of Black women's embodiment as sacred was read by many (most notably by Rudolph Guiliani, mayor of New York at the time) as irrefutably *profane* and repulsive. The patently racist-sexist logics underlying established sacred/profane binaries rendered her ideas implausible: her aesthetic intervention became legible (and thus dismissable) as an affront to (ostensibly universal) faith, beauty, civility, and human decency.

Similarly, though they tried to mock and disrupt the colonial gaze of human display and to expose the violence of Columbus' "discovery" via their performance art, Coco Fusco and Guillermo Gomez-Peña found many audiences could not perceive beyond the frame of settler-colonial imperial logics and thus were unable to engage with their critiques. Instead of recognizing their work as an ironic performance, one of talking back to coloniality, many audiences just saw Fusco and Gomez-Peña as "authentic" specimens of caged difference on display for the audience's edification (or sexual needs, or cultural curiosity). Alternatively, others (particularly elite viewers) indignantly charged Fusco and Gomez-Peña with being unscrupulous and deceptive (Fusco 1995, 52–59). Either way, most could not perceive their performative challenge to five hundred years of violence and genocide in the name of (ostensibly universal values of) modernity, progress, art/culture, civilization, and knowledge.

With regard to the politics of interpreting and applying intersectionality, it is imperative to understand this twinned epistemic dynamic, wherein consensus reality and dominant logics are granted epistemic safeguarding (akin to an impervious protective coating) and a *surfeit* of cognitive authority, while insurgent ideas and resistance politics face a significant credibility *deficit* and can be treated as wholly illegible or illogical. These linked epistemic circumstances help explain, in part, how single-axis norms continue to preside in ways that render matrix orientations implausible or unintelligible (and how intersectionality's roots and origins in Black and women of color feminisms continue to get treated cursorily or even discarded).

Here, Code's notion of a "social imaginary" (which I contend single-axis logics should be understood to constitute), and how it helps to sustain status quo relations, is useful. As she explains it, a social imaginary "is a loosely integrated system of metaphors, images, assumptions, ways of thinking, with powerful if tacit features that generate and underwrite possibilities of knowledge production, interpretation, uptake, and implementation." A social imaginary thus serves to render "some ideas, practices, and projects plausible, intelligible, and others not" (Code 2011, 210). In other words, to better understand the intransigence of single-axis mindsets, it is useful to approach them as akin to "settled expectations" (Campbell 1999).

Like alluvial deposits that accumulate and harden over time, single-axis logics become "sedimented" (Code 2006) and hard to shake because they are intimately connected to wider social norms, structural asymmetries, historical forces, and material practices. They are also often hidden: like a substratum, single-axis mindsets constitute the invisible basis upon which are built a host of violating practices. Susan Campbell explains how established beliefs "settle" or solidify into sets of expectations that actively structure our attention and shape our responses. They have a "normative force" and impose epistemological obligations—on self and others—in ways that buttress power inequity and bolster dominant identities (Campbell 1999, 224–225). To counter this force, intersectionality offers tools for denaturalizing and piercing dominant logics (via its same/different thesis, antisubordination roots, and attention to enmeshment).

For instance, consider Fiona Campbell's questioning of how Disability Studies is named as a field—she argues for a shift to Studies in Ableism (SiA). Using a same/different reading (of the self, the other, and the social world as permeable) that attends to power's multiple forces, Campbell argues that ableism's bodily and intellectual norms should be understood as central to the logics of oneness and, hence, fundamental to dominion. These corporeal and cognitive standards have an "aspirational benchmark" that values and reinforces sameness. This benchmark pivots on a "hermeneutics of the desirable and the disgusting," or a hierarchy of the worthy versus the unworthy: however, it is usually presented as a utopian narrative of medical promise and progressive development (not as a murderous tale of disappearance or as a eugenic nightmare) (Campbell 2012, 214). The aspirational, of course, is simultaneously encoded by myriad other signs or markers used to map out worthy citizen-subjects: whiteness/lightness, normative sexual practices/identities/positionalities (heteronormative and, increasingly, homonormative), privileged class positions, and dominant gender norms/roles.

Campbell calls for a dual accounting, one that focuses on epistemic and embodied defiance against normative (and normalizing) forces while also attending to the "production of ableism" as a systematic process inculcating us into hegemonic body logics and, likewise, into what Puar describes as global economies of productivity versus "debility" (Puar 2012a). This, in turn, offers ways to challenge widespread notions of pathology, reasonableness, productivity, deficiency, healthiness, and well-being that are both specific to ableism and part of the shared logics used to animate and justify myriad ontological hierarchies (Campbell 2012, 218). In attending to ableism's permeability with/in other systems of oppression, Campbell also rejects the common impetus to create universalizable knowledge about disability (as an obverse of narrow norms of wellness and corporeal uniformity) because such knowledge could readily align with ableist Western/modern/colonial epistemic practices, forms of governance, and systems of economic expropriation (Campbell 2012, 222–223; see also Grech 2012).

In other words, part of what an intersectional approach emphasizes is how established beliefs exert considerable power by obscuring (as meaningful or relevant), or by eradicating (as unworthy or lesser), the different subjectivities, knowledges, bodies, cosmologies, memories, histories, or worldviews being presented (and that have long been present, even if denied or suppressed). Attending to structured absences and epistemic opacities is therefore imperative because they impact knowledge dynamics and political possibilities not only with regard to margin/center power relations but also within-group relations and margin-to-margin knowledge dynamics and political possibilities.

In other words, intersectionality's focus on simultaneous privilege and oppression, combined with its attention to multiplicity (in terms of subjectivity and power relations) via a same/different, both/and lens, means that epistemic relations among (and within) differently marginalized communities can also be fraught: marginalized spaces, bodies, and knowledges are not free from relations of dominance. As Lugones explains, "Since our journeys to the limen are different, often at odds, often in great tension *given that we are among each other's oppressors*, the freeing spaces where we attempt to chisel our own faces are not readily accessible to each other" (Lugones 2006, 77, italics added). Single-axis logics can thus lead to cognitive or political outcomes that are more than just partial or incomplete: they render intersectional worldviews unintelligible and serve as an obstacle to understanding and to enacting intersectional ways of knowing and being.

Given the range of harms and violations incited and sustained by pop-bead, hierarchical mindsets, why is it that single-axis gender frameworks endure within feminist projects at large and in debates about and uses of intersectionality in particular? Certainly, on one hand, as a means to understand bodies, map power, unpack social relations, and historicize ideas, gender, taken up within critical feminist contexts, seems a potentially expansive (or at least salvageable) category. On the other hand, it can be profoundly narrow, not only in terms of its historical uses, but also its current deployments. For instance, an "ongoing myopia of hegemonic concepts of gender" continues to occlude and to discount the "cross-border dimensions of gender dynamics, and the continued power of the geographies of colonial modernity" (Patil 2013, 848).

Despite repeated evidence of their fundamental distortions, diachronically and presently, common-denominator gender logics continue to exert a considerable political and philosophical force. Even when used in the name of radical critique and resistance, gender-primary logics continue to "govern" (regulate and rule) many feminist practices in ways that carry on hegemony and replicate normative/deviant hierarchies. Gender, then, might well need to be understood as a remarkably persistent example of the single-axis logics and practices intersectionality contests and, equally, a powerful factor in keeping intersectional ideas and worldviews contained, sidelined, or just out of reach.

## How Might Gender Be Epistemically Unjust on Intersectional Terms?[7]

From its earliest formations, intersectionality has underscored the inadequacy of seeking recognition (from the state, the law, one's allies in resistance movements, or within one's "home" communities) via categorical terms, knowledge norms, or political practices that deny multiplicity, disarticulate enmeshed identities and systems, and artificially parse vectors of power and pathways to meaningful social change. Reflecting back on her earlier writings, Crenshaw has explained how "Demarginalizing" was, in great part, about revealing and critiquing how U.S. antidiscrimination law, civil rights activism, and feminist politics required certain categories and frameworks for claims to be legible, even if these, in turn, violated complexity, denied multiplicity, and undermined justice. The law established "interpretive templates that any discrimination claim needed to engage in order to be cognizable" (Crenshaw 2011c, 228): however, these single-axis terms of recognition repeatedly (and variously) violated Black women's claims.

In the context of feminism, intersectionality has shown how (common-denominator) gender, though used to render sexism "cognizable" as a (fluid, constructed, lived) process and system, nevertheless operates as an inadequate, even violating "interpretive template," because gender (in its Western, modern, dimorphic iterations) continues to be a key means by which modernity's singular logics and divisive practices live on.[8] Gender remains central to identifying and facilitating feminist projects even as it also has been a fundamental means by which inequalities among women have been created and reinforced. It may, therefore, be integral to the patterns of imaginative intransigence vis-à-vis intersectionality mapped out herein and pivotal to the persistent (and peculiar) dismissal and distortion of intersectional logics and practices.

Code outlines how "governing imaginaries" (here, with regard to the fields of law and medicine) reinforce a philosophical order and also sustain the larger social order. The figure of the "reasonable man" offers a condensation of the law's imaginary, while for medicine it is the "science-obedient diagnostician" (Code 2006, 106). Code does not discuss the implications of gender as a "governing imaginary" for women's and gender studies. However, if we consider gender-primary logics, or the collective figure "women," to be, in fact, akin to a governing imaginary, then we must consider the coercive force exerted by gender upon intersectional logics and politics. In turn, since "Western gender discourse embeds us in and is embedded in colonial formations" (Hoagland 2010, 227) that are saturated by Western "body logics" (Oyěwùmí 1997), by heteronormative somatics and reproductive frames (Hall 2005; Lugones 2007, 2010), and by ableist fantasies of productivity and capacity (Campbell 2012; Goodley 2014; Puar 2012a), this should lead to questioning whether gender should remain feminism's primary "legitimating discursive structure" (Gedalof 2012, 3).

As Hoagland argues, gender actively "enters us into a cognitive framework," one that "permeate[s] our thinking" (Hoagland 2010, 237) in ways that distort, even as it has been used to shed light on unequal social relations, exclusionary philosophical norms, and harmful power structures, presently and historically. In the end, then, how illuminating is gender for analyzing and/or contesting existing inequalities and oppressive social relations, and what are its costs or erasures if one accounts for gender intersectionally, transnationally, and also decolonially?

The "flattening effect" of gender on feminist theory (Alarcón 1990, 361) comes even more sharply into focus via a decolonial lens that accounts for what Lugones (2007) describes as the "light" side of modernity as well as the "dark" side—the Enlightenment's underside (i.e., coloniality, slavery, and conquest). Western modernity's binary gender system was devised and instituted as an exclusive set of categories and processes, carefully reserved in the social contract's partitioned social ontology only for those considered full persons (not subpersons). Modernity's logics understand male/female binaries (sexual dimorphism) as relevant to all beings (human and animal), but simultaneously *degender* or deny gender to all but those males and females understood (and designated) as human in the social contract—that is, reserved only for those *most* privileged within modernity's "light" side (Lugones 2007, 2010).

Within modernity's "light" side, there are also hierarchical ontologies and declensions of personhood—if one's white/light racial status is intertwined with poverty, non-normative sexuality, or bodily difference or disability, for instance, one is placed lower on the established human hierarchy. One's gendered status is likewise also mitigated: one can be degendered or categorized as outside of or as deviating from gender by myriad factors. For modernity's "dark" side, and for the light side's shadows, so to speak, "sex was made to stand alone." Modernity's dark side was understood to be *without gender* yet still sexed (male and female) (Lugones 2007; see also Morgan 2004; Taylor-García 2008).

This Western modern gender-race-ability logic also generated classifications for a wide range of what appear as/get constructed as anomalies: notions of the monstrous or animal-like body, for instance, were used to mark deviance and ascribe depravity. Though at times "the colonial gaze gender[ed] Indigenous people as hermaphrodites or intersexed" (Bailey 2010, 66), peculiar or abnormal genders are understood to not correspond to being gendered in the dual/light/modern/human sense. Rather, as the outer limits of gender, or as beyond gender, anomalies and abnormalities buttress normative bourgeois, civilized, human gender. Ostensible lack of gender, or aberrant or deviant gender, is then used to rationalize ungendered/degendered bodies being brutalized (as hypersexual or animal flesh), caged or incarcerated, exploited as surplus labor, or destroyed because expendable.

Across time and place, gender has functioned as a category or means of understanding that, minimally, flattens and distorts and, maximally, erases and violates: it was conceived and devised, in the context of coloniality, slavery, and empire, to "facilitate the destruction of frameworks, epistemes, economies and cosmologies of conquered cultures" (Hoagland 2010, 228). Furthermore, once one takes up an interpretive frame shaped by decolonial and intersectional feminist commitments, the ostensible historical *break* from coloniality (the "post" colonial)—a declared fiction which is part of the social contract's epistemology of ignorance—comes to be understood as definitively not "over" but still happening. As Hoagland explains, "This is the coloniality of power. . . . [T]he 'after' of 'post-colonialism' is an aftermath that includes virtually seamless continuations of colonial reorderings: identity formation, economic exploitation, epistemic ordering, and patterns of violence. This aftermath informs U.S. academic institutions, including its intellectual canons, and even thrives in progressive intellectual productions" (Hoagland 2010, 228).

Thinking diachronically, via a heterogeneous temporality that "supplants the claims of a singular history" tied to linear/colonial/modern time (Alcoff 2004a, 111), creates room to document how coloniality endures (and, likewise, how departures from or resistances alongside coloniality are also ongoing). For instance, Barbara Heron (2007) maps out continuities between Victorian colonial gender discourses of feminine virtue (ideologies/norms meant for the elite, "light" side of modernity—for the gendered) and contemporary ideas about the moral goodness of NGO development and women's organizations from the Global North. Heron unpacks "constructions of gender, which position white middle-class women as simultaneously subjects and non-subjects who may enhance their hold on bourgeois subjectivity through the performance of 'goodness'" (Heron 2007, 7). Women from the Global North, working in feminized and racialized NGO and development contexts, often reanimate colonial logics (of time, productivity, capital, embodiment, gender, and race) in the name of ostensibly universal forms of gender progress that privilege modernity's "light"/bourgeois subjectivities.

Legacies of (modern Western) gender processes and ideologies thus play out in new ways that may appear, on the surface, disconnected from (or wholly discontinuous from) colonial/modern gender. At present, for instance, gender, as an oppressive tool of the state's practices, has clear ties to the logics of coloniality, though at face value, contemporary rationales for regulating genders, or current sites of policing gender, may not seem linked to these legacies and histories. To illustrate, Dean Spade delineates how, in the U.S. context, dimorphic gender norms used today by the criminal justice system (and the medical establishment) to police trans* bodies can be traced to the history of prisons and to carceral logics that emerged after slavery. He asserts that from the nation's founding, "the legal rules governing Indigenous and enslaved people articulated their subjection through the imposition of violent racialized gender norms. . . . [T]he laws governing slavery, land ownership, labor, health, mobility, punishment, and family create very specific statuses and norms according to specific race/gender positions" (Spade 2012, 189; see also Davis 2003, 2005).

Likewise, gender, coloniality, and conquest can be read, retroactively, in ways that expose sites of contestation and historical discontinuity that have been smoothed over or ignored. In this vein, C. Alejandra Elenes uses a decolonial, intersectional approach to examine the historical emergence and current practices of Mexican nationalism. Specifically focusing on the figure of Malintzin, in combination with powerful romantic myths of Mexico's Indigenous "past," Elenes traces how the Western/modern colonial gender logics of the missionary priests and the conquistadores continue in current Mexican national imaginaries and state ideologies and practices. A masculinist, settler-colonial nationalism and teleology artificially parse time and treat identities as atomized: this impedes meaningful acknowledgment of the ongoing exploitation of Indigenous communities in the present and, at the same time, forecloses historical consideration of Malintzin's struggle and survival as an enslaved Indigenous woman (Elenes 2011, 150–155).

Refusing to separate the workings of race, gender, and coloniality, Elenes contends that "to reduce Malintzin's gender as the primary source that marks her as a traitor is . . . reductive" (156), even though this is the conventional reading of/story about her legacy. In other words, "Mexican nationalism and patriarchy do not forgive her, not because she was a woman, but because she was a woman who acted outside the narrow confines of gender ideology through her sexuality and the possession of knowledge held only by a few" (157). However, warns Elenes, conventional ideas about gender, agency, and resistance also may not hold here, as a means of reclaiming "Malintzin as a decolonial figure," since she "made choices under untenable conditions" (161): attending to structural constraints and processes, in terms of state ideology, but also in terms of Malintzin's lived realities as an enslaved woman, means a "both/and" accounting of her life and actions is requisite (162).[9]

From an intersectional disposition, more adequately and meaningfully considering how gender can operate as a kind of constraining, even violent imaginary for feminist theory, politics, research, and activism (and for many other intellectual/political movements for social change more broadly) would require granting more than just nominal plausibility to the fact that gender has long been a highly delimited, narrowly conceived, racialized, ableist, bourgeois concept and thus equally long attached to multiple, intermingled systems of dominance. In other words, just as "the colonial move interpellates others into a Western discourse" (Hoagland 2010, 235), gender may well interpellate us deep into these colonial legacies.

As Lugones explains, "historicizing gender and heterosexualism is thus an attempt to move, dislodge, complicate what has faced me and others engaged in liberatory/decolonial projects as hard barriers that are both conceptual and political. . . . Liberatory possibilities that emphasize the light side of the colonial/modern gender system affirm rather than reject an oppressive organization of life" (Lugones 2007, 187). Approaching gender as an interpretive template derived from lenses shaped by decolonial, intersectional, anti-ableist, queer dispositions, it is clear that gender needs to be still more "troubled," further unsettled, and more fully disarticulated from dominant sensibilities and histories.

## Epistemic Injustice, Testimonial Voids, and Intersectionality

Despite myths of equal (and equally accessed) "rhetorical space," where everyone can have a voice, speak up, be heard, and be understood, cognitive authority, as a form of social and political power, is unequal and disproportionately distributed (Code 1995). Crenshaw thus maps out how Black women are silenced (in that their testimony or claims are refused) by the courts, by civil rights paradigms, and by feminist politics (Crenshaw 1989). Power asymmetries shape perception and impact assessments of the reasonableness of claims (Narayan 1997; Schutte 2000): as a consequence, resistant ways of knowing repeatedly encounter a highly structured and carefully maintained "intelligibility gap" (Alcoff 2012, 27). Credibility among and between knowers is also differential, not uniform. Some groups have been systematically rendered unrecognizable as knowers: in turn, alternative ways of knowing engaged in by such groups are frequently disregarded or, if noted, tend to be viewed, from within dominant frames, as proof of deficiency, as evidence of epistemic disqualification and incapacity, not as viable knowledge practices (Heldke 2006).

As Miranda Fricker (2007) illustrates, inequality narrows the domain of socially available meanings and negatively impacts the interpretation, reception, and overall perception of knowledges generated by disenfranchised groups: those who are marginalized do not participate equally in the construction or definition of what counts as meaningful. In other words, hermeneutic inequality and marginalization are epistemological effects of structural and political inequality. Furthermore, Fricker underscores that "testimonial injustice" and "hermeneutic marginalization" are intertwined factors—one is unable to render one's experience/knowledge legible to those with more power, and those with more power are unable to read/interpret beyond the frameworks they have created (Fricker 2007). Though not specifically named in Fricker's discussion, I would argue intersectionality should more explicitly be taken up in philosophical analyses of epistemic injustice and testimonial inequality. Crenshaw, for instance, clearly accentuates how hermeneutic bias and interpretive injustice intertwine when describing how, like numerous Black feminists before her, she still finds herself "speaking into the void" decades after first delineating intersectional analyses (Crenshaw 2011c, 228).

To illustrate this dynamic, consider Elena Marchetti's (2008) analysis of the Australian Royal Commission into Aboriginal Death in Custody (RCIADIC). Marchetti highlights how a predisposition toward a facially neutral (but fundamentally biased) liberal legal ideology skewed the commission's findings: their approach did not take up an intersectional and decolonial orientation toward community, testimony, sovereignty, or justice. Adhering to liberal legal frames led to a systemic inability to recognize complex within-group differences, cultural hegemony, and violence at work in the commission's practices and in Australia's history. Instead, the commission reinforced the state's settler colonial foundations.

While their approach appeared inclusive, since "Indigenous people were employed to ensure that an Indigenous voice was included in the RCIADIC's investigations," the commission did not adequately account for power—i.e., systematic subjugation, institutionalized harm, and testimonial injustice. They also failed to recognize, in contexts of trauma, that the usual measures of knowledge may not suffice *and* that not everything can be articulated: there may be no language or framework adequate to name the historical experience, cultural knowledge, or collective memory at hand (Simon and Eppert 1997). The Commission engaged in a *demographic* modification to systematic exclusion but without meaningful epistemological transformation or historical accounting: their method was inadequately intersectional and decolonial in its orientation toward testimony, power, and temporality. Though included, Indigenous participants' "lack of power to direct and influence the research and recommendations ultimately inhibited the nature of the data collected." Furthermore, Marchetti found, "Only voices that imitated non-Indigenous cultural norms and that fell within liberal legal understandings" emerged in the data and were included in reports (Marchetti 2008, 167).

In contexts of structural inequality, then, some limited recognition may occasionally be granted or some degree of cognitive authority "conferred" (e.g., if one is willing to take up the speaking position of a native informant or cultural insider, or to mimic hegemonic norms of knowledge and testimony). However, bestowed authority is precarious and usually still functions as a place of unhearability, since one is asked to speak in ways that align with (and fortify) dominant explanations or established assumptions (Narayan 1997). As Alcoff elucidates, while assimilation in all its guises (political, linguistic, ontological, epistemological) may offer the "promise of intelligibility," this promise is contingent upon adhering to majority ways of thinking/being/speaking. Furthermore, adopting majority logics and vocabularies usually results in a one-way accommodation or absorption—an enfolding into a "monotopic horizon" (Alcoff 2012, 27). Nevertheless, the desire for recognition, the yearning to be heard, can lead one to align with dominance, even as one aims to contest it. In fact, Lugones describes this dynamic as a major aspect of the "the resisting ↔ oppressing relation." She asserts, "As subjected, we fear standing outside the bounds of the ordinary even though the ordinary oppresses us into servility" (Lugones 2005, 94–95).

Of course, feminist knowledge practices are not exempt from questions of testimonial injustice or from the normative force of presuppositions. For instance, in terms of transnational feminist politics, much of "western feminism still harbors the hope that its own views of emancipation are universally valid for all the world's women, if only because western thought generally does not mark itself as culturally specific. Instead, it engages in the discursive mode of a universal *logos*, which it takes to be applicable to all rational speakers" (Schutte 2000, 59). To a large extent, what Alarcón pinpointed decades ago holds: the "linguistic status" of feminist subjectivity, rationality, and recognition remains bound to monological Enlightenment norms (Alarcón 1990, 363–365). This is, in part, why Lee Maracle (1994) connects language to a means of force and why Anzaldúa describes, metaphorically, having her (multilingual, carnal, borderland) tongue cut out (Anzaldúa 1999, 75–86). Rejecting purity and the logics of oneness, at the level of language and subjectivity, Trinh T. Minh-ha advocates, instead, "saying at least two, three things at a time," as it is "vital to assume one's radical 'impurity' and to recognize the necessity of speaking from a hybrid place" (Minh-ha 1992, 140).

However, in ways overt and subtle, many aspects of feminist cognitive authority continue to be wedded to discourses, worldviews, and assumptions tied to legacies of conquest and coloniality: as a result, different orientations and contesting claims often cannot be perceived, much less heard or supported (Narayan 1997, 144–145). Ofelia Schutte describes how being understood or recognized as a Latina feminist philosopher (even in limited ways) requires her to take up knowledge norms and forms of language that, before she even begins, *already mark her as a less capable knower*. She explains, to claim "my position as a cultural agent in terms recognized by the dominant cultural group . . ., I need to be knowledgeable in the language and epistemic maneuvers of the dominant culture." However, this is "the same culture that in its everyday practice marks me as culturally 'other' than itself" (Schutte 2000, 53–54).

When using alternative lenses, memories, experiences, and presuppositions, liminal speakers often have normative logics imposed that flatten or silence significant differences in meanings, goals, or worldviews. As a consequence, marginalized subjects may seek recognition on conventional terms, even as such paths to communication and understanding can violate by requiring the adoption of processes, expectations, and lenses that distort. Being understood or becoming legible can entail being "hermeneutically marginalized, systemically and systematically" (Code 2011, 209). Intersectionality thus calls for reading conventional frameworks or approaches against the grain and, simultaneously, for thinking in more than one register and attending to more than one world of meaning/being at once.

Developing, interpreting, and applying intersectional knowledge, derived from and crafted in marginalized locations, requires recognizing this many-sided struggle. First is the sustained effort to articulate what cannot readily be conveyed (if at all) in conventional terms. Second is the attempt to navigate interpretive distortion and bias—to be understood without being (mis)translated into dominant logics that obstruct and block out the meanings being presented. Third is the endeavor not to slide into hegemonic knowledge practices, margin-to-margin or within-group, thereby replicating the normative force and violation of hierarchical and divisive knowledge practices. Acknowledging these narrative/interpretive politics is requisite for understanding the material, ontological, and epistemological asymmetries of power which have shaped intersectionality's historical emergence, which it has continually sought to name and transform, and which continue to impact its reception and use.

Grounded in and derived from knowledge gained living at the crossroads of multiple identities and in the crosshairs of power and privilege, intersectionality names and seeks to address the conundrum of having inadequate frames for expressing or representing compound subjectivity, knowledge, experience, and political orientations—or of being *read into* or *assimilated into* frameworks that occlude and discount the complexities at hand. Yet (differently) privileged knowers regularly treat as immaterial or extraneous many of the factors intersectionality insists are deeply relevant, including the contexts of knowledge production, the impact of structural power upon knowers and knowledges, and knowers' social locations. In other words, commonplace beliefs about understanding in general, and many approaches to reading/interpreting intersectional knowledge in particular, are unable to meet the multiplicity that informs intersectionality's overall analytical orientation and political commitments. We need more adequate forms of interpretation that can better account for its critical and reflexive stance toward dominant sensibilities and established categories.

## Intersectionality and the Politics of Understanding

When it comes to intersectionality, as a disposition or orientation, two issues must be thought through more fully: how it is *understood* and how it is *misunderstood* or thought of as implausible both need consideration. Sometimes, people seem to have understood intersectionality but then use it in anti-intersectional or assimilative ways, folding it into conventional frameworks: intersectionality's different meanings, politics, assumptions, and aims disappear. Alternatively, intersectional mindsets can be written off simply as illogical. Either way, "dominant expectations"—about rationality, subjectivity, or narrative style—tend to "rule out the meaningfulness of important struggles" from marginalized locations and communities and thus significantly impede their ability to be heard and understood (Babbitt 2001, 298).

Susan Babbitt suggests ideas, lives, and stories which diverge from dominant expectations (about what reason looks like, about what a life trajectory should entail, or what an adequate narrative or storyline offers) often are just "not able to be heard" (Babbitt 2001, 300). For instance, as Sandoval argues, women of color feminist theorizing tends to operate at the level of the implausible, such that its "kinetic motion" does not register whatsoever (Sandoval 2000, 44). In other words, due to institutionalized power asymmetries and systematic injustices, some lives and stories unfold so far outside the bounds of dominant narrative frameworks and life trajectories they are, from conventional mindsets, fundamentally unimaginable (Babbitt 2001, 308). Furthermore, there tends to be little to no curiosity, from dominant locations, about the inconceivable: this implausibility is rarely questioned or contested—it just "is."

At the same time, epistemological and political erasure can also unfold *in seeming to be heard* or "understood": however, the means of understanding distort by erasing divergences from prevailing norms (and ignoring challenges to established worldviews). Understanding can enact a kind of assimilationist cognitive move—as in "boomerang perception" (Spelman 1988, 12) and other forms of recognition that are demonstrably "weighted toward the dominant culture" (Alcoff 2012, 32). This absorption (that erases while enfolding) derives in part from the fact that "those of us educated in Western traditions are taught, when we wish to explore something new, to translate it into something we know and understand" (Hoagland 2010, 237). In such circumstances, "people *think* they have understood . . . when they have not" (Babbitt 2001, 303).

Differences between epistemological frames thus tend to be treated as irrelevant, insignificant, or just nonexistent. That there are "residues" that do not (and cannot) readily translate (Schutte 2000, 49; see also Alcoff 2004b), or key ideas and insights at hand that remain *not yet understood* (and which require different forms of perception, knowing, and interpretation even to be perceived, much less understood), falls away. In thinking about understanding more complexly, and about asymmetrical cognitive authority and structural power more adequately, Code contends we must repudiate Enlightenment assumptions about "human sameness, about a matter-of-course ease of 'putting oneself in someone else's shoes' and knowing his/her/their circumstances accordingly. Such assumptions impede possibilities of knowing people and their situations well enough to recognize when and how sameness can in fact *not* be assumed: they make it difficult to see how differences make a difference" (Code 2011, 208).

In other words, many Enlightenment norms of understanding or knowing suppress the differences present (and being presented). Any epistemological *departure* or political *struggle* required to comprehend the world from alternative or contestatory views is also foreclosed—whether something is not understood (because illegible, irrational, inconceivable) or whether it is understood (but in ways that absorb it into the already-known, enfold it into dominant epistemes). A lack of comprehension, or an inadequate understanding arrived at by adhering to established explanations or imaginaries, is not seen as epistemologically significant: there is a fundamental "failure to explain what ought to be explained," which means that "expectations that ought to be questioned cannot be questioned" (Babbitt 2005, 9).

Whether by taking difference into the fold, by treating it as insignificant, or by ignoring the residues of lives or ideas that do not translate across boundaries, many commonplace means of interpreting and narrating experience (and the parameters for defining what constitutes experience in the first place) constrain (or even foreclose) perception of divergent worlds, imaginaries, or life trajectories. Privileged knowers may thus believe they have understood marginalized lives, stories, and ideas by incorporating them into dominant frames of rationality or, alternatively, by categorizing what they don't understand merely as odd, esoteric, or even irrational—and thus as not worth knowing because outside of reason or so "different" they cannot be absorbed into the logic of the same. This ensures established worldviews and privileged subjectivities remain one and whole—not fragmented, split, or contested. Understanding, paradoxically, becomes an exercise in willful ignorance, enforcing the silences and asymmetries of power that marginalized groups aim to render visible and transform.

Thinking from within multiplicity, though it can entail engaging with frames and norms that are conflicting, or with ideas and lives not fully comprehensible within the usual terms, is fundamental to intersectional forms of understanding (and to understanding intersectionality). As Code explains, "fostering an imaginative openness" entails more than "receptivity": it requires "a willingness to grant conceivability to the seemingly implausible. It also involves attention to perceptual habits and peripheries" (Code 2006, 112–125). It is thus important to allow for the fact that what one does not (and maybe cannot) understand, via established frameworks or by conventional logics, still can have meaningfulness and importance, particularly as we reside in different "worlds" (see Lugones 1987, 2005, 2010) that do not necessarily align in terms of basic presuppositions about time, space, and reality, for instance.

### Intersectionality and the "Resistant Oppressed"[10]

For marginalized and resistant knowers, being subjected to monological, nonintersectional ways of knowing can lead to a splitting. Schutte, for instance, explains that, as a Latina, she has "become a split subject.

Even when 'recognized,' it's still a misrecognition. . . . What remains to be understood in the statements of the culturally differentiated other—that is, *the incommensurable something* not subject to perfect cultural translation—may actually be the most important part" of what she has to say (Schutte 2000, 54–55, italics added). The "incommensurable something" is fundamental: to overlook it or to categorize it as inconsequential is to deny Schutte's personhood and ideas.

Furthermore, while dominant groups may inaccurately view the "incommensurable" as insignificant, or erroneously equate split subjectivity and consciousness with a kind of fragmentation-as-brokenness, Lugones contends that the complex subject's splintered perception and split existence should be understood not as fragmented (or fragmentable) but as "curdled." Curdled subjects and curdled logics indicate resistance and resilience at the level of the individual (that is, curdling evinces a refusal to let go of the "incommensurable something," an insistence on its meaningfulness and relevance): they also signal that alternative worlds, ways of being, and mindsets have long existed, thanks to collective efforts, and these, too, live on alongside hegemony (Lugones 1994).[11] She explains, "as we exercise double vision, it is clear that this gives us a way of rejecting the reality of the oppressor as true even when we recognize that it rules our lives, even from the inside" (Lugones 2006, 79). Building on Lugones, Alison Bailey argues that curdled/resisting subjects "take hold of the double meaning" of their actions, selves, and ideas: reality is not unified, but is comprised of multiple worlds—and within each, "both dominant and resistant logics are present" (Bailey 2007, 84–90).

In this vein, Alcoff discusses the merits of thinking about time against the linearity of colonial chronology and asserts that a people's history and lived experience simply cannot be "captured by the colonial narrative" (Alcoff 2004a, 109). Furthermore, the violence exerted by coloniality's dimorphic gender norms (Lugones 2007, 2010) and by what Elizabeth Freeman (2010) might call its "chrononormativity," cannot be accounted for in the colonial episteme. In discussing queer temporalities, Freeman explains that the chrononormative is a key "technique by which institutional forces come to seem like somatic facts. Schedules, calendars, time zones, and even wristwatches inculcate . . . forms of temporal experience that seem natural. . . . Manipulations of time convert historically specific regimes of asymmetrical power into seemingly ordinary bodily tempos and routines, which in turn organize the value and meaning of time" (Freeman 2010, 3). Freeman's discussion thus further illuminates Lugones' emphasis on the decolonial (as persistent, ongoing), and her rejection of frames such as the post- and/or pre-colonial which align with coloniality's temporal mappings (Lugones 2007, 2010).

To illustrate, consider Hoagland's discussion of Sylvia Marcos' (2006) research with contemporary *curanderas*, midwives, and shamans. Marcos, "drawing on primary sources, colonial documents and ethnographies," contests long-standing distortions and mistranslations of Indigenous concepts of eros and gender and renders visible "a precolonial cosmology," built on a porous "Nahua worldview [that] involves duality, fluidity, and balance" which is still practiced. More than simply trace this cosmology and recognize this continuous practice (which is discontinuous with dominant historical narratives and logics), Hoagland contends it is imperative to recognize that what Marcos delineates "*is not translatable into Western cosmology*" and that the gender roles and experiences presented are "*not commensurable with Western gender*" (Hoagland 2010, 238, italics added). Thus, while prevailing logics exert considerable political and epistemological force that must be acknowledged, at the same time, it is equally vital to recognize that governing imaginaries are rarely completely successful. Resistant, incommensurable bodies, lives, ideas, and practices exist alongside and against these forces.

Since resistance to dominance is, obviously, possible, learning to perceive this potential (in oneself and in others), and to engage with this lived (historical and ongoing) complexity, is imperative. Maria Jastrzębska's poem about lying in a hospital bed in a pink robe, seemingly inert and inactive, is illustrative: the protagonist is perceived by others, particularly by medical staff and hospital managers, as passive, weak, and still, not as a "warrior." However, she states, "I have never been/as slow/or as deadly." Imperceptible to the dominant eye is the fact that she is "watching/with the stillness/of a lizard or snake" and is "lying in wait/ready to pounce" (Jastrzębska 1996, 189–191). Likewise, in discussing Anzaldúa's writings, and particularly the notion of "conocimiento" (Anzaldúa 1999), Lugones analogizes Anzaldúa's state of thinking/being as like that of a "serpent coiled" (Lugones 2005, 90), that is, taking an internal journey, recoiling from dominant logics. Extending this analogy, Lugones asserts we must always presume that "the subjected form intentions against the grain," even if we have been carefully taught not to see this fact readily (or at all) (86).

In reading Anzaldúa as akin to a coiled serpent, Lugones illustrates that, while she may be unable to act in ways that align with conventional ideas about agency, since those norms can require the subjugated to perform kinds of action that are merely "oppressed activity carrying out servile intentions," Anzaldúa is, nonetheless, working to "concoct sense away from dominant sense." Actively "coiled," she should be understood to be in a state of "germinative stasis" (Lugones 2005, 95–96). To clarify, Lugones does not ignore the onus or cost of having to navigate incommensurable worlds. However, she emphasizes that it is a mistake to assume hegemonic interpretations and systems are so powerful as to hold us all "captive" all of the time, in every way (90). Here, the value of intersectionality's capacity to attend to relational power and privilege, across and within intermingled systems, comes to the fore: via its same/different thesis and both/and logics, an intersectional disposition does not see notions of "germinative stasis" or categories such as "the resistant oppressed" as illogical contradictions.

Intersectionality acknowledges that lived complexity is often not representable or visible in standard terms: to meet (rather than suppress or ignore) multiplicity, it is vital to develop both a desire and a capacity to understand each other otherwise and to read texts, archives, social reality, life stories, institutions, and systems of power on different terms. Concerted efforts to read against the grain are pivotal for taking up intersectionality's "matric" thinking against "single-axis" forces. Intersectional oppositional epistemic/political approaches derive from, and build upon, resistant cognitive skills forged in the perceptual and embodied horizons of marginalization (Lugones 1994, 2005; Hoagland 2001; Sandoval 2000) and are not meant to be extracted from their communities/histories/contexts of origin, then commoditized and traded.

Unfortunately, matrix mindsets often are not pursued but dropped: in turn, opportunities to understand the world and each other differently fall away. bell hooks contends, for instance, that "resistant" Black feminist ideas and forms of speech, especially ones that cannot be readily appropriated or effortlessly understood, are often ignored: assessed via same/different binary frames, if noted, they tend to be categorized simply as unusual (and their difference is not taken to be meaningful) (hooks 1990, 147). In other words, argues Lugones, the "monologism of the colonizer" exerts an ongoing interpretive/political force that has a "way of silencing all contestatory interlocution. There is no place for conversation that includes the colonized tongue—the one you and I hold in our mouths—as a centrifugal force altering the society's language and its map of reality" (Lugones 2006, 81–82).

Yet, and still, the "resistant oppressed" exist and continue to defy the singular (Lugones 2006), though often in alternative forms, voices, genres, or locations. Such non-cooperation requires developing an "epistemology of resistance" in the face of systematic ignorance (Bailey 2007, 87), which I would argue intersectionality should be understood to constitute. It also necessitates taking up different reading practices and requirements, for which Lugones stipulates a key proviso: "Recognition of another as liminal, as standing in a borderlands, is a necessary condition for reading their words and gestures differently. If I think you are in a limen, I will know that, at least some of the time, you do not mean what you say but something else" (Lugones 2006, 79).

This means, for example, that "the language of writers from oppressed groups, for whom forthrightness is a dangerous luxury, is rarely literal, and is generally multi-layered," as Kristin Waters delineates in the history of Black women writers (Waters 2007, 368). Likewise, Lugones contends, "the Chicana's resistance is exercised from outside a shared linguistic domain. . . . As colonized subjects are rendered alien and contained both spatially and linguistically in barrios and on reservations, these become liminal sites for the fashioning of intensely contestatory speech" (Lugones 2006, 82).

## Intersectionality and Opacity

As with intersectional political orientations, intersectional approaches to understanding or perception are not based on a presupposition of transparency and underlying sameness, particularly as monological models impede meaningful coalitions and undermine coalitional knowing by setting aside difference. Intersectionality underscores that a many-horizoned way of perceiving and a multifaceted, complex form of being is necessary: such a "pluritopic" approach emphasizes that "other truths" exist, and always have, "but their visibility is reduced by the continuing power asymmetry, which is based on the coloniality of knowledge, power, being, and gender" (Tlostanova and Mignolo 2009, 18).

Moreover, an intersectional disposition entails acknowledging and learning to read both multiplicity and opacity, but "not through assimilating the text of others to our own" (Lugones 2006, 84). Rather than offering intelligibility via transparency, the knowledges and stories that we share (or attempt to share with one another) can be understood to "remind us of 'our' (whoever we are) relative opacity to one another" (Code 2011, 271). Opaqueness and incomprehensibility are thus not to be ignored or eradicated but followed. Given intersectionality's emphasis on multiplicity, not only in terms of subjectivity and knowledge but also domains of power and relational privilege and oppression, this lesson about opacity—as something to learn to read, and to pursue as meaningful, is key. Furthermore, attending to and inhabiting/entering opacity is necessary not only between center(s) and margin(s) but also within-group and margin-to-margin (Lugones 2006). An active commitment to potential meaningfulness, even if well beyond the bounds of what one knows, or on terms far different from what one understands as logical, is essential from an intersectional approach.

This interrogative, open orientation toward opacities and absences creates space for lives, meanings, histories, memories, and knowledges to surface and be engaged with, but not via assimilative gestures. The intersectional question becomes, then, how to perceive each other, and each other's ideas/lives/histories, as complex, even as resistant or disruptive, without resorting to sameness or transparency as the primary path to understanding: an assimilative enfolding or a boomerang logic that erases difference can also happen in margin-to-margin relations. In other words, "we know that liminal lives are led and created against the grain of dominating power. If we know that about each other, we have good reason *not to assimilate what we hear and see to the oppressor's meaning or to our own*" (Lugones 2006, 84, italics added).

To clarify, the interpretive demands that stem from intersectional orientations are not merely about an "empathetic recognition" that "manages rather than transforms the subject/object distinction" (Hemmings 2011, 204, 196–197). Intersectionality entails forms of perception, and relations of reading, that do not aim to comprehend "the other [only] through sympathy and fancy" (Boler 1999, 156). In fact, "passive empathy" breaches intersectional dispositions because it "produces no action towards justice but situates the powerful Western eye/I as the judging subject, never called upon to cast her gaze at her own reflection" (Boler 1999, 161). In addition, as Hemmings suggests, more adequate forms of (feminist) thinking "may also require an acknowledgment that one is already in the history of the other-subject and not in ways that fit with the desire for heroism," which can function as another iteration of a desire for sameness in terms of the agentic/feminist subject (Hemmings 2011, 224).

For example, in discussing recent debates about the *foulard* or veil in France, Bilge analyses how Western feminist conceptions of agency, though offering "an essential antidote to previous hegemonic accounts obliterating subjectivities and experiences of subordinated groups," can, nevertheless, "significantly impoverish the analysis of power" by denying agency in subjectivities/lives that are simplistically read as compliant with the status quo (because not resistant in recognizable ways): any "social action" tagged as complicit becomes illegible as agentic (Bilge 2010, 19). By finding complicity, or a "lack" of agency, to be (the only) viable explanation (from a Western/modern feminist perspective or measure), such models recenter Western feminist subjects as agential and, simultaneously, erase or discount rationales offered by the women themselves about religion, piety, etc.—in fact, religious motivations in particular are often excluded from Western feminist notions of the rational and the agential (22). Though aimed at unearthing resistance to dominance, such narrow notions of feminist agency do not adequately depart from dominant epistemes and the workings of power embedded therein; rather, they bolster a Eurocentric (light/bourgeois) notion of gendered subjectivity and citizenship.

Rather than engage in assimilative logics or resort to monological sameness, two epistemological strategies are key to pursuing an intersectional model of understanding. One must continually endeavor to "bracket" governing imaginaries or cordon off dominant logics. Additionally, and simultaneously, one must actively pursue intersectional meanings, or be "biased" toward intersectional logics and orientations, even if doing so disorients and unsettles. In other words, to adequately note and engage opacity, and to "develop commitments" toward its potential meaningfulness, requires, in part, actively excluding or turning away from conventional mindsets (Babbitt 2001, 305–309).

### Engaging Intersectionality Requires Both "Bracketing" and "Bias"

Gaile Pohlhaus Jr. explores what is required to actively *follow* another's reasoning, particularly across asymmetries of power or incommensurable worlds. The kind of understanding she has in mind entails far more than being open-minded: it requires both substantial "re-orientation" and considerable "rehabituation" (Pohlhaus 2012, 237). She explains, "understanding another's reasoning requires one to do more than hold a particular set of claims in mind. It requires one to follow the sense of those claims. . . . To follow the sense of a claim is to *comport oneself* toward the world in particular ways and to participate within the 'grammar' which structures the sense of the claim" (225, italics added). Sarah Hoagland, too, has underscored that adequate feminist knowing needs to actively pursue decolonial and intersectional mindsets, which requires "working to enter a distinct conceptual framework, a different cosmology, rather than [merely] working to inhabit and move among disparate logics" (Hoagland 2010, 237).

Rather than simply urge open-mindedness, in the usual sense, toward intersectionality's alternative logics and political commitments, I suggest, instead, that what may be requisite is a twofold practice: actively *bracketing* conventional ways of knowing and, at the same time, engaging in focused *bias toward* intersectionality in ways that do not seek to "understand" it simply by folding it into conventional logics, since this is a violation, a means of refusing or not-knowing intersectionality. In other words, to practice intersectional orientations requires in many ways that we practice "epistemic disobedience" (Roshanraven 2014) and engage in "[] bracketing." As Lugones explains, "only in [] bracketing can we appreciate the different logic that organizes the social in the resistant response." Ideas, persons, cosmologies, and actions that are defiant to the logics of oneness, she contends, are simply not perceptible without "[] bracketing" (Lugones 2010, 749).

I would argue, then, that understanding, via an intersectional disposition or orientation, calls for an active "refusal of dominant worlds of sense" (Pohlhaus 2012, 238): it requires a vigorous (and ongoing) rejection of hegemonic rationality. Understanding across epistemological, political, and structural forms (and structured asymmetries) of power requires "explicitly refusing to think within certain structural contexts" (226) so that the different logics, the contours of another's reasoning, have a chance to come to the fore (and not just in familiar/translatable/comfortable terms). In fact, one can find a near chorus of voices underscoring how practicing active refusal is vital for more adequate feminist (and, I would argue, intersectional) knowledge practices and politics.

Schutte, for instance, stipulates that "deactivation" of hegemonic logics is imperative (Schutte 2000, 61). To better to address the normative force of invisible frames of reference, and to allow for resistant ideas/lives to flourish, Anzaldúa contends status quo frameworks must not just be stretched but may need rupturing or breaking (Anzaldúa 1990b). Heldke advocates "traitorous" ways of thinking and being so as to more effectively defy dominance, since "overprivilege and ignorance combine" in pernicious ways to impede transformation and change (Heldke 2006, 159). Lugones likewise asserts it is necessary to learn to separate or isolate one's self from the "pulls toward normalcy" and subordination: this happens in part by learning "to block the effectiveness of oppressive meanings and logics" (Lugones 2005, 85).

Alarcón (1990) thus calls for practicing "disidentification," rather than identification and commonality, as a path to understanding and affiliation, while José Esteban Muñoz examines queer-of-color "disidentifications" as a means of negotiating and resisting via performances that "scramble" and "recircuit" dominant cultural norms and expectations (Muñoz 1999, 31). Hoagland advocates engaging in "refusal and disruption," practicing "disloyalty" to dominance via "conceptual separatism," and actively departing from cognitive norms (Hoagland 2001, 129). These tactics, she explains, arise out of her political interests and intents as a lesbian philosopher: from her lived experiences, she knows of the capacity for and need to think against the grain when one is a member of a disenfranchised group. She thus became "interested in strategies of resisting rationality both in the sense of resisting (dominant) rationality and also of finding nondominant resisting rationalities" (140).

It is this double pursuit (of disturbing and resisting hegemonic rationalities while also noting and fostering resisting rationalities) that is at the heart of intersectional orientations. We must both depart from (or "[] bracket") default frameworks and hegemonic imaginaries *and* take up "bias" toward intersectional logics. To explain the kind of bias I mean, Babbitt's discussion of how knowers dedicated to eradicating inequality can practice politically committed interpretive "bias" when reading across power asymmetries (e.g., from positions of privilege or geopolitical dominance) is useful.

By "relevantly" biased, Babbitt means taking up bias *away from* dominant mindsets and *toward* outlooks one may not fully (or even ever) understand. This is not the same as simply "appreciating difference" (Babbitt 2001, 305), or pluralizing perspectives, since these approaches, grounded in monological premises, tend to obscure any challenge to dominant views. Rather, Babbitt describes a contextually situated and politically and epistemically committed bias toward persons/stories/places/practices that, normatively, would be denied meaningfulness. This requires shutting out the dominant story while also disrupting and departing from established ideas about rationality, understanding, and objectivity (Babbitt 2001).

Likewise, Hoagland discusses how only going so far as "developing critical discourse within Western ideology," but still foreclosing or refusing "ways of thinking and engaging that might leave our worldviews and our place in them scathed," is not enough (Hoagland 2010, 236). It is in this vein that Hemmings calls for "a consideration of how one might figure in another's history" (and not just how another does or does not figure in one's own worldview and sense of self/history/

reality). Provocatively, she queries, "What about those practices that cannot be recognized as part of agency . . . without the concomitant demise of the status of the one who recognizes?" The Western feminist subject, then, may well need "to encounter a history in which she is not recognized or not recognized in ways that she may be content to rest with"; furthermore, "she may not be the subject of history" (Hemmings 2011, 214) and thus also not the definitive/emblematic protagonist of feminism.

Intersectionality helps illuminate how instilled notions of rationality, time, subjectivity, agency, and reality, grounded in Enlightenment ideals, are, more often that not, ill-considered in contexts of asymmetrical cognitive authority, geopolitical inequalities, and partitioned social ontologies. Nevertheless, these established ideas inculcate us as knowers. Babbitt's urging to engage in forms of "relevant" bias, as both an interpretive and applied tactic, necessitates being committed to the *possibility* of meaningfulness, even if one cannot fully grasp it or readily perceive it by the usual terms of knowing. An intersectional disposition thus requires confronting more than the incompleteness of one's worldview: it can also mean encountering the peripheral nature, if not the irrelevance, of one's episteme and sense of self, in an/other's view. Intersectionality can be considered to be both incommensurable with *and* resistant to dominant logics: however, these dual aspects of its disposition are generally not perceptible within conventional interpretive, policy, research, or theoretical strategies.

Intersectional pursuits, therefore, are not necessarily achievable within hegemonic spaces/practices without actively engaging in "[] bracketing" and "bias": both are needed to animate intersectionality's different analytical dispositions and political commitments. First, we must *meet* rather than *suppress* intersectionality's multidimensional analytics, politics, and insights: then, we must take up intersectionality, as a sensibility or disposition, in ways that do not blunt heterogeneity, contestation, and difference. So, what might be some strategies for disrupting the recurring epistemic misrecognition (or backlash) that both distorts intersectionality and impedes its application? The concluding chapter offers some tactics for engaging in the "[] bracketing" and "bias" needed to inhabit an intersectional disposition and to more adequately pursue and practice intersectionality as a critical orientation.

## Notes

1. Mills' discussion of the racial contract engages with Carole Pateman's idea of a "sexual contract" (Pateman 1988). Both authors' formulations, however, are fairly "pop-bead" in approach, rather than intersectional, even in their later collaborative work (e.g., Pateman and Mills 2007).
2. To clarify, I am not suggesting there is no racial contract. If the idea of an asymmetrical racial contract, as central to the social contract, seems implausible or overstated, the dynamics surrounding Trayvon Martin's death, George Zimmerman's acquittal for Martin's murder, and the discounting of Rachel Jeantel as a witness during the 2013 trial, surely suggest otherwise. However, the structural inequalities at work cannot be explained adequately without attending to the politics of class, gender, and sexuality operative within race and also infusing the asymmetries of harm sanctioned and practiced by the state.
3. See Hoagland (2010), Lugones (2007), Mignolo (2003), Morgan (2004), Quijano (2000), Smith (2003, 2008).
4. Alcoff describes an intelligibility gap facing Latino/as as knowers, in terms of content and style: Latino/as are both "alien" and "alienated" and thus often unable to name ideas or describe the world in ways that will be understood or taken seriously (Alcoff 2012, 27).
5. For more recent examples of science being hindered by powerful cultural norms and dominant epistemic frames, Emily Martin (1991) examines how sexist ideas about sperm and eggs (e.g., anthropomorphizing heteronormative romance plots [with princes/sperm pursuing and rescuing princesses/eggs] or sexist imagery of vengeful and retaliatory femme-fatale eggs) skew and even undermine new research in cell biology and human reproduction. Keely Savoie (2006) also offers a brief discussion of how evolutionary biology, as a default framework, prevents new facts about animal sexuality (that do not fit within a heteronormative, reproductive frame) from being engaged with, published, or understood.
6. For high-resolution images of Cox's work, see http://reneecox.org/. See also www.brooklynmuseum.org/eascfa/feminist_art_base/gallery/renee_cox.php
7. I began to explore this question to some degree in May (2014a).
8. Many categories operate/turn on exclusionary logics, in overlapping and divergent ways: in other words, "gender" is not alone in terms of its historical moorings or its categorical practices and processes tied to dominance. I focus on it here in the interests of thinking through what a more adequately intersectional imaginary might be for feminist work at large because gender (in its single-axis formulation) seems to continue to govern much of our political, ontological, and epistemological capacities/orientations.
9. For a classic first-person account of what it means to make choices in untenable and violating conditions, see Jacobs' *Incidents in the Life of a Slave Girl* (Jacobs 1987) and Spelman's insightful discussion of Jacobs' textual and ethical strategies (Spelman 1998).
10. Lugones 2006, 78.
11. Lugones' concept of curdling, as it relates to intersectional ideas about subjectivity and complex ontology, is discussed more fully in Chapter 1.

# 6

# Fostering an Intersectional Disposition

## *Strategies for Pursuing and Practicing Intersectionality*

In accord with intersectionality's both/and thinking and matrix orientation, we need to understand it as malleable and broadly applicable, be accountable to its political and intellectual genealogies, and not presume its radical origins guarantee liberatory outcomes (or ensure that there are no elisions in its legacy to address). It is imperative to understand intersectionality in this threefold way (as grounded in a particular intellectual/political history and set of commitments, not bound to specific groups yet oriented toward dismantling oppression and seeking justice on multiple fronts, and as flexible and open to critique). Otherwise, we risk reducing it to a descriptor of intricacies, a demographic factor, or a depoliticized matrix device with no commitment to eradicating injustice or to transforming ways of being and knowing.

Doing intersectional work, then, is not about performing a theatrics of inclusion, wherein intersectionality is employed chiefly as an ornamental device or as an empty gesture. Symbolic uses or perfunctory readings of intersectionality flatten its complexity and ignore the interpretive and political demands it places on us as knowers (e.g., to unsettle governing imaginaries, cut across boundaries, attend to gaps and silences, and create links): they also depoliticize intersectionality by overlooking its goals of forging radical justice and crafting a world in which all can flourish (i.e., to achieve more than just the capacity to exist or survive, though this baseline criterion is important as it remains *not* equally available to all).

An intersectional disposition requires actively orienting ourselves, and expressly developing interpretive inclinations, modes of being, and political commitments in ways that disrupt, trouble, and fundamentally depart from mainstream logics, ontological habits, and perceptual practices. Intersectionality's both/and orientation encourages developing and honing the capacity to exercise ruptures with hegemony and to embark on (coalitional) journeys toward each other's worlds/selves/histories/meanings/imaginaries. At the same time, we must attend to significant structural disparities within and between group and consider the impact (and import) of our different positionings in multiple and relational systems of power.

Importantly, each of us, from our divergent positionalities, has the capacity to reorient, to "concoct sense" away from dominance (Lugones 2005). As Alcoff underscores, because "perceptual practices are dynamic even when congealed into habit," epistemic departures *can* be initiated and political/coalitional "dynamism can be activated," even in seemingly intransigent circumstances, fixed social relations, or sedimented practices (Alcoff 2006b, 189). In this vein, intersectional praxis invites us to strive to relinquish atomization and to forswear hierarchical mindsets: furthermore, its matrix, multidimensional, antisubordination orientation (and history) is not optional.

To lay the ground for realizing intersectional social change, then, it is imperative to develop "a disposition to read each other away from structural, dominant meaning." As Lugones contends, we need "both to be able to recognize liminality and to go from recognition to a deciphering of resistant codes" (Lugones 2006, 79). As a critical heuristic, intersectionality offers many valuable tools and skills in this regard. For instance, in the interests of "deciphering" power, it directs our attention to gaps, inconsistencies, opacities, and discontinuities and insists that such omissions or silences be treated as (potentially) meaningful and significant, not just as obstacles to work around or anomalies to set aside.

Drawing from diverse interdisciplinary literatures, this concluding chapter offers some strategies for pursuing intersectionality as a matric, justice-oriented "disposition" (Bowleg 2013; Cho, Crenshaw, and McCall 2013). Gleaned from myriad examples and genres of intersectional thought and action, these tactics are not offered as guarantees or as some kind of fail-safe formula for practicing intersectionality: they are more akin to brushstrokes in an in-process, many-layered portrait of intersectional orientations and politics. Intersectional practices, in other words, are both recursive and flexible, rather than fixed or set in stone.

Furthermore, several of the suggestions condensed below delineate what practicing/inhabiting intersectionality is *not* about, but my method here is intended as more than simply negative: it is more akin to what in drawing is understood as a "negative space" approach. In a positive space/object-oriented way of observing and drawing, one delineates the outer boundaries (or outline) of something to render its likeness or image. A negative space approach focuses on the interrelationships and dynamism between different objects and placements in space and approaches the edges of something from its peripheries and beyond. A focus on the interstices, on context, and on interacting forces renders meaning and crafts renderings at the boundaries where (supposed) opposites meet: it also requires that the background (which the eye/I is often trained not to note or attend to) be brought to the foreground.

### Remember What Intersectionality Entails . . . and Does Not Entail

Intersectionality is a justice-oriented approach to be taken up for social analysis and critique, for political strategizing and organizing, for generating new ideas, and for excavating suppressed ones, all with an eye toward disrupting dominance and challenging systematic inequality. This entails actively finding ways to perceive/interpret/act against the pull of established, single-axis imaginaries and to engage in an ongoing effort to realize meaningful, collective justice via epistemic, ontological, economic, and structural change. There is also, therefore, a need to be wary of overly instrumental models of intersectionality and/or depoliticized applications that negate its political history and subversive potential.

As a critical heuristic, intersectionality is far more than a complexity device, a key word, a demographic factor, a dummy variable, a descriptive tool, a pluralizing impetus, a multicultural/(neo)liberal gesture, or a means to highlight (but not contest) how oppressive power works. Such simplistic notions or uses of intersectionality violate its radical politics, flout its historical roots, flatten its epistemological interventions, and ignore its ontological complexities. Furthermore, these are key means by which intersectionality is not only depoliticized but also repackaged, made ready to be absorbed into empiricism as usual, taken up as a means of extending state surveillance, adopted as an essentialist, categorical logic, used as an insipid managerial rhetoric, or deployed as a cosmetic discourse to mask ongoing inequalities.[1]

In the interests of pursuing and practicing an intersectional disposition, and being "relevantly biased" (Babbitt 2001) toward intersectionality's alternative methods and orientations, it is necessary to shift one's energies, imagination, and practices toward four interrelated commitments:

1. Honor and foster intersectionality's antisubordination orientation;
2. Draw on intersectionality's matrix approach to meaningfully engage with heterogeneity, enmeshment, and divergence;
3. Take up intersectionality's invitation to follow opacities and to read against the grain;
4. Set aside norm emulation as a philosophical/political/research/policy strategy.

## Honor and Foster Intersectionality's Antisubordination Orientation

Opportunities to meaningfully apply an intersectional disposition are all around us. Since dominant logics exert considerable normative force (but are also often relatively invisible), expect to find them at work in unexpected places. Both ongoing and new forms of harm and erasure connected to single-axis legacies may well be operative, despite assertions and commitments otherwise, including in feminist work and in other justice-oriented contexts (including intersectional ones, as well). A historicized, contextual approach is thus imperative to understanding how intersectionality's antisubordination impetus has been forged (and, in turn, also continually resisted). Use its both/and logics to ferret out, examine, and contest the various, sometimes hidden workings of power and to unsettle the either/or imaginaries that help to rationalize and reinforce systemic domination.

- Established and accepted social roles, analytic tools, research norms, public discourses, market rationales, representations, political goals, historical frames, affective states, and philosophical presuppositions can all, in different ways, collude with single-axis, hierarchical practices or reinforce systematic, asymmetrical patterns of harm, violation, and inequality. Unmarked logics and transparent categories therefore need to be interrogated, as do conventional frames of legibility and legitimacy. This often requires, for example, "eliciting counterfactual questions that disturb the naturalness of existing arrangements" (Choo and Ferree 2010, 139–142). Ask what the underlying "legitimating discursive structure" is, in a policy, a study, a philosophical frame, a disciplinary model, or an activist strategy, because "discursive underpinnings structure what questions can be asked, and what answers are looked for" (Gedalof 2012, 2–3).
- Question progress narratives and declared breaks from past violences or from historical instances of inequality that have ostensibly been transcended or transformed (Spade 2013). Angela Davis' and Juan Cartenega's analyses of the normalization of mass incarceration and resultant forms of civil death, whereby convicted felons are not allowed to vote (felon disenfranchisement), for instance, show how seemingly antiquated classifications of personhood/nonpersonhood, with regard to citizenship and the social contract, continue in new iterations that many do not notice, or, alternatively, find wholly acceptable (Cartagena 2009; Davis 2005; Ewald, 2002). Likewise, Sherene Razack's extensive analysis of the politics of "states of exception" and "camps of abandoned or 'rightless' people" illustrates how seemingly old global racial orders are presently operating to contain Muslims in the West (Razack 2008).

- Though some have used or understood intersectionality in ways that align with liberal multiculturalism, reinforce and rationalize state surveillance, further settler colonial logics, or ignore the coloniality of gender, doing so undermines its antisubordination impetus and ignores its long-standing focus on the (settler) state's founding brutalities and ongoing abuses. Instead, intersectionality *can* be taken up in ways that align with (and ally with) decolonial feminisms—and thus "unsettle" its practices from those of settler colonialism (Dhamoon 2014; Egan 2014; Smith 2005b). For instance, it is possible to refuse linear historical frames that treat Indigeneity as "disappeared" or as past/gone (Hoagland 2010). From an intersectional disposition, it is also possible to engage with and think through Native ideas, identities, and histories without assimilating them to settler logics of race, gender, sexuality, citizenship, and the state that erase sovereignty issues and deny ongoing decolonial resistances and realities (Barker 2006; Smith 2005b, 2010).

Picking up one pathologizing lens or objectifying mindset to explain or dismantle another is not intersectional and undermines its antisubordination philosophy. Doing so not only falsely disaggregates and obscures enmeshment but reinforces atomization and false universals, impedes coalition, and animates the hierarchical logics that cut across intermingled systems of harm and inequality, diachronically and presently, thereby buttressing (not contesting) subordination.

- For instance, avoid relying on homophobia to forge racial solidarities or to advocate for civil rights (Collins 2004). Likewise, do not adhere to homonationalism or pinkwashing[2] as avenues to queer recognition or rights, as these tactics rationalize state violence, justify harm, and retain (or simply shift) the normative/deviant binary (Puar 2006, 2007, 2011). Whether one is talking about activism or research, intersectional dispositions are not about seeking visibility/legibility, or rights and recognition, via terms that pathologize others and leave intact a worthy/unworthy human hierarchy or partitioned social ontology. Since, for instance, "disabled people have not yet established their entitlement to exist unconditionally as disabled people" (Campbell 2012, 215), an intersectional approach to disability analysis and rights would not emphasize add-and-stir inclusion. Instead, for example, one might ask: does the work attend to (and encourage valuing, engaging, and also inhabiting) what Fiona Campbell (2012) calls "anti-social" bodies (228), rather than merely seek to integrate disability into the existing social imaginary or body politic?

- Beware of analogical limits: early intersectionality scholars and activists underscored how nineteenth-century race-sex analogies (in the abolition and suffrage movements) required a series of erasures and silences to function—they also retained masculinity as the normative center of "blackness" and whiteness at the heart of gender. Contemporary usage of ableist metaphors to delineate the contours of anti-racist feminisms is, likewise, insufficiently intersectional (May and Ferri 2005; Shalk 2013), as is analogizing homophobia to racism to advocate for gay rights (Carbado 2013).
- Disparaging disability to promote reproductive rights, or ignoring forced sterilization of Native, poor, disabled, and/or incarcerated women, while fighting for (narrowly defined parameters of) bodily autonomy or choice, is both common and highly problematic. An intersectional approach to reproductive justice shifts to an orientation that allows for "movement intersectionality" (Roberts and Jesudason 2013), values heterogeneous embodiment, accounts for systematic, state-sanctioned anti-natalism (Mingus and Talley 2013; Spade 2013), and recognizes "outlaw" ontologies (Campbell 2012), not just "normate" bodies and lives.

Keep an antisubordination impetus front and center by aligning form, content, and outcome (i.e., intersectional approaches emphasize that form/content correspondence is fundamentally a political question, not just a formal one). The meanings and consequences of the categories, methods, and interpretive approaches used all need to be considered: furthermore, each of these aspects must be taken up in ways that attend to broad structural patterns and to various dimensions of power. To whom is the project accountable, and how? What is intersectionality doing (and not doing) in the work—for whom/with whom, by what means or methods, and to what end(s)? If the interpretive tools or modes of applying intersectionality are reliant on ideas, values, methods, or logics that have been identified as fundamentally violent by intersectionality scholars/activists, this should give pause and not be brushed aside as inevitable or acceptable (May 2014a).

- When operationalizing intersectionality, it is imperative not to facilitate "the spread of a depoliticized intersectionality." It is equally crucial to assess the contexts of use: "ask what the introduction of this particular tool does for . . . subordinated groups in the local context of its introduction" (Bilge 2013, 410–411). Recognize that many established and commonly used categories, aims, or frames may not be relevant to, or may even violate, majority world experiences and issues (Grech [2012], for example, questions prevailing disability studies lenses in this regard).
- Unwittingly, many of us rely on categories, logics, social imaginaries, timelines, or modes of understanding that "presuppose the continued imposition of Western ontology, episteme, economics, politics, and cosmology" (Hoagland 2010, 235). Use intersectionality to generate new insights and to push "against hegemonic disciplinary, epistemological, theoretical, and conceptual boundaries" (Dhamoon 2011, 230). When applying an intersectional lens, it is important, for instance, to actively work against norms and values that (re)enact (Western) "rescue feminism" (Bilge 2014), whereby gender "operates as a kind of technology of empire" that demarcates the modern/free Western gendered subject from non-modern/not-free others (Razack 2008).
- It is possible, in some measure, to deactivate legacies of dominance in our work. This requires an interrogative, reflexive assessment of intersectional projects. Ask, for instance, does the approach, analysis, or outcome "destabilize and displace the subject of modernity"? (Schutte 2000, 64). Are the citational practices, research methods, political strategies, or policy aims "absorptive," superficial, or assimilative (Bilge 2014; Tomlinson 2013a)? How are the relationships among different identity categories and systems of power modeled and conceived (Harnois 2005)? How/Does the project disrupt the status quo (Collins 2014)? How/Does it lay the ground for furthering oppression or reinscribing the settler state (Williams 2009)?

### Draw on Intersectionality's "Matrix" Approach to Meaningfully Engage with Heterogeneity, Enmeshment, and Divergence

From an intersectional lens, heterogeneity is not just a pluralization of the singular, or a diversification of sameness: via both/and logics, intersectionality attends to selves/worlds/embodiments/imaginaries that are understood to be inextricably intermingled *and* divergent. Intersectionality entails learning both to recognize enmeshment and to refrain from atomizing multiplicity. When using its multidimensional, matrix approach, do not artificially parse complexity, fragment compoundedness, or treat multifacetedness as a hindrance or problem. Turn from either/or logics and single-axis explanations: presume that heterogeneity and incommensurability are present (even if not apparent or understandable on conventional terms) and pursue multiplicity/compoundedness as having significance and meaning.

- Break open categorical seamlessness and trace how systems of power "secure one another," such that "women" can be understood to have been "produced into positions that exist symbiotically but hierarchically" (Razack 1998, 13; see also Alarcón 1990; Crenshaw 1989). Rather than enforce rigid boundaries between resistant logics (as if their histories and goals are wholly unrelated), or collapse them as undifferentiated, transnational, decolonial, and intersectional orientations to questions of race, gender, nation, and power can be taken up relationally, for instance.
- Focus on the forces and implications of within-group differences is requisite. Harnois, for instance, offers some formulas to measure within- and between-imputation variances (Harnois 2005, 826–827, n6). In addition, Bowleg describes transcription and coding strategies which allow for multiplicity and interaction, recognize identities as social processes, account for community contexts, explore unstated/implicit factors, and acknowledge variable and contextual forms of micro-aggressions and stereotyping negotiated by the Black gay men in her study (Bowleg 2013). Since attention to historical context, structural processes, and local dynamics is pivotal to thinking about within-group and between-group differences simultaneously, Dhamoon also

encourages using "situated comparisons" to account for intersectional processes, interactions, and relational power (Dhamoon 2011).

- Many existing data sets and conventional methods are mired in additive, sequential norms that neither attend to contexts of power and inequality sufficiently nor meaningfully engage with heterogeneity (within or between group). As a consequence, noting and interpreting "the seemingly un-measurable and unanalyzable . . . becomes one of the most substantial tools of the intersectionality researcher (Bowleg 2008, 322). In addition to asking what is "noted but not explained?" it is also imperative to focus on what is "not linked to . . . processes" and structural dynamics (Clarke and McCall 2013, 354). Examine what definitions and examples of, say, gender and sexism *are* included in the data, findings, or policy frame, but also those that *are not* present or accounted for (Cole 2009; Harnois 2005, 2013; Springer, Hankivsky, and Bates 2012).

Pry open structured occlusions—whether in institutional practices, in the architecture of an argument, or in liberation politics. Use intersectionality's both/and same/different approach to render visible complex heterogeneities that may have been overlooked or suppressed. Find shared logics and trace continuities across contexts and practices where, from single-axis mindsets, we have been taught not to notice meaningful connections. At the same time, avoid homogenizing differences and collapsing divergences.

- Using intersectionality as an interpretive lens, look for evidence of "layers of suppressed meaning" and unpack the workings of taken-for-granted epistemological assumptions, conventional turns of phrase, or dominant explanations (Code 2011, 206). In other words, identify (and ask) unasked questions: unsettle everyday logics and conventional expectations (Dhamoon 2014) and ask unsettling questions about established ideas and practices that seem wholly unproblematic or even laudatory. For example, Mieke Verloo finds intersectional approaches useful for ferretting out undemocratic principles and harmful practices embedded in Western democracies (Verloo 2014). Try to name problems without a name (Narayan 1997): measure the unmeasurable, analyze the seemingly un-analyzable (Bowleg 2008), and pinpoint critical but overlooked insights by bringing contextual dynamics and backgrounds into focus (Pohlhaus 2012).

- Pivot the usual lenses or expected methods to account for intersectional complexities and avoid relying on readily available frames without question. As Kathy Ferguson explains, "when we are busy arguing about the questions that appear within a certain frame, the frame itself becomes invisible; we become enframed within it" (Ferguson 1993, 7). For example, do not impose or presume a single historical time—note, instead, discrepancies in concepts of time (without mapping them back into a singular frame—that is, as 'backward' or 'primitive'/prior ideas about time explained within modernity's linear trajectory and logics). As Alcoff delineates, thinking through Panamanian history, "the West imposed a 'single' historical time through which the experience in the colonies would be viewed from the perspective of the colonial centers. This means that, for example, Panamanian history is marked as beginning with the U.S. intervention to build the canal in the early twentieth century, in which Panama was broken from Colombia to form an independent nation" (Alcoff 2004a, 109). On the flip side, this also means that "divergences in periodization" should be recognized as a key "form of resistance" and not just as happenstance or curious (110).
- Read histories and practices alongside each other, in relation, even if they are usually conceived of as unrelated. Ben-Moshe, for example, shows how "using combined data on containment to include medical/psychiatric institutions . . . reveals that incarceration rates in the US have long been extremely high—but with shifting locations." This, in turn, pinpoints "the need to reconceptualize institutionalization and imprisonment as not merely analogues but as in fact interconnected, in their logic, historical enactment and social effects" (Ben-Moshe 2013, 390). She then disrupts conventional logics once more, by mapping out the interconnections between capitalism, the prison, and the medical establishment. Ben-Moshe argues, "the forces of incarceration of disabled people should be

understood under the growth of both the prison industry and the institution-industrial complex, in the form of a growing private industry of nursing homes, boarding homes, for-profit psychiatric hospitals and group homes" (393).

Intersectionality understands oppression and resistance to be ongoing, relational processes: this offers possibilities for reading resistance, reconceptualizing agency, and working around (rather than accepting) structural, epistemic, and ontological obstacles that impede coalitions. Although power asymmetries reduce opposition's discernibility, intersectional dispositions presume the possibility for dissent even if it has not been noted, seems unwarranted, or looks to be structurally/historically impossible. Look for departures from dominance and identify sites of resistance, alternative knowledges, and different histories that may be imperceptible from within the usual frames. Gain fluency in resistant logics and develop the skills to engage intricacy.

- Approaching heterogeneity as meaningful, from an intersectional position, entails perceiving multiply and engaging with multidimensionality. For instance, consider Lugones' reading of Anzaldúa's "germinative stasis"—a state of being undertaken on her intellectual/political journey to *conocimiento*. This active state does not necessarily entail action in a conventional sense: it may, in fact, be (mis)interpreted as one of lack, passivity, or inaction. Yet, her active subjectivity is understandable and logical from within both/and borderland logics and worlds, even if illogical or illegible otherwise. Anzaldúa is "both the one oppressed and the one resisting" (i.e., she is ontologically plural and engaged in a dynamic relation). Furthermore, "both of these selves exist in different worlds of sense, meaning, logics" (Lugones 2005, 90) (i.e., worlds, imaginaries, cosmologies, space, time, and place are also plural and not necessarily aligned). In short, taking up an intersectional disposition means one commits to pursuing and perceiving incommensurable pluralities.
- Shift foci so that oppressive forms of power can be rendered visible and understood as existing in tension with dissent, not just as unidirectional, totalizing forces. In this vein, Anzaldúa invites readers to perceive multiply as she traverses and mines historical memory: she

highlights, for instance, how Indigenous women across the Americas continue to "tend the flame" despite having been "silenced, gagged, caged . . . bludgeoned for 300 years" (Anzaldúa 1999, 44–45). This is resistance, ongoing—an unsettling of "settled"/settler-colonial questions of nation, time, place, memory, race, and gender.

- Consider how Kristie Dotson's metaphor of "concrete flowers" pivots debates in philosophy to ask, from a Black feminist position, what counts as philosophy, who counts as a knower, and what minimal conditions are required (though mainly still absent) for mere survival when it comes to "diverse philosophers." Like weeds growing in the cracks of concrete sidewalks, Black feminist philosophers should not be understood as accepting these harsh environs but as surviving in a context "that was never meant to sustain" or even acknowledge their existence (Dotson 2011b, 408). Furthermore, Dotson does not romanticize this resilience. "Concrete flowers" are "malnourished": when they manage to sprout forth, they exist in the barest sense, on "grisly ground" (408). Her metaphor offers a both/and portrait of the "oppressing ↔ resisting relation," highlighted by Lugones (2005, 90), and focuses attention on the field's absences and failures, including the regular exodus of "diverse philosophers" from philosophy itself (Dotson 2011b).
- To understand the relational nature of power and privilege, and the enmeshed complexities of lived subjectivity, an intersectional disposition recognizes the value of engaging different forms of knowing: a wide range of epistemic/political resources have value and can offer key lessons in learning to perceive/think otherwise. As Nikol Alexander-Floyd has observed, for example, use of "nontraditional writing genres has been a primary strategy for critical race theorists in general, and black feminist critical race theorists in particular, in developing their analyses and challenging legal methodology. Many critical race theorists, for instance, employ irony, storytelling, and the relaying of personal experiences in an effort to affront and expose the law's false presentation of itself as linear, objective, unyielding, and timeless" (Alexander-Floyd 2012, 812).
- Lived experience can thus offer insights needed to think/act at variance, and both fiction and narrative can provide lessons in

reading/taking up resilience. For instance, echoing Dotson, and her metaphor of devalued weeds as overlooked evidence of splendor, resilience, and persistence (but also of structural harm and systematic neglect), consider the scraggy trees that reach toward the sky from the barrio sidewalks in Sandra Cisneros' (1984) novel *The House on Mango Street*, despite inhospitable conditions, or the bright yellow dandelions that sprout up in Gwendolyn Brooks' Bronzeville yards (in her 1953 novella *Maud Martha*). Both authors craft complex views of subjectivity, power, and place from within spaces of urban containment.

### Take Up Intersectionality's Invitation to Follow Opacities and to Read Against the Grain

Intersectionality directs our attention to referents/lives/worlds that may not be understandable or perceivable within the bounds of usual cognition. Following opacities requires noting signs, even seemingly insignificant ones, of lives lived "nonmonologically" (Lugones 2006, 82). Intersectional orientations to understanding, therefore, are not about expecting, or enforcing, transparency or full translatability, whereby intelligibility, rationality, and meaning are measured only (or primarily) in relationship to dominant norms, hegemonic categories, or singular logics. An intersectional interpretive method needs to be flexible and destabilizing, capable of engaging concurrent, simultaneous factors by reading in an athwart or transverse manner, whether one is reading texts, each other, and/or the political landscape. Identifying and addressing epistemological injustice, testimonial inequality, and asymmetries in intelligibility are also paramount to an intersectional approach, which treats opacities and silences as meaningful: engaging the limits of what can be said and understood in conventional/normative terms is therefore also requisite.

- By using a "doubled attentiveness" (Simon and Eppert 1997, 6), and presuming from the start that "'It's not everything you can talk, . . . but . . .'" (Davies 1994, 339, ellipses in original), an intersectional disposition attends to small signs of withholding, untellability, or unheardness. In this vein, I have found Anna Julia

Cooper's liberal use of ellipses in her nineteenth-century writing a significant aspect of her delineation of Black feminist subjectivity, voice, and systemic silencing/erasure (see May 2007, 2009 ). In other words, look for signs within syntax or genre that "mark liminality" (Lugones 2006, 82) and note performances of "disidentification" within the bounds of everyday life (Muñoz 1999).

- By acknowledging "incommensurability" between speaking positions or worldviews, an intersectional approach requires attending to "residues" that do not travel or translate across contexts. An intersectional disposition aims "not to foreclose the meanings of statements only to those meanings that are readily available" (Schutte 2000, 57) or that are easily expressible/explainable with the usual communicative/knowledge tools.
- Recognize residues and treat them as meaningful: do not dismiss the meanings at hand as irrelevant or insignificant if they do not mesh with what is readily known or already understood. If something is not apparent or explainable on conventional terms, develop an openness toward the opaque possibilities (Code 2011; Smith 1994)—pursue being "relevantly biased" toward meanings/lives/stories that cannot be made familiar via established lenses or explanations (Babbitt 2005, 2001).
- Break open, investigate, and work the opacities from an intersectional, matrix disposition (rather than accept them as inevitable or unworkable). For instance, in the interests of trying to think comparatively and transnationally about domestic violence, and in particular the question of death by domestic violence in the United States and in India, Uma Narayan uncovered important statistical and structural absences in both countries. In the United States, she found there are no data aggregated to reveal numbers of deaths by domestic violence—there are data accounting for domestic violence rates across a spectrum and for conviction rates for murder, but these are not cross-fertilized or thought through together. In both India and the United States, Narayan found that the politics of nation impacted the information gathered (and the political organizing strategies developed) to such a degree that trying to think comparatively, via the usual mechanisms, was akin to comparing "apples and oranges." However, rather than give up,

she underscored the merits of continuing her analysis by using an intersectional method of "comparing fruit" (Narayan 1997, 99).

Reading history, via an intersectional approach, requires entering archives with a healthy skepticism and working to render visible worlds/selves that exist or persist alongside and against dominance (Lugones 2005; Taylor-García 2008; Walker 1983). Listen to utterances that contest "annihilating silence" (Morris 2006, 146): at the same time, listen to silences as expressive as well (Kadi 2003; Kogawa 1994). An intersectional archival strategy, then, exposes both the processes of dominance, and the challenges to dominance, embedded in the historical record's own presences and absences.

- Intersectionality calls for reworking established methods or reinterpreting sedimented stories from different angles of vision: this can involve rereading the already "known" and/or unpacking an author's overlooked textual strategies pedagogies. Saavedra and Nymark, for instance, discuss how Chicana feminists and writers reframe the history, narrative, and meanings of Malintzin/La Malinche away from simplistic traitor/whore nationalist (and settler-colonial) frames and toward understandings of Malintzin as a historical figure who negotiated specific forms of power and who worked the constrained possibilities available in the contexts of conquest and enslavement (Saavedra and Nymark 2008, 259; see also Townsend 2006).
- Consider also Elizabeth Spelman's reading of Harriet Jacobs' 1861 *Incidents in the Life of a Slave Girl* (see Jacobs 1987). Spelman treats Jacobs as a knower in her own right and treats her autobiography as artful, not as formulaic or mimetic. She thus identifies rhetorical strategies used by Jacobs to act upon readers' imaginations and to negotiate the raced, classed, and gendered minefields of reader reception. Spelman underscores how Jacobs presents herself and seeks to be understood as a complex subject, directs her white reading audience to understand slavery as a system in a particular way and to see their complicity in its violence and exploitation, and, simultaneously, aims to have her readers understand themselves as capable of change and, thus, capable of working to eradicate the slave system (Spelman 1998, 59–89).

- Intersectionality's attention to what gets dismissed or left out means that one's historical/textual focus may need to shift. In terms of queer histories and memories, Ann Cvetkovich advises attending to miscellany and marginalia, or "ephemera, the term used by archivists and librarians to describe occasional publications and paper documents, material objects, and items that fall into the miscellaneous category when being catalogued" (Cvetkovich 2003, 243). Judith Halberstam, writing about transgender archives, asks us to actively engage, and not just accept, the archive. In other words, attend to the fact that "the archive is not simply a repository; it is also a theory of cultural relevance, a construction of collective memory, and a complex record of queer activity. In order for the archive to function, it requires users, interpreters, and cultural historians to wade through the material and piece together the jigsaw puzzle of queer history in the making" (Halberstam 2005, 169–70).
- Intersectionality's matrix lens is thus imperative for plumbing the historical record because it helps render a more complex portrait of power and subjectivity from the traces left behind. Barbara Bush's (2000) reading of Thomas Thistlewood's eighteenth-century Jamaica diaries is illustrative of how a both/and reading productively blurs and refuses Thistlewood's reliance on dichotomous and dehumanizing stereotypes of Black/African womanhood, specifically that of the monstrous "'She Devil'" versus the "eroticised 'Sable Venus.'" Bush's approach to Thistlewood's writings (and to British colonial/patriarchal imagination) renders visible this "contemporary racist discourse" from the time period *and* also ample evidence of dissent, of the means by which enslaved women developed relationships beyond the parameters of slavery and "asserted their 'personhood' through a complex interplay between 'collaboration,' survival strategies, an African-derived women's culture, and active resistance" (Bush 2000, 764).

Instead of adhering to established frameworks that have been systematized and elevated to "the status of arbiter of truth and reality" (Lugones 2006, 81), intersectionality reminds us that the demand for simplicity, for example, is often a hegemonic move. Intersectionality thus invites us to pursue the incommensurable, the eclipsed, and the untranslatable as sites of political meaning, ontological possibility, and rich epistemic potential. This, in turn, often requires broadening the scope of what counts as an epistemic or political resource, devising new materials, and (re)working genres to accommodate multiple/moving selves and narrative forms of knowing.

- If the available data or archives are insufficient, try looking elsewhere—or, following Alice Walker's lead, start writing the histories, the stories, or the policies that you should be able to find or that need to exist (see Walker 1983, 13). In addition, since "key insights into the social world are not found only in peer-reviewed journal articles and monographs" (Harnois 2013, 21), look to other expressive/knowledge genres, including art, orature, performance, music, and narrative. Fiction, for instance, can encapsulate a both/and intersectional worldview and offer nuanced ways of thinking about relational power, complex subjectivity, and structural inequality: it can sometimes offer what traditional empirical or philosophical work may not (as the discussion above of Cisneros' and Brooks' novels suggests).
- Entering the gaps or interstices of dominant logics from an intersectional approach can require interpretive methods like "poetic association" rather than dominant norms of rationality (Anzaldúa 1990a, xvii). Code, for instance, advocates a "scavenger approach" as a philosophical/political orientation to epistemic resources, including novels and narratives, rather than empiricism as usual, which is ill-equipped in terms of many of its cognitive assumptions and foundational premises. Code explains that "diverse textual resources [can] point toward an epistemic stance from which to think away from the taken-for-granted structural inequalities, whose lived meanings a viable politics of difference and post-colonial resistance has to understand better than ready-made formulas or accumulations of information—of facts—can allow" (Code 2011, 218–219).

- Develop genres and/or methods that can draw upon the plurilogical, engage self and other in ways that take up different imaginaries, and that can enter/inhabit counternarratives. Reworking genre, specifically, is a strategy Anzaldúa identifies for productively "exploding" neat boundaries and categories (Anzaldúa 1990a, xvi). She urges use of "montage," "fragmented discourse," and anthologizing to account for "cacophony" (multiple voices that do not necessarily adhere to the harmonious or singular) (xvii). Likewise, Barbara Christian (1990) points to the productive ambiguities opened up by using and reading riddles, proverbs, and hieroglyphs: narrative can be written and read in ways that disrupt the theory/story divide (Maracle 1994) that intersectionality rejects.

An intersectional interpretive strategy engages the untranslatable or incommensurable without necessarily trying to render it understandable or legible on familiar terms. This also means, however, that seemingly positive approaches or lenses may need to be re-evaluated, reworked, or even abandoned—there may be significant violations or occlusions which the usual frames enforce that need to be challenged.

- Intersectionality's both/and approach helps expose how frameworks used to unearth resistance can also distort. For example, "agency" as a concept can reinscribe, rather than contest or unsettle, narrowly conceived notions of gender, resistance, and subjectivity (masquerading as universal concepts).[3] Calling for alternative feminist reading strategies that do not reinforce racist and civilizationist thinking, Kathleen Zane (1998) and Sirma Bilge (2010) pinpoint different forms of subtle arrogance embedded in transnational feminist analyses which rely on definitions of agency that dismiss women on their own terms and which presume oppression to be "totalizing" if the subjectivity at hand is "hybrid" (Zane 1998) or is not recognizable as agential in ways that align with Western/modern gendered subjectivity.
- An intersectional approach also underscores how focusing on an individual's capacity to resist, without attending to systematic harm and institutionalized oppression, obscures that to "act," in the conventional sense, may not be possible or desirable: the terms of agency (conventionally conceived) deny, from the start, different/

divergent subjectivities and undertheorize enmeshed, structural relations of power (Frye 1983; Lugones 2005). For instance, Anneliese Singh's research on resilience among transgender youth of color fills in gaps left by conventional resilience frames which have not necessarily accounted for both transprejudice and racism simultaneously, and thus obscure contextually-specific resiliency tactics, important questions of school intolerance and community dynamics, and subtle uses of social media that an intersectional model can reveal (Singh 2013).

- When it comes to iconic historical figures, justifiably celebrated for resisting multiple systems of oppression—such as Harriet Tubman in the U.S. context, an intersectional reading can help illustrate how such figures are often (paradoxically and problematically) memorialized in ways that distort, curtail, or flatten. For example, while "Tubman's resilience frequently is hailed and even celebrated," it is often done so via the lens of "an exceptional but lone figure" that relies on "stereotypes of Black women's unparalleled strength." In addition, by means of other seemingly positive lenses (e.g., maternal or salvific frameworks), the multidimensional aspects of Tubman's life can be flattened: furthermore, her "militancy is often made over or made ready to be embraced into the folds of the nation's progress narrative, a triumphal tale . . . that erases the ongoing, tenacious nature of many forms of systemic oppression Tubman fought against and sought to transform" (May 2014b, 32).

### Set Aside Norm Emulation as a Philosophical/Political/ Research/Policy Strategy

Taking up intersectional orientations can require one to question, problematize, and even dispense with widely accepted (and regularly rewarded) disciplinary parameters, research norms, and methodological practices. Outwardly inclusive approaches, neutral categories, or objective methods can introduce ideological assumptions and can import or institute hierarchical imaginaries that intersectionality contests. In short, the operative mindsets at work in an array of common practices can naturalize inequality and animate hierarchy.

- Immersing in an intersectional approach can lead to questioning ubiquitous research standards of generalizability (Singh 2013). Furthermore, typical descriptors or categories may come to be understood as inadequate, or inadequately conceived, for the particular contexts and situational dynamics under examination (Cole 2008; Harnois 2013; Warner 2008). Likewise, norms of parsimony can come to seem highly problematic, because disparaging of heterogeneity (Bailey 2009; Hancock 2007b). The way research questions are developed may thus need reformulating (Bowleg 2008), or the usual scales intervened in, to account for heterogeneity and variance in meaningful ways, not just nominal or demographic ones (Harnois 2013).
- To illustrate how single-axis logics can creep into research modeling and findings, Harnois shows how an independent variable model can significantly impede the research process and distort the findings. For example, race is often merely a "dummy variable" in much gender research, and a host of studies on feminist identity formation "assume that the independent variables (e.g., generation, marital status, parental status, employment status, income) affect (or do not affect) feminist identity in exactly the same way" for all women (Harnois 2005, 810). She draws on intersectionality to devise a different portrait, to ask different questions, and to introduce doubt as to the veracity of widely accepted frames, thereby rejecting explanations that "make the assumption that the meaning of feminist identity and feminism is identical for women of different racial and ethnic groups" (810).
- Expectations to pinpoint causality, or to search for the greatest single variable or main effect, "sometimes imposed through methodological means, such as use of covariates" (Artiles 2013, 337), may well come (and need) to be doubted from an intersectional disposition (Choo and Ferree 2010). For example, in discussing racial disproportionality in special education (high numbers of minority students placed in special education), Alfredo Artiles argues that searching for "the one variable that has the greatest explanatory power in predicting special education placement" tends to uphold a deficit-based "medical model of disability" and ignores how numerous "structural conditions in the special education

field offer incentives for a unitary approach," one that "naturalizes the racialization of disabilities" (Artiles 2013, 337–338). This also cuts questions of socioeconomic difference, cultural context, and gender dynamics out of the picture (Ferri and Connor 2014): the quest to tease out a main effect can naturalize inequality and even block "intersectional analyses of disabilities with other markers of difference" that are not understood as racial signifiers (Artiles 2013, 338).

- Intersectionality requires focusing on the contexts of knowledge production and reception and also bringing background forces or dynamics to the fore. It should be used to read texts, perceive each other's possibilities, interpret data, and formulate methods, but also to attend to the contexts of discovery and develop more adequate theorizing. For instance, using intersectionality as a research analytic and epistemic frame demands more than "critical reinterpretation of statistical 'evidence.'" An intersectional approach requires "rethinking our basic approach to *doing* statistical research . . . but also how these statistics are produced" (Harnois 2013, 103).
- Critical interdisciplinarity is another means of animating intersectionality's cross-cutting analytics and of disrupting the epistemologies, ontologies, and ideological values that disciplinary norms can uphold. Intersectional interdisciplinarity entails more than rendering disciplinary bounds permeable—though this is important: it also means refusing disciplinary divides that falsely atomize linked struggles, histories, and knowledges (Maldonado-Torres 2012). For instance, critical interdisciplinarity can create room for disengaging from "disciplinary demarcations of Europe/EuroAmerica as *the* site of knowledge-production": it generates opportunities "to disobey exclusionary disciplinary boundaries that separate, insulate, and universalize singular (white/Anglo) ways of knowing" (Roshanravan 2014, 14).

Single-axis logics have a long history and continue to exert a considerable force: they constitute a naturalized social imaginary that "governs" everyday practices, processes, and possibilities. At the same time, an intersectional disposition reveals how they have also long been contested. We need not be bound by monological mindsets: it is important to recognize their normative force, yet not give single-axis logics too much power. Certainly, it also is not easy to come to see the foundations of one's practice (as a researcher, policy worker, or activist), or of one's sense of self/personhood, as grounded in violent logics and anti-intersectional premises: it can be even harder to begin to practice one's craft against the grain, since established norms of thinking and being tend to be rewarded. Nevertheless, it is possible to use intersectionality's same/different orientation as an analytical or political means to refuse atomization, reject false universals, and forswear hierarchical practices.

- Taking intersectionality's matrix politics and interrogative orientation seriously requires careful consideration of potential biases, distortions, and erasures built into commonly used measurement tools, research models, or interpretive lenses. Ask how a study, policy, or advocacy plan is framed and implemented: what does the model account for, from an intersectional approach, and what does it exclude or excise? Does it atomize or rank forms of power? Which categories and what explanations does it take as givens? Does the model presume internal coherence or falsely universalize identities (e.g., homogenize gendered experience)?
- Intersectionality requires reflexivity about citational practices and the knowledge resources one draws on (and does not draw on). Try to reference literatures, use research materials and methods, and devise political strategies that do not presuppose single-axis thinking. If one must rely on single-axis materials (or if others do so), *work to render visible their limits (do not just accept them at face value and without question)*. Ange-Marie Hancock, for example, challenges Derrick Bell (2004) not only for "depending on two discrete literatures" (on gender and violence and on race and violence) but also for accepting and reinforcing their atomized logics. Hancock argues that his approach is additive in nature and erroneously in search of a singular policy solution: it also furthers a "deeply patriarchal view of heterosexual relationships" (Hancock 2007b, 70), reinforces, rather than contests, a competitive distributive model of rights, and erases as meaningful any lived differences for those who

fall between or are erased by the additive/sequential formulations (70). In other words, Bell unnecessarily forecloses intersectional analytic possibilities in terms of race, class, and gender in debates about school reform because his analytic lenses and research frames treat the categories, lived experiences, and the historical origins/foundations for each lived/structural category as separate.

- Assess whether the form or syntax aligns with intersectionality's valuing of heterogeneity and enmeshed multiplicities: avoid atomization or hierarchy as formal principles or analytic lenses. Bowleg cautions, for example, if you "ask an additive question," you are more likely to "get an additive answer," meaning participants may well take up the invitation, embedded in a hierarchical question, to rank identities or separate out systems of oppressive power (Bowleg 2008, 314). She explains, "if I were to ask a question about day-to-day challenges today, . . . I would not use a phrase such as 'race, gender and/or sexual orientation' in which the presence of the conjunctions *and/or* could imply that I wanted the experience recounted serially (race, then gender, then sexual orientation) or that these identities could or should be separated" (316, italics in original). At the same time, it is essential to note, and analyze, when participants *deviate* from the researcher's lead and redirect the operative assumptions. To illustrate, Bowleg describes one interviewee who rejected her either/or logics and replied: "'there is no higher political repression. So I personally don't ascribe to that I'm Black first, lesbian second, woman third. I'm all those'" (314).

Intersectionality attends to existing interstices, gaps, and omissions in dominant logics, yet is equally focused on finding ways to create (new) fissures in sedimented imaginaries, ones that can be "worked" toward an intersectional, both/and sense of collective possibilities and justice. If the available resources or usual methods are problematical (e.g., single-axis and hierarchical), an intersectional disposition looks for ways to, nevertheless, break from the singular. In other words, one may well be confronted with (single-axis) constraints or asked to engage with anti-intersectional materials: however, full compliance and/or total resignation are not the only responses available. An intersectional approach can be used to contest and to reformulate dominant imaginaries. Furthermore, its both/and frame allows for the possibility that what may appear to be full acceptance of or compliance with single-axis norms might well be sites where these imaginaries are being reworked or resignified from within.

- Intersectionality invites us to find ways to draw on matrix thinking so as to attend to and intervene in normative logics and forces. Harnois, for instance, discusses how a widely used data set, like the Schedule of Sexist Events (SSE), can be rooted in single-axis, universalizing approaches to "gender" and "sexism." More than simply limiting, the embedded assumptions, measurement tools, and resultant data can be *anti*-intersectional and thus mask how people experience and navigate both privilege and discrimination as simultaneous, relational dynamics (Harnois 2013, 53–55). Yet since many researchers must still engage with this data, Harnois identifies some modes of intervening: disaggregating data to uncover difference, particularity, and complexity within-group (64–79); creating "multiplex" models to reflect compound experiences and enmeshed power dynamics (e.g., split samples [93–97]), use of interaction terms (97–101), and multinomial logistics regressions (117–123); and situating forms of inequality and aspects of identity not only as (overtly and indirectly) interactive but also as tied to wider social contexts and structures (75–79, 82–85).
- An intersectional disposition invites us to find ways to break singular logics and foster both/and solidarities, even if outwardly adhering to single-axis rules and principles. Consider Suzanne Goldberg's analysis of the use of amicus briefs in U.S. courts. When studying identity-based law reform organizations in the United States, she noted something especially interesting, from an intersectional perspective, about the practice of cross-category *amicus* briefs. Despite an established social movement orientation and "organizational landscape" still characterized predominantly by "single identity-based advocacy," and notwithstanding antidiscrimination law's single-axis norms for litigation, Goldberg found that *amicus* brief participation is one strategy used to create collective and coalitional dynamics by traversing (and thus in some

ways refusing) single-axis frames. She explains, "By virtue of their participation, *amici* signal that the identity group members whose rights are at issue in the case before the court are not alone in their quest for justice." In other words, despite "instrumental concerns that shape participation in both litigation and social movements, identity groups have broad expressive leeway for achieving their strategic aims through *amicus* briefs" (Goldberg 2009, 128–135).

## An Open-Ended Ending

In closing, it is important to note that pursuing an intersectional disposition entails, fundamentally, a recursive intellectual/political commitment. Rather than a fixed method or a predetermined set of principles, an intersectional approach is open-ended, dynamic, and "biased" toward realizing collective justice. Pursuing and practicing intersectionality is not about norm emulation or alignment but unsettling and contesting norms: it is not about add and stir inclusion, or assimilation into status quo (hierarchical, asymmetrical, monological) socialities, embodiments, epistemes, affects, and structures, but about interrupting, unsettling, reworking, and transforming them.

Given intersectionality's Black feminist and women of color historical roots, and owing to its ongoing intellectual/political/structural commitments and practices, an intersectional disposition is, in essence, oriented toward radical social change. However, it does not come with any political or epistemological guarantees. Intersectionality is not a "one-off" political tactic or research strategy, a magic wand for eliminating willful ignorance and epistemic inequality, or a cure-all for eradicating dominance. Intersectional approaches do not (and cannot) provide a magic bullet, or offer a "panacea" (Bailey 2010, 53), methodologically or politically.

Pursuing intersectionality entails committing to a transformative collective vision and finding ways to confound and dismantle dominance by drawing on same/different logics, focusing on multiple domains of power, and attending to enmeshed identities and systems. It requires pivoting critical energies and political efforts toward unearthing suppressed complexities, contesting hidden norms and exclusions, tracing shared logics across disparate domains, and pinpointing unexpected sites of complicity or unwitting forms of collusion with dominance.

Going about doing intersectional work can therefore be "unsettling," not just in an intellectual way, or in an abstract sense, but also disquieting on a personal level. And yet, inhabiting and engaging an intersectional disposition can nonetheless serve as an essential driving force, can impel us, collectively, to find ways to realize a more just world. Given ongoing systemic inequalities and persistent and widespread violence, there is much work to be done: intersectionality not only has continued relevance but also has an important role to play in fostering the many possibilities that lie before us.

## Notes

1. See Bailey (2007), Bilge (2013), Brah and Phoenix (2004), Carbado (2013), Cho, Crenshaw, and McCall (2013), Cole (2008, 2009), Collins (2014), Crenshaw (2011c), Dhamoon (2011), Hancock (2007a, 2007b, 2014), Harnois (2005, 2013), Lewis (2013), Phoenix and Pattynama (2006), Puar et al. (2008), Shields (2008), Smooth (2013), Warner and Shields (2013), Yuval-Davis (2012).
2. Katherine Franke, discussing Israel's marketing of its gay-friendly governmental ethos, offers a succinct explanation of "pinkwashing." She writes, "A state's posture with respect to the rights of "its" homosexuals has become an effective foreign policy tool . . . to portray a progressive reputation when their other policies relating to national security, immigration, income inequality, and militarism are anything but progressive." Pinkwashing's rhetorics of persuasion and management of image go as follows: "Modern states recognize a sexual minority within the national body and grant that minority rights-based protections. Pre-modern states do not. Once recognized as modern, the state's treatment of homosexuals offers cover for other sorts of human rights shortcomings. So long as a state treats its homosexuals well, the international community will look the other way when it comes to a range of other human rights abuses" (Franke 2012, 3).
3. See Bilge (2010), Elenes (2011), Hemmings (2011), Lugones (2005), Mahmood (2005), Zane (1998).

# REFERENCES


Adell, Sandra. 1994. *Double-Consciousness/Double Bind: Theoretical Issues in Twentieth-Century Black Literature*. Champagne: Univ of Illinois Press.

Aguilar, Delia D. 2012. From Triple Jeopardy to Intersectionality: The Feminist Perplex. *Comparative Studies of South Asia, Africa and the Middle East* 32 (2): 415–428.

Ahmed, Sara. 2004. Declarations of Whiteness: The Non-Performativity of Anti-Racism. *Borderlands* 3 (2): http://www.borderlandsejournal.adelaide.edu.au/vol3no2_2004/ahmed_declarations.

———. 2007. The Nonperformativity of Antiracism. *Meridians* 7 (1): 104–126.

———. 2008. The Politics of Good Feeling. *ACRAWSA e-Journal (Australian Critical Race and Whiteness Studies Association)* 4 (1): http://www.acrawsa.org.au/files/ejounralfiles/57acrawsa5-1.pdf.

———. 2009. Embodying Diversity: Problems and Paradoxes for Black Feminists. *Race Ethnicity and Education* 12 (1): 41–52.

———. 2010. *The Promise of Happiness*. Durham, NC: Duke Univ Press.

———. 2012. *On Being Included: Racism and Diversity in Institutional Life*. Durham, NC: Duke Univ Press.

Alarcón, Norma. 1990. The Theoretical Subjects of *This Bridge Called My Back* and Anglo-American Feminism. In *Making Face, Making Soul/Haciendo caras: Creative and Critical Perspectives by Feminists of Color*, ed. Gloria Anzaldúa, 356–369. San Francisco: Aunt Lute.

Alcoff, Linda Martín. 2001. On Judging Epistemic Credibility: Is Social Identity Relevant? In *Engendering Rationalities*, eds. Nancy Tuana, Sandra Morgen, 53–80. Albany, NY: SUNY Press.

———. 2004a. Against "Post-Ethnic" Futures. *The Journal of Speculative Philosophy* 18 (2): 99–117.

———. 2004b. Schutte's Nietzschean Postcolonial Politics. *Hypatia* 19 (3): 144–156.

———. 2006a. The Unassimilated Theorist. *PMLA* 121 (1): 255–259.

———. 2006b. *Visible Identities: Race, Gender, and the Self*. New York: Oxford Univ Press.

———. 2011. An Epistemology for the Next Revolution. *Transmodernity* 1 (2): 67–78.

. 2012. Alien and Alienated. In *Reframing the Practice of Philosophy: Bodies of Color, Bodies of Knowledge*, ed. George Yancy, 23–44. Albany: SUNY Press.

Alcoff, Linda Martín and Eva Feder Kittay. 2007. Introduction: Defining Feminist Philosophy. In *The Blackwell Guide to Feminist Philosophy*, eds. Linda Martín Alcoff, Eva Feder Kittay, 1–13. Hoboken, NJ: Wiley Blackwell.

Alexander, Jacqui M. and Chandra Talpade Mohanty. 1997. Introduction: Genealogies, Legacies, Movements. In *Feminist Genealogies, Colonial Legacies, Democratic Futures*, eds. Jacqui M. Alexander, Chandra Talpade Mohanty, xiii–xlii. New York: Routledge.

Alexander-Floyd, Nikol G. 2012. Disappearing Acts: Reclaiming Intersectionality in the Social Sciences in a Post-Black Feminist Era. *Feminist Formations* 24 (1): 1–25.

Allen, Paula Gunn. 1986. *The Sacred Hoop: Recovering the Feminine in American Indian Traditions*. Boston: Beacon Press.

Alsultany, Evelyn. 2002. Los intersticios: Recasting Moving Selves. In *This Bridge We Call Home: Radical Visions for Transformation*, ed. AnaLouise Keating, 106–110. New York: Routledge.

Anderson-Bricker, Kristin. 1999. "Triple Jeopardy": Black Women and the Growth of Feminist Consciousness in SNCC, 1964–1975. In *Still Lifting, Still Climbing: African American Women's Contemporary Activism*, ed. Kimberly Springer, 46–69. New York: NYU Press.

Anzaldúa, Gloria. 1983. La Prieta. In *This Bridge Called My Back: Writings by Radical Women of Color*, eds. Cherríe Moraga, Gloria Anzaldúa, 198–209. New York: Kitchen Table Press.

———. 1990a. Haciendo caras, una entrada. In *Making Face, Making Soul/Haciendo caras: Creative and Critical Perspectives by Feminists of Color*, ed. Gloria Anzaldúa, xv–xxviii. San Francisco: Aunt Lute.

———. 1990b. En Rapport, In Opposition: Cobrando cuentas a las nuestras. In *Making Face, Making Soul/Haciendo caras: Creative and Critical Perspectives by Feminists of Color*, ed. Gloria Anzaldúa, 142–148. San Francisco: Aunt Lute.

———. 1999. *Borderlands/La frontera*. 2nd ed. San Francisco: Aunt Lute.

———. 2002. Now Let Us Shift . . . The Path of Conocimiento . . . Inner Work, Public Acts. In *This Bridge We Call Home: Radical Visions for Transformation*, ed. AnaLouise Keating, 540–578. New York: Routledge.

Artiles, Alfredo J. 2013. Untangling the Racialization of Disabilities. *Du Bois Review* 10 (2): 329–347.

Arya, Lakshmi. 2009. Imagining Alternative Universalisms: Intersectionality and the Limits of Liberal Discourse. In *Intersectionality and Beyond: Law, Power and the Politics of Location*, eds. Emily Grabham, Davina Cooper, Jane Krishnadas, Didi Herman, 326–351. Abingdon, UK: Routledge Cavendish.

Asch, Adrienne and Michelle Fine. 1988. Shared Dreams: A Left Perspective on Disability Rights and Reproductive Rights. In *Women with Disabilities: Essays in Psychology, Culture, and Politics*, eds. Michelle Fine, Adrienne Asch, 297–305. Philadelphia: Temple Univ Press.

Axelsson, Per and Peter Sköld. 2011. Epilogue: From Indigenous Demographics to an Indigenous Demography. In *Indigenous Peoples and Demography: The Complex Relation between Identity and Statistics*, eds. Per Axelsson, Peter Sköld, John P. Ziker, David G. Anderson, 295–308. New York: Berghan Books.

Aylward, Carol. 2010. Intersectionality: Crossing the Theoretical and Praxis Divide. *Journal of Critical Race Inquiry* 1 (1): 1–48.

Babbitt, Susan E. 2001. Objectivity and the Role of Bias. In *Engendering Rationalities*, eds. Nancy Tuana, Sandra Morgen, 297–314. Albany: SUNY Press.

———. 2005. Stories from the South: A Question of Logic. *Hypatia* 20 (3): 1–21.

Bagilhole, Barbara. 2009. *Understanding Equal Opportunities and Diversity: The Social Differentiations and Intersections of Inequality*. Bristol, UK: Policy Press.

———. 2010. Applying the Lens of Intersectionality to UK Equal Opportunities and Diversity Policies. *Canadian Journal of Administrative Sciences/Revue Canadienne des sciences de l'administration* 27 (3): 263–271.

Bailey, Alison. 1998. Privilege: Expanding on Marilyn Frye's "Oppression." *Journal of Social Philosophy* 29 (3): 104–119.
———. 2007. Strategic Ignorance. In *Race and Epistemologies of Ignorance*, eds. Shannon Sullivan, Nancy Tuana, 77–94. Albany: SUNY Press.
———. 2009. On Intersectionality, Empathy and Feminist Solidarity: A Reply to Naomi Zack. *Journal of Peace and Justice Studies* 18 (2): 14–37.
———. 2010. On Intersectionality and the Whiteness of Feminist Philosophy. In *The Center Must Not Hold: White Women Philosophers on the Whiteness of Philosophy*, ed. George Yancy, 51–76. Lanham, MD: Lexington Books.
Baldwin, James. 1981. *Go Tell It on the Mountain*. New York: Random House.
———. 1993. *Nobody Knows My Name*. New York: Vintage.
Barker, Joanne. 2006. Gender, Sovereignty, and the Discourse of Rights in Native Women's Activism. *Meridians* 7 (1): 127–161.
———. 2008. Gender, Sovereignty, Rights: Native Women's Activism against Social Inequality and Violence in Canada. *American Quarterly* 60 (2): 259–266.
Bartky, Sandra Lee. 1990. *Femininity and Domination: Studies in the Phenomenology of Oppression*. New York: Routledge.
Barvosa, Edwina. 2008. *Wealth of Selves: Multiple Identities, Mestiza Consciousness, and the Subject of Politics*. College Station: Texas A&M Univ Press.
Bassel, Leah. 2012. *Refugee Women: Beyond Gender versus Culture*. New York: Routledge.
Bassel, Leah and Akwugo Emejulu. 2010. Struggles for Institutional Space in France and the United Kingdom: Intersectionality and the Politics of Policy. *Politics and Gender* 6 (4): 517–544.
Baynton, Douglas. 2005. Slaves, Immigrants, and Suffragists: The Uses of Disability in Citizenship Debates. *PMLA* 120 (2): 562–567.
Beale, Frances. 1970. Double Jeopardy: To Be Black and Female. In *The Black Woman*, ed. Toni Cade, 90–100. New York: Signet.
Beauboeuf-Lafontant, Tamara. 2009. *Behind the Mask of the Strong Black Woman: Voice and the Embodiment of a Costly Performance*. Philadelphia: Temple Univ Press.
Beaulieu, Elizabeth Ann. 1999. *Black Women Writers and the American Neo-Slave Narrative: Femininity Unfettered*. Westport, CT: Greenwood Press.
Bell, Derrick. 2004. *Silent Covenants: Brown v. Board of Education and the Unfulfilled Hopes for Racial Reform*. New York: Oxford Univ Press.
Ben-Galim, Dalia, Mary Campbell, and Jane Lewis. 2007. Equality and Diversity: A New Approach to Gender Equality Policy in the UK. *International Journal of Law in Context* 3 (1): 19–33.
Ben-Moshe, Liat. 2013. Disabling Incarceration: Connecting Disability to Divergent Confinements in the USA. *Critical Sociology* 39 (3): 385–403.
Berger, Michele Tracy and Kathleen Guidroz. 2009. Introduction. In *The Intersectional Approach: Transforming the Academy through Race, Class, and Gender*, eds. Michele Tracy Berger, Kathleen Guidroz, 1–25. Chapel Hill: Univ of North Carolina Press.
Bhavnani, Kum-Kum and Krista Bywater. 2009. Dancing on the Edge: Women, Culture, and a Passion for Change. In *On the Edges of Development: Cultural Interventions*, eds. Kum-Kum Bhavnani, John Foran, Priya A. Kurian, Debashish Munshi, 52–66. New York: Routledge.
Bilge, Sirma. 2010. Beyond Subordination vs. Resistance: An Intersectional Approach to the Agency of Veiled Muslim Women. *Journal of Intercultural Studies* 31 (1): 9–28.
———. 2013. Intersectionality Undone. *Du Bois Review* 10 (2): 405–424.
———. 2014, April 25. Confronting the Undoing of Intersectionality within Disciplinary Academic Feminism. Paper presented at International Intersectionality Conference, Vancouver, BC, Canada.

Blackwell, Maylei. 2011. *¡Chicana Power! Contested Histories of Feminism in the Chicano Movement*. Austin: Univ of Texas Press.
Blackwell, Maylei and Nadine Naber. 2002. Intersectionality in an Era of Globalization: The Implications of the UN World Conference against Racism for Transnational Feminist Practices—A Conference Report. *Meridians* 2 (2): 237–248.
Boler, Megan. 1999. *Feeling Power: Emotions and Education*. New York: Routledge.
Borchorst, Anette and Mari Teigen. 2009. Who Is at Issue, What Is at Stake? Intersectionality in Danish and Norwegian Gender Equality Policies. Paper presented at the ECPR Joint Session of Workshops, Lisbon, Portugal.
Bose, Christine E. 2012. Intersectionality and Global Gender Inequality. *Gender and Society* 26 (1): 67–72.
Bowleg, Lisa. 2008. When Black + Lesbian + Woman ≠ Black Lesbian Woman: The Methodological Challenges of Qualitative and Quantitative Intersectionality Research. *Sex Roles* 59 (5–6): 312–325.
———. 2013. "Once You've Blended the Cake, You Can't Take the Parts Back to the Main Ingredients": Black Gay and Bisexual Men's Descriptions and Experiences of Intersectionality. *Sex Roles* 68 (11–12): 754–767.
———. 2014, April 26. Keynote panelist for Intersectionality Research and Practice: Challenges and Possibilities panel. International Intersectionality Conference, Vancouver, BC, Canada.
Brah, Avtar and Ann Phoenix. 2004. Ain't I A Woman? Revisiting Intersectionality. *Journal of International Women's Studies* 5 (3): 75–86.
Brooks, Gwendolyn. 1993. *Maud Martha: A Novel.* 50th Anniversary ed. Chicago: Third World Press.
Brown, Damita and Kim Sánchez. 1994. Transforming Organizing Strategies for the Nineties: The Women of Color Resource Center. *Inscriptions* 7. http://culturalstudies.ucsc.edu/PUBS/Inscriptions/vol_7/Brown.html.
Burri, Susanne and Dagmar Schiek. 2009. *Multiple Discrimination in EU Law: Opportunities for Legal Responses to Intersectional Gender Discrimination?* European Commission Directorate-General for Employment, Social Affairs and Equal Opportunities. http://ec.europa.eu/justice/gender-equality/files/multiplediscriminationfinal7september2009_en.pdf.
Bush, Barbara. 2000. "Sable Venus," "She Devil" or "Drudge"? British Slavery and the "Fabulous Fiction" of Black Women's Identities, c. 1650–1838. *Women's History Review* 9 (4): 761–789.
Bustelo, Maria. 2008, September. Spain: A Better Performer in Gender than in Intersectionality. Paper presented at Fourth Pan-European Conference on EU Politics, Riga, Latvia.
———. 2009. Spain: Intersectionality Faces the Strong Gender Norm. *International Feminist Journal of Politics* 11 (4): 530–546.
Butler, Judith. 1993. *Bodies That Matter: On the Discursive Limits of "Sex."* New York: Routledge.
———. 2009. *Frames of War: When Is Life Grievable?* London: Verso.
Cabrera, Patricia Muñoz. 2010. *Intersecting Violences: A Review of Feminist Theories and Debates on Violence against Women and Poverty in Latin America.* London: Central American Women's Network.
Cade, Toni. 1970. On the Issue of Roles. In *The Black Woman*, ed. Toni Cade (Bambara), 101–112. New York: Signet.
Caldwell, Kia Lilly. 2009. Black Women, Cultural Citizenship, and the Struggle for Social Justice in Brazil. In *Gendered Citizenships: Transnational Perspectives on Knowledge Production, Political Activism, and Culture*, eds. Kia Lilly Caldwell, Renya K. Ramirez, Kathleen Coll, Tracy Fisher, Lok Siu, 55–74. New York: Palgrave.

Campbell, Fiona Kumari. 2012. Stalking Ableism: Using Disability to Expose "Abled" Narcissism. In *Disability and Social Theory: New Developments and Directions*, eds. Dan Goodley, Bill Hughes, Lennard J. Davis, 212–230. New York: Palgrave.

Campbell, Susan E. 1999. Dominant Identities and Settled Expectations. In *Racism and Philosophy*, eds. Susan E. Babbitt, Susan Campbell, 216–234. Ithaca, NY: Cornell Univ Press.

Caputi, Jane A. 2010. Crises of Representation: Hate Messages in Campaign 2008 Commercial Paraphenalia. In *Who Should Be First? Feminists Speak Out on the 2008 Presidential Campaign*, eds. Beverly Guy-Sheftall, Johnnetta Betsch Cole, 121–154. Albany: SUNY Press.

Carastathis, Anna. 2008. The Invisibility of Privilege: A Critique of Intersectional Models of Identity. *Revue les ateliers de l'éthique/The Ethics Forum* 3 (2): 23–38.

———. 2013a. Identity Categories as Potential Coalitions. *Signs* 38 (4): 941–965.

———. 2013b. Basements and Intersections. *Hypatia* 28 (4): 698–715.

———. 2014. The Concept of Intersectionality in Feminist Theory. *Philosophy Compass* 9 (5): 304–314.

Carbado, Devon W. 1999a. Black Rights, Gay Rights, Civil Rights. *UCLA Law Review* 47: 1467–1519.

———. 1999b. Epilogue: Straight Out of the Closet: Men, Feminism, and Male Heterosexual Privilege. In *Black Men on Race, Gender, and Sexuality: A Critical Reader*, ed. Devon W. Carbado, 417–448. New York: NYU Press.

———. 2001. Race to the Bottom. *UCLA Law Review* 49: 1283–1313.

———. 2013. Colorblind Intersectionality. *Signs* 38 (4): 811–845.

Carby, Hazel V. 1985. "On the Threshold of Woman's Era": Lynching, Empire, and Sexuality in Black Feminist Theory. *Critical Inquiry* 12: 262–277.

———. 1987. *Reconstructing Womanhood: The Emergence of the Afro-American Woman Novelist*. New York: Oxford Univ Press.

Cartagena, Juan. 2009. Lost Votes, Lost Bodies, Lost Jobs: The Effects of Mass Incarceration on Latino Civic Engagement. In *Behind Bars: Latino/as and Prison in the United States*, ed. Suzanne Oboler, 133–148. New York: Palgrave Macmillan.

Chang, Robert S. and Jerome McCristal Culp Jr. 2002. After Intersectionality. *UMKC Law Review* 71: 485–492.

Cho, Sumi. 2013. Post-Intersectionality. *Du Bois Review* 10 (2): 385–404.

Cho, Sumi, Kimberlé W. Crenshaw, and Leslie McCall. 2013. Toward a Field of Intersectionality Studies: Theory, Applications, and Praxis. *Signs* 38 (4): 785–810.

Choo, Hae Yeon and Myra Marx Ferree. 2010. Practicing Intersectionality in Sociological Research: A Critical Analysis of Inclusions, Interactions, and Institutions in the Study of Inequalities. *Sociological Theory* 28 (2): 129–149.

Christensen, Ann-Dorte and Sune Qvotrup Jensen. 2012. Doing Intersectional Analysis: Methodological Implications for Qualitative Research. *NORA-Nordic Journal of Feminist and Gender Research* 20 (2): 109–125.

Christian, Barbara. 1990. The Race for Theory. In *Making Face, Making Soul/Haciendo caras: Creative and Critical Perspectives by Feminists of Color*, ed. Gloria Anzaldúa, 335–345. San Francisco: Aunt Lute.

Chun, Jennifer Jihye, George Lipsitz, and Young Shin. 2013. Intersectionality as a Social Movement Strategy: Asian Immigrant Women Advocates. *Signs* 38 (4): 917–940.

Cisneros, Sandra. 1984. *The House on Mango Street*. New York: Knopf Doubleday.

Clare, Eli. 2001. Stolen Bodies, Reclaimed Bodies: Disability and Queerness. *Public Culture* 13 (3): 359–365.

Clark, Natalie. 2012. Perseverance, Determination and Resistance: An Indigenous Intersectional-Based Policy Analysis of Violence in the Lives of Indigenous Girls. Institute for

Intersectionality Research and Practice, Simon Fraser Univ, Vancouver, BC, Canada. http://www.sfu.ca/iirp/documents/IBPA/7_Indigenous%20Girls_Clark%202012.pdf.
Clarke, Averil Y. and Leslie McCall. 2013. Intersectionality and Social Explanation in Social Science Research. *Du Bois Review* 10 (2): 349–363.
Clarke, Cheryl. 1983a. The Failure to Transform: Homophobia in the Black Community. In *Home Girls: A Black Feminist Anthology*, ed. Barbara Smith, 197–208. New York: Kitchen Table Press.
———.1983b. Lesbianism: An Act of Resistance. In *This Bridge Called My Back: Writings by Radical Women of Color*, eds. Cherríe Moraga, Gloria Anzaldúa, 128–137. New York: Kitchen Table Press.
———. 2008, October 4. Why Harriet Tubman Project. http://www.blogster.com/cherylclarke/why-harriet-tubman-project-black-feminist-blog-041008102104.
Code, Lorraine. 1995. *Rhetorical Spaces: Essays on Gendered Locations*. New York: Routledge.
———. 2001. Rational Imaginings, Responsible Knowings: How Far Can You See from Here? In *Engendering Rationalities*, eds. Nancy Tuana, Sandra Morgen, 261–282. Albany: SUNY Press.
———. 2006. *Ecological Thinking: The Politics of Epistemic Location*. New York: Oxford Univ Press.
———. 2011. "They Treated Him Well": Fact, Fiction, and the Politics of Knowledge. In *Feminist Epistemology and Philosophy of Science: Power in Knowledge*, ed. Heidi E. Grasswick, 205–221. London: Springer Dordrecht Heidelberg.
Cohen, Cathy J. 1997. Punks, Bulldaggers, and Welfare Queens: The Radical Potential of Queer Politics? *GLQ: A Journal of Lesbian and Gay Studies* 3 (4): 437–465.
———. 1999. *The Boundaries of Blackness: AIDS and the Breakdown of Black Politics*. Chicago: Univ of Chicago Press.
Cole, Elizabeth R. 2008. Coalitions as a Model for Intersectionality: From Practice to Theory. *Sex Roles* 59 (5–6): 443–453.
———. 2009. Intersectionality and Research in Psychology. *American Psychologist* 64 (3): 170–180.
Collins, Patricia Hill. 1990. *Black Feminist Thought: Knowledge, Consciousness, and the Politics of Empowerment*. London: Unwin Hyman.
———. 1998. *Fighting Words: Black Women and the Search for Justice*. Minneapolis: Univ of Minnesota Press.
———. 2000. What's Going On? Black Feminist Thought and the Politics of Postmodernism. In *Working the Ruins: Feminist Poststructural Theory and Methods in Education*, eds. Elizabeth St. Pierre, Wanda S. Pillow, 41–73. New York: Routledge.
———. 2003. Some Group Matters: Intersectionality, Situated Standpoints, and Black Feminist Thought. In *A Companion to African-American Philosophy*, eds. Tommy L. Lott, John P. Pittman, 205–209. Oxford: Blackwell.
———. 2004. *Black Sexual Politics: African Americans, Gender, and the New Racism*. New York: Routledge.
———. 2008. Reply to Commentaries: *Black Sexual Politics* Revisited. *Studies in Gender and Sexuality* 9 (1): 68–85.
———. 2014, April 24. Intersectionality as an Interpretation of the Social World. Keynote address presented at International Intersectionality Conference, Vancouver, BC, Canada.
Combahee River Collective. 1983. The Combahee River Collective Statement. In *Home Girls: A Black Feminist Anthology*, ed. Barbara Smith, 272–282. New York: Kitchen Table Press.
Conaghan, Joanne. 2007. Intersectionality and UK Equality Initiatives. *South African Journal on Human Rights* 23 (2): 317–334.
———. 2009. Intersectionality and the Feminist Project in Law. In *Intersectionality and Beyond: Law, Power and the Politics of Location*, eds. Emily Grabham, Davina Cooper, Jane Krishnadas, Didi Herman, 21–48. Abingdon, UK: Routledge Cavendish.

Coogan-Gehr, Kelly. 2011. The Politics of Race in US Feminist Scholarship: An Archaeology. *Signs* 37 (1): 83–107.

Coomaraswamy, Radhika. 2001. Report of the Special Rapporteur on Violence against Women, Its Causes and Consequences: Mission to Bangladesh, Nepal and India on the Issue of Trafficking of Women and Girls (28 October–15 November 2000). Report E/CN.4/73. New York: UN Office of the High Commissioner for Human Rights.

Cooper, Anna Julia. 1988. *A Voice from the South by a Black Woman of the South* (1892). New York: Oxford Univ Press.

———. 1998a. The Ethics of the Negro Question (1902). In *The Voice of Anna Julia Cooper: Including* A Voice from the South *and Other Important Essays, Papers, and Letters*, eds. Charles Lemert, Esme Bhan, 206–215. Lanham, MD: Rowman and Littlefield.

———. 1998b. Angry Saxons and Negro Education (1938). In *The Voice of Anna Julia Cooper: Including* A Voice from the South *and Other Important Essays, Papers, and Letters*, eds. Charles Lemert, Esme Bhan, 259–261. Lanham, MD: Rowman and Littlefield.

———. 2006. *Slavery and the French and Haitian Revolutionists*, trans. and ed. Frances Richardson Keller. Lanham, MD: Rowman and Littlefield.

Cooper, Davina. 2004. *Challenging Diversity: Rethinking Equality and the Value of Difference.* Cambridge: Cambridge Univ Press.

———. 2009. Intersectional Travel through Everyday Utopias: The Difference Sexual and Economic Dynamics Make. In *Intersectionality and Beyond: Law, Power and the Politics of Location*, eds. Emily Grabham, Davina Cooper, Jane Krishnadas, Didi Herman, 299–325. Abingdon, UK: Routledge Cavendish.

Crenshaw, Kimberle W. 1988. Race, Reform, and Retrenchment: Transformation and Legitimation in Antidiscrimination Law. *Harvard Law Review* 101 (7): 1331–1387.

———. 1989. Demarginalizing the Intersection of Race and Sex: A Black Feminist Critique of Antidiscrimination Doctrine, Feminist Theory and Antiracist Politics. *University of Chicago Legal Forum*: 139–168.

———. 1991. Mapping the Margins: Intersectionality, Identity Politics, and Violence against Women of Color. *Stanford Law Review* 43 (6): 1241–1299.

———. 2011a. The Curious Resurrection of First Wave Feminism in the US Elections: An Intersectional Critique of the Rhetoric of Solidarity and Betrayal. In *Sexuality, Gender and Power: Intersectional and Transnational Perspectives*, eds. Anna G. Jónasdóttir, Valerie Bryson, Kathleen B. Jones, 227–242. London: Routledge.

———. 2011b. Twenty Years of Critical Race Theory: Looking Back to Move Forward. *Connecticut Law Review* 43 (5): 1253–1352.

———. 2011c. Postscript. In *Framing Intersectionality: Debates on a Multi-Faceted Concept in Gender Studies*, eds. Helma Lutz, Maria Teresa Herrera Vivar, Linda Supik, 221–234. Farnham, UK: Ashgate.

Cruells, Marta and Gerard Coll-Planas. 2013. Challenging Equality Policies: The Emerging LGBT Perspective. *European Journal of Women's Studies* 20 (2): 122–137.

Cvetkovich, Ann. 2003. *An Archive of Feelings: Trauma, Sexuality, and Lesbian Public Cultures.* Durham, NC: Duke Univ Press.

Davies, Carole Boyce. 1994. *Black Women, Writing and Identity: Migrations of the Subject.* New York: Routledge.

———. 2008. *Left of Karl Marx: The Political Life of Black Communist Claudia Jones.* Durham, NC: Duke Univ Press.

Davis, Angela Y. 1972. Reflections on the Black Woman's Role in the Community of Slaves. *The Massachusetts Review* 13 (1–2): 81–100.

———. 1983. *Women, Race, and Class.* New York: Vintage.

———. 2003. *Are Prisons Obsolete?* New York: Seven Stories Press.

———. 2005. *Abolition Democracy: Beyond Empire, Prisons, and Torture.* New York: Seven Stories Press.

Davis, Kathy. 2008. Intersectionality as Buzzword: A Sociology of Science Perspective on What Makes a Feminist Theory Successful. *Feminist Theory* 9 (1): 67–85.
Davis, Lennard J. 1995. *Enforcing Normalcy: Disability, Deafness, and the Body*. London: Verso.
Delphy, Christine. 2006. Antisexisme ou antiracisme? Un faux dilemme. *Nouvelles questions féministes* 25 (1): 59–83.
Desai, Jigna, Danielle Bouchard, and Diane Detournay. 2010. Disavowed Legacies and Honorable Thievery: The Work of "Transnational" in Feminist and LGBTQ Studies. In *Critical Transnational Feminist Praxis*, eds. Amanda Lock Swarr, Richa Nagar, 46–64. Albany: SUNY Press.
Dhamoon, Rita Kaur. 2011. Considerations on Mainstreaming Intersectionality. *Political Research Quarterly* 64 (1): 230–243.
———. 2014, April 25. Keynote Panelist on Intersectionality: Where Have We Been, Where Are We Now panel. International Intersectionality Conference, Vancouver, BC, Canada.
Diaz, Sara, Rebecca Clark Mane, and Martha González. 2013. Intersectionality in Context: Three Cases for the Specificity of Intersectionality from the Perspective of Feminists in the Americas. In *Intersectionality und kritik: Neue perspektiven für alte fragen*, eds. Vera Kallenberg, Jennifer Meyer, Johanna M. Müller, 75–102. Wiesbaden: Springer.
Dill, Bonnie Thornton and Ruth Enid Zambrana. 2009. Critical Thinking about Inequality: An Emerging Lens. In *Emerging Intersections: Race, Class, and Gender in Theory, Policy, and Practice*, eds. Bonnie Thornton Dill, Ruth Enid Zambrana, 1–21. New Brunswick, NJ: Rutgers Univ Press.
Doetsch-Kidder, Sharon. 2012. *Social Change and Intersectional Activism: The Spirit of Social Movement*. New York: Palgrave Macmillan.
Dotson, Kristie. 2011a. Concrete Flowers: Contemplating the Profession of Philosophy. *Hypatia* 26 (2): 403–409.
———. 2011b. Tracking Epistemic Violence, Tracking Practices of Silencing. *Hypatia* 26 (2): 236–257.
Du Bois, W.E.B. 2007. *The Souls of Black Folk*. New York: Oxford Univ Press.
———. 2013. *Black Reconstruction in America: Toward a History of the Part which Black Folk Played in the Attempt to Reconstruct Democracy in America, 1860–1880*. New Brunswick, NJ: Transaction Publishers/Rutgers Univ Press.
DuCille, Ann. 1994. The Occult of True Black Womanhood: Critical Demeanor and Black Feminist Studies. *Signs* 19 (3): 591–629.
Dunye, Cheryl. 1996. *The Watermelon Woman*. New York: First Run/Icarus Films.
Duong, Kevin. 2012. What Does Queer Theory Teach Us about Intersectionality? *Politics and Gender* 8 (3): 370–386.
Egan, Gabrielle. 2014, April 26. Unsettling Discourses of Intersectionality: Moving Forward. Paper presentation. Paper presented at International Intersectionality Conference, Vancouver, BC, Canada.
Ehrenreich, Nancy. 2002. Subordination and Symbiosis: Mechanisms of Mutual Support between Subordinating Systems. *UMKC Law Review* 71: 251–324.
Elenes, Alejandra C. 2011. *Transforming Borders: Chicana/o Popular Culture and Pedagogy*. Lanham, MD: Lexington Books.
Ellison, Ralph. 1995. *Invisible Man*. New York: Vintage Random House.
Erel, Umut, Jin Haritaworn, Encarnación Gutiérrez Rodríguez, and Christian Klesse. 2011. On the Depoliticisation of Intersectionality Talk: Conceptualising Multiple Oppressions in Critical Sexuality Studies. In *Theorizing Intersectionality and Sexuality*, eds. Yvette Taylor, Sally Hines, Mark E. Casey, 56–77. Basingstoke, UK: Palgrave Macmillan.
Ertürk, Yakın and Bandana Purkayastha. 2012. Linking Research, Policy and Action: A Look at the Work of the Special Rapporteur on Violence against Women. *Current Sociology* 60 (2): 142–160.

Ewald, Alec. 2002. "Civil Death": The Ideological Paradox of Criminal Disenfranchisement Law in the United States. *Wisconsin Law Review*: 1045–1132.

Falcón, Sylvanna M. 2012. Transnational Feminism and Contextualized Intersectionality at the 2001 World Conference against Racism. *Journal of Women's History* 24 (4): 99–120.

Fausto-Sterling, Anne. 2000. *Sexing the Body: Gender Politics and the Construction of Sexuality*. New York: Basic Books, Perseus.

———. 2012. *Sex/Gender: Biology in a Social World*. New York: Routledge.

Ferguson, Kathy E. 1993. *The Man Question: Visions of Subjectivity in Feminist Theory*. Berkeley: Univ of California Press.

Ferguson, Roderick A. 2012. *The Reorder of Things: The University and Its Pedagogies of Minority Difference*. Minneapolis: Univ of Minnesota Press.

Ferree, Myra Marx. 2009. Inequality, Intersectionality and the Politics of Discourse. In *The Discursive Politics of Gender Equality: Stretching, Bending and Policy-Making*, eds. Emanuela Lombardo, Petra Meier, Mieke Verloo, 86–104. London: Routledge.

Ferree, Myra Marx and Elaine J. Hall. 1996. Rethinking Stratification from a Feminist Perspective: Gender, Race, and Class in Mainstream Textbooks. *American Sociological Review* 61: 929–950.

Ferri, Beth A. and David J. Connor. 2014. Talking (and Not Talking) about Race, Social Class and Dis/Ability: Working Margin to Margin. *Race Ethnicity and Education* 17 (4): 471–493.

Feyerabend, Paul K. 1975. *Against Method: Outline of an Anarchistic Theory of Knowledge*. London: Humanities Press.

Foreman, P. Gabrielle. 2013. A Riff, a Call, and a Response: Reframing the Problem That Led to Our Being Tokens in Ethnic and Gender Studies; Or, Where Are We Going Anyway and with Whom Will We Travel? *Legacy: A Journal of American Women Writers* 30 (2): 306–322.

Foster, Frances Smith. 1990. *A Brighter Day Coming: A Frances Ellen Watkins Harper Reader*. New York: Feminist Press.

———. 1993. *Written by Herself: Literary Production by African American Women, 1746–1892*. Bloomington: Indiana Univ Press.

Franke, Katherine. 2012. Dating the State: The Moral Hazards of Winning Gay Rights. *Columbia Human Rights Law Review* 44: 1–46.

Frankenberg, Ruth and Lata Mani. 1993. Crosscurrents, Crosstalk: Race, "Postcoloniality" and the Politics of Location. *Cultural Studies* 7 (2): 292–310.

Franklin, Jessica H. 2013. *Building from and Moving beyond the State: The National and Transnational Dimensions of Afro-Brazilian Women's Intersectional Mobilization*. PhD dissertation, McMaster Univ.

Freeman, Elizabeth. 2010. *Time Binds: Queer Temporalities, Queer Histories*. Durham, NC: Duke Univ Press.

Fricker, Miranda. 2007. *Epistemic Injustice: Power and the Ethics of Knowing*. New York: Oxford Univ Press.

Froc, Kerri A. 2010. Multidimensionality and the Matrix: Identifying Charter Violations in Cases of Complex Subordination. *Canadian Journal of Law and Society* 25 (1): 21–49.

Frye, Marilyn. 1983. *The Politics of Reality: Essays in Feminist Theory*. Trumansburg, NY: Crossing Press.

Fusco, Coco. 1995. *English Is Broken Here: Notes on Cultural Fusions in the Americas*. New York: New Press.

García, Alma M. 1989. The Development of Chicana Feminist Discourse, 1970–1980. *Gender and Society* 3 (2): 217–238.

———, ed. 1997. *Chicana Feminist Thought: The Basic Historical Writings*. New York: Routledge.

Garry, Ann. 2011. Intersectionality, Metaphors, and the Multiplicity of Gender. *Hypatia* 26 (4): 826–850.
Gatta, Mary. 2009. Developing Policy to Address the Lived Experiences of Working Mothers. In *Emerging Intersections: Race, Class, and Gender in Theory, Policy, and Practice*, eds. Bonnie Thornton Dill, Ruth Enid Zambrana, 101–122. New Brunswick, NJ: Rutgers Univ Press.
Gedalof, Irene. 2012. Sameness and Difference in Government Equality Talk. *Ethnic and Racial Studies* 36 (1): 117–135.
Gianettoni, Lavinia and Patricia Roux. 2010. Interconnecting Race and Gender Relations: Racism, Sexism and the Attribution of Sexism to the Racialized Other. *Sex Roles* 62 (5–6): 374–386.
Giddings, Paula J. 1984. *When and Where I Enter: The Impact of Black Women on Race and Sex in America*. New York: Bantam Books.
———. 2009. *Ida: A Sword among Lions*. New York: Amistad Harper Collins.
Gillman, Laura. 2007. Beyond the Shadow: Re-Scripting Race in Women's Studies. *Meridians* 7 (2): 117–141.
Gimenez, Martha E. 2001. Marxism, and Class, Gender, and Race: Rethinking the Trilogy. *Race, Gender, and Class* 8 (2): 23–33.
Gines, Kathryn T. 2011. Black Feminism and Intersectional Analyses: A Defense of Intersectionality. *Philosophy Today* 55, SPEP Supplement: 275–284.
———. 2014. Race Women, Race Men and Early Expressions of Proto-Intersectionality, 1830s–1930s. In *Why Race and Gender Still Matter: An Intersectional Approach*, eds. Namita Goswami, Maeve M. O'Donovan, Lisa Yount, 13–25. Brookfield, VT: Pickering and Chatto.
Glenn, Evelyn N. 1999. The Social Construction and Institutionalization of Gender and Race: An Integrative Framework. In *Revisioning Gender*, eds. Myra M. Ferree, Judith Lorber, Beth B. Hess, 3–43. New York: Sage.
Goldberg, Suzanne B. 2009. Intersectionality in Theory and Practice. In *Intersectionality and Beyond: Law, Power and the Politics of Location*, eds. Emily Grabham, Davina Cooper, Jane Krishnadas, Didi Herman, 124–158. Abingdon, UK: Routledge Cavendish.
Goodley, Dan. 2014. *Dis/ability Studies: Theorising Disablism and Ableism*. New York: Routledge.
Gordon-Chipembere, Natasha, ed. 2011. *Representation and Black Womanhood: The Legacy of Sarah Baartman*. New York: Palgrave.
Grabham, Emily. 2009. Intersectionality: Traumatic Impressions. In *Intersectionality and Beyond: Law, Power and the Politics of Location*, eds. Emily Grabham, Davina Cooper, Jane Krishnadas, Didi Herman, 183–202. Abingdon, UK: Routledge Cavendish.
Grabham, Emily, Davina Cooper, Jane Krishnadas, and Didi Herman. 2009. Introduction. In *Intersectionality and Beyond: Law, Power and the Politics of Location*, 1–18. Abingdon, UK: Routledge Cavendish.
Grech, Shaun. 2012. Disability and the Majority World: A Neocolonial Approach. In *Disability and Social Theory: New Developments and Directions*, eds. Dan Goodley, Bill Hughes Lennard Davis, 52–69. New York: Palgrave.
Greenwood, Ronni Michelle. 2008. Intersectional Political Consciousness: Appreciation for Intragroup Differences and Solidarity in Diverse Groups. *Psychology of Women Quarterly* 32 (1): 36–47.
Grewal, Inderpal and Caren Kaplan. 1994. Introduction: Transnational Feminist Practices and Questions of Postmodernity. In *Scattered Hegemonies: Postmodernity and Transnational Feminist Practices*, eds. Inderpal Grewal, Caren Kaplan, 1–34. Minneapolis: Univ of Minnesota Press.
———. 2003. Warrior Marks: Global Womanism's Neo-Colonial Discourse in a Multicultural Context. In *Multiculturalism, Postcoloniality, and Transnational Media*, eds. Ella Shohat, Robert Stam, 256–278. New Brunswick, NJ: Rutgers Univ Press.

Grosz, Elizabeth. 1994. *Volatile Bodies: Toward a Corporeal Feminism*. Bloomington: Indiana Univ Press.

———. 2010. Differences Disturbing Identity: Deleuze and Feminism. In *Working with Affect in Feminist Readings: Disturbing Differences*, eds. Marianne Liljeström, Susanna Paasonen, 101–111. New York: Routledge.

Grundy, John and Miriam Smith. 2005. The Politics of Multiscalar Citizenship: The Case of Lesbian and Gay Organizing in Canada. *Citizenship Studies* 9 (4): 389–404.

Guidroz, Kathleen and Michele Tracy Berger. 2009. A Conversation with Founding Scholars of Intersectionality: Kimberlé Crenshaw, Nira Yuval-Davis, and Michelle Fine. In *The Intersectional Approach: Transforming the Academy through Race, Class and Gender*, eds. Kathleen Guidroz, Michele Tracy Berger, 61–78. Chapel Hill: Univ of North Carolina Press.

Gunnarsson, Lena. 2011. A Defense of the Category "Women." *Feminist Theory* 12 (1): 23–37.

Guy-Sheftall, Beverly. 1990. *Daughters of Sorrow: Attitudes toward Black Women, 1880–1920*. Brooklyn, NY: Carlson.

———. 1995. The Evolution of Feminist Consciousness among African American Women. In *Words of Fire: An Anthology of African-American Feminist Thought*, ed. Beverly Guy-Sheftall, 1–22. New York: New Press.

———. 2002. The Body Politic: Black Female Sexuality and the Nineteenth-Century Euro-American Imagination. In *Skin Deep, Spirit Strong: The Black Female Body in American Culture*, ed. Kimberly Wallace-Sanders, 13–36. Ann Arbor: Univ of Michigan Press.

———. 2009. Black Feminist Studies: The Case of Anna Julia Cooper. *African American Review* 43 (1): 11–15.

Halberstam, Judith. 2005. *In a Queer Time and Place: Transgender Bodies, Subcultural Lives*. New York: NYU Press.

Hall, Kim Q. 2005. Queerness, Disability, and the Vagina Monologues. *Hypatia* 20 (1): 99–119.

Hamilton, Jennifer A. 2009. *Indigeneity in the Courtroom: Law, Culture, and the Production of Difference in North American Courts*. New York: Routledge.

Han, Sora. 2006. The Politics of Race in Asian American Jurisprudence. *UCLA Asian Pacific American Law Journal* 11 (1): 1–40.

Hancock, Ange-Marie. 2004. *The Politics of Disgust: The Public Identity of the Welfare Queen*. New York: NYU Press.

———. 2007a. Intersectionality as a Normative and Empirical Paradigm. *Politics and Gender* 3 (2): 248–254.

———. 2007b. When Multiplication Doesn't Equal Quick Addition: Examining Intersectionality as a Research Paradigm. *Perspectives on Politics* 5 (1): 63–79.

———. 2013. Empirical Intersectionality: A Tale of Two Approaches. *UC Irvine Law Review* 3: 259–296.

———. 2014, April 25. Keynote panelist on Intersectionality: Where Have We Been, Where Are We Now panel. International Intersectionality Conference, Vancouver, BC, Canada.

Hankivsky, Olena, ed. 2011. *Health Inequities in Canada: Intersectional Frameworks and Practices*. Vancouver, BC, Canada: UBC Press.

Hankivsky, Olena and Renee Cormier. 2011. Intersectionality and Public Policy: Some Lessons from Existing Models. *Political Research Quarterly* 64 (1): 217–229.

Harnois, Catherine E. 2005. Different Paths to Different Feminisms? Bridging Multiracial Feminist Theory and Quantitative Sociological Gender Research. *Gender and Society* 19 (6): 809–828.

———. 2013. *Feminist Measures in Survey Research*. Thousand Oaks, CA: Sage.

Harris, Cheryl L. 1993. Whiteness as Property. *Harvard Law Review* 106: 1707–1791.

Harris, Duchess. 1999. "All of Who I Am in the Same Place": The Combahee River Collective. *Womanist Theory and Research* 2 (1–2): 9–22.

Harris, Trudier. 1982. *From Mammies to Militants: Domestics in Black American Literature.* Philadelphia: Temple Univ Press.

Hawkesworth, Mary E. 1989. Knowers, Knowing, Known: Feminist Theory and Claims of Truth. *Signs* 14 (3): 533–557.

Hearn, Jeff. 2011. Neglected Intersectionalities in Studying Men: Age/ing, Virtuality, Transnationality. In *Framing Intersectionality: Debates on a Multi-Faceted Concept in Gender Studies*, eds. Helma Lutz, Maria Teresa Herrera Vivar, Linda Supik, 89–104. Farnham, UK: Ashgate.

Heldke, Lisa. 2006. Farming Made Her Stupid. *Hypatia* 21 (3): 151–165.

Hemmings, Clare. 2011. *Why Stories Matter: The Political Grammar of Feminist Theory.* Durham, NC: Duke Univ Press.

Henderson, Debra A. and Ann R. Tickamyer. 2009. The Intersection of Poverty Discourses: Race, Class, Culture, and Gender. In *Emerging Intersections: Race, Class, and Gender in Theory, Policy, and Practice*, eds. Bonnie Thornton Dill, Ruth Enid Zambrana, 50–72. New Brunswick, NJ: Rutgers Univ Press.

Heron, Barbara. 2007. *Desire for Development: Whiteness, Gender, and the Helping Imperative.* Waterloo, ON, Canada: Wilfrid Laurier Univ Press.

Hoagland, Sarah L. 2001. Resisting Rationality. In *Engendering Rationalities*, eds. Nancy Tuana, Sandra Morgen, 125–150. Albany: SUNY Press.

———. 2010. Colonial Practices/Colonial Identities: All the Women Are Still White. In *The Center Must Not Hold: White Women on the Whiteness of Philosophy*, ed. George Yancy, 227–244. Lanham, MD: Lexington Books.

Hobson, Janell. 2013. *Venus in the Dark: Blackness and Beauty in Popular Culture.* New York: Routledge.

Holloway, Karla F.C. 2006. "Cruel Enough to Stop the Blood": Global Feminisms and the US Body Politic, Or: "They Done Taken My Blues and Gone." *Meridians* 7 (1): 1–18.

———. 2011. *Private Bodies, Public Texts: Race, Gender, and a Cultural Bioethics.* Durham, NC: Duke Univ Press.

hooks, bell. 1981. *Ain't I a Woman? Black Women and Feminism.* Boston: South End Press.

———. 1989. *Talking Back: Thinking Feminist, Thinking Black.* Boston: South End Press.

———. 1990. *Yearning: Race, Gender, and Cultural Politics.* Boston: South End Press.

Hornschiedt, Antje, Cecilia Åsberg, Katherine Harrison, Björn Pernrud, and Malena Gustavson. 2009. Intersectional Challenges to Gender Studies—Gender Studies as a Challenge to Intersectionality. In *Gender Delight: Science, Knowledge, Culture and Writing . . . For Nina Lykke*, eds. Cecilia Åsberg, Katherine Harrison, Björn Pernrud, Malena Gustavson, 33–46. Linköping, Sweden: Linköping Univ.

Hulko, Wendy. 2009. The Time- and Context-Contingent Nature of Intersectionality and Interlocking Oppressions. *Affilia* 24 (1): 44–55.

Hunt, Krista and Kim Rygiel, eds. 2008. *(En) Gendering the War on Terror: War Stories and Camouflaged Politics.* Burlington, VT: Ashgate.

Hunter, Rosemary and Tracey de Simone. 2009. Identifying Disadvantage: Beyond Intersectionality. In *Intersectionality and Beyond: Law, Power and the Politics of Location*, eds. Emily Grabham, Davina Cooper, Jane Krishnadas, Didi Herman, 159–182. Abingdon, UK: Routledge Cavendish.

Hurtado, Aida. 1997. Understanding Multiple Group Identities: Inserting Women into Cultural Transformations. *Journal of Social Issues* 53 (2): 299–327.

Hutchings, Kimberly. 2013. Choosers or Losers? Feminist Ethical and Political Agency in a Plural and Unequal World. In *Gender, Agency, and Coercion*, eds. Sumi Madhok, Anne Phillips, Kalpana Wilson, Clare Hemmings, 14–28. New York: Palgrave Macmillan.

Hutchinson, Darren Lenard. 1999. Ignoring the Sexualization of Race: Heteronormativity, Critical Race Theory, and Anti-Racist Politics. *Buffalo Law Review* 47 (1): 1–116.

———. 2000. Identity Crisis: Intersectionality, Multidimensionality, and the Development of an Adequate Theory of Subordination. *Michigan Journal of Race and Law* 6: 285–318.
———. 2002. New Complexity Theories: From Theoretical Innovation to Doctrinal Reform. *UMKC Law Review* 71 (2): 431–446.
Incite! Women of Color against Violence. 2007. *The Revolution Will Not Be Funded: Beyond the Non-Profit Industrial Complex*. Boston: South End Press.
Isoke, Zenzele. 2013. *Urban Black Women and the Politics of Resistance*. New York: Palgrave.
Jacobs, Harriet A. 1987. *Incidents in the Life of a Slave Girl: Written by Herself*, ed. Jean Fagan Yellin. Cambridge, MA: Harvard Univ Press.
Jaggar, Alison M. 1989. Love and Knowledge: Emotion in Feminist Epistemology. *Inquiry: An Interdisciplinary Journal of Philosophy* 32 (2): 151–176.
James, Joy. 1996. *Resisting State Violence: Radicalism, Gender, and Race in US Culture*. Minneapolis: Univ of Minnesota Press.
———. 2002. *Shadowboxing: Representations of Black Feminist Politics*. New York: Palgrave.
Jastrzębska, Maria. 1996. Warrior Woman. In *"What Happened to You?" Writings by Disabled Women*, ed. Lois Keith, 189–191. New York: New Press.
Jones, Martha S. 2007. *All Bound Up Together: The Woman Question in African American Public Culture, 1830–1900*. Chapel Hill: Univ of North Carolina Press.
Jordan-Zachery, Julia S. 2007. Am I a Black Woman or a Woman Who Is Black? A Few Thoughts on the Meaning of Intersectionality. *Politics and Gender* 3 (2): 254–263.
Kadi, Joanna. 2003. Speaking (about) Silence. In *Sing, Whisper, Shout, Pray: Feminist Visions for a Just World*, eds. M. Jacqui Alexander, Lisa Albrecht, Sharon Day, Mab Segrest, 539–545. San Francisco: EdgeWork Books.
Kafer, Alison. 2013. *Feminist, Queer, Crip*. Bloomington: Indiana Univ Press.
Kantola, Johanna. 2009. Tackling Multiple Discrimination: Gender and Crosscutting Inequalities in Europe. In *Teaching Intersectionality: Putting Gender at the Centre*, eds. Martha Franken, Alison Woodward, Anna Cabó, Barbara Bagilhole, 15–30. Utrecht: ATHENA3 Advanced Thematic Network in Women's Studies in Europe, Univ of Utrecht and Centre for Gender Studies, Stockholm Univ.
Kantola, Johanna and Kevät Nousiainen. 2012. The European Union: Initiator of a New European Anti-Discrimination Regime? In *Institutionalizing Intersectionality: The Changing Nature of European Equality Regimes*, eds. Andrea Krizsan, Hege Skjeie, Judith Squires, 33–58. New York: Palgrave.
Kelley, Robin D.G. 2002. *Freedom Dreams: The Black Radical Imagination*. Boston: Beacon Press.
Kende, Mark S. 2009. *Constitutional Rights in Two Worlds: South Africa and the United States*. Cambridge: Cambridge Univ Press.
King, Deborah K. 1988. Multiple Jeopardy, Multiple Consciousness: The Context of a Black Feminist Ideology. *Signs* 14 (1): 42–72.
Kluchin, Rebecca M. 2009. *Fit to Be Tied: Sterilization and Reproductive Rights in America, 1950–1980*. New Brunswick, NJ: Rutgers Univ Press.
Knapp, Gudrun-Axeli. 2005. Race, Class, Gender: Reclaiming Baggage in Fast Travelling Theories. *European Journal of Women's Studies* 12 (3): 249–265.
———. 2011. Intersectional Invisibility: Inquiries into a Concept of Intersectionality Studies, trans. Rebecca van Dyck. In *Framing Intersectionality: Debates on a Multi-Faceted Concept in Gender Studies*, eds. Helma Lutz, Maria Teresa Herrerra-Vivar, Linda Supik, 187–206. Farnham, UK: Ashgate.
Kóczé, Angéla. 2009. *Missing Intersectionality: Race/Ethnicity, Gender, and Class in Current Research and Policies on Romani Women in Europe*. Budapest, Hungary: Center for Policy Studies, Central European Univ.
Kogawa, Joy. 1994. *Obasan*. New York: Anchor.

Koldinská, Kristina. 2009. Institutionalizing Intersectionality: A New Path to Equality for New Member States of the EU? *International Feminist Journal of Politics* 11 (4): 547–563.

Krizsan, Andrea, Hege Skjeie, and Judith Squires. 2012. Institutionalizing Intersectionality: A Theoretical Framework. In *Institutionalizing Intersectionality: The Changing Nature of European Equality Regimes*, eds. Andrea Krizsan, Hege Skjeie, Judith Squires, 1–32. New York: Palgrave.

Kuhn, Thomas. 1962. *The Structure of Scientific Revolution*. Chicago: Univ of Chicago Press.

Kwan, Peter. 1997. Intersections of Race, Ethnicity, Class, Gender and Sexual Orientation: Jeffrey Dahmer and the Cosynthesis of Categories. *Hastings Law Journal* 48: 1257–1387.

———. 1999. Complicity and Complexity: Cosynthesis and Praxis. *DePaul Law Review* 49: 673–690.

Largent, Mark A. 2008. *Breeding Contempt: The History of Coerced Sterilization in the United States*. New Brunswick, NJ: Rutgers Univ Press.

LaRue, Linda. 1995. The Black Movement and Women's Liberation. In *Words of Fire: An Anthology of African-American Feminist Thought*, ed. Beverly Guy-Sheftall, 164–174. New York: New Press.

Lewis, Gail. 2009. Celebrating Intersectionality? Debates on a Multi-Faceted Concept in Gender Studies: Themes from a Conference. *European Journal of Women's Studies* 16 (3): 203–210.

———. 2013. Unsafe Travel: Experiencing Intersectionality and Feminist Displacements. *Signs* 38 (4): 869–892.

Lindsay, Keisha. 2013. God, Gays, and Progressive Politics: Reconceptualizing Intersectionality as a Normatively Malleable Analytical Framework. *Perspectives on Politics* 11 (2): 447–460.

Linton, Simi. 1998. *Claiming Disability: Knowledge and Identity*. New York: NYU Press.

Logan, Shirley Wilson. 1999. *We Are Coming: The Persuasive Discourse of Nineteenth-Century Black Women*. Carbondale: Southern Illinois Univ Press.

Lombardo, Emanuela and Lise Rolandsen Agustín. 2012. Framing Gender Intersections in the European Union: What Implications for the Quality of Intersectionality in Policies? *Social Politics: International Studies in Gender, State and Society* 19 (4): 482–512.

Lombardo, Emanuela and Elena Del Giorgio. 2013. EU Antidiscrimination Policy and Its Unintended Domestic Consequences: The Institutionalization of Multiple Equalities in Italy. *Women's Studies International Forum* 39: 12–21.

Lombardo, Emanuela and Mieke Verloo. 2009. Institutionalizing Intersectionality in the European Union? Policy Developments and Contestations. *International Feminist Journal of Politics* 11 (4): 478–495.

Lorde, Audre. 1984. *Sister Outsider: Essays and Speeches*. Trumansburg, NY: Crossing Press.

Loutfy, Mona R., Carmen H. Logie, Yimeng Zhang, Sandra L. Blitz, Shari L. Margolese, Wangari E. Tharao, Sean B. Rourke, Sergio Rueda, and Janet M. Raboud. 2012. Gender and Ethnicity Differences in HIV-Related Stigma Experienced by People Living with HIV in Ontario, Canada. *PloS One* 7 (12): e48168.

Lugones, Maria. 1987. Playfulness, "World"-Travelling, and Loving Perception. *Hypatia* 2 (2): 3–19.

———. 1994. Purity, Impurity, and Separation. *Signs* 19 (2): 458–479.

———. 2005. From within Germinative Stasis: Creating Active Subjectivity, Resistant Agency. In *Entremundos/Amongworlds: New Perspectives on Gloria Anzaldúa*, ed. AnaLouise Keating, 85–100. New York: Palgrave.

———. 2006. On Complex Communication. *Hypatia* 21 (3): 75–85.

———. 2007. Heterosexualism and the Colonial/Modern Gender System. *Hypatia* 22 (1): 186–219.

———. 2010. Toward a Decolonial Feminism. *Hypatia* 25 (4): 742–759.

Lutz, Helma, Maria Teresa Herrera Vivar, and Linda Supik, eds. 2011. *Framing Intersectionality: Debates on a Multi-Faceted Concept in Gender Studies*. Farnham, UK: Ashgate.
Lykke, Nina. 2006. Intersectionality—A Useful Concept for Feminist Theory? In *Gender Studies: Trends/Tensions in Greece and Other European Countries*, eds. S. Pavlidou Stella Vosniadou, Vasiliki Dendrinou, Lydia Vaiou, 151–160. Thessaloniki, Greece: Univ of Thessaloniki.
———. 2010. *Feminist Studies: A Guide to Intersectional Theory, Methodology and Writing*. New York: Routledge.
———. 2011. Intersectional Analysis: Black Box or Useful Critical Feminist Thinking Technology? In *Framing Intersectionality: Debates on a Multi-Faceted Concept in Gender Studies*, eds. Helma Lutz, Maria Teresa Herrerra-Vivar, Linda Supik, 207–221. Farnham, UK: Ashgate.
Madhok, Sumi. 2013. Action, Agency, Coercion: Reformatting Agency for Oppressive Contexts. In *Gender, Agency, and Coercion*, eds. Sumi Madhok, Anne Phillips, Kalpana Wilson, Clare Hemmings, 102–121. New York: Palgrave.
Mahmood, Saba. 2005. *Politics of Piety: The Islamic Revival and the Feminist Subject*. Princeton, NJ: Princeton Univ Press.
Maldonado-Torres, Nelson. 2011. Thinking through the Decolonial Turn: Post-Continental Interventions in Theory, Philosophy, and Critique—An Introduction. *Transmodernity* 1 (2): 1–15.
———. 2012. Epistemology, Ethics, and the Time/Space of Decolonization: Perspectives from the Caribbean and the Latina/O Americas. In *Decolonizing Epistemologies: Latina/o Theology and Philosophy*, eds. Ada María Isasi-Díaz, Eduardo Mendieta, 193–206. New York: Fordham Univ Press.
Malveaux, Julianne. 2013. Still Slipping: African-American Women in the Economy and in Society. *The Review of Black Political Economy* 40 (1): 13–21.
Mann, Regis. 2011. Theorizing "What Could Have Been": Black Feminism, Historical Memory, and the Politics of Reclamation. *Women's Studies* 40 (5): 575–599.
Maracle, Lee. 1994. Oratory: Coming to Theory. *Essays on Canadian Writing* 54: 7–11.
Marchetti, Elena. 2008. Intersectional Race and Gender Analyses: Why Legal Processes Just Don't Get It. *Social and Legal Studies* 17 (2): 155–174.
Marcos, Sylvia. 2006. *Taken from the Lips: Gender and Eros in Mesoamerican Religions*. Boston: Brill Academic.
Martin, Biddy. 1996. *Femininity Played Straight: The Significance of Being Lesbian*. New York: Routledge.
Martin, Biddy and Chandra Talpade Mohanty. 1986. Feminist Politics: What's Home Got to Do with It? In *Feminist Studies, Critical Studies*, ed. Teresa De Lauretis, 191–212. Bloomington: Indiana Univ Press.
Martin, Emily. 1991. The Egg and the Sperm: How Science Has Constructed a Romance Based on Stereotypical Male-Female Roles. *Signs* 16 (3): 485–501.
Martinez, Elizabeth. 1993. Beyond Black/White: The Racisms of Our Time. *Social Justice* 20 (1): 22–34.
Martínez, Georgina. 2012, Spring. Feminist Theory. Research paper, Syracuse University, NY.
Matsuda, Mari J. 1989. When the First Quail Calls: Multiple Consciousness as Jurisprudential Method. *Women's Rights Law Reporter* 11 (1): 7–10.
May, Vivian M. 1996. Ambivalent Narratives, Fragmented Selves: Performative Identities and the Mutability of Roles in James Baldwin's *Go Tell It on the Mountain*. In *New Essays on Go Tell It on the Mountain*, ed. Trudier Harris, 97–126. New York: Cambridge Univ Press.
———. 2004. Thinking from the Margins, Acting at the Intersections: Anna Julia Cooper's *A Voice from the South*. *Hypatia* 19 (2): 74–91.

———. 2006. Trauma in Paradise: Willful and Strategic Ignorance in *Cereus Blooms at Night. Hypatia* 21 (3): 107–135.
———. 2007. *Anna Julia Cooper, Visionary Black Feminist: A Critical Introduction*. New York: Routledge.
———. 2008a. "By a Black Woman of the South": Race, Place, and Gender in the Work of Anna Julia Cooper. *Southern Quarterly* 45 (3): 127–152.
———. 2008b. "It Is Never a Question of the Slaves": Anna Julia Cooper's Challenge to History's Silences in Her 1925 Sorbonne Thesis. *Callaloo* 31 (3): 903–918.
———. 2009. Writing the Self into Being: Anna Julia Cooper's Textual Politics. *African American Review* 43 (1): 17–34.
———. 2012a. Historicizing Intersectionality as a Critical Lens: Returning to the Work of Anna Julia Cooper. In *Interconnections: Gender and Race in American History*, eds. Carol Faulkner, Alison M. Parker, 17–48. Rochester, NY: Boydell and Brewer, Univ of Rochester Press.
———. 2012b. Intersectionality. In *Rethinking Women's and Gender Studies*, eds. Catherine Orr, Ann Braithwaite, Diane Lichtenstein, 155–172. New York: Routledge.
———. 2014a. "Speaking into the Void?" Intersectionality Critiques and Epistemic Backlash. *Hypatia* 29 (1): 94–112.
———. 2014b. Under-Theorized and Under-Taught: Re-Examining Harriet Tubman's Place in Women's Studies. *Meridians* 12 (2): 28–49.
May, Vivian M. and Beth A. Ferri. 2005. Fixated on Ability: Questioning Ableist Metaphors in Feminist Theories of Resistance. *Prose Studies* 27 (1–2): 120–140.
McCall, Leslie. 2005. The Complexity of Intersectionality. *Signs* 30 (3): 1771–1800.
McClintock, Anne. 1995. *Imperial Leather: Race, Gender, and Sexuality in the Colonial Contest*. New York: Routledge.
McDowell, Deborah E. 1987. "The Changing Same": Generational Connections and Black Women Novelists. *New Literary History* 18 (2): 281–302.
McGinley, Ann C. and Frank Rudy Cooper. 2013. Identities Cubed: Perspectives on Multidimensional Masculinities Theory. *UNLV Law Journal* 13 (2): 326–340.
McKay, Nellie. 1992. Remembering Anita Hill and Clarence Thomas: What Really Happened When One Black Woman Spoke Out. In *Race-ing Justice, En-Gendering Power: Essays on Anita Hill, Clarence Thomas, and the Construction of Social Reality*, ed. Toni Morrison, 269–289. New York: Pantheon.
McKay, Nellie and Toni Morrison. 1994. An Interview with Toni Morrison. In *Conversations with Toni Morrison*, ed. Danille Taylor-Guthrie, 138–155. Jackson: Univ Press of Mississippi.
McKittrick, Katherine. 2006. *Demonic Grounds: Black Women and the Cartographies of Struggle*. Minneapolis: Univ of Minnesota Press.
McWhorter, Ladelle. 2009. *Racism and Sexual Oppression in Anglo-America: A Genealogy*. Bloomington: Indiana Univ Press.
Mehrotra, Gita Rani. 2012. *Diasporic Intersectionalities: Exploring South Asian Women's Narratives of Race, Ethnicity, and Gender through a Community-Based Performance Project*. PhD dissertation, Univ of Washington.
Mignolo, Walter. 2003. *The Darker Side of the Renaissance: Literacy, Territoriality, and Colonization*. 2nd ed. Ann Arbor: Univ of Michigan Press.
———. 2012. *Local Histories/Global Designs: Coloniality, Subaltern Knowledges, and Border Thinking*. Princeton, NJ: Princeton Univ Press.
Mills, Charles W. 1997. *The Racial Contract*. Ithaca, NY: Cornell Univ Press.
Minh-ha, Trinh T. 1992. *Framer Framed*. New York: Routledge.
Mingus, Mia and Heather L. Talley. 2013. Feminists We Love: Mia Mingus. *The Feminist Wire*. http://thefeministwire.com/2013/11/feminists-we-love-mia-mingus/.

Mirza, Heidi. 2006. Transcendence over Diversity: Black Women in the Academy. *Policy Futures in Education* 4 (2): 101–113.
Mitchell, David T. and Sharon L. Snyder. 2000. *Narrative Prosthesis: Disability and the Dependencies of Discourse*. Ann Arbor: Univ of Michigan Press.
Mohanty, Chandra Talpade. 2003. *Feminism without Borders: Decolonizing Theory, Practicing Solidarity*. Durham, NC: Duke Univ Press.
———. 2013. Transnational Feminist Crossings: On Neoliberalism and Radical Critique. *Signs* 38 (4): 967–991.
Moody-Turner, Shirley. 2013. *Black Folklore and the Politics of Racial Representation*. Jackson: Univ Press of Mississippi.
Moraga, Cherríe. 1983. *Loving in the War Years*. Boston: South End Press.
Moraga, Cherríe and Gloria Anzaldúa. 1983. *This Bridge Called My Back: Writings by Radical Women of Color*. New York: Kitchen Table Press.
Morgan, Jennifer. 2004. *Laboring Women: Reproduction and Gender in New World Slavery*. Philadelphia: Univ of Pennsylvania Press.
Morris, Charles E. 2006. Archival Queer. *Rhetoric and Public Affairs* 9 (1): 145–151.
Morris, Monique W. 2012. Race, Gender and the School-to-Prison Pipeline: Expanding Our Discussion to Include Black Girls. African American Policy Forum. http://aapf.org/wp-content/uploads/2012/08/Morris-Race-Gender-and-the-School-to-Prison-Pipeline.pdf.
Mulvihill, Mary Ann, Louise Mailloux, and Wendy Atkin. 2001. *Advancing Policy and Research: Responses to Immigrant and Refugee Women's Health in Canada*. Winnipeg: Canadian Women's Health Network.
Muñoz, José Esteban. 1999. *Disidentifications: Queers of Color and the Performance of Politics*. Minneapolis: Univ of Minnesota Press.
Murphy, Kevin P. and Jennifer M. Spear, eds. 2011. *Historicising Gender and Sexuality*. New York: John Wiley.
Murray, Pauli. 1995. The Liberation of Black Women. In *Words of Fire: An Anthology of African-American Feminist Thought*, ed. Beverly Guy-Sheftall, 186–197. New York: New Press.
Mutua, Athena D. 2006. The Rise, Development and Future Directions of Critical Race Theory and Related Scholarship. *Denver University Law Review* 84: 329–394.
———. 2013. Multidimensionality Is to Masculinities What Intersectonality Is to Feminism. *UNLV Law Journal* 13 (2): 343–347.
Narayan, Uma. 1997. *Dislocating Cultures: Identities, Traditions, and Third World Feminism*. New York: Routledge.
Nash, Jennifer C. 2008a. Re-Thinking Intersectionality. *Feminist Review* 89 (1): 1–15.
———. 2008b. Strange Bedfellows: Black Feminism and Antipornography Feminism. *Social Text* 26 (497): 51–76.
———. 2009. Review Essay: Un-disciplining Intersectionality. *International Feminist Journal of Politics* 11 (4): 587–604.
———. 2010. On Difficulty: Intersectionality as Feminist Labor. *The Scholar and Feminist Online* 8 (3). http://sfonline.barnard.edu/polyphonic/nash_01.htm – text5.
———. 2011. Home Truths on Intersectionality. *Yale Journal of Law and Feminism* 23: 445–470.
———. 2014. Institutionalizing the Margins. *Social Text* 32 (1 118): 45–65.
Neal, Mark Anthony. 2005. *New Black Man*. New York: Routledge.
Neverdon-Morton, Cynthia. 1989. *Afro-American Women of the South and the Advancement of the Race, 1895–1925*. Knoxville: Univ of Tennessee Press.
Newman, Louise Michele. 1999. *White Women's Rights: The Racial Origins of Feminism in the United States*. New York: Oxford Univ Press.

Ocen, Priscilla A. 2013. Unshackling Intersectionality. *Du Bois Review* 10 (2): 471–483.
O'Grady, Lorraine. 1992. Olympia's Maid: Reclaiming Black Female Subjectivity. *Afterimage* 20 (1): 14–20.
Oliverio, Katie E. 2011. Thresholds of Vulnerability: Gesturing beyond the Sensational. Paper presented at the Emory Univ School of Law, Vulnerability and Human Condition Initiative, Atlanta, GA.
Onwuachi-Willig, Angela. 2005. The Return of the Ring: Welfare Reform's Marriage Cure as the Revival of Post-Bellum Control. *California Law Review* 93 (6): 1647–1696.
Ortega, Mariana. 2006. Being Lovingly, Knowingly Ignorant: White Feminism and Women of Color. *Hypatia* 21 (3): 56–74.
Oyěwùmí, Oyèrónké. 1997. *The Invention of Women: Making an African Sense of Western Gender Discourses*. Minneapolis: Univ of Minnesota Press.
Parent, Mike C., Cirleen DeBlaere, and Bonnie Moradi. 2013. Approaches to Research on Intersectionality: Perspectives on Gender, LGBT, and Racial/Ethnic Identities. *Sex Roles* 68 (11–12): 639–645.
Parker, Pat. 1999. *Movement in Black*. Trumansburg, NY: Crossing Press.
Pateman, Carole. 1988. *The Sexual Contract*. Stanford, CA: Stanford Univ Press.
Pateman, Carole and Charles Mills. 2007. *The Contract and Domination*. Malden, MA: Polity Press.
Patil, Vrushali. 2013. From Patriarchy to Intersectionality: A Transnational Feminist Assessment of How Far We've Really Come. *Signs* 38 (4): 847–867.
Pérez, Emma. 1999. *The Decolonial Imaginary: Writing Chicanas into History*. Bloomington: Indiana Univ Press.
Peterson, Carla L. 1995. *Doers of the Word: African-American Women Speakers and Writers in the North (1830–1880)*. New York: Oxford Univ Press.
Phoenix, Ann and Pamela Pattynama. 2006. Intersectionality. *European Journal of Women's Studies* 13 (3): 187–192.
Platero, Raquel. 2008. Outstanding Challenges in a Post-Equality Era: The Same-Sex Marriage and Gender Identity Laws in Spain. *International Journal of Iberian Studies* 21 (1): 41–49.
Pohlhaus, Gaile. 2012. Relational Knowing and Epistemic Injustice: Toward a Theory of Willful Hermeneutical Ignorance. *Hypatia* 27 (4): 715–735.
Pough, Gwendolyn. 2012, September 28. Rethinking Sapphire: The Angry Black Woman and Contemporary Black Feminisms. Paper presented at Association for the Study of African American Life and History, Pittsburgh, PA.
Pratt-Clarke, Menah. 2010. *Critical Race, Feminism, and Education: A Social Justice Model*. New York: Palgrave.
———. 2013. A Radical Reconstruction of Resistance Strategies: Black Girls and Black Women Reclaiming Our Power Using Transdisciplinary Applied Social Justice©, Ma'at, and Rites of Passage. *Journal of African American Studies* 17 (1): 99–114.
Price, Margaret. 2006. Queer and Pleasant Danger: What's Up with the Mainstreaming of Gay Parents? In *Bitchfest: Ten Years of Cultural Criticism from the Pages of Bitch Magazine*, eds. Margaret Cho, Lisa Jervis, Andi Zeisler, 232–239. New York: Farrar, Strauss, and Giroux.
Prins, Baukje. 2006. Narrative Accounts of Origins: A Blind Spot in the Intersectional Approach? *European Journal of Women's Studies* 13 (3): 277–290.
Puar, Jasbir K. 2005. Queer Times, Queer Assemblages. *Social Text* 23 (3–4): 121–139.
———. 2006. Mapping US Homonormativities. *Gender, Place, and Culture* 13 (1): 67–88.
———. 2007. *Terrorist Assemblages: Homonationalism in Queer Times*. Durham, NC: Duke Univ Press.
———. 2011. Citation and Censorship: The Politics of Talking about the Sexual Politics of Israel. *Feminist Legal Studies* 19 (2): 133–142.

———. 2012a. Coda, The Cost of Getting Better: Suicide, Sensation, Switchpoints. *GLQ: A Journal of Lesbian and Gay Studies* 18 (1): 149–158.

———. 2012b. "I Would Rather Be a Cyborg Than a Goddess": Becoming-Intersectional in Assemblage Theory. *Philosophia* 2 (1): 49–66.

Puar, Jasbir K., Ben Pitcher, and Henriette Gunkel. 2008. Q&A with Jasbir Puar. *Darkmatter* 3: www.darkmatter101.org/site/2008/05/02/qa-with-jasbir-puar/.

Puar, Jasbir K. and Amit Rai. 2002. Monster, Terrorist, Fag: The War on Terrorism and the Production of Docile Patriots. *Social Text* 20 (3): 117–148.

Puentes, Jennifer and Matthew Gougherty. 2013. Intersections of Gender, Race, and Class in Introductory Textbooks. *Teaching Sociology* 41 (2): 159–171.

Purdie-Vaughns, Valerie and Richard P. Eibach. 2008. Intersectional Invisibility: The Distinctive Advantages and Disadvantages of Multiple Subordinate-Group Identities. *Sex Roles* 59 (5–6): 377–391.

Purkayastha, Bandana. 2012. Intersectionality in a Transnational World. *Gender and Society* 26 (1): 55–66.

Quijano, Aníbal. 2000. Coloniality of Power and Eurocentrism in Latin America. *International Sociology* 15 (2): 215–232.

———. 2007. Questioning "Race." *Socialism and Democracy* 21 (1): 45–53.

Rahman, Momin. 2009. Theorising Intersectionality: Identities, Equality, and Ontology. In *Intersectionality and Beyond: Law, Power and the Politics of Location*, eds. Emily Grabham, Davina Cooper, Jane Krishnadas, Didi Herman, 352–372. Abingdon, UK: Routledge Cavendish.

Razack, Sherene. 1998. *Looking White People in the Eye: Gender, Race, and Culture in Courtrooms and Classrooms*. Toronto: Univ of Toronto Press.

———. 2008. *Casting Out: The Eviction of Muslims from Western Law and Politics*. Toronto: Univ of Toronto Press.

Reagon, Bernice Johnson. 1983. Coalition Politics: Turning the Century. In *Home Girls: A Black Feminist Anthology*, ed. Barbara Smith, 343–356. New York: Kitchen Table Press.

Reddy, Chandan. 2011. *Freedom with Violence: Race, Sexuality, and the US State*. Durham, NC: Duke Univ Press.

Rich, Adrienne C. 1979. *On Lies, Secrets, and Silence: Selected Prose, 1966–1978*. New York: W.W. Norton.

Riggs, Marlon T. 1983. *Ethnic Notions*. San Francisco: California Newsreel.

Riley, Robin L. 2013. *Depicting the Veil: Transnational Sexism and the War on Terror*. London: Zed.

Riley, Robin L., Chandra Talpade Mohanty, and Minnie Bruce Pratt, eds. 2008. *Feminism and War: Confronting US Imperialism*. London: Zed.

Ringrose, Jessica. 2007. Troubling Agency and "Choice": A Psychosocial Analysis of Students' Negotiations of Black Feminist "Intersectionality" Discourses in Women's Studies. *Women's Studies International Forum* 30 (3): 264–278.

Roberts, Dorothy. 1997. *Killing the Black Body*. New York: Pantheon.

———. 2011. *Fatal Invention: How Science, Politics, and Big Business Re-Create Race in the Twenty-First Century*. New York: New Press.

Roberts, Dorothy and Sujatha Jesudason. 2013. Movement Intersectionality. *Du Bois Review* 10 (2): 313–328.

Robertson, Mary A. and Arlene Sgoutas. 2012. Thinking beyond the Category of Sexual Identity: At the Intersection of Sexuality and Human-Trafficking Policy. *Politics and Gender* 8 (3): 421–429.

Roediger, David R. 1999. *The Wages of Whiteness: Race and the Making of the American Working Class*. London: Verso.

Roggeband, Conny. 2010. The Victim-Agent Dilemma: How Migrant Women's Organizations in the Netherlands Deal with a Contradictory Policy Frame. *Signs* 35 (4): 943–967.

Rollock, Nicola. 2012. The Invisibility of Race: Intersectional Reflections on the Liminal Space of Alterity. *Race Ethnicity and Education* 15 (1): 65–84.
Rooks, Noliwe M. 2000. Like Canaries in the Mines: Black Women's Studies at the Millennium. *Signs* 25 (4): 1209–1211.
Roshanravan, Shireen. 2014. Motivating Coalition: Women of Color and Epistemic Disobedience. *Hypatia* 29 (1): 41–58.
Roth, Benita. 2004. *Separate Roads to Feminism: Black, Chicana, and White Feminist Movements in America's Second Wave.* New York: Cambridge Univ Press.
Roth, Julia. 2013. *Entangled Inequalities as Intersectionalities: Towards an Epistemic Sensibilization.* Working Paper 43. Berlin: Research Network on Interdependent Inequalities in Latin America. http://www.desigualdades.net/Resources/Working_Paper/43_WP_Roth_Online.pdf.
Rottmann, Susan B. and Myra Marx Ferree. 2008. Citizenship and Intersectionality: German Feminist Debates about Headscarf and Antidiscrimination Laws. *Social Politics: International Studies in Gender, State, and Society* 15 (4): 481–513.
Rowe, Aimee M. Carrillo. 2000. Locating Feminism's Subject: The Paradox of White Femininity and the Struggle to Forge Feminist Alliances. *Communication Theory* 10 (1): 64–80.
Russo, Ann and Melissa Spatz. 2010. Stop the False Race-Gender Divide. In *Who Should Be First? Feminists Speak Out on the 2008 Presidential Campaign*, eds. Beverly Guy-Sheftall, Johnnetta Betsch Cole, 17–20. Albany: SUNY Press.
Saavedra, Cinthya M. and Ellen D. Nymark. 2008. Borderland-*Mestizaje* Feminism: The New Tribalism. In *Handbook of Critical and Indigenous Methodologies*, eds. Norman K. Denzin, Yvonna S. Lincoln, Linda Tuhiwai Smith, 255–270. Thousand Oaks, CA: Sage.
Saldanha, Arun. 2010. Politics and Difference. In *Taking Place: Non-Representational Theories and Human Geography*, eds. Ben Anderson, Paul Harrison, 283–303. Surrey, UK: Ashgate.
Saldívar-Hull, Sonia. 2000. *Feminism on the Border: Chicana Gender Politics and Literature.* Berkeley: Univ of California Press.
Samuels, Ellen. 2014. *Fantasies of Identification: Disability, Gender, Race.* New York: NYU Press.
Sandoval, Chela. 1990. Feminism and Racism: A Report on the 1981 National Women's Studies Association Conference. In *Making Face, Making Soul/Haciendo caras: Creative and Critical Perspectives by Feminists of Color*, ed. Gloria Anzaldúa, 55–71. San Francisco: Aunt Lute.
———. 2000. *Methodology of the Oppressed.* Minneapolis: Univ of Minnesota Press.
Savoie, Keely. 2006. Unnatural Selection: Questioning Science's Gender Bias. In *Bitchfest: Ten Years of Cultural Criticism from the Pages of Bitch Magazine*, eds. Margaret Cho, Lisa Jervis, Andi Zeisler, 134–143. New York: Farrar, Strauss, and Giroux.
Saxton, Marsha. 2013. Disability Rights and Selective Abortion. In *The Disability Studies Reader*, ed. Lennard J. Davis, 87–99. New York: Routledge.
Schalk, Sami. 2013. Metaphorically Speaking: Ableist Metaphors in Feminist Writing. *Disability Studies Quarterly* 33 (4). http://dsq-sds.org/article/view/3874/3410.
Schueller, Malini Johar. 2005. Analogy and (White) Feminist Theory: Thinking Race and the Color of the Cyborg Body. *Signs* 31 (1): 63–92.
Schutte, Ofelia. 2000. Cultural Alterity: Cross-Cultural Communication and Feminist Theory in North-South Contexts. In *Women of Color and Philosophy: A Critical Reader*, ed. Naomi Zack, 44–68. Malden, MA: Blackwell.
Sewall, May Wright, ed. 1894. *World's Congress of Representative Women.* Chicago: Rand McNally.
Shapiro, Joseph P. 1994. Disability Rights as Civil Rights: The Struggle for Recognition. In *The Disabled, the Media, and the Information Age*, ed. Jack A. Nelson, 59–72. Westport, CT: Greenwood Press.

Shields, Stephanie A. 2008. Gender: An Intersectionality Perspective. *Sex Roles* 59 (5–6): 301–311.
Shotwell, Alexis. 2010. Appropriate Subjects: Whiteness and the Discipline of Philosophy. In *The Center Must Not Hold: White Women on the Whiteness of Philosophy*, ed. George Yancy, 117–130. Lanham, MD: Lexington Books.
Siim, Birte. 2013. Gender, Diversity and Migration: Challenges to Nordic Welfare, Gender Politics and Research. *Equality, Diversity and Inclusion* 32 (6): 615–628.
Simien, Evelyn M. 2007. Doing Intersectionality Research: From Conceptual Issues to Practical Examples. *Politics and Gender* 3 (2): 264–271.
Simmons, Aisha Shahida. 2010. Feminists Must Heal the Wounds of Racism. In *Who Should Be First? Feminists Speak Out on the 2008 Presidential Campaign*, eds. Beverly Guy-Sheftall, Johnnetta Betsch Cole, 115–118. Albany: SUNY Press.
Simon, Roger I. and Claudia Eppert. 1997. Remembering Obligation: Pedagogy and the Witnessing of Testimony of Historical Trauma. *Canadian Journal of Education/Revue canadienne de l'éducation* 22 (2): 175–191.
Simpson, Joanna. 2009. *Everyone Belongs: A Toolkit for Applying Intersectionality*. Ottawa: CRIAW/CRIEF. http://criaw-icref.ca/sites/criaw/files/Everyone_Belongs_e.pdf.
Singh, Anneliese A. 2013. Transgender Youth of Color and Resilience: Negotiating Oppression and Finding Support. *Sex Roles* 68 (11–12): 690–702.
Skjeie, Hege and Trude Langvasbråten. 2009. Intersectionality in Practice? Anti-Discrimination Reforms in Norway. *International Feminist Journal of Politics* 11 (4): 513–529.
Smith, Andrea. 2003. Not an Indian Tradition: The Sexual Colonization of Native Peoples. *Hypatia* 18 (2): 70–85.
———. 2004. Beyond the Politics of Inclusion: Violence against Women of Color and Human Rights. *Meridians* 4 (2): 120–124.
———. 2005a. *Conquest: Sexual Violence and American Indian Genocide*. Boston: South End Press.
———. 2005b. Native American Feminism, Sovereignty, and Social Change. *Feminist Studies* 31 (1): 116–132.
———. 2008. American Studies without America: Native Feminisms and the Nation-State. *American Quarterly* 60 (2): 309–315.
———. 2010. Queer Theory and Native Studies: The Heteronormativity of Settler Colonialism. *GLQ: A Journal of Lesbian and Gay Studies* 16 (1–2): 41–68.
———. 2012. Indigeneity, Settler Colonialism, White Supremacy. In *Racial Formation in the Twenty-First Century*, eds. Daniel Martinez HoSang, Oneka LaBennett, Laura Pulido, 66–90. Berkeley: Univ of California Press.
Smith, Barbara. 1983. Introduction. In *Home Girls: A Black Feminist Anthology*, ed. Barbara Smith, xix–lvi. New York: Kitchen Table Press.
Smith, Linda Tuhiwai. 2012. *Decolonizing Methodologies: Research and Indigenous Peoples*. 2nd ed. London: Zed.
Smith, Valerie. 1994. Black Feminist Theory and the Representation of the "Other." In *The Woman That I Am: The Literature and Culture of Contemporary Women of Color*, ed. D. Soyini Madison, 671–687. New York: St. Martin's.
———. 1998. *Not Just Race, Not Just Gender: Black Feminist Readings*. New York: Routledge.
Smooth, Wendy G. 2013. Intersectionality: From Theoretical Framework to Policy Intervention. In *Situating Intersectionality: Politics, Policy, and Power*, ed. Angelia R. Wilson, 11–42. New York: Palgrave.
Sokoloff, Natalie J. 2008. The Intersectional Paradigm and Alternative Visions to Stopping Domestic Violence: What Poor Women, Women of Color, and Immigrant Women Are Teaching Us about Violence in the Family. *International Journal of Sociology of the Family* 34 (2): 153–185.

Sokoloff, Natalie J. and Ida Dupont. 2005. Domestic Violence at the Intersections of Race, Class, and Gender: Challenges and Contributions to Understanding Violence against Marginalized Women in Diverse Communities. *Violence against Women* 11 (1): 38–64.

Soldatic, Karen and Lucy Fiske. 2009. Bodies "Locked Up": Intersections of Disability and Race in Australian Immigration. *Disability and Society* 24 (3): 289–301.

Somerville, Siobhan B. 2005. Queer Loving. *GLQ: A Journal of Lesbian and Gay Studies* 11 (3): 335–370.

Soto, Sandra K. 2010. *Reading Chican@ Like a Queer: The De-Mastery of Desire.* Austin: Univ of Texas Press.

Spade, Dean. 2012. Notes toward Race and Gender Justice Ally Practice in Legal Education. In *Presumed Incompetent: The Intersections of Race and Class for Women in Academia*, eds. Gabriella Gutiérrez y Muhs, Yolanda Flores Niemann, Carmen G. González, Angela P. Harris, 186–197. Boulder: Univ Press of Colorado.

———. 2013. Intersectional Resistance and Law Reform. *Signs* 38 (4): 1031–1055.

Spelman, Elizabeth V. 1988. *Inessential Woman: Problems of Exclusion in Feminist Thought.* Boston: Beacon Press.

———. 1998. *Fruits of Sorrow: Framing Our Attention to Suffering.* Boston: Beacon Press.

Springer, Kimberly. 1999. *Still Lifting, Still Climbing: Contemporary African American Women's Activism.* New York: NYU Press.

———. 2005. *Living for the Revolution: Black Feminist Organizations, 1968–1980.* Durham, NC: Duke Univ Press.

Springer, Kristen W., Olena Hankivsky, and Lisa M. Bates. 2012. Gender and Health: Relational, Intersectional, and Biosocial Approaches. *Social Science and Medicine* 74 (11): 1661–1666.

Squires, Judith. 2007. The Challenge of Diversity: The Evolution of Women's Policy Agencies in Britain. *Politics and Gender* 3 (4): 513–530.

———. 2008. Intersecting Inequalities: Reflecting on the Subjects and Objects of Equality. *Political Quarterly* 79 (1): 53–61.

———. 2009. Intersecting Inequalities: Britain's Equality Review. *International Feminist Journal of Politics* 11 (4): 496–512.

Staunæs, Dorthe. 2003. Where Have All the Subjects Gone? Bringing Together the Concepts of Intersectionality and Subjectification. *NORA: Nordic Journal of Women's Studies* 11 (2): 101–110.

Staunæs, Dorthe and Dorte Marie Søndergaard. 2010. Intersectionality—A Theoretical Adjustment. In *Theories and Methodologies in Postgraduate Feminist Research: Researching Differently*, eds. Rosemarie Buikema, Gabriele Griffin, Nina Lykke, 45–59. London: Routledge.

Strid, Sofia, Sylvia Walby, and Jo Armstrong. 2008. *Report Analysing Intersectionality in Gender Equality Policies for the United Kingdom and the EU, QUING Project.* Vienna: Institute for Human Sciences.

Stryker, Susan and Stephen Whittle, eds. 2006. *The Transgender Studies Reader.* New York: Routledge.

Swan, Elaine. 2010. States of White Ignorance, and Audit Masculinity in English Higher Education. *Social Politics: International Studies in Gender, State and Society* 17 (4): 477–506.

Tarver, Erin C. 2011. Rethinking "Intersectionality": Michelle Obama, Presumed Subjects, and Constitutive Privilege. *Philosophia* 1 (2): 150–172.

Taylor, Chloë. 2012. Genealogies of Oppression: A Response to Ladelle Mcwhorter's *Racism and Sexual Oppression in Anglo-America: A Genealogy. Philosophia* 2 (2): 207–215.

Taylor, Yvette, Sally Hines, and Mark E. Casey. 2011. Introduction. In *Theorizing Intersectionality and Sexuality*, eds. Yvette Taylor, Sally Hines, Mark E. Casey, 1–14. Basingstoke, UK: Palgrave.

Taylor-García, Daphne V. 2008. *The Emergence of Racial Schemas in the Americas: Sexuality, Sociogeny, and Print Capital in the Sixteenth Century Atlantic*. PhD dissertation, University of California, Berkeley.

Terborg-Penn, Rosalyn. 1997. Discrimination against Afro-American Women in the Women's Movement, 1830–1920. In *The Afro-American Woman: Struggles and Images*, eds. Sharon Harley, Rosalyn Terborg-Penn, 17–27. Baltimore: Black Classic Press.

Thomas, Susan L. 1998. Race, Gender, and Welfare Reform: The Antinatalist Response. *Journal of Black Studies* 28 (4): 419–446.

Thomas, Tracy A. 2010. Sex versus Race, Again. In *Who Should Be First? Feminists Speak Out on the 2008 Presidential Campaign*, eds. Beverly Guy-Sheftall, Johnnetta Betsch Cole, 33–40. Albany: SUNY Press.

Tlostanova, Madina and Walter Mignolo. 2009. Global Coloniality and the Decolonial Option. *Kult 6* (1): 11–27.

Tolhurst, Rachel, Beryl Leach, Janet Price, Jude Robinson, Elizabeth Ettore, Alex Scott-Samuel, Nduku Kilonzo, Louis P. Sabuni, Steve Robertson, and Anuj Kapilashrami. 2012. Intersectionality and Gender Mainstreaming in International Health: Using a Feminist Participatory Action Research Process to Analyse Voices and Debates from the Global South and North. *Social Science and Medicine* 74 (11): 1825–1832.

Tomlinson, Barbara. 2013a. Colonizing Intersectionality: Replicating Racial Hierarchy in Feminist Academic Arguments. *Social Identities* 19 (2): 254–272.

———. 2013b. To Tell the Truth and Not Get Trapped: Desire, Distance, and Intersectionality at the Scene of Argument. *Signs* 38 (4): 993–1017.

Torres, Edén. 2003. *Chicana without Apology: The New Chicana Cultural Studies*. New York: Routledge.

Townsend, Camilla. 2006. *Malintzin's Choices: An Indian Woman in the Conquest of Mexico*. Albuquerque: Univ of New Mexico Press.

Townsend-Bell, Erica. 2011. Intersectional Advances? Inclusionary and Intersectional State Action in Uruguay. Paper presented at APSA Conference, Seattle, WA.

Trujillo, Carla. 1998. *Living Chicana Theory*. San Antonio, TX: Third Women Press.

Truth, Sojourner. 1995. Woman's Rights. In *Words of Fire: An Anthology of African-American Feminist Thought*, ed. Beverly Guy-Sheftall, 36. New York: New Press.

Tuana, Nancy. 2006. The Speculum of Ignorance: The Women's Health Movement and Epistemologies of Ignorance. *Hypatia* 21 (3): 1–19.

Urbanek, Doris. 2009. *Towards a Processual Intersectional Policy Analysis*. QUING (Quality in Gender + Equality Policies) Report 028545-2. Vienna: Institute for Human Sciences.

Valdes, Francisco. 1995. Sex and Race in Queer Legal Culture: Ruminations on Identities & (and) Inter-Connectivities. *Southern California Law Review and Women's Studies* 5: 25.

Valentine, Gill. 2007. Theorizing and Researching Intersectionality: A Challenge for Feminist Geography. *The Professional Geographer* 59 (1): 10–21.

Van der Hoogte, Liesbeth and Koos Kingma. 2004. Promoting Cultural Diversity and the Rights of Women: The Dilemmas of "Intersectionality" for Development Organisations. *Gender and Development* 12 (1): 47–55.

Verloo, Mieke. 2006. Multiple Inequalities, Intersectionality and the European Union. *European Journal of Women's Studies* 13 (3): 211–228.

———. 2014, April 26. Keynote panelist for Institutionalizing Intersectionality panel. International Intersectionality Conference, Vancouver.

Walby, Sylvia, Jo Armstrong, and Sofia Strid. 2012. Intersectionality: Multiple Inequalities in Social Theory. *Sociology* 46 (2): 222–240.

Walgenbach, Katharina. 2007. Gender als interdependente kategorie. In *Neue perspektiven auf intersektionalität, diversität und heterogenität*, eds. Katharina Walgenbach, Gabrille Dietze, Antje Hornscheidt, Kerstin Palm, 23–64. Opladen, Germany: Barbara Budrich.

Walker, Alice. 1983. *In Search of Our Mothers' Gardens: Womanist Prose.* New York: Harcourt Brace Jovanovich.
Wallace-Sanders, Kimberly. 2008. *Mammy: A Century of Race, Gender, and Southern Memory.* Ann Arbor: Univ of Michigan Press.
Ward, Stephen. 2006. The Third World Women's Alliance: Black Feminist Radicalism and Black Power Politics. In *The Black Power Movement: Rethinking the Civil Rights-Black Power Era,* ed. Peniel E. Joseph, 119–144. New York: Routledge.
Warner, Leah R. 2008. A Best Practices Guide to Intersectional Approaches in Psychological Research. *Sex Roles* 59 (5–6): 454–463.
Warner, Leah R. and Stephanie A. Shields. 2013. The Intersections of Sexuality, Gender, and Race: Identity Research at the Crossroads. *Sex Roles* 68 (11–12): 803–810.
Wasserman, David, ed. 2006. Disability, Capability, and Thresholds for Distributive Justice. In *Capabilities Equality: Basic Issues and Problems,* ed. Alexander Kaufman, 214–234. New York: Routledge.
Waters, Kristin B. 2007. Some Core Themes of Nineteenth-Century Black Feminism. In *Black Women's Intellectual Traditions: Speaking Their Minds,* eds. Kristin B. Waters, Carol B. Conway, 365–392. Lebanon, NH: Univ Press of New England.
Waters, Kristin B. and Carol B. Conway, eds. 2007. *Black Women's Intellectual Traditions: Speaking Their Minds,* Lebanon, NH: Univ Press of New England.
Weigand, Kate. 2001. *Red Feminism: American Communism and the Making of Women's Liberation.* Baltimore: Johns Hopkins Univ Press.
Wells-Barnett, Ida B. 1893. *The Reason Why the Afro-American Is Not at the World's Columbian Exposition: The Afro-American's Contribution to Columbian Literature.* Chicago: Privately published.
———. 2014. *On Lynchings.* New York: Courier Dover.
Wells-Barnett, Ida B. and Miriam DeCosta-Willis. 1995. *The Memphis Diary of Ida B. Wells,* ed. Miriam DeCosta-Willis. Boston: Beacon Press.
Whitten, Barbara L. 2001. Standpoint Epistemology in the Natural Sciences: The Case of Michael Faraday. In *Engendering Rationalities,* eds. Nancy Tuana, Sandra Morgen, 361–371. Albany: SUNY Press.
Wiegman, Robyn. 2010. The Intimacy of Critique: Ruminations on Feminism as a Living Thing. *Feminist Theory* 11 (1): 79–84.
Williams, Patricia J. 1991. *The Alchemy of Race and Rights.* Cambridge, MA: Harvard University Press.
———. 2010. It's Not as Simple as White Trumping Black or Man Trumping Woman. In *Who Should Be First? Feminists Speak Out on the 2008 Presidential Campaign,* eds. Beverly Guy-Sheftall, Johnnetta Betsch Cole, 29–32. Albany: SUNY Press.
Williams, Toni. 2009. Intersectionality Analysis in the Sentencing of Aboriginal Women in Canada. In *Intersectionality and Beyond: Law, Power and the Politics of Location,* eds. Emily Grabham, Davina Cooper, Jane Krishnadas, Didi Herman, 79–104. Abingdon, UK: Routledge Cavendish.
Wylie, Alison. 2011. What Knowers Know Well: Women, Work and the Academy. In *Feminist Epistemology and the Philosophy of Science,* ed. Heidi E. Grasswick, 157–179. New York: Springer.
Yeğenoğlu, Meyda. 1998. *Colonial Fantasies: Towards a Feminist Reading of Orientalism.* New York: Cambridge Univ Press.
Young, Iris Marion. 1990. *Justice and the Politics of Difference.* Princeton, NJ: Princeton Univ Press.
Yuval-Davis, Nira. 2006. Intersectionality and Feminist Politics. *European Journal of Women's Studies* 13 (3): 193–209.
———. 2007. Intersectionality, Citizenship and Contemporary Politics of Belonging. *Critical Review of International Social and Political Philosophy* 10 (4): 561–574.

———. 2011a. Beyond the Recognition and Re-Distribution Dichotomy: Intersectionality and Stratification. In *Framing Intersectionality: Debates on a Multi-Faceted Concept in Gender Studies*, eds. Helma Lutz, Maria Teresa Herrera Vivar, Linda Supik, 155–170. Farnham, UK: Ashgate.

———. 2011b. *The Politics of Belonging: Intersectional Contestations.* Thousand Oaks, CA: Sage.

———. 2012. Dialogical Epistemology—An Intersectional Resistance to the "Oppression Olympics." *Gender and Society* 26 (1): 46–54.

Zack, Naomi. 2005. *Inclusive Feminism: A Third Wave Theory of Women's Commonality.* Lanham, MD: Rowman and Littlefield.

Zambrana, Ruth Enid and Bonnie Thornton Dill. 2009. Conclusion: Future Directions in Knowledge Building and Sustaining Institutional Change. In *Emerging Intersections: Race, Class, and Gender in Theory, Policy, and Practice*, eds. Bonnie Thornton Dill, Ruth Enid Zambrana, 274–290. New Brunswick, NJ: Rutgers Univ Press.

Zane, Kathleen. 1998. Reflections on a Yellow Eye: Asian I (\Eye/)Cons and Cosmetic Surgery. In *Talking Visions: Multicultural Feminism in a Transnational Age*, ed. Ella Shohat, 161–192. Boston: MIT Press.

Zinn, Maxine Baca, Lynn Weber Cannon, Elizabeth Higginbotham, and Bonnie Thornton Dill. 1986. The Costs of Exclusionary Practices in Women's Studies. *Signs* 11 (2): 290–303.

Zinn, Maxine Baca and Bonnie Thornton Dill. 1996. Theorizing Difference from Multiracial Feminism. *Feminist Studies* 22 (2): 321–331.

Zinn, Maxine Baca, Pierrette Hondagneu-Sotelo, and Michael A. Messner. 1997. Sex and Gender through the Prism of Difference. In *Gender through the Prism of Difference*, eds. Maxine Baca Zinn, Pierrette Hondagneu-Sotelo, Michael A. Messner, 147–156. Boston: Allyn and Bacon.

# Index